SPANISH
ENGLISH
POCKET DICTIONARY

SPANISH ENGLISH

POCKET DICTIONARY

Houghton Mifflin Company

Boston New York

CONTENTS

A SHORT GUIDE TO SPANISH GRAMMAR

Stress

The two fundamental rules of stressing are:

1. Words ending in a *vowel*, in *n* or in *s*, are stressed on the next to the last syllable, e.g. *Pedro, Rosita, examen, Carlos.*

2. Words ending in *any other* consonant are stressed on the last syllable, e.g. *señor, Madrid, nacional.*

If a word does not conform with these two rules, an acute accent (') is written over the vowel of the stressed syllable, e.g. *médico, capitán, inglés.*

In some words a written accent serves only to distinguish words which are pronounced alike, but have a different meaning, e.g. *si* (if), *sí* (yes); *te* (you), *té* (tea), *¿dónde?* (where?) *donde* (where).

Syllables

The vowels *i* and *u* may occur unstressed before or after another vowel, in which case they do not form a separate syllable and are pronounced like English *y* and *w* respectively: *muy bien* (very well), *bueno* (good), *automóvil* (automobile); cf. *continuo* (continuous), *continúo* (I continue), *continuó* (he or she continued).

A single consonant, two letters representing a single sound (like *ch, ll, qu, rr*), or a consonant followed by *l* or *r*, belong to the next syllable: *na-cio-nal, mu-cha-cho, ca-rro, do-ble, Ma-drid.*

Sounds and Spelling

Spanish Letter Sounds	Their pronunciation, like English
a	*a* in father: *Málaga*
b	1. *b*, at the beginning of group or after *m* or *n*: *bomba*
	2. *v*, between two vowels: *estaba*
c	1. *c* in cat, before *a, o, u* or a consonant: *café, clima*
	2. *th* in thin, before *e* and *i*: *Cervantes, nación*
ch	*ch* in child: *muchacha*
d	1. *d* in dog: *dan*
	2. softer than 1., like *th* in with: *nada*
	3. at end of word softer than 2., or even omitted: *hablad*
e	*e* in they or *e* in bed (if a consonant follows in the same syllable: *enero, negro, respuesta*
f	*f*: *África*
g	1. *g* in go, before *a, o, u* or a consonant: *Congo, grande*
	2. *h* in host, before *e* or *i*: *Argentina, página*
h	is silent, only written: *La Habana*
i	*i* in machine, each: *China*
j	*h* in host: *José*
k	(= qu): *kilómetro*
l	*l*: *Irlanda*
ll	*lli* in billiard: *Antillas*
m	*m*: *Méjico*
n	*n*: *banana*
ñ	*ni* in onion: *España*
o	*o* in or (very short): *Bogotá*
p	*p*: *Pepito*
qu	*k* in king: *química*

r	1. *r* in road (trilled *r*): *sombrero*	
	2. at end, weak: *cantar*	
	3. at beginning trilled like *rr*: *río*	
rr	*r* (doubled): *perro*	
s	*s* in so: *sistema*	
t	*t*: *patata*	
u	*oo* in boot: *uno* (it is silent in the syllables *que, gui*): *Miguel, guía*	
v	1. *b*: *Valencia*	
	2. *v*, (like Spanish *b*, see there): *uvas*	
x	1. *x*: *taxi*	
	2. *s* in so, before a consonant: *extra*	
y	*y* in yes: *mayo*	
	i in been, in the word: *y* (and)	
z	*th* in thin: *zoólogo*	

The Articles

1. *The Definite Article*

Before a masculine noun
s. **el** *muchacho* the boy
p. **los** *muchachos* the boys
Before a feminine noun*
s. **la** *muchacha* the girl
p. **las** *muchachas* the girls
Before adjectives with abstract meaning
s. **lo** *hermoso* the beautiful
s. **lo** *útil* all that is useful

2. *The Indefinite Article*

Before a masculine noun
s. **un** *libro* a book
p. **unos** *libros* some books
Before a feminine noun
s. **una** *mesa* a table
p. **unas** *mesas* some tables

*The form *el, un* is used before a feminine noun beginning with the stressed sound *a (ha)*; *el agua fresca* the fresh water; *un hacha afilada* a sharp axe.

The Noun

Gender

Nouns belong either to the masculine or the feminine gender.

Nouns ending in -o are masculine: *el libro*, the book
Exceptions: la mano, the hand; *la (el) radio*, the radio; *la foto*, the photo

Nouns ending in -a, -d, -ez are feminine: *la ventana*, the window; *la ciudad*, the town; *la nuez*, the nut
Exceptions: el día, the day; *el tranvía*, the tram; and nouns of Greek origin ending in -ma; e.g. *el problema*, the problem; *el sistema*, the system

No special rules for nouns ending otherwise: m. *el cohete*, the rocket; *el lápiz*, the pencil; *el papel*, the paper. f. *la clase*, the class; *la crisis*, the crisis; *la imagen*, the image

The natural gender is maintained in nouns like:
el amigo friend
la amiga (girl)friend
el inglés Englishman
la inglesa Englishwoman
el pianista pianist
la pianista pianist (woman)
el guía guide
la guía guide (woman)
el hermano brother
la hermana sister

(*los hermanos* brothers and sisters; *los padres* the parents; *los abuelos* the grandparents)

The Plural of Nouns

The plural of nouns is formed by adding

—S

to nouns ending in unstressed vowel or stressed -é: *el libro* the book, *los libros* the books; *el poeta* the poet, *los poetas* the

poets; *el café* the coffee, *los cafés* the coffee (-houses)
—ES

to nouns ending in a consonant: *el tren* the train, *los trenes* the trains; *la edad* the age, *las edades* the ages

Nouns ending in *-es*, and family names remain unchanged: *el lunes* Monday, *los lunes* on (every) Monday; *el análisis* analysis, *los análisis* the analyses; *López, los López* the family López

Note: The letter *c* is replaced by *qu*, and *z* by *c*, before *-es:* *el frac: los fraques* (dress-coat); *el lápiz: los lápices* (pencil).

The Declension of Nouns

The single cases are formed by prepositions.

The Accusative. Nouns denoting persons form the accusative with *a;* *veo a mi amigo* I see my friend; *no vemos al profesor* we don't see the professor (*al* = *a* + *el*). — Nouns denoting inanimate objects have the same form in the nominative and the accusative: *pongo el libro en la mesa* I put the book on the table.

The Genitive. It is formed by *de:* *el cuarto de las señoritas* the room of the girls; *el sombrero del médico* the doctor's hat (*del* = *de* + *el*).

The Dative is formed by the preposition *a;* *doy una manzana al muchacho* I give the boy an apple; *escriben muchas cartas a los padres* they write many letters to their parents.

The Adjective

The attributive as well as the predicate adjectives agree with their nouns. Adjectives and nouns are inflected alike; e.g. *he comido una naranja muy bonita* I've eaten a very good orange; *estas naranjas son muy bonitas* these oranges are very good.

Adjectives ending in *-o, -án, -or* have a special form in *-a* for the feminine*: *largo, larga* long; *largos, largas holgazán, holgazana* lazy; *holgazanes, holgazanas madrugador, -a* early riser; *madrugadores -as mejor* better, *mejores* better.

Most other adjectives have the same forms for both genders: *verde* green, *verdes, fácil* easy, *fáciles.*

But the adjectives denoting a nationality have the form in *-a* for the feminine: *alemán, alemana; alemanes, alemanas—francés, francesa; franceses, francesas—español, española; españoles, españolas*

Note: *el inglés* the Englishman or the English language; *la inglesa* the Englishwoman; *los ingleses* the English (men); *las inglesas* the English women.

Adjectives generally follow their noun: *la corbata azul* the blue tie.

Some adjectives standing before a masculine singular noun lose their final vowel or syllable:

bueno: un buen vino, a good wine

malo: mal tiempo, bad weather

grande: un gran palacio, a big palace

Santo: San Pedro, Saint Peter

primero: en el primer piso, on the first floor

*Except the irregular comparatives.

tercero: el tercer hombre, the third man	ciento: cien pesetas, a hundred pesetas

Comparison of Adjectives

Positive	Comparative	Superlative I (relative)	Superlative II (absolute)
largo long	*más largo*	*el más largo*	*larguísimo*
larga	*más larga* longer	*la más larga* the longest	very long
bueno good	*mejor* better	*el mejor* the best	*óptimo* very good, excellent
malo bad	*peor* worse	*el peor* the worst	*pésimo* very bad
grande great	*mayor* greater	*el mayor* the greatest	*máximo* very big or great
pequeño little, small	*menor* less, smaller	*el menor* least, the smallest	*mínimo* very little
alto high	*superior* higher	*el superior* the highest	*supremo* very high
bajo low	*inferior* lower	*el inferior* the lowest	*ínfimo* very low
mucho much, many	*más* more	*lo más* the most	*muchísimo* very much
poco little	*menos* less	*lo menos* the least	*poquísimo* very little

Diminutives and augmentatives

Spanish nouns and adjectives may receive diminutive and augmentative suffixes.

The suffixes *-ito*, *-illo*, *-cito*, *-cillo* imply small size or affectionate interest: *Pedrito* little Peter; *chiquillo* kid; *mujercita* dear little wife; *camisas bonitas* nice and good shirts.

The more frequent augmentative suffixes are *-ón*, *-ote*, *-azo*, *-acho*, which give the meaning of large size or contempt: *la sala: el salón* hall; *la palabra: la palabrota* term of abuse; *grandote* very large; *la manaza* huge hand; *ricacha, ricachona* a (very) rich woman.

Pronouns

Personal Pronouns

The Nominative is used only when stressed: *Tú te quedarás, pero yo me iré.* You'll remain, but I'm going away.— *Como. I eat, I'm eating.*— *Llegarán mañana.* They'll arrive tomorrow.

Tú (plural: *vosotros*) is used only between relatives, intimate friends and in addressing children, servants and animals.

The word *usted* (plural: *ustedes*) is used when speaking to somebody, and takes a verb in the third person: *Es usted muy amable.* You're very kind. — *¿Qué desean ustedes?* What do you want? (An inverted question-mark or an inverted exclamation mark is put at the beginning of an interrogative or exclamatory sentence respectively, in written Spanish.)

The conjunctive pronouns can be used only with verbs. These pronouns precede the verb: *Te espero.* I'm waiting for you.— But they are placed after the verb and written together with it after an infinitive, a gerund and an imperative: *Quiero verlo.* I want to see it.—

Viéndome me saludó. On seeing me he greeted me.— *Démelo.* Give it to me.

The disjunctive pronouns can be used apart from verbs: *¿A quién doy la llave?* To whom am I to give the key? *A mí.* — All prepositions have after them the disjunctive forms: *con él* with him (but *conmigo* with me, *contigo* with you, *consigo* with himself, with herself); *para mí* for me; *sin ti* without you etc.

Accusative

Nominative		Conjunctive	Disjunctive
yo	I	me	a mí
tú	you	te	a ti
él	he	le, lo	a él
ella	she	la	a ella
ello	it	lo	a ello
usted	you	le, la	a usted
nosotros	we	nos	a nosotros
nosotras			a nosotras
vosotros	you	os	a vosotros
vosotras			a vosotras
ellos	they	les, los	a ellos
ellas	they	las	a ellas
ustedes	you	los, las	a ustedes

Dative

Conjunctive		Disjunctive	
me	me	a mí	to me
you	te	a ti	to you
him	le	a él	to him
her	le	a ella	to her
it	le	a ello	to it
you	le	a usted	to you
us	nos	a nosotros	to us
		a nosotras	
you	os	a vosotros	to you
		a vosotras	
them	les	a ellos	to them
them	les	a ellas	to them
you	les	a ustedes	to you

Reflexive pronouns

The reflexive pronouns differ only in the third person from the personal pronouns. They are chiefly used with the reflexive verbs, e.g. *lavar* to wash; *lavarse* to wash oneself:

me lavo	I wash (myself)
te lavas	you wash (yourself)
se lava	he washes (himself) she washes (herself)
nos lavamos	we wash (ourselves)
os laváis	you wash (yourselves)
se lavan	they wash (themselves)

Disjunctive forms: *a sí (mismo), a. sí (misma)*: *Las muchachas se compran las medias para sí mismas.* The girls buy the stockings for themselves.

The form *se* is used impersonally with the 3rd pers. sing. of the verb, cf. Fr. *on*, Ger. *man*; *se dice* it is said; *no se sabe nunca* you never can tell.

Demonstrative pronouns

The *"neuter"* forms are:

esto this (here);

eso that (near you);

aquello that (over there).

E.g. *¿Qué es eso?* What's that? —*¿Esto? Es una revista inglesa.* This? It's an English magazine. The "personal" forms are:

m.: *éste, éstos*

ése, ésos

aquél, aquéllos

f.: *ésta, éstas*

ésa, ésas

aquélla, aquéllas

E.g. *Mi libro es éste.* My book is this one. — *Tus lápices son ésos.* Your pencils are those —

Sus hermanas son aquéllas. His or her or their sisters are those there.

The demonstrative adjectives are the same as the demonstrative pronouns but do not bear a written accent and precede the noun:

Este libro es de él. This book belongs to him.

No puede escribir con esa pluma. He can't write with that pen.

¿Por qué están abiertas aquellas ventanas? Why are those windows open?

Possessive adjectives and pronouns

mi libro my book

Este libro es mío. This book is mine.

tu libro your book

Este libro es tuyo. This book is yours.

su libro his (her) book

Este libro es suyo. This book is his (hers).

nuestro libro our book

Este libro es nuestro. This book is ours.

vuestro libro your book

Este libro es vuestro. This book is yours.

su libro their (your) book

Este libro es suyo. This book is theirs (or) yours.

mi carta my letter

Esa carta es mía. That letter is mine.

tu carta your letter

Esa carta es tuya. That letter is yours.

su carta his (her) letter

Esa carta es suya. That letter is his (hers).

nuestra carta our letter

Esa carta es nuestra. That letter is ours.

vuestra carta your letter

Esa carta es vuestra. That letter is yours.

su carta their (your) letter

Esa carta es suya. That letter is theirs (or yours.)

In the plural: *mis libros* my books; *estos libros son nuestros* these books are ours; *sus cartas* his (her, their, your) letters; *esas cartas son suyas* those letters are his (hers, theirs, yours.)

In case of ambiguity instead of *su, suyo* a paraphrase is used:

su carta; la carta de él (de ella, de usted, de ellos, de ellas, de ustedes).

esas cartas son suyas; esas cartas son de él (de ella, de usted, de ellos, de ellas, de ustedes).

Interrogative and relative pronouns

All interrogative adjectives and pronouns bear a written accent mark to distinguish them from the corresponding relative:

¿quién? who?

Interrogative

¿quién? who?

R: quien who

¿quiénes? who? (plural)

R: quienes who (plural)

¿qué? what?

R: que that, which, who

¿cuál? which one?

R: el cual, la cual he who, that which

¿cuáles? which ones?

R: los cuales, las cuales they who, those which

¿cuánto? how much?

R: cuanto all that, as much as

¿cuántos? how many?

R: cuantos all that, as many as

¿cómo? how?

R: como how, as, like

¿cuándo? when?

R: cuando when(ever)

The Adverb

Adverbs are formed from adjectives by adding the suffix *-mente* (to the feminine form): *claro* clear, *claramente* clearly *fácil* easy, *fácilmente* easily *cortés* polite, *cortésmente* politely

If there are more adverbs only the last receives this suffix: *habla clara y distintamente* he speaks clearly and distinctly.

Some adjectives and participles may be used as adverbs: *hable usted más alto* speak up; *se fue contento* he went happily away. **The Verb**

According to the way in which they are conjugated Spanish verbs fall into three conjugations:

I. Verbs ending in —AR: *hablar* to speak, *trabajar* to work;

II. Verbs ending in —ER: *comer* to eat, *beber* to drink;

III. Verbs ending in. —IR: *vivir* to live, *escribir* to write.

All verbal terminations are added to the radical which you get by omitting the ending *-ar, -er, -ir* respectively: *habl-, trabaj-, com-, beb-, viv-, escrib-.*

Regular Verbs
A) Simple tenses
1. *Indicative Mood*

| **Present tense** | I. (-ar) -o | II. (-er) -o | III. (-ir -o |

	-as	-es	-es
	-a	-e	-e
	-amos	-emos	-imos
	-áis	-éis	-ís
	-an	-en	-en
Future tense	-aré	-eré	-iré
	-arás	-erás	-irás
	-ará	-erá	-irá
	-aremos	-eremos	-iremos
	-aréis	-eréis	-iréis
	-arán	-erán	-irán
Past tense	-é	-í	-í
	-aste	-iste	-iste
	-ó	-ió	-ió
	-amos	-imos	-imos
	-asteis	-isteis	-isteis
	-aron	-ieron	-ieron
Imperfect tense	-aba	-ía	-ía
	-abas	-ías	-ías
	-aba	-ía	-ía
	-ábamos	-íamos	-íamos
	-ábais	-íais	-íais
	-aban	-ían	-ían

2. Conditional

Present tense	-aría	-ería	-iría
	-arías	-erías	-irías
	-aría	-ería	-iría
	-aríamos	-eríamos	-iríamos
	-aríais	-eríais	-iríais
	-arían	-erían	-irían

3. Subjunctive mood

Present tense	-e	-a	-a
	-es	-as	-as
	-e	-a	-a
	-emos	-amos	-amos
	-éis	-áis	-áis
	-en	-an	-an

Past tense	I.		II. and III.	
	-ase or	-ara	-iese or	-iera
	-ases	-aras	-ieses	-ieras
	-ase	-ara	-iese	-iera
	-ásemos	-áramos	-iésemos	-iéramos
	-aseis	-arais	-ieseis	-ierais
	-asen	-aran	-iesen	-ieran

4. Imperative Mood

Present tense	-a	-e	-e
	-ad	-ed	-id

5. Non-finite forms

	-ar	-er	-ir
Present Infinitive	-ar	-er	-ir
Gerund	-ando	-iendo	-iendo
Past Participle	-ado	-ido	-ido

B) Compound tenses

They are formed by means of the corresponding tense of the auxiliary verb *haber* (see List of Irregular Verbs) and the past participle of the verb.

1. Indicative Mood

Present Perfect Tense

I have spoken (eaten, lived) etc.
he hablado (comido, vivido)
has hablado (comido, vivido)
ha hablado (comido, vivido)
hemos hablado (comido, vivido)
habéis hablado (comido, vivido)
han hablado (comido, vivido)

Past Perfect Tense
habia hablado I had spoken

2. Conditional

Past Tense
habría hablado
I should have spoken

3. Subjunctive Mood

Present Perfect Tense
haya hablado
that I have spoken

Past Perfect Tense
hubiese or *hubiera hablado*
(if) I had spoken

4. Non-finite forms

Past Infinitive
haber hablado to have spoken

Past Gerund
habiendo hablado having spoken

Use of the single Tenses

The *present* tense of the Indicative refers to the present but it is often used instead of the future tense: *Mañana salgo para Londres*. Tomorrow 'll leave for London.

The *future* tense refers not only to action in future time but also to probability: ¿*Qué hora es? Serán las diez*. What time is it? It may be ten o'clock.

The *past* tense refers to action at a specific point in past time: *Llegué ayer*. I arrived yesterday.

The *imperfect* tense refers to past action that was going on at the same time as some other action or that was habitual: *Mientras yo leía él jugaba*. While I was reading he was playing. — *Me levantaba siempre temprano*. I used to get up early.

The *present perfect* tense refers to a past action which continues in the present: *He venido para verle a usted*. I have come to see you.

The *imperative* is used to give commands; the courteous form of the imperative is expressed by the *present subjunctive; coma usted más* eat more; *vengan ustedes a verme* come to see me; *escríbame una carta* write me a letter (in negative sentences: *no me escriba cartas* don't write me any letters).

The *conditional* is used as in English: *desearía una habitación en el primer piso* I should like to have a room on the first floor; *habríamos ido con ustedes* we should have gone with you. — In subordinate clauses the *subjunctive* is used: *Me ale-*

graría si me escribiese (or
escribiera). I'd be glad if he
wrote me; — *Me habría ale-
grado si me hubiese* (or *hubiera*)
escrito. I'd have been glad if he
had written me.

Irregular Verbs

I. *Radical-changing verbs* are
such as have the regular end-
ings of the conjugation to
which they belong, but have
certain changes in the vowel of
the last syllable of the root.
There are two main types of
radical-changing verbs:

a) The root-vowel is changed
into a diphthong (*e* into *ie* and
o into *ue*) when it is stressed:

  pensar to think
pienso I think
piensas you think
piensa he thinks
pensamos we think
pensáis you think
piensan they think

  contar to count
cuento I count
cuentas you count
cuenta he counts
contamos we count
contáis you count
cuentan they count

The same occurs in the present subjunctive and in the
imperative (*piense*, *cuente*,
etc.). Some verbs ending in
-ir change the root-vowel in
other tenses too; so, for in-

stance, the root-vowel *e* is
changed into *i*, and *o* into *u*,
wherever the root is un-
stressed but followed by *a*, *ie*,
or *ió*:

  sentir to feel
sentí I felt
sentiste you felt
sintió he felt
sentimos we felt
sentisteis you felt
sintieron they felt
sintiese or *sintiera* if I felt
sintiendo feeling

  dormir to sleep
dormí I slept
dormiste you slept
durmió he slept
dormimos we slept
dormisteis you slept
durmieron they slept
durmiese or *durmiera* if I slept
durmiendo sleeping

b) The root-vowel *e* is
changed into *i* both in forms
where the last syllable of the
root is stressed and where the
root is unstressed but followed
by *a*, *ie*, or *ió*:

  pedir to ask
pido I ask
pides you ask
pide he asks
pedimos we ask
pedís vou ask
piden they ask
pidió he asked
pidiese or *pidiera* if he asked
pidiendo asking

A

a, un *m.*, una *f.*

abandon, *v. a.* abandonar.

abbey, *s.* abadía *f.*

abbot, *s.* abad *m.*

abbreviate, *v. a.* abreviar.

abbreviation, *s.* abreviación *f.*

abdicate, *v. a. & n.* abdicar.

abhor, *v. a.* detestar, aborrecer.

abide, *v. n.* permanecer.

ability, *s.* habilidad *f.*, capacidad *f.*

able, *adj.* hábil, capaz.

aboard, *adv.* a bordo.

abolish, *v. a.* abolir.

abolition, *s.* abolición *f.*

abominable, *adj.* abominable.

abound, *v. n.* abundar.

about, *adv.* alrededor; *prep.* sobre, de; hacia, a eso de; *be ~ to* prepararse a.

above, *adv.* en alto, arriba; *prep.* sobre, encima de.

abroad, *adv.* en el extranjero.

absence, *s.* ausencia.

absent, *adj.* ausente.

absolute, *adj.* absoluto.

absolutely, *adv.* absolutamente.

absolve, *v. a.* absolver.

absorb, *v. a.* absorber.

abstain, *v. n.* abstenerse.

abstract, *adj.* abstracto; — *s.* extracto *m.*, resumen *m.*

absurd, *adj.* absurdo.

abundance, *s.* abundancia *f.*

abundant, *adj.* abundante.

abusive, *adj.* abusivo; injurioso.

academic, *adj.* académico.

academy, *s.* academia *f.*

accent, *s.* acento *m.*; — *v. a.* acentuar.

accept, *v. a.* aceptar.

access, *s.* acceso *m.*

accessible, *adj.* accesible.

accessory, *s. & adj.* accesorio *(m.).*

accident, *s.* accidente *m.*

accidental, *adj.* accidental.

accommodate, *v. a.* acomodar; *~ oneself to* acomodarse a.

accommodation, *s.* acomodamiento *m.*; alojamiento *m.*

accompany, *v. a.* acompañar.

accomplish, *v. a.* acabar, terminar.

accord, *s.* acuerdo *m.*; — *v. n.* concordar; *v. a.* conceder.

according: *~ to prep.* según, de acuerdo con.

account, *s.* cuenta *f.*; — *v.n.* dar cuenta de; *on ~ of* con motivo de; *on no ~* de ningún modo.

accuracy, *s.* exactitud *f.*

accusation, *s.* acusación *f.*

accuse, *v. a.* acusar.

accustom, *v. a.* acostumbrar.

ache, *s.* dolor *m.*; — *v. n.* *my head ~s* tengo dolor de cabeza, me duele la cabeza.

achieve, *v. a.* ejecutar, realizar; conseguir.

acknowledge, *v. a.* reconocer.

acquaint, *v. a.* hacer conocer; informar.

acquaintance, *s.* conocimiento *m.*; conocido *m.*

acquire, *v. a.* adquirir.

acquisition, s. adquisición f., compra f.

across, prep. a través de.

act, s. acción f.; (law) ley f.; (theatre) acto m. — v. n. actuar.

action, s. acción f., acto m.

active, adj. activo, ágil.

activity, s. actividad f.

actor, s. actor m.

actress, s. actriz f.

actual, adj. actual.

adapt, v. a. adaptar.

add, v. a. añadir; sumar.

addition, s. añadidura f.; suma f., adición f.; in ~ to por añadidura. además de.

additional, adj. adicional.

address, s. dirección f., señas f. pl.;—v. a. dirigir a.

adjoining, adj. lindante, contiguo.

adjust, v. a. ajustar, arreglar.

administration, s. administración f.

administrative, adj. administrativo.

admirable, adj. admirable.

admiral, s. almirante m.

admiration, s. admiración f.

admire, v. a. admirar.

admission, s. admisión f.; entrada f.; concesión f.

admit, v. a. admitir.

adore, v. a. adorar.

adult, adj. &s. adulto (m.).

advance, v. n. avanzar, adelantarse.

advantage, s. ventaja f.

adventure, s. aventura f.

adversary, s. adversario m.

adverse, adj. adverso.

adversity, s. contrariedad f.

advertise, v. a. anunciar, avisar.

advertisement, s. anuncio m., aviso m.

advice, s. consejo m.; aviso m.

advise, v. a. aconsejar.

aerodrome, s. aeródromo m.

aeroplane, s. avión m, aeroplano m.

affair, s. negocio m; asunto m.

affect, v. a. interesar; tocar; afectar.

affection, s. afecto m.; cariño m.

affectionate, adj. afectuoso, cariñoso.

affirm, v. a. afirmar.

affirmative, adj. afirmativo; — s. afirmativa f.

afford, v. a. dar, conferir; can ~ permitirse.

afraid, adj. inquieto; be ~ tener miedo de.

African, adj. &s. africano.

after, adv. luego; — prep. después de.

afternoon, s. tarde f.

afterwards, adv. luego; más tarde, después.

again, adv. de nuevo, nuevamente, otra vez.

against, prep. contra.

age, s. edad f.

aged, adj. anciano, viejo.

agency, s. agencia f.; actividad f.

agent, s. agente m., representante m.

aggression, s. agresión f.

ago, adv. hace, a week ~ hace una semana.

agree, v. n. concordar; estar de acuerdo; ~ on concordarse; ~ to consentir a; ~ with estar de acuerdo con.

agreeable, adj. agradable.

agreement, s. concordancia f., acuerdo m.

agricultural, adj. agricola.

agriculture, *s.* agricultura *f.*

ahead, *adv.* adelante.

aid, *s.* ayuda *f.*, socorro *m.* – *v. a.* ayudar.

aim, *s.* fin *m.*; propósito *m.*; – *v. n.* tender (a); *v. a.* apuntar.

air, *s.* aire *m.*

air-line *s.* línea *(f.)* aérea.

air-mail, *s.* correo *(m.)* aéreo.

airport, *s.* aeropuerto *m.*, aeródromo *m.*

alarm, *v. a.* alarmar; — *s.* alarma *f.*

alcoholic, *adj.* alcohólico.

ale, *s.* cerveza *f.*

alike, *adj.* igual; — *adv.* igualmente.

alive, *adj.* vivo.

all, *adj.* todo; *s.* todos *m.* pl.; *adv.* del todo: *not at ~* de ningún modo.

alley, *s.* avenida *f.*; paseo *m.*, callejón *m.*

all ed, *adj.* aliado.

allow, *v. a.* permitir, conceder; *~ for* tomar en consideración.

ally, *s.* aliado *m.*; – *v. a.* unir; *v. n.* aliarse.

almost, *adv.* casi.

alms, *s. pl.* limosna *f.*

alone, *adj.* solo; — *adv.* sólo.

along, *prep.* a lo largo de.

aloud, *adv.* en voz alta.

already, *adv.* ya.

also, *adv.* también.

alter, *v. a. & n.* cambiar, mudar.

although, *conj.* aunque.

altitude, *s.* altitud *f.*

altogether, *adv.* enteramente.

always, *adv.* siempre.

amaze, *v. a.* asombrar.

amazing, *adj.* asombroso.

ambassador, *s.* embajador *m.*

ambition, *s.* ambición *f.*

ambitious, *adj.* ambicioso.

ambulance, *s.* ambulancia *f.*

amend, *v. a.* corregir, rectificar.

American, *adj. & s.* americano *(m.).*

amid(st), *prep.* en medio de.

among, *prep.* entre.

amount, *s.* importe *m.*; cantidad *f.*; importancia *f.*; – *v. n.* elevarse a, importar.

ample, *adj.* amplio.

amuse, *v. a.* divertir.

amusement, *s.* divertimiento *m.*

an, *see* a.

anatomy, *s.* anatomía *f.*

ancestor, *s.* abuelo *m.*, antepasado *m.*

anchor, *s.* ancla *f.*; *v. a. & n.* anclar.

ancient, *adj.* antiguo.

and, *conj.* y.

anecdote, *s.* anécdota *f.*

angel, *s.* ángel *m.*

anger, *s.* cólera *f.*, ira *f.*, enojo *m.*; *v. a.* enojar.

angle[1], *s.* ángulo *m.*; punto *(m.)* de vista.

angle[2], *v. n.* pescar con el anzuelo.

Anglican, *adj.* anglicano.

angry, *adj.* iracundo, enojado, enfadado.

animal, *adj. & s.* animal *(m.).*

ankle, *s.* tobillo *m.*

annex, *s.* anejo *m.*, anexo *m.*; dependencia *f.*; —*v. a.* anexar.

anniversary, *s.* aniversario *m.*

announce, *v. a.* anunciar, avisar.

announcement, *s.* anuncio

m., aviso *m.*

announcer, *s.* locutor *m.*, anunciante *m.*

annoy, *v. a.* enfadar, molestar; *be ~ed at* estar enfadado con.

annoying, *adj.* enojoso, molesto.

annual, *adj.* anual.

annul, *v. a.* anular.

another, *adj.* otro.

answer, *s.* respuesta *f.*, contestación *f.*; *v. a.* & *n.* responder, contestar.

antibiotic, *s.* antibiótico *m.*

anticipate, *v. a.* anticipar.

antipathy, *s.* antipatía *f.*

antiquity, *s.* antigüedad *f.*

antiseptic, *adj.* & *s. m.* antiséptico *(m.).*

anxiety, *s.* angustia *f.*, congoja *f.*; inquietud *f.*

anxious, *adj.* angustioso; inquieto; *he ~ to* querer (hacer algo).

any, *pron.* algún *m.*, alguna *f.*; *not ~* ninguno.

anybody, *pron.* alguien; *(at all)* cualquiera.

anyhow, *adv.* de cualquier modo.

anyone, *see* anybody.

anything, *pron.* algo; todo; *(at all)* cualquiera.

anyway, *see* anyhow.

anywhere, *adv.* en todas partes.

apart, *adv.* aparte; solo; *~ from* aparte de.

apartment, *s.* habitación *f.*

ape, *s.* mono *m.*

apologize, *v. n.* pedir perdón, disculparse.

apology, *s.* perdón *m.*, disculpa *f.*

apparent, *adj.* aparente; manifiesto.

appeal, *s.* apelación *f.*; llamamiento *m.*; fuerza *(f.)* atractiva; — *v. n.*

apelar; atraer.

appear, *v. n.* aparecer, presentarse.

appearance, *s.* aparición *f.*, *(look)* aspecto *m.*

appendix, *s.* apéndice *m.*

appetite, *s.* apetito *m.*

applaud, *v. n.* aplaudir.

applause, *s.* aplauso *m.*

apple, *s.* manzana *f.*

applicant, *s.* solicitante *m.*

application, *s.* aplicación *f.*; solicitud *f.*

apply, *v. a.* aplicar, utilizar; *v. n.* cuadrar (con); *~ for* solicitar; *~ to* dirigirse a.

appoint, *v. a.* fijar; destinar; nombrar, designar.

appointment, *s.* destino *m.*; cita *f.*; nombramiento *m.*

appreciate, *v. a.* apreciar.

appreciation, *s.* estimación *f.*, estima *f.*

apprentice, *s.* aprendiz *m.*

approach, *s.* aproximación *f.*; acceso *m.*; *v. a.* acercar, aproximar; *v. n.* acercarse, aproximarse.

appropriate, *v. a.* apropiarse; *adj.* apropiado.

approval, *s.* aprobación *f.*

approve, *v. a.* aprobar.

approximate, *v. a.* & *n.* aproximar(se); — *adj.* aproximativo.

apricot, *s.* albaricoque *m.*, damasco *m.*

April, *s.* abril *m.*

apron, *s.* delantal *m.*

apt, *adj.* apto.

Arab, *adj.* & *s.* árabe *(m).*

arbitrary, *adj.* arbitrario.

arcade, *s.* arcada *f.*

arch, *s.* bóveda *f.* arco *m.*

architect, *s.* arquitecto *m.*

architecture, *s.* arquitectura *f.*

area, *s.* área *f.*

Argentine, *adj.* argentino.

argue, v. a. & n. discutir; argüir.

argument, s. argumento m.; discusión f.

arid, adj. árido.

arise, v. n. levantarse; (come from) resultar.

aristocratic, adj. aristocrático.

arm¹, s. brazo m.

arm², s. (weapon) arma f.

armament, s. armamento m.

armchair, s. sillón m., butaca f.

army, s. ejército m.

around, adv. alrededor; prep. alrededor de.

arouse, v. a. despertar.

arrange, v. a. ordenar, arreglar; v. n. disponer.

arrangement, s. orden f., arreglo m.; disposición f.

arrest, v. a. detener, arrestar; parar; — s. detención f., arresto m.

arrival, s. llegada f.

arrive, v. n. llegar.

arrow, s. flecha f.

art, s. arte m.

artery, s. arteria f.

article, s. artículo m.

artificial, adj. artificial.

artillery, s. artillería f.

artist, s. artista m. & f.

artistic, adj. artístico.

as, conj. como, cuando; pron. tan; ~ young ~ tan joven como.

ascend, v. n. ascender.

ascent, s. ascensión f.

ascertain, v. a. averiguar; establecer.

ash(es), s. ceniza f.

ashamed, adj. avergonzado; be ~ of avergonzarse de.

ashore, adv. en la costa; go ~ desembarcar.

Asiatic, adj. asiático.

aside, adv. de lado; aparte.

ask, v. a. preguntar; pedir, rogar; ~ about informarse.

asleep, adv. durmiendo; fall ~ quedarse dormido, dormirse.

aspect, s. aspecto m.; punto de vista.

aspire, v. n. aspirar a.

ass, s. asno m., burro m.

assail, v. a. atacar, asaltar.

assemble, v. a. reunir; v. n. reunirse.

assembly, s. reunión f., asamblea f.

assign, v. a. asignar.

assist, v. a. ayudar.

assistance, s. asistencia f.

assistant, s. asistente m.

associate, v. a. asociar; v. n. asociarse.

association, s. asociación f.

assume, v. a. asumir.

assumption, s. suposición f.; asunción f.

assure, v. a. asegurar.

astonish, v. a. sorprender.

astonishing, adj. sorprendente.

astonishment, s. sorpresa f.

at, prep. en; ~ the station en la estación; ~ six o'clock a las seis.

athlete, s. atleta m. & f.

athletic, adj. atlético.

athletics, s. pl. atletismo m.

atmosphere, s. atmósfera f.

atom, s. átomo m.

atomic, adj. atómico; ~ bomb bomba (f.) atómica; ~ energy energía (f.) atómica.

atrocity, s. atrocidad f.

attach, v. a. atar.

attaché, s. agregado m.; ~ case maletín m.

attack, v. a. atacar, asaltar; — s. ataque m., a-salto m.

attain, v. a. alcanzar, lograr.

attempt, v. a. intentar; — s. intento m.

attend, v. a. atender a; ~ school ir a la escuela.

attendance, s. asistencia f.

attention, s. atención f.; pay ~ prestar atención.

attentive, adj. atento.

attic, s. buhardilla f.

attitude, s. postura f.; conducta f.

attorney, s. abogado m.

attract, v. a. atraer.

attribute, v. a. atribuir; — s. atributo m.

auction, s. subasta f.

audience, s. audiencia f.; auditorio m.

auditorium, s. auditorio m.; aula f.

August, s. agosto m.

aunt, s. tía f.

Australian, adj. & s. australiano (m.).

Austrian, adj. & s. aus-triaco (m.).

authentic, adj. auténtico

author, s. autor m.

authority, s. autoridad f.; autorización f.

authorize, v. a. autorizar.

automatic, adj. automá-tico.

automation, s. automati-zacion f.

autumn, s. otoño m.

avail, s. be of no ~ no servir para nada; ser inútil.

available, adj. disponible; (estar) en venta.

avalanche, s. avalancha f.

avenge, v. a. vengar.

avenue, s. avenida f.

average, s. término (m.) medio; on the ~ por tér-mino medio; — adj.

medio.

aversion, s. aversión f.

avoid, v. a. evitar.

await, v. a. esperar, aguar-dar.

awake, v. a. despertar; v. n. despertar(se); — adj. despierto.

aware, adj. consciente (de); become ~ hacerse cargo (de).

away, adv. ausente; go ~ irse, marcharse.

awful, adj. horrible.

awhile, adv. un rato.

awkward, adj. torpe; pe-noso.

axe, s. hacha f.

axis, s. eje m.

axle, s. eje m.

azure, adj. & s. azul (m.).

B

baby, s. nene m.; bebé m.

baby-sitter, s. aya f., niñe-ra f. por horas.

bachelor, s. soltero m.; (arts) bachiller m.

back, s. espalda f.; (football) defensa m.; — adj. trasero; — adv. (hacia) atrás; come ~ volver, regresar; some years ~ hace unos años; — v. n. (car) dar mar-cha atrás; (bet) apos-tar (por).

background, s. fondo m.; segundo plano m.

backward, adv. (hacia) atrás; — adj. atrasado.

bacon, s. tocino m.

bad, adj. malo; that's too ~ ! ¡qué lástima!; ~ luck mala suerte f.

badly, adv. mal.

bag, s. saco m.; bolsa f.

baggage, s. bagaje m.; equipaje m.

bake, v. a. & n. cocer;

asar.
baker. s. panadero m.
bakery, s. panadería f.
balance, s. balanza f.;
equilibrio m.; — v. a.
sopesar; equilibrar.
balcony, s. balcón m.
bald, adj. calvo.
bale, s. bala f.; fardo m.
ball, s. pelota f.; bola f.;
globo m.; (dance) baile
m.
ballet, s. bailete m.; ballet
m.
balloon, s. balón m.
ball(-point) pen, s. bolí-
grafo m.
Baltic, adj. báltico.
banana, s. plátano m.;
banana f.
band, s. lazo m.; cinta f.;
banda f.; — v. a.
~ together unirse.
bandage, s. venda f.; ven-
daje m.; — v. a. ven-
dar.
bandit, s. bandido m.
bank¹, s. (river) orilla f.
bank², s. banca f.; banco
m.
banknote, s. billete m.
(de banco).
bankruptcy, s. bancarrota
f.; quiebra f.
banner, s. bandera f.
banquet, s. banquete m.
baptism, s. bautismo
m.
baptize, v. a. bautizar.
bar, s. (iron) barra f.;
tribunal m.; (place for
drink) bar m.; — v. a.
barrear.
barber, s. barbero m.;
peluquero m.
bare, adj. desnudo; —
v. a. desnudar.
barefoot, adv. descalzo.
bargain, s. negocio m.;
into the ~ por añadi-
dura; compra (f.) de
lance; — v. n. regatear.

barge, s. barcaza f.
bark, s. ladrido m.;
—v. n. ladrar.
barley, s. cebada f.
barman, s. barman m.
barn, s. granero m.
barometer, s. barómetro m.
baron, s. barón m.
baroness, s. baronesa f.
barrack(s), s. (pl.) cuartel m.
barrel, s. barril m.; (of
gun) cañón m.
barren, adj. árido, estéril.
barrier, s. barrera f.; obstáculo m.
barrister, s. abogado m.
base, s. base f.; — v. a.
basar.
basement, s. fundamento
m.; sótano m.
basic, adj. básico. fundamental.
basin, s. palangana f.; jofaina f.; cuenca f.
basis, s. base f.
basket, s. cesta f.; canasta
f., cesto m.
basket-ball, baloncesto m.
bass, s. bajo m.
bath, s. baño m.; take a ~
tomar un baño.
bathe, v. a. bañar; —v. n.
bañarse.
bather, s. bañista m., f.
bathing-costume, s. traje
(m.) de baño.
bathroom, s. cuarto (m.)
de baño.
battery, s. batería f.
battle, s. batalla f.
bay, s. golfo m.; bahía f.
be, v. n. ser, estar; how
are you? ¿cómo está
usted?; I am twenty
tengo veinte años.
beach, s. playa f.
bead, s. perla f.; cuenta f.
beam, s. (timber) viga f.;
(light) rayo m.; — v. n.
(ir)radiar.

bean, s. judía f.; French
~s judías (f. pl.) ver-
des.

bear,¹ s. oso m.

bear², v. a. (carry) llevar;
(suffer) sufrir, sopor-
tar; (child) dar a luz;
when were you born?
¿cuándo nació usted?

beard, s. barba f.

bearing, s. conducta f.;
relación f.; beyond all ~
insoportable.

beast, s. bestia f.

beat, v. a. batir, golpear;
vencer.

beautiful, adj. hermoso,
guapo.

beauty, s. hermosura f.;
belleza f.; ~ parlour
salón (m.) de belleza.

because, conj. porque.

beckon, v. n. hacer señas,
llamar con señas.

become, v. n. hacerse,
llegar a ser; convenir.

bed, s. cama f.; go to ~ ir
a la cama, acostarse.

bedclothes, s. pl. ropa (f.)
de cama.

bedroom, s. dormitorio
m.; alcoba f.

bee, s. abeja f.

beef, s. carne (f.) de vaca.

beef-steak, s. bistec m.

beer, s. cerveza f.

beetle, s. escarabajo m.

beetroot, s. remolacha f.

before, adv. antes; —
prep. ante, delante de; —
conj. antes de (que).

beg, v. a. rogar, pedir;
I ~ your pardon?
¡Perdone! ¿Qué dijo
usted?

beggar, s. mendigo m.

begin, v. a. & n. empezar,
comenzar.

beginner, s. principiante
m.,f.

beginning, s. comienzo m.;
principio m.

behalf, prep. on ~ of en
interés de; en nombre
de.

behave, v. n. portarse,
conducirse.

behaviour, s. conducta f.

behind, adv. detrás;
atrás; — prep. detrás
de, tras.

being, s. existencia f.;
ser m., criatura f.

Belgian, adj & s. belga.

belief, s. creencia f.

believe, v. a. creer; pensar.

bell, s. timbre m.; campanilla f.; ring the ~ tocar
el timbre.

belly, s. vientre m.

belong, v. n. pertenecer.

belongings, s. pl. efectos
m. pl.; trastos m. pl.

beloved, adj. querido,
amado.

below, adv. abajo, hacia
abajo.

belt, s. cinturón m.

bench, s. banco m.

bend, v. a. curvar; — v. n.
curvarse; — s. (road)
curva f.

beneath, adv. abajo; —
prep. debajo de.

benefit, s. beneficio m.; —
v. a. & n. beneficiar.

bent, s. inclinación f.; —
adj. ~ on empeñado en.

berry, s. baya f.

berth, s. litera f.; cama f.;
camarote m.

beside, prep. al lado de.

besides, adv. además; —
prep. además de.

best, adj. el (la) mejor; —
adv. lo mejor

best-seller, s. libro (m.)
de gran éxito.

bet, v. a. apostar; — s.
apuesta f.

better, adj. mejor; all the

~ tanto mejor; — v. a. mejorar.

between, *prep.* entre, por entre.

beware, *v. n.* cuidarse de;

— *int.* ~! ¡cuidado!

beyond, *prep.* más allá de; ~ doubt sin duda.

Bible, *s.* Biblia *f.*

bicycle, *s.* bicicleta *f.*

bid, *v. a.* mandar; ofrecer; — *s.* oferta *f.*

big, *adj.* grande; vasto.

bill, *s.* cuenta *f.*; ~ of fare lista (*f.*) de platos, menú *m.*; (*poster*) cartel *m.*

bin, *s.* recipiente *m.* dust~ basurero *m.*

bind, *v. a.* atar; *fig.* obligar.

biography, *s.* biografía *f.*

biological, *adj.* biológico.

biology, *s.* biología *f.*

bird, *s.* pájaro *m.*, pajarillo *m.*

birth, *s.* nacimiento *m.*; parto *m.*

birthday, *s.* cumpleaños *m.*

birth-place, *s.* lugar (*m.*) de nacimiento.

biscuit, *s.* bizcocho *m.*; galleta *f.*

bishop, *s.* (*church*) obispo *m.*; (*chess*) alfil *m.*

bit, *s.* pedazo *m.*; pedacito *m.*

bite, *v. a.* morder; — *s.* mordedura *f.*; bocado *m.*

bitter, *adj.* amargo.

bitterness, *s.* amargura *f.*

black, *adj.* negro; ~ coffee café *m.*; — *v. a.* ennegrecer; ~ shoes limpiar los zapatos.

blackberry, *s.* zarzamora *f.*

blackbird, *s.* mirlo *m.*

blackboard, *s.* pizarra *f.*; encerado *m.*

blackmail, *s.* chantaje *m.*; — *v. a.* hacer chantaje, chantajear.

blacksmith, *s.* herrero *m.*

bladder, *s.* vejiga *f.*

blade, *s.* (*grass*) brizna *f.*; (*knife*) hoja *f.*; razor ~ hoja de afeitar.

blame, *v. a.* echar la culpa a, culpar; —*s,* culpa *f.*; reproche *m.*

blank, *s.* formulario *m.*

blanket, *s.* manta *f.*

bleed, *v. n.* sangrar; — *v. a.* desangrar.

blend, *v. a.* mezclar; — *v. n.* mezclarse; — *s.* mezcla *f.*

bless, *v. a.* bendecir; — *me!* ¡cielos!

blind, *adj.* ciego ~ alley callejón (*m.*) sin salida.

block, *s.* (*buildings*) manzana *f.*; cuadra *f.*; bloque *m.*; (*traffic*) obstáculo *m.*; *v. a.* bloquear, obstruir.

blood, *s.* sangre *f.*

bloody, *adj.* sangriento.

bloom, *s.* floración *f.*; *fig.* prosperidad *f.*; — *v. n.* florecer; *fig.* prosperar.

blossom, *s.* flor *f.*; capullo *m.*; — *v. n.* estar en flor.

blot, *s.* mancha *f.*; — *v. a.* manchar.

blouse, *s.* blusa *f.*

blow¹, *v. n.* soplar; ~ up volar, hacer estallar.

blow², *s.* golpe *m.*

blue, *adj.* azul.

blunder, *s.* equivocación *f.* — *v. n.* cometer una equivocación, equivocarse.

blunt, *adj.* romo, obtuso.

board, *s.* tabla *f.*; plancha

f.;(meals) alimento m.,
comida f.; (council)
concejo m., comisión f.;
— v. a. alimentar; ~
the ship embarcar; —
v. n. comer.

boarder, s. huésped m.

boarding-house, s. casa
(f.) de huéspedes, pen-
sión f.

boarding-school, s. inter-
nado m.

boast, v. n. jactarse; — s.
jactancia f.

boat, s. barca f.; buque
m., barco m.

boat-train, s. tren (m.)
de enlace con el buque.

bodily, adj. corporal.

body, s. cuerpo m.

boil¹, v. a. & n. hervir,
cocer.

boil², s. furúnculo m.

boiler, s. caldera f.; ter-
mosifón m.

bold, adj. atrevido.

bolt, s. cerrojo m.; — v. a.
echar el cerrojo; v. n.
lanzarse.

bomb, s. bomba f.; — v.
a. bombardear.

bond, s. lazo m.; obliga-
ción f.; contrato m.

bone, s. hueso m.

bonnet, s. gorra f.; cu-
bierta (f.) del motor.

book, s. libro m.; — v. a.
reservar, prenotar;
(ticket) sacar, comprar.

bookcase, s. armario (m.)
para libros, librería
f.

booking-office, s. taquilla
f.

book-keeper, s. contable
m.; tenedor (m.) de
libros.

book-keeping, s. conta-
bilidad f.

book-maker, s. corredor
(m.) de apuestas.

bookseller, s. librero m.

bookshelf, s. librería f.,
estante (m.) para li-
bros.

bookshop, librería f.

boot, s. bota f.

booth, s. barraca f.

booty, s. botín m.

border, s. frontera f., borde m.; — v. a. orlar,

boring, adj. aburrido.

born, pp. nacido; be ~
nacer.

borrow, v. a. pedir pres-
tado.

bosom, s. seno m.; pecho
m.

boss, s. jefe m., patrón m.

botanical, adj. botánico.

botany, s. botánica f.

both, s. ambos m., ambas
f.; los dos; — conj.
~ ... and tanto ...
como.

bottle, s. botella f.; — v.
a. embotellar.

bottom, s. fondo m.

bough, s. rama f.; ramo
m.

boundary, s. límite m.

bouquet, s. ramillete (m.)
de flores.

bow,¹ s. arco m.; (knot)
nudo m.

bow², v. n. inclinarse; hacer una reverencia; —
s. reverencia f.; (ship)
proa f.

bowels, s. pl. intestinos m.
pl. .

bowl, s. tazón m.

box, s. caja f., cajón m.;
(theatre) palco m.

box-office, s. taquilla f.

boy, s. niño m., muchacho
m.; ~ scout explorador
m.

bra, s. sostén m.

bracelet, s. pulsera f.; brazalete m.

brain, s. seso m.; cerebro m.

brainy, listo, cuerdo.

brake, s. freno m.; — v. a. frenar.

branch, s. rama f.; ramo m.; sucursal f.; — v. n. ramificarse, bifurcarse.

brand, s. marca f.; género m.; — v. a. marcar con hierro.

brave, adj. valiente; v. n. afrontar.

brawl, s. alboroto m., pelea f.; v. n. alborotar, pelear.

bread, s. pan m.; ~ and butter pan con mantequilla.

breadth, s. anchura f.

break, v. a. romper; — v. n. romperse.

break-down, s. depresión (f.) nerviosa; (car) avería f.

breakfast, s. desayuno m.; have ~ desayunar(se).

breast, s. pecho m.; seno m.; mama f.

breath, s. respiración f.; aliento m.; soplo m.

breathe, v. a. & n. respirar.

breed, v. a. criar; — v. n. reproducirse.

breeze, s. brisa f.

bribe, s. soborno m.; — v. a. sobornar.

brick, s. ladrillo m.

bricklayer, s. albañil m.

bride, s. novia f.; recién casada f.

bridegroom, novio m.; recién casado m.

bridge, s. puente m.

brief, adj. breve, sucinto.

briefcase, s. cartera f.

briefly, adv. brevemente.

bright, adj. brillante; claro; listo.

brighten, v. a. pulir; v. n.

despejarse; iluminarse.

brightness, s. brillo m.; serenidad f.

brilliant, adj. brillante; — s. brillante m.

bring, v. a. traer; ~ up educar.

brisk, adj. ágil, vivo.

British, adj. británico.

broad, adj. ancho.

broadcast, v. a. transmitir, radiar; s. emisión f., transmisión f.

broadcasting, s. emisión f.

broken, pp. roto, quebrado.

bronze, s. bronce m.

brooch, s. broche m.

brook, s. arroyo m.

broom, s. escoba f.

brother, s. hermano m.

brother-in-law, s. cuñado m

brown, adj. pardo, moreno.

bruise, s. contusión f.; — v. a. contusionar.

brush, cepillo m.; — v. a. cepillar.

brute, s. bruto m., bestia f.

bucket, s. cubo m., balde m.

bud, s. capullo m., brote m.; — v. n. brotar.

budget, s. presupuesto m.; — v. a. asignar.

buffet, s. buffet m., aparador m.; ambigú m.

bug, s. chinche f.

build, v. a. construir, edificar; — s. figura f.

builder, s. arquitecto m.

building, s. edificio m.

built-in, adj. ~ wardrobe armario (m.) empotrado.

bulb, s. tubérculo m.; bombilla f.

bull, s. toro m.

bullet, *s.* bala *f.*

bulletin, *s.* boletín *m.*

bun, *s.* bollo *m.*; panecillo *m.*

bunch, *s.* ~ *of flowers* ramillete *(m.)* de flores; ~ *of keys* manojo *(m.)* de llaves.

bundle, *s.* lío *m.*; manojo *m.*; — *v. a.* atar.

buoy, boya *f.*

burden, *s.* carga *f.*; peso *m.*; — *v. a.* cargar.

burglar, *s.* ladrón *m.*

burial, *s.* entierro *m.*; funeral *m.*

burn, *v. a. & n.* quemar; — *s.* quemadura *f.*

burst, *v. a. & n.* reventar, estallar; — *s.* estallido *m.*

bury, *v. a.* enterrar, sepultar.

bus, *s.* autobús *m.*

bush, *s.* arbusto *m.*, maleza *f.*

business, *s.* ocupación *f.*, oficio *m.*; asunto *m.*; negocio *m.*

businessman, *s.* hombre *(m.)* de negocios.

bus-stop, parada *(f.)* del autobús.

bust, *s.* busto *m.*

busy, *adj.* diligente; ocupado.

but, *conj.* pero; *next door* ~ *one* de aquí a la segunda puerta.

butcher, *s.* carnicero *m.*

butter, *s.* mantequilla *f.*

butterfly, *s.* mariposa *f.*

button, *s.* botón *m.*; — *v. a.* abotonar, abrochar.

buy, *v. a.* comprar.

buyer, *s.* comprador *m.*

by, *prep.* cerca de; por; según; ~ *car* en coche; ~ *heart* de memoria; ~ *chance* casualmente; — *adv.* cerca; ~ *the way* a propósito; *close* ~ muy cerca.

C

cab, *s.* coche *(m.)* de punto; taxi *m.*

cabbage, *s.* col *f.*

cabin, *s.* cabaña *f.*; camarote *m.*; barraca *f.*

cabinet, *s.* armario *m.*; gabinete *m.*, caja *f.*; consejo *(m.)* de ministros.

cabinet-maker, *s.* ebanista *m.*

cable, *s.* cable *m.*; cablegrama *m.*; — *v. a.* mandar un cable, cablegrafiar.

café, *s.* café *m.*

cage, *s.* jaula *f.*; — *v. a.* enjaular.

cake, *s.* bizcocho *m.*, pastel *m.*

calculate, *v. a.* calcular.

calendar, *s.* calendario *m*

calf, *s.* ternero *m.*; becerro *m.*; *(anatomy)* pantorrilla *f.*

call, *v. a.* llamar; ~ *on* visitar, ir a ver; ~ *up* llamar por teléfono; *to be* ~*ed for* en lista de correos; — *s.* llamada *f.*; visita *f.*

call-box, *s.* cabina *(f.)* telefónica.

calm, *adj.* calmoso, tranquilo; — *s.* calma *f.*; — *v. a.* calmar, tranquilizar.

camel, *s.* camello *m.*

camera, *s.* aparato *(m.)* fotográfico, cámara *(f.)* fotográfica.

camp, *s.* campo *m.*, campamento *m.*, colonia *f.*; — *v. n.* campar.

campaign, *s.* campaña *f.*

camping, *s.* camping *m.*

can¹, *I ~ do it* puedo
hacerlo; *you ~ go*
puede irse.

can², *s.* jarro *m.; (car)*
bidón *m.*

canal, *s.* canal *m.*

canary, *s.* canario *m.*

cancel, *v. a.* cancelar,
anular.

cancer, *s.* cancro *m.*

candle, *s.* vela *f.;* bugía *f.*

cane, *s.* cana *f.;* bastón
m.

cannon, *s.* cañón *m.*

canoe, *s.* canoa *f.*

can-opener, *s.* abrelatas
m.

canteen, *s.* cantina *f.;* ambigú *m.; (bottle)* can-
timplora *f.*

canvas, *s.* lona *f.; (picture)* lienzo *m.*

cap, *s.* gorro *m.;* gorra *f.;*
tapa *f.*

capable, *adj.* capaz (de).

capacity, *s.* capacidad *f.*

cape¹, *s.* capa *f.*

cape², *s.* cabo *m.,* promon-
torio *m.*

capital, *s. (money)* capital *m.; (town)* capital
f.; — adj. capital.

captain, *s.* capitán *m.*

caption, *s.* leyenda *f.*

capture, *s.* captura *f.; —
v. a.* capturar.

car, *s.* coche *m.,* automóvil *m.,* auto *m.*

caravan, *s.* caravana *f.;*
coche *(m.)* vivienda.

carbon-paper, *s.* papel
(m.) carbón.

card, *s.* naipe *m.,* carta *f.;*
tarjeta *(f.)* de visita.

cardboard, *s.* cartón *m.*

cardigan, *s.* chaqueta *(f.)*
de lana.

cardinal, *s.* cardenal *m.;
— adj.* cardinal; *~
number* número *(m.)*
cardinal: *the ~ points*

los puntos cardinales.

care, *s.* preocupación *f.;*
cuidado *m.; take ~ !*
¡cuidado!; *c/o* al cui-
dado de; *— v. n.* pre-
ocuparse de; *I don't ~ !*

¡qué me importa! *~
for* interesarse por.

career, *s.* carrera *f.*

careful, *adj.* cuidadoso;
prudente, cauteloso.

careless, *adj.* descuidado,
desatento.

caress, *s.* caricia *f.; — v.
a.* acariciar.

cargo, *s.* cargamento *m.*

carnation, *s.* clavel *m.*

carpenter, *s.* carpintero *m.*

carpet, *s.* alfombra *f.*

carriage, *s.* vehículo *m.,*
coche *m.*

carriage-way, *s.* autopista
f.; dual ~ carretera *(f.)*
con dos pistas.

carrot, *s.* zanahoria *f.*

carry, *v. a.* llevar.

cart, *s.* carretón *m.;* ca-
rretilla *f.; — v. a.*
transportar.

cartoon, *s.* caricatura *f.;*
película *(f.)* de dibu-
jos animados.

cartridge, *s.* cartucho *m.;*
rollo *(m.)* de película.

carve, *v. a.* cortar; ta-
llar.

case¹, *s.* caso *m.;* asunto
m.; in ~ caso que; *in
any ~* de todos modos.

case², *s.* estuche *m.,* caja
f.

cash, *s.* caja *f.;* metálico
m.; moneda *(f.)* con-
tante; *pay ~* pagar al
contado; *~ on delivery*
por reembolso; *— v. a.*
cobrar.

cash-book, *s.* libro *(m.)*
de caja.

cashier, *s.* cajero *m.*

cask, *s.* barril *m.*

cast, v. a. echar; ~ a vote votar; s. tiro m., lance m. (theatre) reparto m.; (mould) fundición f.

castle, s. castillo m.; ~s in Spain castillos en el aire; — v. a. enrocar (chess).

casual, adj. casual.

cat, s. gato m.

catalog(ue), s. catalogo m.

cataract, s. catarata f.

catastrophe, s. catástrofe f.

catch, v. a. coger, atrapar; (arrest) capturar; ~ the train alcanzar el tren; ~ cold coger un catarro.

category, s. categoría f.

cater, v. a. abastecer; cuidar de.

caterpillar, s. oruga f.

cathedral, s. catedral f.

catholic, adj. & s. católico (m.); liberal.

cattle, s. ganado m.

cauliflower, s. coliflor f.

cause, s. causa f.; asunto m.; — v. a. causar.

caution, s. prudencia f., precaución f.; ~ money caución f.; (warning) advertencia f.; — v. a. advertir.

cautious, adj. cauto, prudente.

cave, s. cueva f.

cavern, s. caverna f.

cavity, s. cavidad f.

cease, v. a. &. n. cesar.

ceaseless, adj. incesante.

cedar, s. cedro m.

ceiling, s. techo m., cielo raso m.

celebrate, v. a. celebrar.

celebration, s. celebración f.

celery, s. apio m.

cell, s. celda f.; (biology) célula f.

cellar, s. sótano m.

cello, s. violoncelo m.

cement, s. cemento m.

cemetery, s. cementerio m.

centenary, s. centenario m.

central, adj. central; ~ heating calefacción (f.) central; — adj. céntrico.

centre, s. centro m.; — v. a. centralizar, concentrar.

century, s. siglo m.

cereal, s. cereales m. pl.

ceremony, s. ceremonia f.

certain, adj. seguro, cierto; for ~ sin falta; make ~ of sg cerciorarse de.

certainly, adv. ciertamente.

certificate, s. certificado m.; ~ of birth acta (f.) de nacimiento.

certify, v. a. certificar.

chain, s. cadena f.; — v. a. encadenar.

chair, s. silla f.; presidencia f. — v. n. presidir.

chairman, s. presidente m.

chalk, s. tiza f.

challenge, s. desafío m.; — v. a. desafiar.

chamber, s. cámara f.

champagne, s. champaña m.

champion, s. campeón m.

championship, s. campeonato m.

chance, s. oportunidad f.; posibilidad f.

chancellor, s. canciller m.

change, s. cambio m.; for a ~ para variar; — v. a. cambiar; (clothes) mudarse; ~ train cambiar de tren.

channel, s. canal m.; the English ~ La Mancha.

chap, s. mozo m.
chapel, s. capilla f.
chapter, s. capítulo m.
character, s. carácter m.; *(novel)* personaje m.
characteristic, s. característica f.; *adj.* característico.
charge, s. *(weapon, electricity)* carga f.; *(office)* posición f.; cargo m.; *(law)* acusación f.; ~ account cuenta (f.) de crédito; take ~ of hacerse cargo de; — v. a. cargar; *(entrust)* encargar; *(expenses)* cobrar; *(law)* acusar.
charity, s. caridad f.; beneficencia f.; limosna f.
charm, s. encanto m.; — v. a. encantar.
charming, adj. encantador.
chase, v. a. cazar; — s. caza f., persecución f.
chassis, s. chasis m.
chat, s. charla f.; plática.
chatter, v. n. charlar; castañetear; — s. charla f.
cheap, adj. barato.
cheat, v. a. engañar; — s. engaño m.
check, s. cheque m.; *(bill)* cuenta f.; *(ticket)* marca f.; — v. a. *(control)* examinar; marcar; *(hinder)* trabar; ~ up control; ~ out marcharse.
checkmate, s. jaque (m.) mate; — v. a. dar jaque mate.
cheek, s. mejilla f.
cheeky, adj. insolente.
cheer, s. alegría f.; give a ~ dar vivas; — v. a. aplaudir.
cheerful, adj. alegre, animado.
cheerio, int. ¡hasta pronto!

(drinking) ¡a su salud!
cheese, s. queso m.
chemical, adj. químico.
chemist, s. boticario m., químico; ~'s shop farmacia f.
chemistry, s. química f.
cheque-book, s. talonario (m.) de cheques.
cherry, s. cereza f.; *(tree)* cerezo m.
chess, s. ajedrez m.
chest, s. cajón m., armario m.; ~ of drawers cómoda f.; *(anatomy)* pecho m.
chestnut, s. castaña f.; — adj. marrón.
chew, v. a. mascar, masticar.
chicken, s. pollo m., gallina f.
chief, adj. principal; — s. jefe m.
chiefly, adv. principalmente, sobre todo.
child, s. niño m., niña f.
childhood, s. infancia f.
childish, adj. pueril.
childless, adj. sin hijos.
chill, s. frío m.; — v. a. helar; *fig.* enfriar.
chilly, adj. frío.
chimney, s. chimenea f.
chin, s. barba f., barbilla f.
china, s. porcelana f.
Chinese, adj. chino.
chip, s. astilla f.; — s. pl. patatas (f.) fritas.
chocolate, s. chocolate m.
choice, s. elección f.; — adj. excelente.
choir, s. coro m.
choke, v. a. ahogar; v. n. atragantarse.
choose, v. a. elegir, escoger.
chop, v. a. cortar; — s. chuleta f.
Christian. adj. & s. cris-

tiano (m.).

Christianity, s. cristianismo m.

Christmas, s. Pascua f., Navidad f.; *Merry* ~! ¡Felices Pascuas! ~ *eve* Nochebuena f.

church, s. iglesia f.

cider, s. sidra f.

cigar, s. cigarro m., puro m., habano m.

cigarette, s. cigarrillo m., pitillo m.

cigarette-case, s. pitillera f.

cigarette-holder, s. boquilla f.

cinder, s. ceniza f.

cine-camera, s. tomavistas m.

cinema, s. cine m.; cinematografía f.

circle, s. círculo m.; — v. n. dar vueltas.

circuit, s. circuito m.; *short* ~ corto circuito.

circular, adj. redondo; — s. circular f.

circulate, v. a. & n. circular.

circumstance, s. circunstancia f.; *under no* ~s en ningún caso.

circus, s. circo m.; plaza (f.) rotunda.

cite, v. a. citar.

citizen, s. ciudadano m., ciudadana f.

citizenship, s. ciudadanía f.

city, s. ciudad f.

civil, adj. civil; ~ *service* servicio (m.) público; (polite) cortés.

civilian, ciudadano m.

civilize, v. a. civilizar.

claim, s. demanda f., pretensión f.; — v. a. reclamar.

clap, v. n. aplaudir; — s. aplauso m.; palmada f.

class, s. clase f.; — v. a. clasificar.

classic, adj. & s. clásico (m.)

classify, v. a. clasificar.

class-room, s. sala (f.) de clase, aula f.

clause, s. cláusula f.

claw, s. garra f.; — v. a. agarrar.

clay, s. greda f., arcilla f.

clean, adj. limpio; — v. a. limpiar; ~ *out* vaciar; ~ *up* arreglar(se).

cleaning, s. limpieza f.

clear, adj. claro, limpio; — adv. por completo, del todo; — v. a. limpiar, aclarar.

clergy, s. clero m.

clergyman, s. clérigo m.

clerk, s. empleado m., dependiente m.; secretario m.

clever, s. listo, inteligente.

client, s. cliente m.

climate, s. clima m.

climb, v. a. subir; — s. subida f.

cling, v. n. agarrarse de.

clinic, s. clínica f.

cloak, s. abrigo m., capote m., capa f.; — v. a. cubrir.

cloak-room, s. guardarropa m.; (station) consigna f., depósito (m.) de equipajes.

clock, s. reloj m.

close, adj. cercano; (shut) cerrado adv. ~ *at hand* muy cerca; ~ s. final m.; — v. a. cerrar, terminar.

closet, s. gabinete m., ropero m., armario m.; (WC) retrete m.

cloth, s. tela f.; *lay the* ~ poner la mesa.

clothe, v. a. vestir.

clothes, s. pl. ropa f.
clothing, s. ropa f.
cloud, s. nube f.; — v. a.
nublarse.
cloudy, adj. nublado.

club, s. club m.; maza
(f.) de golf; (cards)
trébol m.; — v. a. gol-
pear.
clue, s. indicio m., pista f.
clutch, v. a. agarrar; — s.
embrague m.
coach, s. coche m., vagón
m.; (person) entrena-
dor m.; — v. a. entre-
nar.
coal, s. carbón m.
coal-mine, s. hullera f.,
mina (f.) de carbón.
coast, s. costa f.; — v. n.
costear.
coat, s. abrigo m., sobre-
todo m.; (jacket) cha-
queta f., americana f.;
— (paint) mano f.;
~ of arms blasón m.,
escudo m.; ~ v. a.
cubrir.
cock, s. gallo m.; (tap)
grifo m.; (hammer) ga-
tillo m.; — v. a. amar-
tillar.
cockpit, s. cabina (f.) del
piloto.
cocktail, s. coctel m.
cocoa, s. cacao m.
coconut (coco), s. coco m.
cod, s. bacalao m.
code, s. cifras f. pl.;
(law) código m.
coffee, s. café m.
coffee-mill, s. molinillo
(m.) de café.
coffee-pot, s. cafetera f.
coffin, s. ataúd m.
coin, s. moneda f.
coincidence, s. coincidencia f.
coke, s. coque m.
cold, adj. frío; I am ~
tengo frío; — s. frío

m.; catarro m.; ~ in
the head constipado m.,
resfrío m.
collaborate, v. n. cooperar.
collapse, s. colapso m.; —
v. n. hundirse.
collar, s. cuello m.; — v.
a. agarrar.
colleague, s. colega m.,
compañero m.
collect, v. a. recoger; coleccionar; (gather) reu-
nir(se).
collection, s. colección f.
college, s. colegio m.;
universidad f.
collide, v. n. chocar.
collision, s. colisión f.
colon,[1] s. dos puntos.
colon,[2] (anatomy) colón m.
colonel, s. coronel m.
colonial, adj. colonial.
colony, s. colonia f.
colour, s. color m.; ~s
bandera (f.) nacional;
— v. a. colorar.
colourless, adj. incoloro.
column, s. columna f.
comb, s. peine m.; — v. a.
peinar.
combine, v. a. combinar;
v. n. unirse; — s. sega-
dora-trilladora f.; car-
tel m.
come, v. n. venir; (arrive)
llegar; ~ and see me
venga usted a verme;
~ to know llegar a
saber; ~ back volver,
regresar; ~ in entrar;
~ up subir.
comedy, s. comedia f.
comfort, s. comodidad f.;
— v. a. consolar.
comfortable, adj. cómodo.
comic, adj. & s. cómico
(m.); — s. historietas
(f. pl.) cómicas.
comma, s. coma f.
command, v. a. & n. co-
mandar, ordenar; — s.

orden f., mando m.

commander, s. comandante m.

commemorate, v. a. conmemorar.

commence, v. a. & n. empezar, comenzar, principiar.

comment, s. comentario m.; — v. n. hacer comentarios.

commentary, s. comentario m.

commerce, s. comercio m.

commercial, adj. comercial, mercantil.

commission, s. comisión f.; — v. a. encargar; nombrar, designar.

commissioner, s. comisionado m., comisario m.

commit, v. a. cometer, perpetrar; (to prison) encerrar, meter; ~ oneself comprometerse.

committee, s. comisión f., comité m.

common, adj. común.

commonwealth, s. unión (f.) de Estados.

communicate, v. n. comunicar.

communication, s. comunicación f.

communication-cord, s. freno (m.) de alarma.

community, s. comunidad f.

compact, s. contrato m.; m.; (powder) polvera f.; — adj. compacto; fig. conciso, breve.

companion, s. compañero m.

company, s. compañía f.

comparatively, adv. relativamente.

compare, v. a. comparar.

comparison, s. comparación f.

compartment, s. compartimiento m.

compass, s. brújula f.

compasses, s. pl. compás m.

compel, v. a. obligar.

competence, s. competencia f.

competition, s. competición f.

competitor, s. competidor m.

complain, v. n. quejarse.

complaint, s. queja f.; reclamación f.

complete, adj. completo; — v. a. completar, terminar.

complication, s. complicación f.

compliment, s. piropo m., galantería f.; — v. a. felicitar.

comply, v. a. cumplir; ~ with conformarse ∂.

component, s. componente m.

compose, v. a. componer, formar; ~ oneself serenarse.

composer, s. compositor m.

composition, s. composición f.

compound, adj. & pp. compuesto; — s. composición f., compuesto m.; — v. a. componer, mezclar.

comprehend, v. a. comprender.

comprehension, s. comprensión f.

compress, v. a. comprimir; — s. compresa f.

compromise, s. compromiso m.; — v. n. acordarse; comprometer.

compulsory, adj. obligatorio, de rigor.

comrade, s. camarada m., compañero m.

conceal, *v. a.* ocultar, esconder.
conceited, *adj.* presumido
concentrate, *v. a.* concentrar.
concept, *s.* concepto *m.*
conception, *s.* concepción *f.*; opinión *f.*
concern, *v. a.* referirse a, interesar; *be ~ed for* inquietarse por; — *s.* casa *(f.)* comercial, empresa *f.*, *(anxiety)* angustia.
concert, *s.* concierto *m.*; — *v. n.* concertarse.
concession, *s.* concesión *f.*
concise, *adj.* conciso, breve.
conclude, *v. a.* concluir, terminar; *v. n.* llegar a la conclusión.
conclusion, *s.* conclusión *f.*; iinal *m.*, fin *m.*, cabo *m.*
concrete, *adj.* concreto; — *s.* cemento *m.*; hormigón *m.*
condemn, *v. a.* condenar.
condense, *v. a.* condensar.
condition, *s.* condición *f.*; estado *m.*
conduct, *s.* conducta *f.*, — *v. a.* conducir, dirigir.
conductor, *s.* cobrador *m.*, revisor *m.*; *(orchestra)* director *m.*
cone, *s.* cono *m.*
confectioner, *s.* confitero *m.*, pastelero *m.*
confectionery, *s.* confitería *f.*, pastelería *f.*
confer, *v. a. & n.* conferir.
conference, *s.* conferencia *f.*, reunión *f.*
confess, *v. a.* confesar.
confidence, *s.* confianza *f.*
confident, *adj.* seguro; — *s.* confidente *m.*
confidential, *adj.* confidencial.
confine, *v. a.* limitar; *be*

~ed to bed tener que guardar cama.
confirm, *v. a.* confirmar.
conflict, *s.* conflicto *m.*; — *v. n.* luchar, chocar.
confront, *v. a.* confrontar.
confuse, *v. a.* confundir, desorientar.
confusion, *s.* confusión *f.*
congratulate, *v. a.* felicitar.
congratulation, *s.* felicitación *f.*, enhorabuena *f.*
congress, *s.* congreso *m.*
conjecture, *s.* conjetura *f.*; — *v. a.* conjeturar.
connect, *v. a.* conectar, relacionar: *~ with* enlazar con.
connection, *s.* conexión *f.*
conquer, *v. a.* conquistar, vencer.
conqueror, *s.* conquistador *m.*
conquest, *s.* conquista *f.*
conscience, *s.* conciencia *f.*
conscious, *adj.* consciente; *be ~ of* darse cuenta de.
consent, *s.* permiso *m.*; — *v. n.* consentir.
consequence, *s.* consecuencia *f.*
consequent, *adj.* consecuente, consiguiente.
consequently, *adv.* por lo tanto, por eso.
conservation, *s.* conservación *f.*
conservative, *adj.* conservador.
consider, *v. a.* considerar, estudiar, tomar en cuenta.
considerable, *adj.* considerable, bastante.
considerate, *adj.* atento, delicado.
consideration, *s.* consideración *f.*; *(payment)* retribución *f.*; *take into*

~ tener en cuenta.

consign, v. a. consignar; mandar.

consignment, s. consignación f., envío m.

consist, v. n. consistir.

consistent, adj. lógico, razonable.

consolation, s. consuelo m.

consonant, adj. & s. consonante (f.)

conspicuous, adj. conspicuo.

constable, s. agente (m.) de policía, guardia m.

constant, adj. constante.

constitute, v. a. constituir.

constitution, s. constitución f.

construct, v. a. construir.

construction, s. construcción f.

consul, s. cónsul m.

consulate, s. consulado m.

consult, v. a. consultar; v. n. deliberar.

consultation, s. consulta f., deliberación f.

consume, v. a. consumir.

consumer, s. consumidor m.

consumption, s. consumo m.; (illness) tisis f., tuberculosis f.

contact, s. relación f., contacto m.

contain, v. a. contener; ~ oneself contenerse.

container, s. recipiente m.

contemplate, v. a. contemplar; (project) proyectar.

contemporary, adj. & s. contemporáneo (m.).

contempt, s. desprecio m., menosprecio m.

content, adj. contento, satisfecho; — s. contento m., satisfacción f.

contents, s. pl. contenido m.

continent, s. continente m.

continental, adj. continental.

continuation, s. continuación f.

continue, v. a. continuar; ~ reading seguir leyendo; to be ~d continuará.

continuous, adj. continuo.

contract, s. contrato m.; — v. a. contratarse; (debt, illness) contraer.

contradiction, s. contradicción f.

contrary, adj. & s. contrario (m.); ~ to contrario a; on the ~ al contrario.

contrast, s. contraste m., diferencia f.; — v. n. contrastar, hacer contraste; (compare) comparar.

contribute, v. a. contribuir; v. n. colaborar.

contribution, s. contribución f.; colaboración f.

control, s. control m.; dirección f.; ~s mando m.; — v. a. controlar; dirigir.

convenience, s. comodidad f.

convenient, adj. conveniente, cómodo, oportuno.

conversation, s. conversación f.

converse, v. n. conversar.

convert, v. a. convertir, transformar.

convey, v. a. transmitir, llevar.

conveyance, s. transporte m.; (vehicle) vehículo m.

conveyer, s. cinta (f.) transportadora.

convince, v. a. convencer.

cook, v. a. cocinar, gui-

sar; — s. cocinero m.,
cocinera f.

cool, adj. fresco; — v. a.
enfriar; v. n. enfriar-
se.

co-operative, s. coopera-
tiva f.

copper, s. cobre m.

copy, s. copia f.; número
m.; — v. a. copiar.

coral, s. coral m.

cord, s. cuerda f.

cordial, adj. & s. cordial
(m.).

cork, s. corcho m.; — v.
a. tapar con corcho.

cork-screw, s. sacacorchos
m.

corn, s. grano m.; trigo
m.; (on the foot) callo m.

corned-beef, s. adobado
(m.) de carne de vaca.

corner, s. (street) esquina
f.; (room) rincón m.

corporal, s. cabo m.; —
adj. corporal.

corporation, s. corpora-
ción f.

corps, s. cuerpo m.; army
~ cuerpo (m.) de
ejército.

corpse, s. cadáver m.

correct, adj. correcto.
exacto; — v. a. corre-
gir.

correction, s. corrección f.

correspond, v. n. estar
de acuerdo; ~ with
escribir a.

correspondence, s. correspondencia f.

correspondent, s. corresponsal m.

corridor, s. corredor m.,
pasillo m.

corrupt, adj. corrupto; —
v. a. corromper; —
v. n. corromperse.

corruption, s. corrupción
f.

cosmetics, s. pl. cosmético
m.

cost, s. precio m.; —
v. a. costar.

costly, adj. costoso, caro.

costume, s. traje m.; (fancy dress) disfraz m.

cottage, s. casita f.,
chalet m.

cotton, s. algodón m.

couch, s. diván m.

cough, s. tos f.; — v. n.
toser.

council, s. concejo m.,
junta f.

councillor, s. consejero
m., concejal m.

counsel, s. consejo m.;
(lawyer) abogado m.;
— v. a. aconsejar.

count[1], v. a. contar;
— s. recuento m.

count[2], s. conde m.

countenance, s. cara f.,
aspecto m.; (aid) apo-
yo m.; — v. a. apo-
yar.

counter, s. mostrador m.;
— adj. contrario.

countess, s. condesa f.

country, s. país m.; región
f.; in the ~ en el campo,
en provincias.

countryman, s. aldeano
m., campesino m.

countryside, s. paisaje m.

county, s. condado m.,
distrito m.

couple, s. par m.; pareja
f.; — v. a. acoplar.

courage, s. valor m.

courageous, adj. valiente, valeroso, bravo.

course, s. curso m.; (way)
ruta f., dirección f.;
(dish) plato m.; of ~
claro, por supuesto.

court, s. patio m.; (law)
juzgado m.; tribunal
m.; (royal) Corte f.;
— v. a. hacer la corte a.

courteous, adj. cortés.

courtesy, s. cortesía f.

courtyard, s. patio m.

cousin, s. primo m., prima f.

cover, v. a. cubrir, tapar; *(embrace)* abarcar; *(distance)* recorrer; *(with a weapon)* apuntar; — s. tapa f., tapadera f.; *(rug)* manta f.; *(furniture)* funda f.

cow, s. vaca f.

coward, adj. & s. cobarde (m., f.).

crab, s. cangrejo m.

crack s. *(sound)* detonación f.; *(gap)* raja f., grieta f.; — v. a. & n. rajar; forzar, cascar; ~ *jokes* decir chistes; — adj. grande; — int. ¡crac!

cracker, s. galleta f.

cradle, s. cuna f.; — v. a. mecer.

craft, s. habilidad f., astucia f.; *(profession)* profesión f., oficio m. *(conveyance)* embarcación f.

craftsman, s. artesano m.

crane, s. grúa f.; *(bird)* grulla f.

crash, s. choque m.; *(sound)* estrépito m.; — v. n. chocar.

crash-helmet, s. casco (m.) protector.

crave, v. a. anhelar, codiciar.

crawl, v. n. marchar lentamente; *(on all fours)* gatear; — s. *(swim)* crawl m.

crayon, s. lápiz (m.) de color.

crazy, adj. loco, extravagante.

cream, s. crema f.; *fig.* crema y nata f.

create, v. a. crear.

creation, s. creación f.

creator, s. creador m.

creature s. criatura f.; *(beast)* animal m., bicho m.; *fig.* tipo m.

credentials, s. pl. credenciales f. pl.

credit, s. saldo (m.) a favor, crédito m.

creditor, s. acreedor m.

crew, s. tripulación f.; *(group)* cuadrilla f.

cricket, s. grillo m.; *(sport)* cricket m.

crime, s. delito m., crimen m.

criminal, adj. & s. criminal (m.).

crimson, adj. & s. carmesí (m.).

cripple, s. cojo (m.), estropeado (m.); — v. a. estropear.

crisis, s. crisis f.

critic, s. crítico m.

critical, adj. crítico.

criticism, s. crítica f.

criticize, v. a. criticar.

crooked, adj. torcido; *fig.* deshonesto.

crop, s. cosecha f.; — v. a. cosechar; *(hair)* cortar; ~ up surgir.

cross, s. cruz f.; *(crossing)* cruce m.; — v. a. cruzar; atravesar.

crossing, s. cruce m.

crossroad, s. cruce (m.) de caminos.

cross-word (puzzle), s. crucigrama m.

crow, s. cuervo m.; *(cock's)* canto m.; — v. n. cantar.

crowd, s. multitud f., muchedumbre f.; — v. a. abarrotar; — v. n. apiñarse.

crowded, adj. abarrotado, completamente lleno, de bote en bote.

crown, *s.* corona *f.; fig.* cumbre *f.; — v. a.* coronar.

crude, *adj.* bruto; *(rude)* tosco.

cruel, *adj.* cruel.

cruelty, *s.* crueldad *f.*

cruet, *s.* alcuza *f.*, vinagreras *f. pl.*

cruise, *s.* viaje *(m.)* marítimo; — *v. n.* rondar.

crumb, *s.* miga *f.*

crusade, *s.* cruzada *f.*

crush, *v. a.* aplastar; — *v. n.* aplastarse.

crust, *s.* corteza *f.*

cry, *v. n.* gritar; *(weep)* llorar; — *s.* grito *m.;* llanto *m.*

crystal, *s.* cristal *m.*

cub, *s.* cría *f.*, cachorro *m.*

cube, *s.* cubo *m.;* (ice-)cubito *m.;* *(of sugar)* terrón *m.*

cuckoo, *s.* cuclillo *m.*

cucumber, *s.* pepino *m.*

cue [1], *(theatre)* entrada *f.*

cue [2], *(billiards)* taco *m.*

cuff, *s.* puño *m.;* *(slap)* bofetada *f.; — v. a.* dar una bofetada a.

cultivate, *v. a.* cultivar.

cultural, *adj.* cultural.

culture, *s.* cultura *f.*

cup, *s.* taza *f.*, copa *f.*

cupboard, *s.* aparador *m.;* alacena *f.*, armario *m.*

cure, *v. a.* curar; — *v. n.* curarse; — *s.* cura *f.*

curiosity, *s.* curiosidad *f.;* rareza *f.*

curious, *adj.* curioso; *(odd)* raro.

curl, *s.* rizo *m.; — v. a.* rizar.

curly, *adj.* rizado.

currant, *s.* grosella *f.*

currency, *s.* dinero *m.;* *foreign* ~ divisa *f.*, moneda *(f.)* extranjera.

current, *s.* corriente *f.;* — *adj.* corriente, común; ~ *account* cuenta *(f.)* corriente.

curse, *s.* maldición *f.;* — *v. a.* maldecir.

curtain, *s.* cortina *f.;* *(theatre)* telón *m.*

curve, *s.* curva *f.; — v. a.* curvar; *v. n.* hacer una curva.

cushion, *s.* almohada *f.*, cojín *m.*

custard, *s.* natillas *f. pl.*

custom, *s.* costumbre *f.;* ~*s* impuestos *m. pl.;* aduana *f.*

customary, *adj.* usual, acostumbrado.

customer, *s.* cliente *m.*, parroquiano *m.*

customhouse, *s.* aduana *f.*

cut, *v. a.* cortar; *(hay)* segar; *off* cortar; ~ *out* recortar; ~ *up* dividir, cortar — *s.* cortadura *f.;* *(of dress)* corte *m.;* parte *f.;* rebaja *f.;* — *adj.* *(glass)* tallado.

cutlery, *s.* cuchillos *m. pl.*, cubiertos *m. pl.*

cutter, *s.* cortador *m.;* *(ship)* cúter *m.*

cycle, *s.* ciclo *m.;* bicicleta *f.; — v. n.* ir en bicicleta.

cylinder, *s.* cilindro *m.*

D

dad, daddy, *s.* papá *m.*

daily, *adj.* diario; — *adv.* diariamente; — *s.* diario *m.*, periódico *m.*

dainty, *adj.* delicado, fino.

dairy, *s.* lechería *f.*

daisy, *s.* margarita *f.*

dam, *s.* dique *m.*

damage, *s.* daños *m. pl.;* — *v. a.* estropear, averiar.

damages, s. pl. indemnización f.

dame, s. dama f.

damn, v. a. condenar; — int. ¡caray! ~ it! ¡Caramba!

dance, v. n. bailar; — s. baile m.

dancer, s. bailarín m., bailarina f.

Dane, s. dinamarqués m., danés m.

danger, s. peligro m.

dangerous, adj. peligroso.

Danish, adj. danés.

dare, v. n. atreverse.

dark, adj. oscuro; — s. oscuridad f.

darkness, s. oscuridad f.

darling, adj. & s. querido (m.), alma f.

darn, v. a. zurzir; — s. zurcido m.

dash, v. a. echar, tirar; — v. n. salir corriendo; ~ it! ¡demonio!

dash-board, s. salpicadero m.; cuadro (m.) de instrumentos, panel m.

data, s. pl. datos m. pl.

date[1], (fruit) dátil m.

date[2], s. fecha f.

daughter, s. hija f.

daughter-in-law, s. nuera f.

dawn, s. amanecer m., madrugada f.; — v. n. amanecer.

day, s. día m.; ~ by ~ cada día; some ~ un día; by ~ de día; the other ~ hace poco; a ~ off día libre.

day-nursery, s. guardería (f.) infantil.

day-ticket, s. billete (m.) válido un día.

daytime, adv. de día.

deacon, s. diácono m.

dead, adj. & s. muerto

(m.).

deadly, adj. mortal.

deaf, adj. sordo.

deal, v. a. (cards) repartir, dar; ~ in tráficar en; ~ with tratar de; — s. (business) negocio m.; square ~ buen trato (m.); a great ~ of mucho, gran cantidad de.

dealer, s. comerciante m., vendedor m.

dealing, s. distribución f.

dean, s. decano m.; (church) deán m.

dear, adj. querido; oh ~! ¡Dios mío!; Dear Sir Muy Señor Mío.

death, s. muerte f.

debt, s. deuda f.

debtor, s. deudor m.

decease, s. muerte f.; — v. n. morir, fallecer.

deceit, s. engaño m., trampa f.

deceive, v. a. engañar.

December, s. diciembre m.

decent, adj. decente.

deception, s. decepción f.

decide, v. a. decidir.

decidedly, adv. decididamente.

decision, s. decisión f., resolución f.

decisive, adj. decisivo.

deck, s. cubierta f.

deck-chair, s. silla (f.) de tijera.

declare, v. a. declarar; v. n. declararse.

decline, v. a. rehusar; — v. n. decaer; — s. declinación f.

decorate, v. a. decorar.

decoration, s. decoración f.; (distinction) condecoración f.

decrease, v. a. & n. disminuir; — s. disminución f.

decree, *s.* decreto *m.;*
— *v. a.* decretar.

dedicate, *v. a.* dedicar.

deed, *s.* acción *f.,* obra
f.; (contract) con-
trato *m.*

deep, *adj.* hondo, profundo.

deer, *s.* venado *m.*

defeat, *v. a.* vencer; — *s.*
derrota *f.*

defect, *s.* defecto *m.*

defence, *s.* defensa *f.*

defend, *v. a.* defender.

defender, *s.* defensor *m.*

deficient, *adj.* deficiente.

defile, *v. n.* desfilar; —
s. desfile *m.*

define, *v. a.* definir.

definite, *adj.* definitivo.

definition, *s.* definición *f.*

defy, *v. a.* desafiar.

degree, *s.* grado *m.; by
~s* gradualmente; *(ti-
tle)* título *m.*

delay, *v. a.* demorar; —
s. demora *f.*

delegate, *s.* delegado *m.;*
— *v. a.* delegar.

delegation, *s.* delegación
f.

deliberate, *adj.* delibe-
rado; — *v. a.* deliberar.

delicate, *adj.* delicado; —
(wine) exquisito; *(vase)*
frágil

delicious, *adj.* delicioso.

delight, *s.* deleite *m.;* —
v.a. deleitar, encantar.

delightful, *adj.* delicioso;
encantador.

deliver, *v. a.* entregar,
repartir; *(speech)* dar,
pronunciar.

delivery, *s.* entrega *f.*

delusion, *s.* decepción *f.*

demand, *s.* demanda *f.;*
petición *f.;* — *v. a.*
exigir; insistir.

democracy, *s.* democracia
f.

democrat, *s.* demócrata
m., f.

democratic, *adj.* democrático.

demolish, *v. a.* demoler,
derrumbar.

demonstration, *s.* demostración *f.;* manifesta-
ción *f.*

den, *s.* caverna *f.*

denial, *s.* denegación *f.*

denomination, *s.* deno-
minación *f.;* valor *(m.)*
nominal.

denounce, *v. a.* denunciar.

dense, *adj.* denso, espeso.

dental, *adj.* dental.

dentist, *s.* dentista *m.*

denture, *s.* dentadura *f.*

deny, *v. a.* negar.

deodorant, *adj.* deso-
dorante.

depart, *v. n.* irse, partir.

department, *s.* departamento *m.;* ministerio *m.*

departure, *s.* partida *f.,*
salida *f.*

depend, *v. n.* depender;
it ~s depende; *~ on*
confiar en.

dependent, *adj. & s.* dependiente *(m.).*

deplore, *v. a.* deplorar.

depose, *v. a.* deponer.

deposit, *s.* depósito *m.;*
— *v. a.* depositar.

depot, *s.* depósito *m.,* almacén *m.*

depress, *v. a.* deprimir.

depression, *s.* depresión *f.*

deprive, *v. a.* privar.

depth, *s.* profundidad *f.*

deputy, *s.* diputado *m.;*
(substitute) sustituto,
vice-.

derive, *v. a.* derivar; —
v. n. derivarse.

descend, *v. n.* descender, bajar.

descendant, *s.* descendiente *m.*

descent, *s.* descenso *m.;* (*birth*) descendencia *f.*

describe, *v. a.* describir.

description, *s.* descripción *f.*

desert [1], *s.* desierto *m.*

desert [2], *v. n.* desertar.

deserve, *v. a.* merecer.

design, *v. a.* diseñar, proyectar; — *s.* proyecto *m.*

desire, *s.* deseo *m.;* — *v. a.* desear.

desk, *s.* escritorio *m.;* (*office*) despacho *m.*

desolate, *adj.* desolado, despoblado.

despair, *v. n.* desesperar; — *s.* desesperación *f.*

despatch, *see* **dispatch.**

desperate, *adj.* desesperado.

despise, *v. a.* despreciar.

despite, *prep.* a pesar de.

dessert, *s.* postre *m.*

dessert-spoon, *s.* cucharilla *f.*

destination, *s.* destinación *f.*

destine, *v. a.* destinar.

destiny, *s.* destino *m.*

destroy, *v. a.* destruir.

destruction, *s.* destrucción *f.*

detach, *v. a.* separar; destacar.

detachment, *s.* separación *f.;* destacamento *m.*

detail, *s.* detalle *m.;* — *v. a.* detallar.

detain, *v. a.* detener.

detective, *s.* detective *m.*

detergent, *s.* detergente *m.*

deteriorate, *v. a.* deteriorar; — *v. n.* deteriorarse.

determine, *v. a.* determi-

nar; decidir.

detonation, *s.* detonación *f.*

develop, *v. a.* desarrollar; (*film*) revelar.

development, *s.* desarrollo *m.;* (*event*) cambio *m.,* acontecimiento *m.*

device, *s.* (*trick*) recurso *m.,* ardid *m.;* (*mechanism*) dispositivo *m.,* aparato *m.*

devil, *s.* diablo *m.,* demonio *m.*

devoted, *adj.* fiel, aficionado.

devotion, *s.* devoción *f.*

devour, *v. a.* devorar.

dew, *s.* rocío *m.*

diabetes, *s.* diabetes *f.*

diadem, *s.* diadema *f.*

diagnosis, *s.* diagnosis *f.*

diagram, *s.* diagrama *m.*

dial *s.* cuadrante *m.,* esfera *f.;* disco *m.* — *v. a.* marcar.

dialect, *s.* dialecto *m.*

dialogue, *s.* diálogo *m.*

diameter, *s.* diámetro *m.*

diamond, *s.* diamante *m.;* — *adj.* de diamantes.

diaper, *s.* pañal *m.*

diarrhoea, *s.* diarrea *f.*

diary, *s.* diario *m.*

dictate, *v. a.* dictar.

dictation, *s.* dictado *m.*

dictionary, *s.* diccionario *m.*

die [1], *s.* dado *m.*

die [2], *v. n.* morir; (*motor*) pararse.

diet, *s.* dieta *f.;* — *v. n.* estar a dieta.

differ, *v. n.* diferir.

difference, *s.* diferencia *f.;* *it makes no* ~ no importa

different, *adj.* diferente, distinto.

difficult, *adj.* difícil.

difficulty, *s.* dificultad

f.

diffuse, *v. a.* difundir; — *adj.* difuso.

dig, *v. a.* excavar, sacar.

digest, *v. a.* digerir; — *s.* resumen *m.*, reseña *f.*

digestion, *s.* digestión *f.*

dignity, *s.* dignidad *f.*

diligence, *s.* diligencia *f.*

diligent, *adj.* diligente, aplicado.

dimension, *s.* dimensión *f.*

diminish, *v. a.* disminuir.

dine, *v. a.* comer, cenar.

dining-car, *s.* coche comedor *m.*

dining-room, *s.* comedor *m.*

dinner, *s.* cena *f.*, comida *f.*, *have ~* cenar, comer.

dinner-jacket, *s.* smoking *m.*

diphtheria, *s.* difteria *f.*, difteritis *f.*

diploma, *s.* diploma *m.*

diplomacy, *s.* diplomacia *f.*

diplomatic, *adj.* diplomático.

direct, *v. a.* dirigir; — *adj.* directo; *fig.* recto.

direction, *s.* dirección *f.*, rumbo *m.; (command)* instrucción *f.*

directly *adv.* directamente

director, *s.* director *m.*

directory, *s.* libro *(m.)* de señas; guía *f.*

dirt, *s.* suciedad *f.*, basura *f.*

dirty, *adj.* sucio; — *v. a.* manchar.

disadvantage, *s.* desventaja *f.*

disagree, *v. n.* disentir; oponerse.

disagreeable, *adj.* desagradable.

disappear, *v. n.* desaparecer.

disappoint, *v. a.* desengañar.

disappointment, *s.* desengaño *m.*

disapprove, *v. a.* desaprobar.

disarm, *v. a.* desarmar.

disaster, *s.* desastre *m.*

disc, *s.* disco *m.*

discern, *v. a.* discernir.

discharge, *v. a.* descargar; *(duties)* desempeñar, cumplir; *(from the hospital)* dar de alta; — *s.* descarga *f.; (shot)* disparo *m.*

discipline, *s.* disciplina *f.; — v. a.* disciplinar.

discourage, *v. a.* desanimar.

discourse, *s.* discurso *m.; — v. a.* tratar de.

discover, *v. a.* descubrir.

discovery, *s.* descubrimiento *m.*

discreet, *adj.* discreto.

discretion, *s.* discreción *f.*, prudencia *f.*

discuss, *v. a.* discutir.

discussion, *s.* discusión *f.*

disease, *s.* enfermedad *f.*

disembark, *v. a. & n.* desembarcar.

disgrace, *s.* deshonra *f.*

disgraceful, *adj.* deshonroso, vergonzoso.

disguise, *s.* disfraz *m.; — v. a.* disfrazar.

disgust, *s.* disgusto *m.; — v. a.* disgustar; *I'm ~ed* me repugna, me disgusta.

disgusting, *adj.* repugnante.

dish, *s.* plato *m.; — v. a. ~ up* servir.

dishonest, *adj.* deshonesto.

dishonour, *s.* deshonor

m.; — *v. a.* deshonrar.

dish-water, *s.* lavadura *f.,* lavazas *f. pl.*

disinfect, *v. a.* desinfectar.

disk, *see* disc.

dislike, *v. a.* no querer; *I* ~ *it* no me gusta; — *s.* antipatía *f.*

dismiss, *v. a.* despedir.

disobedient, *adj.* desobediente.

disobey, *v. n.* desobedecer.

disorder, *s.* desorden *m.*

dispatch, *v. a.* despachar, enviar; — *s.* despacho *m.*

dispensary, *s.* farmacia *f.;* dispensario *m.*

dispense, *v. a.* dispensar; ~ *with* pasar sin.

disperse, *v. a.* dispersar; — *v. n.* dispersarse.

displease, *v. n.* desagradar.

disposal, *s.* disposición *f.;* for ~ por vender.

dispose, *v. a.* disponer.

disposition, *s.* disposición *f.; (mind)* genio *m.*

dispute, *v. n.* disputar, discutir; — *s.* disputa *f.,* discusión *f.*

disqualify, *v. a.* descalificar.

dissolve, *v. a.* disolver; — *v. n.* disolverse, desaparecer.

distance, *s.* distancia *f.*

distant, *adj.* dis'ante, lejano.

distinct, *adj.* claro, preciso, diferente, distinto.

distinguish, *v. a.* distinguir; ~ *oneself* distinguirse.

distort, *v.a.* torcer.

distract, *v.a.* distraer.

distress, *s.* angustia *f.;*

(danger) peligro *m.,* apuro *m.;* — *v. a.* angustiar.

distribute, *v. a.* distribuir.

distribution, *s.* distribución *f.; (mail)* reparto *m.*

district, *s.* distrito *m.*

disturb, *v. a.* molestar, perturbar.

dive, *v. n.* zambullirse; — *s.* zambullida *f.; (plane)* picada *f.*

diver, *s.* buzo *m.*

divide, *v. a.* dividir.

dividend, *s.* dividendo *m.*

divine, *adj.* divino; — *v. a.* adivinar.

diving, *s.* salto *(m.)* de palanca.

diving-board, *s.* trampolín *m.,* palanca *f.*

division, *s.* división *f.*

divorce, *s.* divorcio *m.;* — *v. n.* divorciarse.

dizzy, *adj.* mareado; *(speed)* vertiginoso.

do, *v. a.* hacer; *what can I* ~ *for you?* ¿en qué puedo servirle? ; *that will* ~ está bien, basta; *that won't* ~ no conviene; ~ *one's best* hacer todo lo posible; *nothing* ~*ing!* ¡qué se le va a hacer!; *I am done* estoy muerto de cansancio; *how* ~ *you* ~? ¡buenos días! (¡buenas noches!); ¡hola!; *he is* ~*ing well* está bien; le va bien; *I don't know* no sé; *so* ~ *I* yo también; *you like coffee, don't you?* le gusta el café, ¿verdad?; ~ *again* repetir.

dock, *s.* muelle *m.;* — *v. n.* atracar.

dockyard, s. astilleros m. pl.

doctor, s. médico m., doctor m.; — v. a. curar, tratar.

document, s. documento m.

documentary, ~ film película (f.) documental.

dog, s. perro m.

doll, s. muñeca f.

dollar, s. dólar m.

dome, s. cúpula f.

domestic, adj. (person) casero; (animal) doméstico; — s. doméstica f., criada f.

dominate, v. n. dominar.

dominion, s. dominio m.

donkey, s. burro m., asno m.

door, s. puerta f; next ~ al lado; out of ~s al aire libre; fuera.

dormitory, s. dormitorio m.

dose, s. dosis f.

dot, s. punto m.

double, adj. doble; ~ bed cama (f.) de matrimonio; ~ bedroom habitación (f.) con dos camas; — v. a. duplicar, doblar.

doubt, s. duda f.; no ~ sin duda; — v. n. dudar.

doubtful, adj. dudoso.

doubtless, adv. sin duda, indudablemente.

dough, s. masa f.

dove, s. paloma f.

down, adv. abajo; go ~ bajar; ~ in the country en el campo; — prep. ~ the river río abajo.

downstairs, adv. (escaleras) abajo.

downward(s), adv. hacia abajo.

dozen, s. docena f.

draft, s. (plan) plano m.; (air) corriente (f.) de aire; (chimney) tiro m.; (bank) giro m.; — v. a. (plan) trazar; (recruit) reclutar.

drain, v. a. desecar; fig. agotar; — s. desagüe m.

drama, s. drama m.

dramatic, adj. dramático.

draper, s. pañero m.

drapery, s. paños m. pl.; (ornament) colgaduras f pl.

draught, s. tiro m.; tracción f.; (drink) trago m.; (air) corriente (f.) de aire; (sketch) esbozo m.; (ship) calado m.

draw, v. a. (fetch) sacar; (at school; sketch) dibujar; ~ to an end llegar a su fin; ~ back retirar(se); ~ near acercarse; ~ out sonsacar; ~ up (sketch) redactar; — s. (lottery) sorteo m.; (game) empate m.

drawer, s. gaveta f.; chest of ~s cajón m.; (person) dibujante m.; s. pl. calzoncillos m. pl.

drawing-pin, s. chinche f.

drawing-room, s. sala f., salón m.

drawn, adj. empatado.

dread, v. n. temer, tener miedo; — s. miedo m.; terror m.

dreadful, adj. espantoso.

dream, s. sueño m.; — v. n. soñar.

dress, s. traje m., vestido m.; — v. a. vestir; (decorate) arreglar; (hair) peinar; (wound) hacer la cura a.

dresser, s. aparador m.

dressing-gown, s. bata f.

dressmaker, s. modista f.

dress-suit s. frac m.

drift, s. corriente f.; propensión f.; − v. a. arrastrar; v. n. dejarse arrastrar; amontonarse.

drill, s. taladro m.; (exercise) entrenamiento m.; − v. a. perforar; entrenar, hacer ejercicios.

drink, v. a. beber; ~ to sy's health brindar por; − s. bebida f.; trago m.

drip, v. n gotear.

drive, v. a. (car) conducir; (nail) clavar; ~ at proponerse; ~ away echar; − s. (road) carretera f.; (by car) paseo (m.) en coche (golf) golpe m.; (campaign) campaña f.

driver, s. chófer m., motorista m.

driving license, s. permiso (m.) de conductor.

drop, s. gota f.; − v. a. dejar caer; v. n. caerse, bajar; ~ in pasar por; venir (a ver).

drown, v. n. ahogarse.

drug, s. droga f., medicina f.; narcótico m.; − v. a. narcotizar.

druggist, s. boticario m.

drunk, adv. borracho; get ~ emborracharse.

dry, adj. seco; ~ land tierra (f.) firme; fig. aburrido; − v. a. secar; ~ up secarse.

dry-clean, v. a. limpiar en seco.

dub, v. a. apodar; (film) sincronizar.

duchess, s. duquesa f.

duck, s. pato m.; − v. n. bajar, agachar; − v. a. zambullir.

due, adj. the train is ~ at noon el tren debe llegar al mediodía; in ~ time a su tiempo; − s. cuota f.; impuesto m.

duel, s. duelo m.

duke, s. duque m.

dull, adj. (knife) romo; (sad) triste; (pain) sordo; (boring) soso, aburrido; (stupid) torpe.

duly, adv. debidamente.

dumb, adj. mudo; strike ~ dejar atónito.

dummy, s. maniquí m., (cards) muerto m.; (theatre) comparsa f.; (imitation) imitación f.; (baby) chupete m.

duplicate, s. copia f.

durable, adj. durable, duradero.

during, prep. durante.

dusk, s. crepúsculo m., oscurecer m.

dusky, adj. oscuro, sombrío.

dust, s. polvo m.; bite the ~ morder el polvo; − v. a. quitar el polvo de.

dustbin, s. lata (f.) para la basura; cubo m.

dustman, s. basurero m.

dusty, adj. polvoriento.

Dutch, adj. holandés.

Dutchman, s. holandés m.

duty, s. deber m.; on ~ de guardia, de servicio; off ~ libre de servicio; (taxes) impuesto m.

duty-free, adj. libre de derechos.

dwarf, s. enano m.

dwell, v. n. vivir, habitar; ~ on insistir en.

dwelling, s. vivienda f.

casa *f.*

dwelling-house, *s.* casa (*f.*) de vivienda.

dye, *v. a.* teñir; — *s.* tinte *m.*

E

each, *pron.* cada; ~ *other* el uno al otro.

ear, *s.* oído *m.*; *I'am all* ~*s* soy todo oídos; *anat.* oreja *f.*

earl, *s.* conde *m.*

early, *adj.* pronto, rápido; ~ *life* juventud *f.*; ~ *riser* madrugador *m.*; — *adv.* temprano.

earn, *v. a.* ganar.

earnest, *adj.* serio; — *s.* in ~ en serio.

earth, *s.* mundo *m.*, tierra *f.*; — *v. a.* dar tierra.

earthquake, *s.* terremoto *m.*

ease, *s.* naturalidad *f.*; *live a life of* ~ llevar una vida desahogada; *be at* ~ estar tranquilo; *with* ~ con soltura; — *v. a.* aliviar.

east, *s.* este *m.*, *the Near East* el Oriente Cercano; *the Far East* el Extremo Oriente.

Easter, *s.* Pascua (*f.*) de Resurrección; Pascua Florida.

eastern, *adj.* del este, oriental.

easy, *adj.* fácil; *feel easier* sentirse mejor; — *adv.* *take it* ~! ¡tómelo con calma!

easy-chair, *s.* sillón *m.*, butaca *f.*

eat, *v. a.* comer; *I want something to* ~ quiero algo para comer.

ebb, *s.* reflujo *m.*; — *v. n.* disminuir, bajar.

echo, *s.* eco *m.*; — *v. a.* & *n.* resonar; repetir.

economic(al), *adj.* económico.

economics, *s pl.* economía (*f.*) política.

economy, *s.* economía *f.*

edge, *s.* (*razor*) filo *m.*; (*book*) borde *m.*

edition, *s.* edición *f.*

editor, *s.* redactor *m.*

editorial, *adj.* & *s.* editorial (*m.*), artículo (*m.*) de fondo.

educate, *v. a.* educar.

education, *s.* educación *f.*

effect, *s.* efecto *m.*, resultado *m.*; *in* ~ en realidad; *go into* ~ entrar en vigor; — *v. a.* efectuar, realizar.

effective, *adj.* de buen efecto; *become* ~ entrar en vigor.

effort, *s.* esfuerzo *m.*; intento *m.*

egg, *s.* huevo *m.*; *boiled* ~ huevo pasado por agua.

egg-cup, *s.* huevera *f.*

Egyptian, *adj.* & *s.* egipcio (*m.*).

eight, *adj.* & *s.* ocho.

eighteen, *adj.* & *s.* diez y ocho, dieciocho.

eighth, *adj.* octavo.

eighty, *adj.* & *s.* ochenta.

either, *adj.* & *pron.* cualquiera de los dos; *on* ~ *side* a ambos lados;

~... *or* o...o.

elastic, *adj.* & *s.* elástico (*m.*); goma *f.*

elbow, *s.* codo *m.*

elder, *adj.* mayor.

elderly, *adj.* de cierta edad.

elect, *v. a.* elegir; — *adj.* electo.

election, *s.* elección *f.*

electric(al), *adj.* eléctrico.
electricity, *s.* electricidad
f.
electron, *s.* electrón *m.*
electronic, *adj.* electró-
nico.
elegance, *s.* elegancia *f.*
elegant, *adj.* elegante.
element, *s.* elemento *m.*
elementary, *adj.* ele-
mental
elephant, *s.* elefante *m.*
eleven, *adj. & s.* once.
eleventh, *adj.* undécimo.
else, *conj.* o; *or* ~ o si
no; - *pron. & adj.* más;
everyone ~ todos los
demás; *nothing* ~ nada
más.
elsewhere, *adv.* en otra
parte.
embankment, *s. (river)*
dique *m.; (railway)*
calzada *f.; (port)* mue-
lle *m.*
embark, *v. a.* embarcar.
embassy, *s.* embajada *f.*
embrace, *v. a.* abrazar;
(contain) abarcar.
embroider, *v. a.* bordar.
emerge, *v. n.* emerger.
emergency, *s.* emergencia
f.
emigrant, *s.* emigrante
m., f.
emigrate, *v. n.* emigrar.
emigration, *s.* emigración
f.
emit, *v. a.* emitir.
emotion, *s.* emoción *f.*
emperor, *s.* emperador *m.*
empire, *s.* imperio *m.*
employ, *v. a.* emplear; -
s. empleo *m.*
employee, *s.* empleado
m.
employer, *s.* patrón *m.*
employment, *s.* empleo *m.*
empty, *adj.* vacío; *I feel* ~
tengo hambre; - *v. a.*

vaciar; *v. n.* vaciarse.
enable, *v. a.* permitir.
enclose, *v. a.* cercar; *(annex)* adjuntar; ~d ad-
junto.
encounter, *s.* encuentro
m.; - *v. a.* encontrar,
dar con.
encourage, *v. a.* estimular,
animar, *fig.* fomentar.
encyclopaedia, *s.* enciclopedia *f.*
end, *s.* final *m.; (aim)*
fin *m.; loose* ~s cabos
m. pl.; - *v. n.* terminar.
endeavour, *v. n.* esforzarse; - *s.* esfuerzo *m.*
ending, *s.* fin *m.; (of a
word)* desinencia *f.*
endless, *adj.* sin fin,
infinito.
endorse, *v. a.* endosar.
endorsement, *s.* endoso *m.*
endow, *v. a.* dotar.
enemy, *s.* enemigo *m.*
energetic, *adj.* enérgico.
energy, *s.* energía *f.*
engage, *v. a. (room)* reservar; *(maid)* tomar.
engagement, *s.* compro-
miso *m.,* cita *f.;* espon-
sales *m. pl.*
engine, *s.* motor *m.;
(train)* locomotora *f.*
engineer, *s.* ingeniero *m.;
(driver)* maquinista *m.*
English, *adj.* inglés; *the* ~
los ingleses.
Englishman, *s.* inglés *m.*
Englishwoman, *s.* inglesa
f.
engrave, *v. a.* grabar.
enjoy, *v. a.* gozar de; ~
oneself divertirse.
enjoyment, *s.* goce *m.;*
placer *m.*
enlarge, *v. a.* ampliar,
agrandar.
enormous, *adj.* enorme.
enough, *adj.* suficiente;

adv. bastante;
that's ~! ¡basta!
enquire, see inquire.
enrich, v. a. enriquecer.
ensign, s. bandera f.,
enseña f.; (person)
alférez m.
enter, v. a. entrar en; ~
the army ingresar en el
ejército; (name) re-
gistrar, anotar.
enterprise, s. empresa f.
entertain, v. a. divertir,
entretener.
entertainment, s. divertimiento m.; (show)
espectáculo m.
enthusiasm, s. entusiasmo
m.
enthusiastic, adj. entusi-
ástico.
entire, adj. entero, todo.
entirely, adv. totalmente,
completamente.
entitle, v. a. titular, de-
nominar; (authorize)
autorizar.
entrails, s. pl. vísceras f.
pl., entrañas f. pl.
entrance, s. entrada f.;
~ examination examen
(m.) de ingreso.
entry, s. entrada f.;
(account) partida f.;
(sports) competidor m.
enumerate, v. a. enume-
rar.
envelop, v. a. envolver,
cubrir.
envelope, s. sobre m.
envious, adj. envidioso.
environment, s. ambiente
m.
envy, s. envidia f.; — v.
a. envidiar.
epidemic, s. epidemia f.;
— adj. epidémico.
equal, adj. & s. igual (m.,
f.); — v. n. equivaler:
— v. n. igualar.
equality, s. igualdad f.
equator, s. ecuador m.

equip, v. a. equipar.
equipment, s. equipo m.
err, v. n. errar, equivo-
carse.
errand, s. recado m.,
mandado m.
error, s. error m.; be in ~
equivocarse.
escalator, s. escalera (f.)
móvil, escalera rodan-
te.
escape, v. n. fugarse, escaparse; v. a. evitar, escapar a; it ~s me no me
viene a la memoria; —
s. fuga f.
escort, s. escolta f.; — v.
a. escoltar.
especial, adj. especial.
especially, adv. especialmente.
essay, s. ensayo m.; — v.
a. ensayar, intentar.
essence, s. esencia f.
essential, adj. esencial.
establish, v. a. establecer.
establishment, s. establecimiento m.
estate, s. estado m.; (property) propiedad f.,
finca f.; real ~ in-
mueble m.
esteem, v. a. estimar; —
s. estima f.
eternal, adj. eterno.
eucharist, s. eucaristía f.
European, adj. & s. euro-
peo.
evacuate, v. a. evacuar.
even, adj. (surface) liso;
(speed) uniforme;
(number) par; (exact)
exacto; — v. a. igua-
lar; — adv. hasta, aún;
not ~ ni siquiera; ~ if
aun cuando.
evening, s. tarde f. (before
sunset); noche f. (after
sunset); ~ dress ves-
tido (m.) de noche,
traje (m.) de etiqueta.

event, *s.* acontecimiento *m.*, suceso *m.*; *(sports)* competición *f.*

eventually, *adv.* eventualmente, finalmente.

ever, *adv.* alguna vez; *(always)* siempre; ~ *since* desde que; *for* ~ por siempre; *Yours* ~ suyo afectísimo; ~ *so much* muchísimo.

every, *adj. & pron.* cada, todos *m.pl.*; ~ *day* cada día, todos los días; ~ *other day* un día sí y otro no.

everybody, *pron.* todo el mundo.

everyday, *adj.* diario, cotidiano.

everyone, *pron.* todo el mundo.

everything, *pron.* todo.

everywhere, *adv.* en todas partes.

evidence, *s.* evidencia *f.*

evident, *adj.* evidente.

evil, *adj.* malo; – *s.* mal *m.*

exact, *adj.* exacto; – *v. a.* exigir.

exactly, *adv.* exactamente.

exaggerate, *v. a.* exagerar.

examination, *s.* examen *m.*; *medical* ~ reconocimiento *(m.)* médico.

examine, *v. a.* examinar; *(doctor)* reconocer; *(judge)* interrogar.

example, *s.* ejemplo *m.*; *for* ~ por ejemplo.

excavation, *s.* excavación *f.*

exceed, *v. a.* exceder.

exceedingly, *adv.* sumamente.

excel, *v. n.* sobresalir.

excellent, *adj.* excelente.

except, *v. a.* exceptuar; – *conj.* excepto.

exception, *s.* excepción *f.*

exceptional, *adj.* excepcional.

excess, *s.* exceso *m.*, sobrante *m.*; – *adj.* ~ *luggage* exceso de equipaje.

excessive, *adj.* excesivo.

exchange, *s.* cambio *m.*; *in* ~ *for* a cambio de; *(building)* bolsa *(f.)* de cambio; *foreign* ~ divisa *f.*; *rate of* ~ curso *m.*, cambio *m.*; *bill of* ~ giro *m.*; *telephone* ~ central *(f.)* telefónica; – *v. a.* cambiar.

excitement, *s.* excitación *f.*; agitación *f.*

exclaim, *v. n.* exclamar.

exclude, *v. a.* excluir.

excursion, *s.* excursión *f.*

excuse, *s.* razón *f.*; – *v. a.* perdonar, dispensar, disculpar; ~ *me* perdóneme.

execute, *v. a.* *(order)* cumplir; *(music)* ejecutar; *(criminal)* ejecutar.

execution, *s.* cumplimiento *m.*; ejecución *f.*

executive, *adj.* ejecutivo, directivo; ~ *board* consejo *(m.)* de administración; – *s.* ejecutor *m.*, director *m.*

exercise, *s.* ejercicio *m.*; – *v. a. & n.* hacer ejercicio, entrenar.

exhaust, *v. a.* agotar; *be* ~*ed* estar exhausto.

exhibit, *v. a.* exhibir; – *s.* exhibición *f.*, exposición *f.*; *(jury)* cuerpo *(m.)* de delito.

exile, *s.* destierro *m.*, exilio *m.*; – *v. a.* desterrar, exilar.

exist, *v. n.* existir.

existence, *s.* existencia *f.*

exit, s. salida f.

expect, v. a. esperar, contar con; I ~ so lo supongo.

expectation, s. expectación f., expectativa f.

expedition, s. expedición f.

expense, s. gasto m.

expensive, adj. caro.

experience, s. experiencia f.; — v. a. pasar por, sufrir.

experiment, s. experimento m.; — v. n. experimentar.

experimental, adj. experimental.

expert, adj. & s. experto (m.).

expire, v. n. expirar.

explain, v. a. explicar; justificar.

explanation, s. explicación f.

exploit, s. hazaña f.; — v. a. explotar.

exploration, s. exploración f.

explore, v. a. explorar.

explosion, s. explosión f.

export, s. exportación f.; — v. a. exportar.

exporter, s. exportador m.

expose, v a. exponer; revelar.

exposure, s. exposición f.; fotografía f.

express, adj. expreso; — s. (train) expreso m.; — v. a. exprimir; ~ oneself expresarse.

expression, s. expresión f.

exquisite, adj. exquisito.

extend, v. a. extender; (visa) prorrogar; (lenghten) prolongar; (congratulations) expresar; — v. n. extenderse.

extension, s. extensión f.; prolongación f.

external, adj. externo.

extinguish, v. a. extinguir, apagar.

extra, adj. adicional, de más; — s. (news-paper) extra m.; (theatre) comparsa f.

extract, s. extracto m.; — v. a. extraer.

extraordinary, adj. extraordinario.

extremely, adv. sumamente.

extremity, s. extremidad f.

eye, s. ojo m.; keep an ~ on vigilar.

eyebrow, s. ceja f.

eyeglasses, s. pl. gafas f. pl.; lentes m. pl.

eyelid, s. párpado m.

eyepiece, s. ocular m.

eyeshade, s. guardavista m.; visera f.

eyesight, s. vis

F

fable, s. fábula f.

face, s. cara f.; ~ down boca abajo; ~ to ~ cara a cara; make ~s hacer muecas; — v. a. hacer frente a; the room ~s the street el cuarto da a la calle.

facility, s. facilidad f.

fact, s. hecho (m.) verídico; as a matter of ~ en realidad.

factory, s. fábrica f.

faculty, s. facultad f.

fade, v. n. desteñirse; (flowers) marchitarse.

fail, v. n. faltar; ~ to

find no poder encontrar; *— s. without* ~ sin falta.

failure, *s.* fracaso *m.*; *heart* ~ ataque *(m.)* al corazón.

faint, *adj.* desfallecido; *(colour)* pálido; *(idea)* vago; *— v. n.* desmayarse.

fair,[1] *s.* feria *f.*

fair,[2] *adj. (hair)* rubio; *(nice)* bueno, bello; *(passable)* ni bien ni mal; ~ *price* precio *(m.)* razonable; *— adv.* honestamente, limpiamente.

fairly, *adv.* bastante.

faith, *s.* confianza *f.*; *in good* ~ de buena fe.

faithful, *adj.* fiel, leal.

faithfully, *adv.* fielmente, lealmente; *yours* ~ *s. s. s.* (su seguro servidor).

falcon, *s.* halcón *m.*

fall, *v. n.* caer, caerse; *(curtain)* bajar; ~ *ill* caer enfermo; ~ *back* retroceder; ~ *for* prenderse de; ~ *in love* enamorarse de; ~ *off* disminuir; ~ *through* fracasar; *— s.* caída *f.*; *(slope)* declive; *(water)* catarata *f.*

false, *adj.* falso; fingido; ~ *teeth* dentadura *(f.)* postiza.

fame, *s.* fama *f.*

familiar, *adj.* conocido, familiar; *be* ~ *with* estar familiarizado con.

family, *s.* familia *f.*; *— adj.* de familia.

famine, *s.* hambre *f.*

famous, *adj.* famoso.

fan,[1] *s.* abanico *m.*; ventilador *m.*; *— v. a.* abanicar.

fan,[2] *(sports)* aficionado *m.*; hincha *m.*

fancy, *s.* fantasía *f.*; imaginación *f.*; *— v. n.* imaginarse.

fantastic, *adj.* fantástico.

far, *adv,* lejos; *so* ~ hasta ahora; *how* ~ *is it?* ¿a qué distancia está? ~ *from it* muy al contrario; *by* ~ con mucho; *as* ~ *lknow* que yo sepa; *as* ~ *as thé town* hasta la ciudad; *— adj.* lejano; *on the* ~ *side of* al otro lado de.

fare, *s.* precio *(m.)* del billete; *(person)* viajero *m.*; *(food)* comida *f.*; *— v. n.* vivir; salir; *(eat)* comer.

farewell, *s.* despedida *f.*; *take one's* ~ *of* sy despedirse de.

farm, *s.* finca *f.*; granja *f.*; hacienda *f.*; *— v. a.* cultivar, labrar.

farmer, *s.* labrador *m.*, agricultor *m.*, granjero *m.*

farther, *adv.* más; más lejos.

fashion, *s.* moda *f.*

fashionable, *adj.* de moda, elegante.

fast,[1] *s.* ayuno *m.*; *— v. n.* ayunar.

fast,[2] *adj. (train)* rápido; *(watch)* estar adelantado; *— adv.* de prisa.

fasten, *v. a.* fijar; *(boat)* amarrar.

fat, *s.* gordo *m.*; *— adj.* grasiento, grueso, gordo.

fate, *s.* fortuna *f.*, suerte *f.*

father, *s.* padre *m.*

father-in-law, *s.* suegro *m.*

fault, *s.* culpa *f.*; defecto *m.*; falta *f.*

faultless, adj. sin defectos, impecable.

faulty, adj. defectuoso.

favour, s. favor m.; ask a ∼ of sy pedir un favor a; − v. a. preferir.

favourable, adj. favorable.

favourite, adj. preferido, favorito.

fear, s. temor m., miedo m.; − v. a. temer.

fearful, adj. (shy) tímido, miedoso; (terrible) terrible, espantoso.

fearless, adj. valiente, intrépido.

feast, s. fiesta f.; banquete m.; − v. a. celebrar; convidar; v. n. deleitarse.

feat, s. hecho m., hazaña f.

feather, s. pluma f.

feature, s. facción f.; − v. a. exhibir.

February, s. febrero m.

federation, s. (con)federación f.

fee, s. honorario m.; cuota f.

feeble, adj. débil.

feed, v. a. dar de comer; ∼ up engordar; I'm fed up estoy harto de; − s. pienso m.

feel, v. a. sentir, palpar, tocar; v. n. sentirse; do you ∼ hungry? ¿tiene usted hambre? I ∼ like a Coca-Cola me apetece una Coca-Cola.

fellow, s. hombre m.; tipo m.

fellowship, s. amistad f.

felt, s. fieltro m.

female, s. hembra f.; − adj. femenino; ∼ child niña f.; chica f.

feminine, adj. femenino.

fencing, s. esgrima f.

ferry, s. ferry m., transbordo m.; − v. n.

transbordar.

ferry-boat, s. transbordador m.

fertile, adj. fértil.

fertilize, v. a. fertilizar.

fertilizer, s. fertilizante m.

festival, s. fiesta f., festival m.

fetch, v. a. traer.

fever, s. fiebre f.

few, adj. & pron. pocos, unos cuantos; quite a ∼ bastante; ∼er menos.

fiancé, s. novio m.

fiancée, s. novia f.

fibre, s. fibra f.

fiction, s. ficción f., fantasía f.; (literature) novela f.

field, s. campo m.; (war) campaña f.

fiery, adj. ardiente, fogoso.

fifteen, adj. & s. quince.

fifth, adj. quinto.

fifty, adj. & s. cincuenta.

fig, s. higo m.; I don't care a ∼ for it ¡no me importa un comino!

fight, v. n. pelear; fig. luchar; − s. pelea f., lucha f.

fighter, s. luchador m.; (plane) avión (m.) de caza, caza m.

figure, s. figura f., tipo m.; línea f.; (number) cifra f.; número m.; (drawing) dibujo m.; − v. a. figurar.

file[1], s. lima f.; − v. a. limar.

file[2], s. archivo m.; fila f.

fill, v. a. llenar; v. n. llenarse.

film, s. película f.; − v. a. & n. filmar.

fin(s), s. aleta f.

final, adj. final, último; − ∼s (sports) final f.; examen (m.) final.

finally, *adv.* finalmente, por último, en fin.

finance, *s.* finanzas *f. pl.;* — *v. a.* financiar.

financial, *adj.* financiero.

find, *v. a.* hallar, encontrar; ~ *out* averiguar; — *s.* hallazgo *m.*

fine¹, *s.* multa *f.;* — *v. a.* multar.

fine², *adj.* fino; *that's* ~! ¡qué bueno!

finger, *s.* dedo *m.;* first ~ índice *m.*

finger-nail, *s.* uña *f.*

finish, *v. a.* terminar, acabar; — *s.* final *m.,* fin *m.*

fir, *s.* abeto *m.*

fire, *s.* fuego *m.;* incendio *m.; be on* ~ arder; *set on* ~ prender fuego a; — *v. a.* disparar.

fire-alarm, *s.* alarma *(m.)* de incendios.

fire-arm, *s.* arma *(f.)* de fuego.

fire-brigade, *s.* cuerpo *(m.)* de bomberos.

fire-engine, *s.* bomba *(f.)* de incendios.

fire-escape, *s.* escalera *(f.)* de salvamento.

fireplace, *s.* chimenea *f.,* hogar *m.*

fire-station, *s.* cuartel *(m.)* de bomberos.

firework(s), *s. (pl.)* fuegos *(m. pl.)* artificiales.

firm¹, *s.* casa *f.*

firm², *adj.* firme.

firmament, *s.* firmamento *m.*

firmness, *s.* firmeza *f.*

first, *adj.* primero; ~ *aid* primeros auxilios *m. pl.;* — *adv.* primero; *por* primera vez.

firstly, *adv.* primeramente.

first-rate, *adj.* de primer orden, de primera categoría.

fish, *s.* pez *m. (alive);* pescado *m. (dish);* — *v. n.* pescar.

fisherman, *s.* pescador *m.*

fish-hook, *s.* anzuelo *m.*

fishing-rod, *s.* caña *(f.)* de pescar.

fist, *s.* puño *m.*

fit¹, *s.* ataque *m.*

fit¹, *adj.* apto; — *v. n.* sentar, encajar; *this key doesn't* ~ esta llave no sirve; *the coat* ~s *me* el abrigo me sienta bien.

five, *adj. &. s.* cinco.

fix, *v. a.* fijar; — *s.* lío *m.*

flag, *s.* bandera *f.;* — *v. a.* embanderar.

flame, *s.* llama *f.* luz *f.;* — *v. n.* llamear.

flank, *s.* costado *m.,* flanco *m.* — *v. a.* flanquear.

flannel, *s.* franela *f.*

flash, *v. n.* destellar, brillar; — *v. a.* proyectar; — *s.* instante *m.;* ~ *of light* destello *m.*

flashlight, *s.* linterna *(f.)* eléctrica.

flat¹, *s.* piso *m.,* apartamiento *m.*

flat², *adj.* plano, llano, liso.

flatter, *v. a.* adular.

flattery, *s.* adulación *f.*

flavour, *s.* sabor *m.;* — *v. a.* sazonar.

flax, *s.* lino *m.*

flea, *s.* pulga *f.*

flee, *v. n.* huir.

fleet, *s.* flota *f.*

flesh, *s.* carne *f.*

flight¹, *s.* vuelo *m.;* ~ *of stairs* escalera *f.*

flight², *s. (escape)* huída *f.,* fuga *f.; put to* ~ poner en fuga.

flirt, *s.* coqueta *f.;* — *v. n.* flirtear.

float, *v. n.* flotar ; — *v. n.* poner a flote; *(loan)* emitir; — *s.* balsa *f.*

flood, *s.* inundación *f.;* — *v. a.* inundar.

floor, *s.* piso *m.*, suelo *m.; ground ~* planta *(f.)* baja, piso bajo.

flour, *s.* harina *f.*

flourish, *v. n.* prosperar.

flow, *v. n.* fluir; — *s.* corriente *f.*, flujo *m.*

flower, *s.* flor *f.;* — *v. n.* florecer.

flower-bed, *s.* macizo *m.*

flu, *s.* gripe *f.*

fluent, *adj.* fluente, fluido.

fluid, *s. & adj.* fluido *(m.)*, líquido *(m.)*

flute, *s.* flauta *f.*

fly¹, *s.* mosca *f.*

fly², *v. n.* volar; ir en avión.

foam(-)rubber, *s.* espuma *(f.)* de goma.

focus, *s.* foco *m.*, centro *m.;* — *v. a.* enfocar.

fog, *s.* neblina *f.*, niebla *f.;* — *v. a.* ofuscar.

fog-horn, *s.* sirena *(f.)* de niebla.

fold, *s.* arruga *f.*, redil *m.; (pleat)* pliegue *m.;* — *v. a.* doblar; *(arms)* cruzar.

foliage, *s.* follaje *m.*

folk, *s.* gente *f.;* familia *f.*

follow, *v. a.* seguir; *do you ~ me?* ¿me entiende usted?; *as ~s* como sigue.

follower, *s.* partidario *m.*

following, *adj.* siguiente.

folly, *s.* tontería *f.*

fond, *adj.* aficionado, cariñoso, tierno; *I'm*

very ~ of flowers me gustan muchísimo las flores.

food, *s.* comida *f.*

fool, *s.* tonto, necio; — *v. a.* engañar.

foolish, *adj.* tonto; *~ thing* tontería *f.*

foot, *s.* pie *m.; on ~* a pie, de pie.

football, *s.* fútbol *m.*

footlight(s), *s. (pl.)* candilejas *f. pl.*

footstep, *s.* huella *f.*, pisada *f.*, paso *m.*

for¹, *prep.* para; por; *leave ~ London* salir para Londres; *~ a year* por un año.

for², *conj.* porque, como.

forbidden, *adj. & pp. it is ~* está prohibido.

force, *s.* violencia *f.; by ~* a la fuerza; *armed ~s* fuerzas *(f. pl.)* armadas; *police ~* policía *f.; legal ~* vigencia *f.; come into ~* entrar en vigor; — *v. a.* forzar, obligar.

forearm, *s.* antebrazo *m.*

forecast, *s.* pronóstico *m.;* — *v. a. & n.* pronosticar.

forefinger, *s.* (dedo) índice *m.*

foreground, *s.* primer plano *m.*

forehead, *s.* frente *f.*

foreign, *adj.* extranjero; *~ affairs* asuntos *(m. pl.)* exteriores; *Foreign Office* Ministerio de Asuntos Exteriores; *~ trade* comercio *(m.)* exterior.

foreigner, *s.* extranjero *m.*, forastero *m.*

forenoon, *s.* mañana *f.*

foresee, *v. a.* prever.

forest, *s.* bosque *m.*

foretell, v. a. predecir, pronosticar.

foreword, s. prefacio m.

forge, s. fragua f.; − v. a. forjar; (falsify) falsificar.

forgery, s. falsificación f.

forget, v. a. olvidar(se); I ~ no recuerdo.

forgive, v. a. perdonar.

fork, s. tenedor m.; (road) empalme m., bifurcación f.; − v. n. bifurcarse.

form, s. forma f.; (school) año m., grado m.; − v. a. formar; ~ a line hacer cola.

formal, adj. formal; ceremonioso.

formality, s. formalidad f.

formation, s. formación f.

former, adj. primero, antiguo, ex-.

formerly, adv. anteriormente.

formula, s. fórmula f.

fortify, v. a. fortificar.

fortnight, s. quince días.

fortunate, adj. afortunado.

fortunately, adj. afortunadamente, por suerte.

fortune, s. fortuna f., dicha f.; (riches) bienes m. pl.

forty, adj. & s. cuarenta.

forward, adj. delantero; − adv. adelante; look ~ to esperar con ilusión; − s. (football) delantero m.; − v. a. reexpedir.

foul, adj. (play) sucio; (air) viciado; (weather) malo; − s. irregularidad f.

found, v. a. fundar.

foundation, s. fundación f.; (base) cimientos m. pl.

founder, s. fundador m.

fountain, s. fuente f.

fountain-pen, s. pluma (f.) fuente, pluma estilográfica.

four, adj. & s. cuatro.

fourteen, adj. & s. catorce.

fourth, adj. & s. cuarto.

fowl, s. aves f. pl., pollo m.

fox, s. zorro m.

fraction, s. fracción f., trozo m.

fracture, s. fractura f.; − v. a. fracturar.

fragile, adj. frágil.

fragrant, adj. fragante.

frail, adj. frágil.

frame, (picture) marco m.; (house) armadura f.; (constitution) constitución f.; complexión f.; − v. a. (picture) poner marco a; (construct) construir.

framework, s. armazón m.; armadura f.

frank, adj. franco.

frankness, s. franqueza f, sinceridad f.

fraternal, adj. fraternal.

fraud, s. fraude m.

free, adj. libre; ~ of charge gratis; ~ of duty libre de derechos aduaneros; − v. a. libertar, poner en libertad.

freedom, s. libertad f.

freely, adv. libremente, con toda libertad.

freeze, v. n. helar; − v. a. congelar.

freight, s. carga f.; (charges) flete m.; − v. a. cargar; fletar.

French, adj. francés.

French-bean, s. judías (f. pl.) verdes.

Frenchman, s. francés m.

Frenchwoman, s. francesa

f.

frequent, adj. frecuente
— v. a. frecuentar.

frequently, adv. frecuentemente.

fresh, adj. fresco; (air) puro, (water) dulce; (new) nuevo; — adv. recién.

friction, s. fricción f.

Friday, s. viernes m.

fridge, s. frigorífico m.; nevera f.

friend, s. amigo m.; make ~s with hacerse amigo.

friendly, adj. amistoso.

friendship, s. amistad f.

fright, s. susto m., miedo m.

frighten, v. a. asustar.

frivolous, adj. frívolo.

frock, s. falda f.; hábito (m.) de fraile.

frog, s. rana f.

from, prep. de; where do you come ~? ¿de dónde es usted?; ~ beginning to end desde el principio al fin; ~ day to day de día en día.

front, s. fachada f.; (war) frente m.; in ~ delante; in ~ of delante de; frente a; — adj. ~ row primera fila f.; — v. n. enfrentarse.

front-door, s. puerta (f.) principal.

frontier, s. frontera f.

frost, s. helada f.; frío m.; — v. a. congelar.

frosty, adj. helado, frío.

frozen, adj. helado, congelado.

fruit, s. fruta f., fruto m.

fruitful, adj. fecundo, fértil.

fruit-tree, s. árbol (m.) frutal.

frustrate, v. a. frustrar.

fry, v. a. freír; fried eggs

huevos (m.) al plato.

frying-pan, s. sartén f.

fuel, s. combustible m.

fulfil, v. a. cumplir.

full, adj. lleno; of ~ age mayor de edad.

fully, adv. enteramente, completamente.

fun, s. diversión f., gracia f.

function, s. función f.; — v. n. funcionar.

fund, s. fondo m.

funeral, s. entierro m.

funnel, s. embudo m.; (of a ship) chimenea f.

funny, adj. gracioso; (strange) extraño, raro.

fur, s. piel f.

fur-coat, s. abrigo (m.) de piel.

furious, adj. furioso.

furnace, s. caldera f.

furnish, v. a. amueblar; (provide) proporcionar.

furnished, adj. amueblado.

furniture, s. muebles m. pl.

furrier, s. peletero m.

further, adv. más; ~ on más lejos.

furthermore, adv. además.

fury, s. furia f.

fuse, v. a. fundir; — v. n. fundirse; — s. fusible m., plomo m.

fuss, s. alboroto m.; — v. n. alborotar.

future, s. futuro m. porvenir m.; — adj. futuro, venidero.

G

gain, v. a. ganar, conquistar; (reach) alcanzar; v. n. (watch) adelantarse; — s. ganancia f.

gait, s. manera (f.) de andar.

gall, s. bilis f.

gallery, s. galería f.; *picture* ~ galería de pinturas.

gallon, s. galón m.

gallop, s. galope m.; — v. n. galopar.

gambling, s. juego (m.) de azar.

game, s. juego m.; *play a* ~ jugar una partida; *(hunting)* caza f.

gamekeeper, s. guardabosque m.

gang, s. pandilla f., cuadrilla f.

gangway, s. pasillo m.; escalerilla (f.) de embarco.

gaol, see **jail.**

garage, s. garaje m., cochera f.

garden, s. jardín m., huerta f.

gardener, s. jardinero m.

garlic, s. ajo m.

garment, s. prenda (f.) de vestir.

garter, s. liga f.

gas, s. gas m.; ~ *stove* cocina (f.) de gas; — v. a. gasear.

gasometer, s. gasómetro m.

gas-pipe, s. tubo (m.) de gas.

gas-range, s. cocina (f.) de gas.

gas-works, s. fábrica (f.) or compañía (f.) de gas.

gate, s. puerta f., entrada f.

gateway, s. puerta (f.) cochera.

gather, v. a. recoger; *(from words)* deducir; v. n. reunirse.

gay, adj. alegre.

gaze, v. a. mirar con fijeza; — s. mirada (f.) fija.

gazetteer, enciclopedia f.; diccionario (m.) geográfico.

gear, s. equipo m.; engranaje m.; *(car)* cambio (m.) de velocidades; — v. n. embragar.

general, s. & adj. general (m.); *in* ~ en general.

generally, adv. general-mente.

generation, s. generación f.

generator, s. generador m.

generosity, s. generosidad f.

generous, adj. generoso.

genial, adj. cordial, afable.

genius, s. genio m.

gentle, adj. *(hand)* cuidadoso; *(knock)* leve; *(person)* apacible, bondadoso.

gentleman, s. caballero m.

gently, adv. delicadamente.

genuine, adj. genuino.

geographical, adj. geográfico.

geography, s. geografía f.

geology, s. geología f.

geometric, adj. geométrico.

geometry, s. geometría f.

germ, s. germen m.

German, adj. & s. alemán.

gesticulate, v. n. gesticular.

gesture, s. gesto m.

get, v. a. recibir, conseguir; *(have)* tener; ~ *me?* ¿me entiende usted?; ~ *one's hair cut* cortarse el pelo; ~ *home* llegar a casa; ~ *better* mejorar; ~ *dress-*

ed vestirse; ~ ill caer
enfermo; it is ~ting
late ya es tarde; ~
married casarse; ~ old
envejecer; ~ tired can-
sarse; ~ along marchar-
se; fig. llevarse bien;
~ at llegar hasta, al-
canzar; ~ away alejar-
se; ~ down bajar; ~ in
meter, entrar; (arrive)
llegar; ~ off apearse;
bajarse; ~ on subir,
proseguir, continuar;
~ out salir, bajarse; ~
up levantarse.

geyser, s. calentador (m.)
de agua.

ghost, s. fantasma m.

giant, s. gigante m.; —
adv. gigantesco.

gift, s. regalo m., obsequio
m.; (talent) talento m.

gifted, adj. talentoso.

gild, v. a. dorar.

gin, s. ginebra f.

ginger, s. jengibre m.

gingerbread, s. pan (m.)
de especies; alajú m.

gipsy, s. gitano m.

giraffe, s. jirafa f.

girdle, s. cinturón m.;
faja f.; — v. a. ceñir,
cercar.

girl, s. niña f.; (older)
muchacha f., chica f;
~ friend amiga f.

give, v. a. dar; (gift) regalar; ~ a toast brindar
por; ~ a hand ayudar;
~ birth dar a luz;
~ away regalar; (se-
cret) divulgar; ~ back
dvolver; ~ up dejar,
aebandonar.

glacier, s. glaciar m.

glad, adj. contento, ale-
gre; be ~ estar contento,
alegrarse.

gladness, s. gozo m.,
alegría f.

glance, v. n. echar una

mirada; ~ through (a
book) hojear; (gleam)
brillar, relucir; — s.
mirada f., ojeada f.

glass, s. vidrio m.; a ~
of wine un vaso or
una copa de vino;
~es gafas f. pl., ante-
ojos m. pl. — v. a.
vidriar.

glazier, s. vidriero m.

gleam, s. destello m.; —
v. n. destellar.

glide, v. n. resbalar, deslizarse; (aviation) pla-
near.

glider, s. planeador m.

glimpse, s. ojeada f.,
vistazo m.; catch a ~ of
avistar; — v. a. dar
un vistazo a.

glitter, v. n. brillar; — s.
resplandor m.

globe, s. esfera f., globo m.

gloom, s. oscuridad f.;
fig. tristeza f.

gloomy, adj. sombrío;
fig. triste, melancólico.

glorious, adj. glorioso.

glory, s. gloria f.; — v. n.
gloriarse.

glove, s. guante m.

glow-worm, s. luciérnaga
f.

glue, s. cola f.

gnat, s. mosquito m.

gnaw, v. a. & n. roer.

go, v. n. ir, andar, mar-
char; let's ~! ¡vámo-
nos!; ~ shopping ir de
compras; ~ bad echarse
a perder; ~ mad
volverse loco; I'm
going to ask you a
favour le pediré a
usted un favor; ~
abroad ir al extranjero;
~ across cruzar; ~
away irse, marcharse;
~ back volver, regresar;
~ down bajar; (sun)
ponerse; ~ on conti-

nuar; ~out salir; (light) apagarse; ~ to pieces romperse en mil pedazos; ~under hundirse; ~

up subir; ~ with acompañar; fig. ir con.
goal, s. meta f.; (sports) gol m., tanto m.
goal-keeper, s. portero m.
goat, s. cabra f.
God, s. Dios m.; ~ bless you! ¡Dios le bendiga!; (sneezing) ¡Salud!

goddess, s. diosa f.
godfather, s. padrino m.
godmother, s. madrina f.
goggles, s. pl. anteojos (m. pl.) de automovilista.
gold, s. oro m.
golden, adj. dorado.
golf, s. golf m.

golf-club, s. palo (m.) de golf.
goloshes, s. pl. chanclos m. pl.
good, adj bueno; (ticket) válido; it is no ~ no sirve para nada; she has ~ looks es muy guapa; very ~! ¡muy bien!; ~ heavens! ¡cielos!; a ~ many mucho; — s. bueno m.; bien m.; ~s bienes m. pl.; ~s train tren (m.) de carga.

good-bye, int. ¡adiós!
good-looking, adj. guapo, bien parecido.
goodness, s. bondad f.
good-tempered, adj. cordial, afable.
goodwill, s. buena voluntad f.
goose, s. ganso m.
gooseberry, s. uva (f.) espina.
gospel, s. evangelio m.

gossip, s. chisme m.; (person) chismoso; — v. n. chismear.
Gothic, adj. gótico.
gout, s. gota f.
govern, v. a. & n. gobernar.
governess, s. institutriz f.
government, s. gobierno m.
governor, s. gobernador m.
gown, s. bata f.; vestido m.
grace, s. gracia f.; with a good ~ de buena gana; with a bad ~ de mala gana; say ~ rezar el benedícite.
graceful, adj. garboso.
gracious, adj. afable.
grade, s. grado m.; — v. a. clasificar.
gradual, aaj. gradual.
graduate, v. n. graduarse; — s. graduado m.
grain, s. grano m.
grammar, s. gramática f.
grammar-school, s. instituto m.
grammatical, adj. gramatical, gramático.
gramme, s. gramo m.
gramophone, s. gramófono m.
grand, adj. magnífico.
grandchild, s. nieto m. nieta f.
granddaughter, s. nieta f.
grandfather, s. abuelo m.
grandma, s. abuelita f.
grandmother, s. abuela f.
grandpa, s. abuelito m.
grandson, s. nieto m.

grape, s. uva f.
grape-fruit, s. toronja f.
grant, v. a. conceder; take for ~ed tomar por cierto: — s. concesión f.;

graph 60. guide-book

subvención f.

graph, s. gráfica f.

graphic, adj. gráfico.

grasp, v. a. agarrar; (meaning) comprender; — s. conocimiento m.

grass, s. hierba f., césped m.

grate, s. parrilla f.; (on the window) reja f.; — v. a. raspar, rayar.

grateful, adj. agradecido.

gratitude, s. gratitud f.

grave,[1] s. sepulcro m., tumba f.

grave,[2] adj. grave.

gravity, s. gravedad f.

gravy, s. salsa f.

gray, adj. gris.

grease, s. grasa f.; — v. a. engrasar.

great, adj. gran, grande; a ~ deal mucho.

greatly, adv. muy; mucho.

greatness, s. grandeza f.

greed, s. codicia f.

greedy, adj. codicioso.

Greek, adj. & s. griego.

green, adj. verde.

greengrocer, s. verdulero m.

greenhouse, s. invernadero m., invernáculo m.

greet, v. a. saludar.

greeting(s), s. (pl.) saludo(s) m. (pl.).

grey, adj. gris.

grief, s. dolor m.

grieve, v. a. afligir, lastimar; v. n. afligirse.

grill s. parrilla f.; v.a. asar a la parrilla.

grim, adj. torvo; horrendo.

grin, s. mueca f.; — v. n. hacer muecas.

grind, v. a. moler; (teeth) rechinar.

grinder, s. molinillo m.; (tooth) muela f.

grip, v. a. agarrarse a; — s. empuñadura f.

grocer, s. especiero m.

grocery, s. tienda (f.) de comestibles, or ultramarinos.

groom, s. mozo (m.) de cuadra; (bride-) novio m.; — v. a. cuidar de.

gross, s. grueso m.; (12 dozens) gruesa f.; — adj. grosero; (error) craso; — ~ weight peso (m.) bruto.

ground, s. tierra f., terreno m.; ~ floor planta (f.) baja.

group, s. grupo m.; — v. a. agrupar.

grow, v. n. crecer; ~ up desarrollarse.

growl, s. gruñido m.; — v. n. gruñir, refunfuñar.

grown-up, adj. & s. adulto m.

growth, s. desarrollo m., crecimiento m.

grudge, v. a. envidiar; — s. rencor m.; bear a ~ against sy guardar rencor a.

gruff, adj. ceñudo, áspero.

grunt, s. gruñido m.; — v. n. gruñir.

guarantee, s. garantía f.;

— v. a. garantizar.

guard, s. guardia m.; (railway) revisor m.; guardatrén m. — v. a. vigilar.

guardian, s. guardián m.

guess, v. a. acertar, adivinar; (think) suponer; — s. conjetura f., suposición f.

guest, s. huésped m., convidado m.

guide, v. a. guiar; — s. guía m., f.

guide-book, s. guía f.

guilt, *s.* delito *m.*, culpa *f.*

guilty, *adj.* culpable; *plead* ~ reconocerse culpable.

guinea, *s.* guinea *f.*

guitar, *s.* guitarra *f.*

gulf, *s.* golfo *m.*

gull, *s.* gaviota *f.*

gullet, *s.* esófago *m.*

gum,[1] *s.* goma *f.*

gum,[2] *(anatomy)* encía *f.*

gun, *s.* fusil *m.*, cañón *m.*

gunpowder, *s.* pólvora *f.*

gust, *s.* ráfaga *f.*

gutter, *s.* canalón *m.*

gymnasium, *s.* gimnasio *m.*

gymnastics, *s. pl.* gimnasia *f.*

gym-shoes, *s. pl.* calzado *(m.)* de gimnasia.

H

haberdashery, *s.* pañería *f.*, mercería *f.*

habit, *s.* costumbre *f.*

hail,[1] *s.* granizo *m.*; — *v. n.* granizar.

hail,[2] *v. a.* aclamar; *(taxi)* llamar; ~ *from* venir de.

hair, *s.* pelo *m.*, cabello *m.*

hairdresser, *s.* peluquero *m.*

hairy, *adj.* velludo, peludo; *(not shaved)* barbudo.

half, *s.* mitad *f.*; — *an hour* media hora *f.*; *an hour and a* ~ una hora y media; — *adj.* medio; — *adv.* medio, a medias.

half-way, *adv.* a medio camino.

hall, *s.* vestíbulo *m.*; salón *m.*; *city* ~ ayuntamiento *m.*

halt, *s.* alto *m.*; *come to a* ~ pararse, interrumpirse; — *v. n.* hacer alto.

ham, *s.* jamón *m.*

hammer, *s.* martillo *m.*; — *v. a.* martillar.

hand, *s.* mano *f.*; *at* ~ a mano; *on* ~ a mano, disponible; *give a* ~ ayudar; *have a* ~ *in* tomar parte en; ~*s off!* ¡quita!; ~*s up!* ¡arriba las manos!; *(on a watch)* manecilla *f.*; *(worker)* obrero *m.*; *(play)* mano *f.*; — *v. a.* entregar, dar; ~ *in* presentar; ~ *on* transmitir, pasar; ~ *out* distribuir.

handbag, *s.* bolso *m.*, cartera *(f.)* de señora.

handbook, *s.* manual *m.*

handful, *s.* puñado *m.*

handicap, *s.* impedimento *m.*, obstáculo *m.*; handicap *m.*; — *v. a.* perjudicar, estorbar.

handkerchief, *s.* pañuelo *m.*

handle, *s.* mango *m.*, palo *m.*; — *v. a.* manejar; tocar, manosear; *(trade)* tener.

hand-made, *adj.* hecho a mano.

handsome, *adj.* guapo; *(generous)* generoso.

handwriting, *s.* letra *f.*, escritura *f.*

handy, *adj.* hábil; *(useful)* útil, a la mano.

hang, *v. a.* colgar; *(head)* bajar, inclinar; ~ *it!* ¡que el diablo se lo lleve!; ~ *up* ahorcar; *v. n.* estar colgado; ~ *about* gandulear, vagar; ~ *back* quedar atrás; *fig.* vacilar; ~ *up* colgar.

hanger, *s.* colgador *m.*,

gancho m.

happen, v. n. pasar, ocurrir, suceder.

happiness, s. felicidad f.

happy, adj. feliz; contento, alegre.

harbour, s. puerto m.; — v. a. abrigar.

hard, adj. duro; (time) difícil; (work) fuerte; (worker) asiduo; (man) severo; (word) injurioso; get ~ endurecerse; ~ cash dinero (m.) contante; — adv. duramente.

hardly, adv. apenas; ~ ever casi nunca.

hardware, s. ferretería f.

hare, s. liebre f.

harm, s. daño m.; — v. a. dañar.

harmful, adj. dañoso, nocivo.

harmless, adj. innocuo, inofensivo.

harmony, s. armonía f.

harp, s. arpa f.

harsh, adj. áspero.

hart, s. ciervo m.

harvest, s. cosecha f.; — v. a. & n. cosechar.

harvester, s. segadora f

haste, s. prisa f.; make ~ apresurarse, darse prisa.

hasty, adj. rápido, precipitado; (decision) ligero, irreflexivo.

hat, s. sombrero m.

hatchet, s. hacha f.

hate, v. a. odiar, aborrecer; — s. odio m.

hateful, adj. odioso.

hatred, s. odio m.

have, v. a. tener; ~ a try intentar; let me ~ your key déme usted su llave; ~ tea tomar un té; ~ dinner comer; ~ lunch almorzar; what will you ~? ¿que desea usted?;

~ a drink tomar un trago; ~ a game jugar un partido; I ~ to leave early tengo que salir temprano; I ~ nothing to do with it no tengo nada que ver con ello; I'd better leave será mejor que me vaya; I ~ a new suit made me hago hacer un nuevo traje.

haversack, s. mochila f.

hawk, s. halcón m.

hay, s. heno m.; make ~ hacer heno.

hazard, s. azar m.

H-bomb, s. bomba (f.) de hidrógeno.

he, pron. él; (animal) macho m.

head, s. cabeza f.; (of the family) cabeza m.; (chief) director m.; (of a page) principio m.; (of cattle) res f.; ~ first de cabeza; keep one's ~ mantener la calma; lose one's ~ perder los estribos; — v. a. estar a la cabeza de.

headache, s. dolor (m.) de cabeza.

heading, s. encabezamiento m., título m.; — (sports) cabezada f.

headlight, s. faro m., linterna (f.) delantera.

headline, s. titular m.

headmaster, s. director (m.) de escuela.

headquarters, s. pl. jefatura f., cuartel (m.) general.

heal, v. a. sanar; v. n. curarse, cicatrizarse.

health, s. salud f.; to your ~! ¡a su salud!

healthy, adj. sano, bien de salud.

heap, s. montón m.; — v.

a. amontonar.

hear, *v. a.* oír; ~ *of* enterarse de; ~ *say* oír decir.

heart, *s.* corazón *m.;* take sg to ~ tomar algo a pecho; *by* ~ de memoria; *in the* ~ *of the town* en el centro de la ciudad; *(cards)* copas *f. pl.*

hearth, *s.* hogar *m.*

hearty, *adj.* cordial; ~ *eater* comilón *m.*

heat, *s.* calor *m.; fig.* acaloramiento *m.; — v. a.* calentar; *v. n.* calentarse.

heating, *s.* calefacción *f.*

heaven, *s.* cielo *m.; Heaven forbid!* ¡no quiera Dios!, ¡Dios me libre!; *Good Heaven!* ¡Dios mío!; *for Heaven's sake!* ¡por amor de Dios!

heavy, *adj.* pesado; *(rain)* fuerte; *(work)* duro; ~ *drinker* muy bebedor.

Hebrew, *adj. & s.* hebreo.

hedge, *s.* seto *m.; — v. a.* cercar con un seto.

heed, *s.* cuidado *m.,* atención *f.;* take ~ *of sg* tener cuidado de; *— v. n.* atender.

heedless, *adj.* desatento.

heel, *s.* talón *m.*

height, *s.* altura *f.; fig.* colmo *m.,* crisis *f.*

heir, *s.* heredero *m.*

heiress, *s.* heredera *f.*

helicopter, *s.* helicóptero *m.*

hell, *s.* infierno *m.; go to* ~! ¡vete al infierno!

hello, *int.* ¡hola!

helm, *s.* timón *m.*

helmet, *s.* casco *m.*

help, *v. a.* ayudar; ~ *yourself* sírvase usted; *it can't be* ~ed! ¡qué se

le va a hacer! ¡no hay remedio!; *I can't* ~ *laughing* no puedo menos de reírme; *— s.* ayuda *f.;* ~! ¡socorro!

helpful, *adj.* útil.

helpless, *adj.* inútil.

hen, *s.* gallina *f.*

hence, *adv.* de aquí; *a week* ~ de hoy en ocho días; *— conj.* por lo tanto, en consecuencia.

her, *pron.* la; I *see* ~ la veo; *give* ~ *it* désela; *to* ~ a ella, le.

herb, *s.* hierba *f.;* planta *(f.)* medicinal.

here, *adv.* aquí.

heritage, *s.* herencia *f.*

hero, *s.* héroe *m.*

heroic, *adj.* heroico.

heroine, *s.* heroína *f.*

herring, *s.* arenque *m.*

hers, *pron.* suyo, de ella.

herself, *pron.* ella misma.

hesitate, *v. n.* vacilar.

hiccough, hiccup, *s.* hipo *m.; — v. n.* hipar, tener hipo.

hide, *v. a.* esconder, ocultar; *v. n.* esconderse, ocultarse.

hiding-place, *s.* escondrijo *m.,* escondite *m.*

high, *adj.* alto; *(opinion, temperature)* elevado; *(note)* agudo; ~ *and low* todo el mundo; *por todas partes; High Street* calle principal; *adv.* en alto; *play* ~ jugar fuerte *or* grueso.

highland, *s.* tierras *(f. pl.)* altas.

highness, *s.* altitud *f.; fig.* majestad *f.,* sublimidad *f.*

highway, *s.* carretera *f.*

hike, *v. n.* caminar; *— s.* caminata *f.*

hiker, *s.* excursionista *m.,*

caminante *m.*, *f.*

hiking, *s.* excursionismo *m.*

hill, *s.* colina *f.*

him, *pron.* le.

himself, *pron.* él mismo.

hinder, *v. a.* impedir.

hindrance, *s.* impedimento *m.*, estorbo *m.*

hint, *s.* indicio *m.*, indirecta *f.*; — *v. n.* insinuar.

hip, *s.* cadera *f.*

hire, *s.* have for ~ alquilar; — *v. a.* alquilar; (person) emplear.

his, *pron.* su, suyo, de él.

hiss, *s.* siseo *m.*; — *v. n.* sisear.

historic, *adj.* histórico.

history, *s.* historia *f.*

hit, *v. a.* pegar, dar en; ~ a blow golpear; ~ it dar en el blanco; — *s.* golpe *m.*; blanco *m.*; it's a ~ es sensacional.

hitch-hiking, *s.* autostop *m.*

hoarse, *adj.* ronco.

hobby, *s.* afición *f.*, pasatiempo *m.*

hockey, *s.* hockey *m.*

hoist, *v. a.* alzar, elevar; (flag) izar.

hold, *v. a.* tener; ~ sy sostener; (meeting) celebrar; (office) ocupar; (opinion) sostener; ~ ~ guilty juzgar culpable; ~ back retener; detenerse; (himself) refrenarse; ~ off mantener(se) alejado; ~ on aguantar; (wait) detenerse; ~ out resistir; ~ up parar, detener; — *s.* get ~ of obtener; take ~ of agarrar.

holder, *s.* mango *m.*; (person) propietario *m.*

hole, *s.* agujero *m.*, hoyo *m.*

holiday, *s.* día (*m.*) festivo, día de fiesta; vacaciones *f. pl.*; go on ~ tomarse unas vacaciones.

holiday-maker, *s.* veraneante *m.*, *f.*

hollow, *adj. & s.* hueco (*m.*), vacío (*m.*); — *v. a.* excavar.

holly, *s.* acebo *m.*

holy, *adj.* sagrado, santo.

home, *s.* casa *f.*; hogar *m.*; asilo *m.*; at ~ en casa; make yourself at ~ esta usted en su casa; — *adj.* casero, doméstico; ~ affairs asuntos (*m. pl.*) internos; Home Office Ministerio de la Gobernación; ~ trade comercio (*m.*) interior; — *adv.* a casa; go ~ volver or regresar a casa.

homeless, *adj.* sin domicilio; sin patria.

homely, *adj.* simple, sencillo.

home-made, *adj.* hecho en casa, casero.

homesick, *adj.* nostálgico.

homeward, *adv.* hacia casa.

honest, *adj.* honrado, honesto.

honesty, *s.* honradez *f.*

honey, *s.* miel *f.*

honeymoon, *s.* luna (*f.*) de miel, viaje (*m.*) de novios.

honour, *s.* honor *m.*; in ~ of en honor de; — *v. a.* honrar.

hood, *s.* capota *f.*

hoof, *s.* casco *m.*

hook, *s.* gancho *m.*; (fishing) anzuelo *m.*; (blow) crochet *m.*; — *v. a.* enganchar.

hooligan, s. gamberro m.

hope, s. esperanza f.; — v. a. & n. esperar.

hopeful, adj. esperanzado, lleno de esperanza.

hopeless, adj. desesperanzado, desesperado.

horizon, s. horizonte m.

horizontal, adj. horizontal.

horn, s. asta f., cuerno m.; bocina f.

horrible, adj. horrible.

horror, s. horror m.

horse, s. caballo m.

horseback, s. on ~ a caballo.

horseman, s. jinete m.

hose, s. calcetines m. pl.; (water-) manguera f.

hospitable, adj. hóspitalario.

hospital, s. hospital m.

hospitality, s. hospitalidad f.

host, s. dueño (m.) de la casa, anfitrión m., patrón m.

hostel, s. refugio m.; youth ~ albergue (m.) juvenil.

hostess, s. dueña (f.) de la casa.

hot, adj. caliente; I'm ~ tengo calor.

hotel, s. hotel m.

hot-water-bottle, s. bolsa (f.) de agua caliente.

hound, s. sabueso m.; — v. a. perseguir.

hour, s. hora f.; ~ by ~ de hora en hora; office ~s horas de servicio.

house, s. casa f.; keep ~ mantener casa; (theatre) teatro m., público m.; — v. a. alojar.

household, s. familia f., casa f.

housekeeper, s. ama (f.) de llaves.

housewife, s. ama (f.) de casa.

housework, s. quehaceres (m. pl.) domésticos.

housing, s. vivienda f.; ~ conditions condiciones (f. pl.) de viviendas; ~ estate colonia f.

hovercraft, barca (f.) de almohada neumática.

how, adv. cómo; ~ are you?¿cómo está usted?; ~ is it? ¿por qué?; ~ much? cuánto (pago)?

however, conj. no obstante; — adv. por muy, por mucho.

huge, adj. enorme.

hullo, int. ¡eh!; (phone) ¡oiga! ¡diga! ¡dígame!

human, adj. humano.

humanity, s. humanidad f.

humble, adj. humilde.

humorous, adj. divertido.

humour, s. humor m.; be in a good ~ estar de buen humor; sense of ~ sentido (m.) de humor.

hundred, adj. & s. ciento.

hundredth, adj. centésimo.

Hungarian, adj. & s. húngaro (m.).

hunger, hambre f.; — v. n. sentir hambre de.

hungry, adj. hambriento; I'm ~ tengo hambre.

hunt, v. a. & s. cazar, buscar; — s. caza f., cacería f.

hunter, s. cazador m.

hurricane, s. huracán m.

hurry, s. prisa f.; I'm in a ~ tengo prisa; — v. n. apresurarse; ~ up! ¡dése prisa!

hurt, v. a. herir; fig. ofender; get ~ estar resentido; — s. herida f.; ofendida f.

husband, s. marido m., esposo m.

hut, *s.* choza *f.*

hydrant, *s.* boca (*f.*) de riego.

hydrogen, *s.* hidrógeno *m.*

hygiene, *s.* higiene *f.*

hymn, *s.* himno *m.*

hyphen, *s.* guión *m.*

I

I, *pron.* yo.

ice, *s.* hielo *m.*; (~ *cream*) helado *m.*, granizado *m.*

icy, *adj.* helado.

idea, *s.* idea *f.*; (*purpose*) intención *f.*

ideal, *adj.* ideal; magnífico; — *s.* modelo *m.*, ideal *m.*

identical, *adj.* idéntico.

identity, *s.* identidad *f.*; ~ *card* documento (*m.*) de identidad.

idle, *adj.* perezoso, holgazán, desocupado; — *v. n.* holgazanear.

idleness, *s.* pereza *f.*

if, *conj.* si; *as* ~ como si; *even* ~ aunque; ~ *I were you* en su lugar.

ignition, *s.* ignición *f.*, encendido *m.*

ignorant, *adj.* ignorante; *be* ~ *of* ignorar.

ignore, *v. a.* no hacer caso.

ill, *adj.* enfermo; — *s.* mal *m.*; — *adv. be* ~ *at ease* no estar a gusto.

illegal, *adj.* ilegal.

illiterate, *adj.* iletrado; — *s.* analfabeto *m.*

illness, *s.* enfermedad *f.*

illusion, *s.* ilusión *f.*

illustrate, *v. a.* ilustrar.

illustration, *s.* ilustración *f.*

image, *s.* imagen *f.*; vivo retrato *m.*

imagine, *v. a.* imaginar.

imitate, *v. a.* imitar.

immediate, *adj.* inmediato; urgente.

immense, *adj.* inmenso, enorme.

immigrant, *adj. & s.* inmigrante (*m.*, *f.*).

immigration, *s.* inmigración *f.*

impact, *s.* impacto *m.*, choque *m.*

impatience, *s.* impaciencia *f.*

impatient, *adj.* impaciente.

impel, *v. a.* empujar.

imperial, *adj.* imperial.

impertinent, *adj.* impertinente.

implement, *s.* herramienta *f.*

implore, *v. a. & n.* implorar.

import, *v. a.* importar; — *s.* importación *f.*

importance, *s.* importancia *f.*

important, *adj.* importante.

importer, *s.* importador *m.*

impose, *v. a.* imponer; ~ *on* engañar.

impossible, *adj.* imposible.

impregnate, *v. a.* impregnar.

impression, *s.* impresión *f.*

imprison, *v. a.* encarcelar.

improve, *v. a.* mejorar, perfeccionar; *v. n.* mejorarse.

improvement, *s.* mejoría *f.*, mejora *f.*

impulse, *s.* impulso *m.*

in, *prep.* en; *a foot* ~ *length* un pie de largo; ~ *all* en todo; ~ *a week* en una semana; ~ *the morning* por la maña-

na; — *adv.* dentro;
come ∼! ¡adelante!
incapable, *adj.* incapaz.
inch, *s.* pulgada *f.*; ∼ *by*
∼ poco a poco, palmo
a palmo.
incident, *s.* incidente *m.*
incidentally, *adv.* inci-
dentalmente.
incline, *v. a.* inducir; *be*
∼*d* inclinarse; — *s.*
pendiente *m.*, cuesta *f.*
include, *v. a.* incluir, comprender.
inclusive, *adj.* inclusivo.
income, *s.* ingresos *m.*
pl.; renta *f.*
income-tax, *s.* impuesto
(m.) sobre la renta.
incompetent, *adj.* incom-
petehte.
inconvenient, *adj.* inconveniente.
increase, *v. a. & n.*
aumentar; — *s.* au-
mento *m.*
incredible, *adj.* increíble.
indeed, *adv.* verdaderamente, claro.
independence, *s.* independencia *f.*
independent, *adj.* inde-
pendiente.
index, *s.* índice *m.*; ∼ *finger* dedo *(m.)* índice
Indian, *adj. & s.* indio
(m.); ∼ *corn* maíz *m.*
india-rubber, *s.* goma *(f.)*
de borrar.
indicate, *v. a.* indicar.
indicator, *s.* indicador *m.*
indifferent, *adj.* indiferente.
indigestion, *s.* indigestión *f.*
indirect, *adj.* indirecto.
indispensable, *adj.* indispensable.
individual, *adj.* individual; orginal; — *s.* indi-
viduo *m.*, individual *m.*

indoors, *adv.* en casa.
induce, *v. a.* inducir.
indulge, *v. a.* mimar, ∼ *in*
permitirse.
indulgence, *s.* indulgen-
cia *f.*
industrial, *adj.* industrial.
industrious, *adj.* Industrio-
so, aplicado, trabaja-
dor.
industry industria *f.*
inevitable, *adj.* inevitable.
inexpensive, *adj.* barato.
inexperienced, *adj.* inexperto.
infamous, *adj.* infame.
infant, *s.* criatura *f.*,
niño *m.*
infantry, *s.* infantería *f.*
infant-school, *s.* escuela
(f.) de párvulos.
infection, *s.* infección *f.*
infinitive, *s.* infinitivo *m.*
infirmary, *s.* enfermería
f.
inflame, *v. a.* inflamar.
inflammable, *adj.* infla-
mable.
inflict, *v. a.* infligir.
influenza, *s.* influenza *f.*,
gripe *f.*
inform, *v. a.* informar,
avisar.
informal, *adj.* familiar,
de confianza.
information, *s.* información *f.*
ingenious, *adj.* ingenioso.
ingenuity, *s.* ingeniosidad
f., inventiva *f.*
ingratitude, *s.* ingratitud
f.
inhabit, *v. a. & n.* habitar.
inhabitant, *s.* habitante *m.*
inherit, *v. a.* heredar.
inheritance, *s.* herencia *f.*
initiative, *s.* iniciativa *f.*
injection, *s.* inyección *f.*
injury, *s.* herida *f.*; *fig.*
injuria *f.*
injustice, *s.* injusticia *f.*

ink, s. tinta f.; – v. a. entintar, echar tinta a.

inland, s. tierra (f.) adentro; ~ trade comercio (m.) interior.

inn, s. posada f., parador m.

inner, adj. interior.

innocent, adj. inocente.

innumerable, adj. innumerable, innúmero, sin número (m).

inoculate, v. a. inocular, vacunar.

in-patient, s. hospitalizado m.

inquire, v. a. & n. preguntar, indagar, averiguar.

inquiry, s. indagación f., averiguación f.; ~ office oficina (f.) de informaciones.

inscription, s. inscripción f.

insect, s. insecto m.

insensible, adj. insensible.

inseparable, adj. inseparable.

insert, v. a. insertar, añadir.

inside, adj. & s. interior (m.); (sports) left, right ~ interior (m.) izquierda, derecha; – adv. por dentro; let's go ~ entremos.

insist, v. n. insistir.

inspect, v. a. inspeccionar.

inspection, s. inspección f.

inspector, s. inspector m.

inspire, v. a. inspirar.

instalment, s. plazo m.; parte f.

instance, s. ejemplo m.; ocasión f.; for ~ por ejemplo.

instant, adj. inmediato; – s. instante m; momento m.; this ~ ahora mismo.

instead, adv. en lugar de esto; prep. ~ of en vez de.

instinct, s. instinto m.

institute, s. instituto m.; – v. a. instituir.

institution, s. institución f.

instruct, v. a. & n. enseñar; (command) dar órdenes.

instruction, s. instrucción f.; enseñanza f.

instructive, adj. instructivo.

instrument, s. instrumento m.; fig. medio m.

insufficient, adj. insuficiente.

insult, s. insulto m.; – v. a. insultar, ofender.

insurance, s. seguro m.

intact, adj. intacto.

integral, adj. integral.

integrity, s. integridad f.

intelligence, s inteligencia f.; ~ serv ce Inteligencia f.

intelligent, adj. inteligente.

intend, v. a. intentar, querer, pensar.

intense, adj. intenso.

intensity, s. intensidad f.

intent, s. intento m.; – adj. resuelto, decidido.

intention, s. intención f.

intercontinental, adj. intercontinental.

interest, s. interés m.; be of ~ tener importancia; rate of ~ tipo (m.) de interés; – v. a. interesar.

interesting, adj. interesante.

interfere, v. n. meterse, intervenir.

interior, adj. & s. interior (m.).

intermission, s. inter-
medio m., descanso m.
internal, adj. interno;
~ combustion engine
motor (m.) de combus-
tión interna.
international, adj. & s.
internacional (m.).
interpret, v. a. interpretar.
interpretation, s. inter-
pretación f.
interpreter, s. intérpre-
te m., f.
interrupt, v. a. interrumpir.
interval, s. intervalo m.
interview, s. entrevista
f.; – v. a. entrevistar.
intimate, adj. íntimo; – v.
a. sugerir; comunicar.
into, prep. en; translate
~ English traducir al
inglés.
introduce, v. a. presen-
tar.
introduction, s. prefa-
cio m., introducción
f.; letter of ~ carta (f.)
de presentación.
invalid¹, adj. indis-
puesto, enfermizo.
invalid², adj. no válido.
invasion, s. invasión f.
invent, v. a. inventar.
invention, s. invento m.
inventor, s. inventor m.
invest, v. a. investir;
(money) invertir.
investigate, v. a. inves-
tigar.
investigation, s. investigación f.
investment, s. inversión f.
invitation, s. invitación
f.
invite, v. a. convidar,
invitar; provocar.
involuntary, adj. invo-
luntario.
inward(s), adv. hacia

adentro.
iris, s. iris m.; (flower)
lirio m.
Irish, adj. irlandés.
Irishman, s. irlandés m.
Irishwoman, s. irlandesa
f.
iron, s. hierro m.; plancha
f.; – v. a. planchar.
ironical, adj. irónico.
ironware, s. ferretería f.
ironworks, s. fundición
(f.) de hierro (m.)
irony, s. ironía f.
irregular, adj. irregular.
irrelevant, adj. insignifi-
cante, fútil.
irresolute, adj. irresoluto.
irrigation, s. irrigación
f., riego m.
irritate, v. a. irritar, molestar.
island, s. isla f.
isle, s. isla f.
isolate, v. a. aislar.
isolation, s. aislamiento
m.
issue, s. edición f.; emisión f.; tema m.;
– v. a. publicar.
it, lo; I don't see it no
lo veo; it's I soy yo;
that's it eso es; it is
cold hace frío.
Italian, adj & s. italiano.
item, s. entrada f., item
m., artículo m.
its, pron. su.
itself, pron. sí mismo.
ivory, s. marfil m.
ivy, s. hiedra f.

J

jack, s. gato m.; ~ of
hearts sota (f.) de cora-
zones; – v. a. ~ up
alzar con gato.
jacket, s. chaqueta f.,
americana f.

jail, s. cárcel f.

jam [1], v. a. atestar; ~med with people atestado de gente; ~ on the brakes frenar bruscamente; — s. atropello m.; be in a ~ estar apurado.

jam [2], s. mermelada f.

January, s. enero m.

Japanese, adj. & s. japonés (m.).

jar, s. tarro m.

jaw, s. quijada f., mandíbula f.

jazz, s. jazz m.

jealous, adj. celoso.

jealousy, s. celos m. pl

jelly, s. jalea f.

jersey, s. jersey m.

jet, s. chorro m.; ~ plane avión (m.) a reacción; ~ propulsion propulsión (f.) a reacción.

Jew, s. judío m.

jewel, s. joya f., alhaja f., piedra (f.) preciosa

jeweller, s. joyero m.

jewellery s. joyería f.

job, s. empleo m., trabajo m. deber m.; ~ work destajo m.; — v. n. destajar.

jockey, s. jockey m., jinete m.

join, v. a. juntar, acoplar; v. n. juntarse; ingresar; ir con, unirse.

joiner, s. carpintero m.

joint, s. empalme m., juntura f.; — adj. mancomunado.

joint-stock company, s. sociedad (f.) anónima.

joke, s. chiste m., broma f.; — v. n. bromear.

jolly, adj. alegre, jovial.

journal, s. revista f., periódico m.

journalist, s. periodista

m., f.

journey, s. viaje m., —v. n. viajar.

joy, s. alegría f., gozo m.

joyful, adj. alegre.

judge, s. juez m.; — v. a. & n. juzgar.

jug, s. jarro m.

Jugoslav, adj. & s. yugoslavo (m.).

juice, s. zumo m., jugo m.

July, s. julio m.

jump, v. n. saltar; — s. salto m.; long ~ salto de longitud; high ~ salto de altura.

jumper, s. blusa (f.) de punto, pulóver m.

junction, s. unión f.; (of roads) cruce m.

June, s. junio m.

junior, adj. menor; I am three years his ~ soy tres años menor que él; John Smith, Jr. John Smith, hijo; — adj. juvenil.

jury, s. jurado m.

juryman, s. jurado m.

just [1], adj. justo, exacto.

just [2], adv. justamente, precisamente; ~ the same da lo mismo; ~ now ahora mismo; ~ in time en buen momento; ~ a minute sólo un minuto; un momento.

justice, s. justicia f.

justify, v. a. justificar.

juvenile, adj. juvenil.

K

keel, s. quilla f.

keen, adj. afilado, aguzado; ~ appetite muy buen apetito; be ~ on tener entusiasmo por.

keep, v. a. guardar, conservar; (family) mantener; (boarders) tener; ~ accounts llevar los libros; ~ one's word cumplir su palabra; v. n. quedarse; (milk, butter) conservarse; ~ working trabajar sin cesar; ~ waiting hacer esperar; ~ away mantener or quedar alejado; ~ back retener; ~ on continuar, seguir.

keeper, s. guardián m.

kennel, s. perrera f.

kerb, s. borde (m.) de la acera.

kernel, s. semilla f., pepita f.; fig. médula f.

kettle, s. caldera f., tetera f., hervidor m.

key, s. llave f.; fig. clave f.; (of typewriter) tecla f.

kid, s. cabrito m.; (child) pequeño m., niño m.; — v. n. bromear.

kidnap, v. a. secuestrar.

kidney, s. riñón m.

kill, s. a. matar; be ~ed perder la vida.

kilogram(me), s. kilogramo m., kilo m.

kilometre, s. kilómetro m.

kind, s. clase f.; raza f., especie f.; all ~s of toda clase de; — adj. amable; be so ~ as to tenga la bondad de.

kindle, v. a. encender.

kindly, adj. bondadoso; — adv. amablemente.

kindness, s. bondad f., amabilidad f.

king, s. rey m.

kingdom, s. reino m.

kipper, s. arenque (m.) ahumado.

kiss, s. beso m; — v. a. besar.

kit, s. equipo m.; herramientas f. pl., caja (f.) de herramientas.

kitchen, s. cocina f.; ~ garden huerta f.

kitchenette, s. nicho (m.) para cocinar.

kite, s. cometa (f.) de papel.

knapsack, s. mochila f.

knee, s. rodilla f.

kneel, v. n. arrodillarse.

knife, s. cuchillo m.; — v. a. apuñalar, dar una cuchillada a.

knight, s. caballero m.

knit, v. a. & n. tejer, hacer punto.

knob, s. tirador m.

knock, s. golpe m., ruido m.; — v. n. llamar a la puerta; v. a. pegar, golpear; ~ against tropezar con; ~ down desarmar; (price) rebajar; ~ out poner fuera de combate.

knocker, s. aldaba f.

knot, s. nudo m.; v. a. anudar.

know, v. a. conocer; ~ by sight conocer de vista; saber; he ~s French sabe francés; let ~ informar.

knowledge, s. conocimiento m.; to my ~ según tengo entendido.

known, adj. conocido; make ~ publicar, comunicar.

knuckle, s. juntura (f.) de los dedos, nudillo m.

L

L, s. libra f.

label, s. rótulo m., etiqueta f.; — v. a. rotular.

laboratory, s. laboratorio m.

labour, s. trabajo m.; — v. n. trabajar; esforzarse.

labourer, s. jornalero m., peón m.

lace, s. encaje m.; cordón m.; — v. a. enlazar.

lack, s. falta f.; for ~ of a falta de; — v. n. faltar; no tener.

lad, s. mozo m., muchacho m.

ladder, s. escalera f.; (on stocking) carrera f.

ladle, s. cucharón m.

lady, s. señora f., dama f.

lake, s. lago m.

lamb, s. cordero m.

lame, adj. cojo.

lamp, s. lámpara f.

lamp-shade, s. pantalla f.

land, s. tierra f.; campo m.; by ~ por tierra; native ~ patria f.; — v. n. (ship) atracar; (plane) aterrizar.

landing, s. desembarco m.; aterrizaje m.

landing-strip, s. pista (f.) de aterrizaje.

landlady, s. propietaria f., casera f.

landlord, s. propietario m., casero m.

landscape, s. paisaje m.

language, s. idioma m., lengua f.

lantern, s. linterna f., farol m.

lard, s. manteca (f.) or grasa (f.) de cerdo; — v. a. mechar.

larder, s. despensa f.

large, adj. grande.

last, adj. último; ~ but one penúltimo; at ~ por fin, al fin; ~ week la semana pasada; ~

night anoche; — v. n. durar.

lasting, adj. duradero.

latch-key, s. llave (f.) de la casa.

late, adj. tardío; (dead) difunto; (news) reciente; — adv. tarde be ~ llegar tarde.

lately, adv. recientemente.

later (on), adv. más tarde.

latest, adj. último; the ~ news últimas noticias f. pl. — adv. por último.

Latin, adj. latino; — s. (language) latín m.

latter, adj. último.

laugh, s. risa f.; — v. n. reir(se); ~ at reirse de.

laughter, s. risa f.

launch, v. a. lanzar; (ship) botar, echar al agua; — s. lancha f.

laundry, s. lavandería f.; ropa (f.) limpia, ropa sucia.

lavatory, s. retrete m., water m.

lavish, adj. pródigo; — v. a. prodigar.

law, s. ley f.; derecho m.

law-court, s. juzgado m., tribunal m.

lawful, adj. legal, lícito.

lawn, s. césped m.

lawn-tennis, s. tenis m.

lawyer, s. abogado m.

lay, v. a. poner, colocar, situar; ~ the cloth poner la mesa; ~ off despedir; dejar, cesar; ~ up acumular.

layer, s. capa f.

lazy, adj. perezoso, holgazán.

lead¹, s. plomo m.; (pencil) mina f.

lead², v. a. conducir; (life) llevar; (orchestra)

dirigir; — *v. n. (street)* llevar; *(cause)* dar lugar a; *(cards)* ser mano; — *s.* delantera *f.,* ventaja *f., (theatre)* papel *(m.)* principal.

leader, *s.* líder *m.;* director *m.;* jefe *m.,* caudillo *m.*

leadership, *s.* direccion *f.*

leaf, *s.* hoja *f.; (of book)* página *f.*

lean [1], *v. n.* inclinarse; *(prop)* apoyarse; *v. a.* apoyar; ~ *back* reclinarse; ~ *on* depender de; ~ *out* asomarse.

lean, [2] *adj.* magro, flaco.

leap, *v. n.* saltar; — *s.* salto *m.*

learn, *v. a.* aprender.

learned, *adj.* culto, erudito.

learning, *s.* estudio *m.,* saber *m.*

least, *adj.* menor; at ~ por lo menos.

leather, *s.* cuero *m.*

leave [1], *v. a.* dejar; ~ *it to me* déjelo de mi cuenta; *v. n.* salir; ~ *behind* dejar atrás; ~ *for* salir para; ~ *out* omitir.

leave, [2] *s.* licencia *f.;* permiso *m.;* take ~ of despedirse de; go on ~ ir de vacaciones.

lecture, *s.* conferencia *f.;* — *v. n.* hablar.

lecturer, *s.* conferenciante *m* ; docente *m.*

left, *adj.* izquierdo; — *s.* izquierda *f.;* to the ~ a la izquierda.

left-luggage office, *s.* depósito *(m.)* de equipajes.

leg, pierna *f.; (of ani-*

mal, of chair) pata *f.*

legal, *adj.* legal.

legend, *s.* leyenda *f.*

legitimate, *adj.* legítimo.

leisure, *s.* horas *(f. pl.)* libres; *be at* ~ estar desocupado.

lemon, *s.* limón *m.*

lemonade, *s.* limonada *f.*

lend, *v. a.* prestar; ~ *an ear* escuchar; ~ *a hand* ayudar.

length, *s.* largo *m.,* longitud *f.*

lengthen, *v. a.* alargar; *v. n.* alargarse.

lens, *s.* lente *f.*

less, *adj. & adv.* menos.

lesser, *adj.* menor.

lesson, *s.* lección *f.;* clase *f.*

lest, *conj.* a fin de que no.

let, *v. a.* dejar; ~ *go* soltar; *let's* o vamos; *have you rooms to let?* ¿tiene usted habitaciones para alquilar?; ~ *alone* dejar en paz; ~ *down* bajar; *fig.* fallar; ~ *off* dejar ir; *(weapon)* descargar; ~ *out* alquilar; — *s.* alquiler *m.*

letter, *s.* carta *f.; (type)* letra *f.;* ~ *of credit* carta de crédito.

letter-box, *s.* buzón *m.*

lettuce, *s.* lechuga *f.*

level, *s.* nivel *m.;* — *adj.* llano; ~ *crossing* paso *(m.)* a nivel; — *v. a.* igualar.

lever, *s.* palanca *f.*

lexicon, *s.* diccionario *m.*

liability, *s.* obligación *f.*

liar, *adj. & s.* mentiroso.

liberal, *adj.* liberal; generoso.

liberty, *s.* libertad *f.*

librarian, *s.* bibliotecario *m.*

library, s. biblioteca f.; lending ~ biblioteca circulante.

licence, license, s. licencia f.; driving ~ carnet (m.) de conductor.

lick, v. a. lamer.

lid, s. tapa f., tapadera f.

lie,[1] s. mentira f.; — v. n. mentir.

lie,[2] v. n. estar acostado or echado; here ~s aquí yace; (be situated) estar situado, quedar; ~ down acostarse, echarse; — s. situación f., posición f.

lieutenant, s. teniente m.

life, s. vida f.; biografía f.

life-belt, s. salvavidas m.

lifeless, adj. inanimado, sin vida.

lift, v. a. levantar; v. n. (fog) disiparse; — s. levantamiento m.; give sy a ~ ayudar a; llevar en su coche.

light,[1] s. luz f.; lumbre f., fuego m.; dar lumbre; turn on the ~ encender la luz; bring to ~ sacar a la luz; — v. a. encender; ~ up iluminar.

light [2] adj. ligero; ~ blue azul claro.

lighten, v. a. aliviar; — v. n. aliviarse.

lighter, s. encendedor m., mechero m.

lighthouse, s. faro m.

lighting, s. alumbrado m.

lightness, s. ligereza f.

lightning, s. relámpago m.

like,[1] adj. igual, parecido; what is he ~? ¿qué aspecto tiene? — s. igual m.

like [2], v.a. querer; I'd ~ to quisiera.

likely, adj. verosímil; — adv. probablemente.

likeness, s. semejanza f., parecido m.

likewise, adv. asimismo.

lily, s. lirio m.

limb, s. miembro m.; (of the tree) rama f.

limit, s. límite m.; — v. a. limitar.

limited, pp. limitado; ~ company compañía (f.) de responsabilidad limitada, sociedad (f.) anónima.

line, s. línea f.; drop a ~ mandar unas líneas; — v. a. (paper) rayar; (coat) forrar; ~ up alinearse.

linen, s. ropa (f.) blanca.

lining, s. forro m.

links, s. pl. campo (m.) de golf.

lion, s. león m.

lip, s. labio m.; (of a pitcher) pico m.

lipstick, barra (f.) or lápiz (m.) de labios.

liquid, adj. & s. líquido.

liquor, s. bebida (f.) alcohólica.

list, s. lista f.; — v. a. hacer una lista.

listen, v. n. oír; escuchar

listener, s. oyente m., f.

literal, adj. literal.

literary, adj. literario.

literature, s. literatura f.

litter, s. basura f.; (stretcher) camilla f.; (animals) camada f.

little, adj. pequeño; ~ money poco dinero.

live, v. n. vivir; long ~! ¡viva!; — adj. vivo.

lively, adj. vivo, animado.

liver, s. hígado m.

living-room, s. sala (f.) de estar.

load, s. carga f.; — v. a. cargar.

loaf, s. pan m.

loan, *s.* préstamo *m.;* — *v. a.* prestar.
lobby, *s.* vestíbulo *m.*
lobster, *s.* langosta *f.*
local, *adj.* local.
locate, *v. a.* situar; hallar.
location, *s.* situación *f.,* ubicación *f.*
lock,[1] *s.* mechón *m.*
lock,[2] *s.* cerradura *f.,* candado *m.; (on river)* esclusa *f.;* — *v. a.* cerrar (con llave).
locksmith, *s.* cerrajero *m.*
lock-up, *s.* calabozo *m.*
lodge, *s.* casucha *f.,* portería *f.;* — *v. a.* alojar; *v. n.* alojarse.
lodger, *s.* inquilino *m.,* huésped *m., f.*
lodging(s), *s. (pl.)* alojamiento *m.,* vivienda *f.*
logical, *adj.* lógico.
loin, *s.* lomo *m.*
lonely, *adj.* solitario, solo.
long,[1] *adj.* largo; *a ~ time ago* hace mucho; — *s. before ~* en poco tiempo; — *adv. all day ~* todo el día; *how ~?* ¿cuánto tiempo? *so ~!* ¡hasta pronto!; *any ~er* más tiempo.
long,[2] *v. n. ~ for* anhelar, codiciar.
long-play(ing), *adj.* (record) disco *(m.)* de larga duración.
look, *v. n.* mirar; *~ here!* ¡escúcheme!; *~ like* parecerse; *~ after* cuidar; *~ at* mirar; *~ for* buscar; *~ forward to* aguardar con impaciencia; *~ up* buscar; *~ out!* ¡cuidado!; — *s.* mirada *f.*
looking-glass, *s.* espejo *m.*
loose, *adj.* flojo, suelto; *(life)* licencioso.
loosen, *v. a.* soltar.

lord, *s.* señor *m.; House of Lords* Cámara *(f.)* de los Lores.
lordship, *s.* autoridades *f. pl.; his ~* su excelencia.
lorry, *s.* camión *m.,* furgón *m.*
lose, *v. a.* perder; *~ heart* desanimarse; *~ the train* perder el tren.
loss, *s.* pérdida *f.; be at a ~* no saber qué hacer.
lost, *adj. & pp.* perdido; *~ property office* sección *(f.)* de objetos perdidos.

lot, *s.* suerte *f.; (ground)* lote *m.; a ~ of* mucho.
loud, *adj.* fuerte; *(colour)* chillón.
loud-speaker, *s.* altoparlante *m.,* altavoz *m.*
lounge, *v. n.* holgazanear; — *s.* salón *m.,* vestíbulo *m.*
lounge-suit, *s.* traje *(m.)* para la tarde.
love, *s.* amor *m.; be in ~* estar enamorado; *fall in ~ with sy* enamorarse de; — *v. a.* querer.
lovely, *adj.* bello, hermoso, guapo.
lover, *s.* amante *m.*
low, *adj.* bajo; *~ gear* primera velocidad *(f.) ~ opinion* mala opinión.
lower, *adj.* más bajo; — *v. a.* bajar; *(flag)* arriar.
lowland, *s.* llanura *f.,* país *(m.)* bajo.
loyal, *adj.* leal, fiel.
loyalty, *s.* lealtad *f.*
lubricate, *v. a.* lubricar.
luck, *s.* suerte *f.; bad ~* mala suerte.
lucky, *adj.* afortunado.
luggage, *s.* equipaje *m.*
luggage-rack, *s.* portaequipajes *m.*

luggage-van, *s.* furgón (*m.*) de equipajes.

luminous, *adj.* luminoso.

lump, *s.* bola *f.*, grumo *m.*, *(of sugar)* terrón *m.*

lunch, *s.* almuerzo *m.;* — *v. n.* almorzar.

luncheon, *s.* almuerzo *m.*

lung, *s.* pulmón *m.*

lustre, *s.* lustre *m.; (lamp)* lustro *m.*

lute, *s.* lira *f.*

luxurious, *adj.* lujoso.

luxury, *s.* lujo *m.*

lyric, *adj.* lírico.

M

macaroni, *s.* macarrones *m. pl.*

machine, *s.* máquina *f.*

machinery, *s.* maquinaria *f.*

mackintosh, *s.* impermeable *m.*

mad, *adj.* loco; *(dog)* rabioso; *be ~ after sg* anhelar.

madam, *s.* señora *f.*

madness, *s.* locura *f.*

magazine, *s.* revista *f.*

magistrate, *s.* magistrado *m.*

magnet, *s.* imán *m.*

magnetic, *adj.* magnético.

magneto, *s.* magneto *m.*

magnificent, *adj.* magnífico.

magnify, *v. a.* ampliar; *~ing glass* lente *(f.)* de aumento, lupa *f.*

maid, *s.* criada *f.*, sirvienta; *old ~* solterona *f.*

maiden, soltera *f.;* *~ name* nombre *(m.)* de soltera.

mail, *s.* correo *m.;* Correos *m.;* — *v. a.* echar al correo.

mail-boat, *s.* buque *(m.)* correo.

main, *adj.* principal; *in the ~* en general.

maintain, *v. a.* mantener; sostener.

majestic, *adj.* majestuoso.

majesty, *s.* majestad *f.*

major, *adj.* mayor; principal; — *s.* comandante *m.*, mayor *m.;* *~ general* general *(m.)* de brigada.

majority, *s.* mayoría *f.*

make, *v. a.* hacer; *(mistake)* cometer; *(money)* ganar; *(peace)* hacer; *(war)* hacer; *~ fun of* burlarse de; *~ a fool of sy* poner en ridículo; *~ known* hacer saber; *~ ready* preparar; *~ sense* tener sentido; *~ sure* cerciorarse; *~ the acquaintance of* conocer a; *~ use of* servirse de; *~ up (face)* pintarse; *(invent)* inventar; — *s.* fabricación *f.*, producto *m.*

maker, *s.* fabricante *m.*

male, *adj. & s.* macho *(m.)*.

mammal, *s.* mamífero *m.*

man, *s.* hombre *m.;* — *v. a.* tripular.

manage, *v. a.* manejar; *~ to do sg* lograr hacer.

management, *s.* administración *f.*, dirección *f.*

manager, *s.* gerente *m.*, director *m.*, administrador *m.*

manhood, *s.* virilidad *f.*

manicure, *s.* manicura *f.* — *v. a.* hacer la manicura.

manifest, *adj.* manifiesto; — *v. a.* manifestar.

manipulate, *v. a.* manipular.

mankind, *s.* humanidad *f.*

manly, *adj.* varonil.

manner, *s.* manera *f.;*

~s costumbres *f. pl.*

manoeuvre, *s.* maniobra *f.; .— v. n.* maniobrar.

manpower, *s.* mano *(f.)* de obra.

manual, *adj. & s.* manual *(m.).*

manufacture, *s.* fabricación *f.; — v. a.* fabricar.

manufacturer, *s.* fabricante *m.*

manuscript, *adj. & s.* manuscrito *(m.).*

many, *adj.* mucho(s); *a good* **~** mucho; *how* **~?** ¿cuántos?; **~** *a time* a menudo.

map, *s.* mapa *m.*

marble, *s.* mármol *m.*

march, *v. n.* marchar; — *s.* marcha *f.*

March, *s.* marzo *m.*

mare, *s.* yegua *f.*

margin, *s.* margen *m.*

marine, *adj.* marino; — *s.* marina *f.*

mariner, *s.* marinero *m.,* marino *m.*

mark, *s.* marca *f.,* seña *f.,* señal *f.; hit the* **~** dar en el blanco; *(school)* punto *m.,* nota *f. price* **~** etiqueta *f.; — v. a.* marcar, señalar.

market, *s.* mercado *m.*

market-price, *s.* precio *(m.)* de mercado.

marmalade, *s.* mermelada *f.*

marriage, *s.* matrimonio *m.*

married, *adj.* casado, casada.

marry, *v. a.* casar; — *v. n.* casarse.

marshal, *s.* mariscal *m.; — v. a.* ordenar, guiar.

marvel, *s.* maravilla *f.; — v. n.* maravillarse.

marvellous, *adj.* maravilloso.

masculine, *adj.* masculino.

mask, *s.* máscara *f.,* careta *f.*

mass,[1] *s.* misa *f.*

mass,[2] *s.* masa *f.,* montón *m.;* **~** *meeting* mítin *(m.)* popular; **~** *production* producción *(f.)* en serie.

mast, *s.* mástil *m.*

master, *s. (school)* maestro *m.; (owner)* amo *m.,* dueño *m.; — v. a.* dominar.

masterpiece, *s.* obra *(f.)* maestra.

match,[1] *s.* fósforo *m.,* cerilla *f.*

match,[2] *s.* encuentro *m.,* competición *f.; (marriage)* partido *m.; (equal)* igual *m.; they're a good* **~** hacen una buena pareja; *I'm no* **~** *for him* no puedo competir con él; — *v. a.* igualar.

match-box, *s.* caja *(f.)* de fósforos, *or* cerillas.

mate,[1] *s. (chess)* mate *m.*

mate,[2] *s.* compañero *m.; (marine)* primer oficial *m.; (wife)* consorte *f.,* mujer *f.; — v. a.* aparear.

material, *s.* materia *f.; raw* **~** materia prima; *writing* **~s** efectos *(m. pl.)* de escritorio; — *adj.* material.

mathematical, *adj.* matemático.

mathematics, *s.* matemáticas *f. pl.*

matrimony, *s.* matrimonio *m.*

matter, *s.* materia *f.; (theme)* tema *m.; (business)* asunto *m.,* causa

f.; what's the ~? ¿qué
pasa?; — v n. im-
portar.
mattress, s. colchón m.
mature, adj. maduro; —
v. a. & n. madurar.
maturity, s. madurez f.
maximum, adj. & s. máximo (m.).
may, v. n. poder; ~ I
come in? ¿puedo en-
trar?; ~ I have this
dance? ¿quiere usted
concederme este baile?
May, s. mayo m.
maybe, adv. tal vez, quizás.
mayor, s. alcalde m.
me, pron. me; give ~ some
of that déme usted un
poco de aquello; it's ~
soy yo; is this for ~ ?
es esto para mí?
meadow, s. pradera f.
meal, s. comida f.
mean¹, s. término (m.)
medio; in the ~ time
entretanto.
mean,² v. a. & n. proponerse, intentar.
mean,³ adj. malo.
meaning, s. sentido m.;
significado m.; what's
the ~ of this? ¿qué
significa esto?
means, s.pl. medios m. pl.;
(money) dinero m.; by
all ~ a todo trance, sin
falta.
meantime, adv. mientras
tanto, entretanto.
meanwhile, see mean-
time.
measure, s. medida f.; in
some ~ hasta cierto
punto; — v. a. medir.
measurement, s. medida
f.; take sy's ~s tomar
las medidas de.
meat, s. carne f.; ~ pie
empanada f.

mechanic, s. mecánico m.
mechanical, adj. mecánico.
mechanics, s. pl. mecánica
f.
mechanism, s. mecanismo m.
mechanize, v. a. mecani-
zar.
medal, s. medalla f.
medical, adj. médico.
medicine, s. medicina f.;
~ chest botiquín m.
mediocre, adj. mediocre.
meditate, v. n. meditar.
medium, s. medio m.;
through the ~ of por
medio de; — adj. me-
dio; ~-sized de tamaño
mediano.
meet, v. a. encontrar;
pleased to ~ you tengo
mucho gusto en cono-
cerle; will the bus ~ the
train? ¿empalmará el
ómnibus con el tren?;
(demands) satisfacer;
— v. n. ~ with an
accident tener un acci-
dente; (assemble) reu-
nirse.
Mexican, adj. & s. meji-
cano (m.).
microbe, s. microbio m.
microfilm, s. microfilm
m.; — v.n. microfilmar.
microphone, s. micrófono
m.
microscope, s. microscopio m.
middle, adj. medio; Middle Ages s. edad (f.)
media; — s. centro m.,
medio m.
middle-aged, adj. de edad
madura.
midnight, s. media noche
f.
might, s. poder m., fuerza
f.
mighty, adj. poderoso.
migrate, v. n. vagar.

mild, *adj. (weather)* templado; *(cheese)* blando, fresco; *(disposition)* suave.

mile, *s.* milla *f.*

mileage, *s.* kilometraje *m.*

military, *adj.* militar.

milk, *s.* leche *f.;* — *v. a. & n.* ordeñar.

milkman, *s.* lechero *m.*

mill, *s.* molino *m.,* molinillo *m.; (factory)* fábrica *f.;* — *v. a.* moler.

miller, *s.* molinero *m.*

milliner, *s.* modista *f.,* sombrérera *f.*

million, *s.* millón *m*

mince, *v. a.* despedazar: — *s.* carne *(f.)* picada.

mind, *s.* mente *f.;* call to ~ recordar; *change one's* ~ cambiar de opinión; *have a* ~ tener

meeting, *s.* sesión *f.,* junta *f.,* mítin *m.*

melody, *s.* melodía *f.*

melon, *s.* melón *m.*

melt, *v. a.* derretir; *v. n.* derretirse, disolverse.

member, *s.* socio *m.,* miembro *m.*

memorial, *s.* monumento *(m.)* conmemorativo; memorial *m.*

memory, *s.* memoria *f.;* in ~ of sy en recuerdo de.

mend, *v. a.* remendar; *v. n.* restablecerse.

mention, *v. a.* mencionar; don't ~ it! no hay de que; — *s.* mención *f.*

menu, *s.* menú *m.,* lista *(f.)* de platos.

merchandise, *s.* mercancía *f.,* mercadería *f.*

merchant, *s.* comerciante *m.*

mere, *adj.* mere, puro.

meridian, *s.* meridiano *m.*

merit, *s.* mérito *m.;* — *v. a.* merecer.

merry, *adj.* alegre; *a* ~ *Christmas!* ¡Felices Pascuas!; *make* ~ estar alegre.

mess, *s.* lío *m.; in a* ~ desarreglado, revuelto; — *v. a.* enredar; ensuciar.

message, *s.* recado *m.,* mensaje *m.*

messenger, *s.* mensajero *m.*

metal, *s.* metal *m.*

meteorology, *s.* meterología *f.*

method, *s.* método *m.*

metre, *s.* metro *m.*

metropolis, *s.* metrópoli *f.*

ganas de; *have in* ~ pensar en; *keep in* ~ tener presente; *make up one's* ~ decidir, resolver; — *v. a.* cuidar, tener cuidado a; *I don't* ~ me da lo mismo; *never* ~ no se moleste.

mine,[1] *pron.* mío; *a friend of* ~ uno de mis amigos.

mine,[2] *s.* mina *f.;* — *v. a.* extraer, explotar.

miner, *s.* minero *m.*

mineral, *adj. & s.* mineral *(m.);* ~ *water* agua *(f.)* mineral.

miniature, *s.* miniatura *f.*

minimum, *adj & s.* mínimo *(m.)*

minister, *s.* ministro *m.;* — *v. n.* atender.

ministry, *s.* ministerio *m.*

minor, *adj.* menor; — *s.* menor *(m. f.)* de edad.

minority, *s.* minoridad *f.*

minus, *adj.* menos, sin.

minute,[1] *s.* minuto *m.*

minute,[2] *adj.* menudo.

miracle, *s.* milagro *m.*

mirror, *s.* espejo *m.*

miscarry, *v. n.* fracasar.

miscellaneous, *adj.* misceláneo.

mischief, s. travesura f., maldad f.

miserable, adj. miserable.

misery, s. miseria f.

misfortune, s. mala suerte f., desgracia f.

miss, v. a. (train) perder; (sy) no encontrar; be ~ing faltar; — s. falta f.

Miss, s. señorita f.

missile, s. cohete m.

mission, s. misión f.

mist, s. niebla f., neblina f.

mistake, s. error m., culpa f., falta f., equivocación f.; sorry, my ~ lo siento, ha sido culpa mía; make a ~ equivocarse, cometer un error; by ~ sin querer; — v. a. confundir.

Mister, s. señor m.

mistress, s. señora f., (of the house) dueña f.; (lover) amante f.

mistrust, s. desconfianza f.; — v. n. desconfiar.

misty, adj. nebuloso, brumoso.

misunderstand, v. a. entender mal.

misunderstanding, s. equivocación f.

mix, v. a. mezclar; (drinks) preparar; v. n. relacionarse, mezclarse.

mixture, s. mezcla f., mixtura f.

mob, s. muchedumbre f., gentío m.

mobility, s. movilidad f.

mock, v. a. burlar; — s. burla f.

mockery, s. burla f., mofa f.

model, s. modelo m.; — v. a. modelar, planear.

moderate, adj. moderado; v. a. moderar.

moderation, s. moderación f.

modern, adj. moderno.

modest, adj. modesto.

modesty, s. modestia f.

modify, v. a. modificar.

moist, adj. húmedo.

moisten, v. a. humedecer; mojar; v. n. mojarse.

moisture, s. humedad f.

molar, s. muela f., molar m.

moment, s. momento m.; in a ~ en seguida; at the ~ por ahora.

momentary, adj. momentáneo.

monarch, s. monarca m.

monarchy, s. monarquía f.

Monday, s. lunes m.

money, s. dinero m.; make ~ ganar dinero.

money-order, s. giro (m.) postal.

monkey, s. mono m.

monograph, s. monografía f.

monopolize, v. a. monopolizar.

monopoly, s. monopolio m.

monstrous, adj. monstruoso.

month, s. mes m.

monthly, adj. mensual; — adv. mensualmente; — s. periódico (m.) mensual.

monument, s. monumento m.

monumental, adj. monumental.

mood, s. humor m., genio m.

moon, s. luna f.; full ~ luna llena; — v. a. ~ about vagar.

moonlight, s. claro (m.) de luna.

moor, s. pantano m., ciénaga f.; — v. a. amarrar.

moral, adj. moral, ético; — s. moraleja f.

more, adj. más; have some ~ sírvase usted.

moreover, adv. además (de eso).

morning, s. mañana f.; in the ~ por la mañana; good ~ buenos días; ~ paper diario (m.) de la mañana.

mortal, adj. mortal.

mortality, s. mortalidad f.

mosquito, s. mosquito m.

moss, s. musgo m.

most, adj. & s. lo máximo, lo más; ~ people la mayoría de la gente; ~ of them la mayor parte de ellos; ~ interesting interesantísimo; ~ likely muy probable.

mostly, adv. en su mayor parte, por lo común.

motel, s. parador m.

moth, s. polilla f.

mother, s. madre f.

mother-in-law, s. suegra f.

mother-tongue, s. lengua (f.) madre.

motion, s. movimiento m., (proposal) moción f., proposición f.; — v. n. hacer señas; indicar.

motionless, adj. inmóvil.

motive, s. motivo m.

motor, s. motor m.; — v. n. ir en automóvil.

motor-bike, s. motocicleta f., moto f.

motor-boat, s. lancha (f.) motora.

motor-car, s. automóvil m.

motor-coach, s. autocar m.

motor-cycle, s. motocicleta f., moto f.

motorway, s. autopista f.

mount, s. monte m.; — v. a. subir; ~ a horse montar a caballo; v. n. subir, aumentar.

mountain, s. montaña f.

mountainous, adj. montañoso.

mountain-range, s. sierra f., cordillera f.

mourn, v. a. deplorar la muerte de, llevar de luto.

mouse, s. ratón m.

moustache, s. bigote m.

mouth, s. boca f.; fig. entrada f.

move, v. a. mover; (propose) proponer; v. n. moverse; keep moving circular; ~ off alejarse; — s. movimiento m., paso m.; (chess) jugada f.; get a ~ on apresurarse.

movement, s. movimiento m.

movie, s. película f.; cine m.

mow, v. a. segar.

mower, s. segador m.; (machine) segadora f.

much, adj. mucho; how ~? ¿cuánto cuesta?; thank you very ~ muchas gracias; too ~ demasiado; so ~ tanto.

mud, s. fango m., cieno m., barro m.

muddy, adj. fangoso.

mug, s. tazón m.

mule, s. mula f.

multiple, adj. múltiple.

multiplication, s. multiplicación f.

multiply, *v. a.* multiplicar.
multitude, *s.* multitud *f.*
municipal, *adj.* municipal.
murder, *s.* asesinato *m.;*
v. a. asesinar.
murderer, *s.* asesino *m.*
muscle, *s.* músculo *m.*
museum, *s.* museo *m.*
mushroom, *s.* seta *f.;*
hongo *m.*
music, *s.* música *f.*
musical, *adj.* musical.
music-hall, *s.* teatro *(m.)*
de variedades.
musician, *s.* músico *m.*
must¹, *v. n.* deber, tener
que; *I ~ go* tengo que
irme; *you ~ not go*
no debe ir.
must², *s.* moho *m.; (of
grape)* mosto *m.*
mustard, *s.* mostaza *f.*
muster, *s.* inspección *f.,*
revista *f.; — v. a.*
pasar revista.
mute, *adj.* mudo; *— v. a.*
hacer callar, silenciar.
mutton, *s.* carnero *m.*
mutual, *adj.* mutuo.
muzzle, *s.* hocico *m.; (of
dog)* bozal *m.; (of
arms)* cañón *m.,* boca
f.; — v. a. silenciar.
my, *pron.* mi, mío; *~
gloves* mis guantes.
myself, *pron.* yo mismo.

mysterious, *adj.* mis-
terioso.
mystery, *s.* misterio *m.*
myth, *s.* mito *m.*

N

nail, clavo *m.; (finger-)*
uña *f.; — v. a. & n.*
clavar.
nail-brush, *s.* cepill(it)o
(m.) de uñas.
naked, *adj.* desnudo.
name, *s.* nombre *m.; (of*

a book) título *m.;*
(fame) fama *f.; by ~*
de nombre; *what's
your~? ¿* cómo se llama
usted?; *— v. a.* nom-
brar.
namely, *adv.* a saber.
nap, *s.* sueñecillo *m.*
napkin, *s.* servilleta *f.*
narrow, *adj.* estrecho; *—
v. a.* reducir; *v. n.*
reducirse, estrecharse.
nation, *s.* nación *f.,* país
m.
national, *adj.* nacional.
nationalization, *s.* nacio-
nalización *f.*
nationality, *s.* nacionalidad *f.*
native, *adj.* nativo; *~
land* patria *f.; ~ lan-
guage* lengua *(f.)* ma-
ternal; *— s.* indígena
m., f.
natural, *adj.* natural.
nature, *s.* naturaleza *f.;
by ~* por naturaleza.
naughty, *adj.* travieso,
díscolo, desobediente.
naval, *adj.* naval.
navigable, *adj.* navega-
ble.
navy, *s.* marina *(f.)* de
guerra, armada *f.*
near, *adv.* cerca; *~ at
hand* próximo; *~ by*
cerca de aquí; *draw
~* acercarse; *— prep.*
cerca de; *~ the station*
cerca de la estación;
— adv. cercano; *— v.
n.* acercarse.
nearly, *adv.* aproximada-
mente, casi.
neat, *adj.* aseado, limpio.
necessary, *adj.* necesario.
necessity, *s.* necesidad *f.*
neck, *s.* nuca *f.; (of a
bottle)* cuello *m.*
necklace, *s.* cadena *f.,*
collar *m.*
necktie, *s.* corbata *f.*

need, s. necesidad f.; — v. a. necesitar; v. n. hacer falta.
needle, s. aguja f.
needless, adj. inútil, innecesario.
negative, adj. & s. negativo (m.), — v. a. negar, refutar.
neglect, v. a. descuidar; — s. abandono m., descuido m.
negligence, s. negligencia, f., descuido m.
negotiation, s. negociación f.
Negro, s. negro m.
neighbour, s. vecino m.
neighbourhood, s. vecindad f.
neither, conj. ~ ... nor ni ... ni; — pron. ninguno de los dos.
nephew, s. sobrino m.
nerve, s. nervio m.
nervous, adj. nervioso; ~ breakdown agotamiento (m.) nervioso.
nest, s. nido m.
net¹, s. red f.; — v. a. enredar.
net², adj. neto.
neutral, adj. neutral.
never, adv. nunca, jamás; ~ again nunca más.
nevertheless, conj. no obstante, sin embargo.
new, adj. nuevo; New Year's Eve Noche (f.) de Año Nuevo.
news, s. noticias f. pl.; what's the ~? ¿qué hay de nuevo?
newspaper, s. periódico m.
next, adj. siguiente, próximo; ~ day el día siguiente; ~ year el año que viene; ~ time la próxima vez; — adv. después; who comes ~? ¿quién sigue?; what

~? ¿y ahora qué?; prep. ~ to al lado de.
nice, adj. agradable; bonito; ~ and warm un calor agradable.
nickname, s. apodo m., — v. a. apodar.
niece, s. sobrina f.
night, s. noche f.; last ~ anoche; good ~! ¡buenas noches!; at ~ de noche; ~ and day día y noche.
night-porter, s. portero (m.) de noche.
nightingale, s. ruiseñor m.
nightmare, s. pesadilla f.
nine, adv. & s. nueve.
nineteen, adv. & s. diecinueve.
ninety, adj. & s. noventa (m.).
ninth, adj. noveno.
nitrogen, s. nitrógeno m.
no, adv.; whether or ~ sí o no; adj. ningún; ~ smoking prohibido fumar.
nobility, s. nobleza f.
noble, adj. & s. noble (m.).
nobody, pron. & s. nadie.
nod, v. a. afirmar con la cabeza, inclinar la cabeza, cabecear.
noise, s. ruido m.
noiseless, adj. silencioso.
noisy, adj. ruidoso.
nomination s. nombramiento m.
none, pron. & s. ningún, ninguno; ~ but únicamente; ~ too no demasiado; ~ too soon a buena hora; ~ the less no obstante, sin embargo.
nonsense, s. tontería f.
non-smoker, s. no-fumador m.
non-stop, adj. continuo, interrumpido.

noon, s. mediodía m.
nor, ni; *neither you ~ I*
ni usted ni yo.
normal, adj. normal.
north, s. norte m.
northern, adj. del norte.
northwest, s. noroeste
m.
nose, s. nariz f.; *fig.*
olfato m.
not, no; ~ *at all* de
ninguna manera; ~ *a*
... ninguno.
notable, adj. notable.
note, s. nota f., anotación
f.; *take ~s* tomar no-
tas; *(music)* nota (f.)
de música; – v. a. ano-
tar; darse cuenta de.
note-book, s. cuaderno
m., libreta f.
noted, adj. célebre, fa-
moso.
nothing, nada; *I have ~*
to do no tengo nada que
hacer; *good for ~*
tunante m.; ~ *else* nada
más; ~ *less than* nada
menos que.
notice, s. aviso m.; *until*
further ~ hasta nueva
orden; *give ~ to sy*
despedir; *at short* ~ a
corto plazo; – v. a.
darse cuenta de.
notify, v. a. notificar.
notion, s. noción f.
nought, nada, cero.
noun, s. substantivo m.,
nombre m.
nourish, v. a. alimentar,
nutrir.
novel, s. novela f.; –
adj. reciente, moderno.
novelist, s. novelista m., f.
novelty, novedad s. f.
November, s. noviembre m.
now, ahora; *by* ~ ya;
from ~ *on* de ahora en
adelante; *just* ~ ahora
mismo; ~ *and then* de

vez en cuando; ~ *that*
ahora que; – *int.* ~
then! ¡ahora bien!
nowadays, adv. hoy día.
nowhere, adv. por nin-
guna parte.
nuclear, adj. nuclear; ~
bomb bomba (f.) nucle-
ar; ~ *fission* fisión (f.)
nuclear; ~ *power sta-*
tion central (f.) de
energía atómica.
number, s. número m.; –
v. a. numerar.
number-plate, s. placa (f.)
de matrícula, or matrí-
cula f.
numerous, adj. numeroso.
nun, s. monja f.
nurse, s. niñera f.; *(sick)*
enfermera f.; – v. a.
cuidar.
nursery, s. cuarto (m.) de
los niños; ~ *school*
jardín (f.) de la in-
fancia; *(of trees)* plan-
tel m.
nut, s. nuez f.; *(screw)* tuerca; ~s loco, chiflado.
nutrition, s. nutrición f.
nylon, s. nailón m.
nilón m.

O

oak, s. roble m.
oar, s. remo m.
oath, juramento m.
obedient, adj. obediente.
obey, v. n. obedecer.
object, s. objeto m.; *(in-*
tention) propósito m.;
– v. n. oponerse a.
objection, s. objeción f.
obligation, s. obligación
f.
oblige, v. a. obligar; *be*
~*d to* tener que; *I am*
much ~*d* estoy muy
agradecido.
obscure, adj. obscuro; –
v. a. obscurecer.

observation, s. observación f.

observe, v. a. observar, advertir, darse cuenta de; *(rules)* cumplir, obedecer.

observer, s. observador m.

obstacle, s. obstáculo m.

obstinate, adj. terco, obstinado.

obtain, v. a. obtener, adquirir.

occasion, s. ocasión f.

occasional, adj. ocasional.

occupation, s. ocupación f.; trabajo m., oficio m.

occupy, v. a. ocupar; tomar; apoderarse de; *be occupied in* estar ocupado con.

occur, v. n. ocurrir; *it ~s to me* se me ocurre.

ocean, s. océano m.

o'clock, adv. *at seven ~* a las siete.

October, s. octubre m.

odd, adj. *(number)* impar; *three shillings ~* tres chelines y pico; *(person)* raro.

of, prep. de; *the book ~ the student* el libro del estudiante; *it is very kind ~ you* es usted muy amable; *two ~ them* dos de ellos; *most ~ all* lo más; *a friend ~ mine* un amigo mío.

off, adv. & prep. *he is ~ to London* salió para Londres; *a mile ~* a una milla de distancia; *day ~* día *(m.)* libre; *~ duty* no estar de servicio.

offence, s. ofensa f.; *(fault)* culpa f., delito m.

offend, v. a. ofender; pecar, cometer una falta.

offensive, adj. ofensivo; *— s.* ofensiva f.

offer, v. a. ofrecer; *— s.* oferta f.

office, s. oficina f.; *(charge)* cargo m.; despacho m.

officer, s. oficial m.

official, adj. oficial; *— s.* oficial m.

often, adv. a menudo, con frecuencia.

oil, s. aceite m.; *— v. a.* engrasar.

ointment, s. unguento m., crema f.

old, adj. viejo; *fig.* antiguo; *grow ~* envejecer; *how ~ are you?* ¿qué edad tiene usted? *I'm thirty years ~* tengo treinta años.

old-fashioned, adj. fuera de moda.

omlet(te) s. tortilla f.

omit, v. a. omitir.

on, prep. & adv. a; *~ the left* a la izquierda; *~ Sunday* el domingo; *~ April 3rd* el tres de abril; *~ sale* de venta; *~ the contrary* a l contrario; *~ credit* al fiado; *~ foot* a pie; *~ duty* de servicio; *~ purpose* de propósito, a sabiendas.

once, adv. una vez; *at ~* en seguida, inmediatamente; *~ more* otra vez.

one, adj. & s. uno; *~ of us* uno de nosotros; *~ has to be careful* hay que tener cuidado; *I prefer this ~* prefiero esto.

onion, s. cebolla f.

onlooker, s. espectador m.

only, adj. único; *— adv.* unicamente, solamente.

open, adj. abierto; *in the ~ air* al aire libre; *be ~ with* ser franco con; — v. a. abrir; v. n. abrirse.

opening, s. abertura f.; *(beginning)* apertura f.; inauguración f.

opera, s. ópera f.

operate, v. a. hacer funcionar; v. n. *~ on* operar, hacer una operación.

operating-theatre, s. sala (f.) de operaciones.

operation, s. funcionamento m.; *(military, medical)* operación f.

operative, adj. operativo, operatorio; — s. operario m.

opinion, s. opinión f.

opponent, s. oponente m.

opportunity, s. oportunidad f.

oppose, v. a. & n. oponer.

opposite, adj. contrario, opuesto.

opposition, s. oposición f.

oppress, v. a. oprimir.

oppression, s. opresión f.

optic, adj. óptico.

optimism, s. optimismo m.

option, s. opción f.

optional, adj. facultativo.

or, conj. o; *either . . . ~* o. . .o.

oral, adj. oral.

orange, s. naranja f.

orator, s. orador m.

orbit, s. órbita f.

orchard, s. huerto m.

orchestra, s. orquesta f.

order, s. orden m.; *(command)* orden f.; *fill an ~* enviar el pedido; — v. a. ordenar, mandar.

ordinary, adj. ordinario, corriente.

organ, s. órgano m.

organic, adj. orgánico.

organism, s. organismo m.

organization, s. organización f.

organize, v. a. organizar.

Orient, adj. oriente; — s. oriente m.; — v. a. orientar; v. n. orientarse.

Oriental, adj. oriental.

origin, s. origen m.

original, adj. original; primero, primitivo; — s. original m.

ornament, s. ornamento m.; — v. a. ornar, decorar.

ornamental, adj. ornamental.

orphan, adj. & s. huérfano (m.), huérfana (f.).

other, adj. otro; *the ~ day* el otro día; *on the ~ hand* por otra parte; *every ~ day* un día sí otro no.

otherwise, adv. de otro modo; si no.

ought, v. n. deber, tener que.

ounce, s. onza f.

our, adj. &. pron. nuestro.

ours, pron. nuestro.

ourself, -ves, pron. nosotros mismos.

oust, v. a. desalojar, expulsar.

out, adv. fuera; *be ~* estar fuera.

outboard-motor, s. motor (m.) fuera de bordo, fuerabordo m.

outdoor(s), adv. al aire libre, fuera.

outer, adj. exterior, más lejano.

outfit, s. equipo m.; ajuar m.

outline, *s.* silueta *f.*, contorno *m.*; *(summing up)* resumen *m.*; — *v. a.* hacer un resumen de.

outlook, *s.* vista *f.*, perspectiva *f.*; modo *(m.)* de ver.

output, *s.* producción *f.*

outrage, *s.* atrocidad *f.*; — *v. a.* ultrajar.

outrageous, *adj.* ultrajoso, infame.

outside, *adj.* exterior, de fuera; — *adv.* fuera; — *s.* exterior *m.*

outsider, *adj. & s.* forastero, extraño.

outskirts, *s. pl.* afueras *f. pl.*, arrabal *m.*

outward, *adj.* externo, exterior.

outwards, *adv.* al exterior.

oven, *s.* horno *m.*

over, *prep. & adv.* sobre; *all ~* por todo; *~ there* allí; *it is ~* ha terminado.

overalls, *s.* mono *(m.)* de mecánico.

overcoat, *s.* abrigo *m.*, gabán *m.*

overcome, *v. a.* vencer.

overcrowded, *adj.* hacinado, atestado.

overdo, *v. a.& n.* exagerar; *(meat) it is overdone* está muy hecho.

overexpose, *v. a.* sobre(e)xponer.

overflow, *v. a.* inundar; *v. n.* desbordar; — *s.* inundación *f.*

overhear, *v. a.* oir por casualidad.

overlook, *v. a.* mirar, dar a; *(miss)* olvidar, pasar por alto; *(forgive)* tolerar.

overseas, *adv.* en ultramar; — *adj.* ultramarino.

overtake, *v. a.* alcanzar, pasar; *fig.* sorprender.

overtime, *s.* horas *(f. pl.)* extra; — *v. n.* trabajar horas extraordinarias.

overturn, *v. a.* derribar, trastornar; — *v. n.* derrumbarse, volcarse.

owe, *v. a.* deber; *how much do I ~ you?* cuánto le debo?

owing to, *prep.* debido a.

own, *adj.* propio; *my ~ mío*; — *v. a.* tener; ser de alguien.

owner, *s.* propietario *m.*

ox, *s.* buey *m.*

oxygen, *s.* oxígeno *m.*

P

pace, *s.* paso *m.*; *(speed)* velocidad *f.*

pacific, *adj.* pacífico; *The Pacific* el Océano Pacífico.

pack, *s.* carga *f.*; *~ of cards* baraja *f.*; — *v. a.* empaquetar.

package, *s.* paquete *m.*

pact, *s.* pacto *m.*

pad, *s.* cojín *m.*; *(writing-)* bloc *(m.)* de papel; — *v. a.* rellenar.

paddle, *s.* canalete *m.*; — *v. n.* impeler con canalete.

page, *s.* página *f.*

pail, *s.* cubo *m.*

pain, *s.* dolor *m.*

painful,. *adj.* doloroso, penoso.

paint, *s.* pintura *f.*; — *v. a.* pintar.

painter, *s.* pintor *m.*;

(*house-*) pintor de brocha gorda.

painting, *s.* pintura *f.*, cuadro *m.*

pair, *s.* par *m.*

palace, *s.* palacio *m.*

palate, *s.* paladar *m.*; *fig.* gusto *m.*

pale, *adj.* pálido.

palm[1], *s.* palma *f.*

palm[2], *s.* (*tree*) palmera *f.*

pan, *s.* cacerola *f.*, olla *f.*

pane, *s.* cristal *m.*, vidrio *m.*

panel, *s.* panel *m.*, tablero *m.*

panic, *s.* pánico *m.*, terror *m.*

panorama, *s.* panorama *m.*

pansy, *s.* pensamiento *m.*

pant, *v. n.* jadear.

pantry, *s.* despensa *f.*

pants, *s. pl.* calzoncillos *m. pl.*

paper, *s.* papel *m.*; documento *m.*

parade, *s.* parada *f.*, desfile *m.*; — *v. n.* desfilar.

paradise, *s.* paraíso *m.*

paragraph, *s.* párrafo *m.*

parallel, *adj. & s.* paralelo *m.*; *draw a ~* establecer un paralelo.

paralize, *v. a.* paralizar.

parcel, *s.* paquete *m.*, bulto *m.*

parchment, *s.* pergamino *m.*

pardon, *s.* indulto *m.*, perdón *m.*; *I beg your ~* perdone usted, dispense usted; *I beg your ~?* no l e he entendido; ¿quiere hacer el favor de repetirlo?; — *v. a.* perdonar.

parent, *s.* progenitor *m.*; *the ~s* los padres.

parish, *s.* parroquia *f.*

Parisian, *adj. & s.* parisiense (*m.*).

park, *s.* parque *m.*; — *v. a.* estacionar, dejar, aparcar.

parking, *s.* estacionamiento *m.*; *no ~* prohibido el estacionamiento.

parliament, *s.* parlamento *m.*

parlour, *s.* salón *m.*, sala *f.*

parrot, *s.* loro *m.*

parsley, *s.* perejil *m.*

parson, *s.* párroco *m.*, cura *m.*

part, *s.* parte *f.*; (*of actor*) papel *m.*; (*for a car*) repuesto *m.*, pieza *f.*; *take ~ in* tomar parte en; — *v. a.* partir; *v. n.* romperse; separarse.

partake, *v. n.* tener parte de, beneficiar de.

partial, *adj.* parcial.

participant, *s.* participante *m.*, *f.*

participation, *s.* participación *f.*

particular, *adj.* particular; — *s.* detalle *m.*

partly, *adv.* en parte, en cierto modo.

partner, *s.* compañero *m.*, socio *m.*; (*dancing*) pareja *f.*

partridge, *s.* perdiz *f.*

party, *s.* partido *m.*; (*feast*) fiesta *f.*

pass, *v. a.* pasar; (*bill, examination*) aprobar; (*sentence*) pronunciar; *v. n.* pasar; *let ~* pasar por alto; *~ away* fallecer; *~ for* tener *or* considerar por; *~ on* pasar, transmitir; *~ out* desmayarse; *~ through* pasar por.

passage, *s.* pasaje *m.*; (*cor-*

ridor) pasillo *m.*

passenger, *s.* pasajero *m.*

passer-by, *s.* transeúnte *m.*

passion, *s.* pasión *f.; be in* ~ estar en cólera.

passive, *adj.* pasivo.

passport, *s.* pasaporte *m.*

past, *adj. & s.* pasado *(m.).; in the* ~ antes; ~ *danger* fuera del peligro; *it's half* ~ *four* son las cuatro y media.

paste, *s.* pasta *f.*

pastime, *s.* pasatiempo *m.*

pastry, *s.* pastel *m.,* pastelito *m.*

pat, *v. a.* acariciar.

patch, *s.* remiendo *m.;* parche *m.; — v. a.* remendar.

patent, *adj.* patente; patentado; *— s.* patente *f.; — v. a.* sacar la patente de.

path, *s.* sendero *m.*

patience, *s.* paciencia *f.*

patient, *adj.* paciente; *— s.* enfermo *m.,* paciente *m.*

patriot, *s.* patriota *m.*

patriotic, *adj.* patriótico.

patron, *s.* parroquiano *m.,* cliente *m.*

pattern, *s.* patrón *m.,* molde *m.,* dibujo *m.*

pause, *s.* descanso *m.,* parada *f.; — v. n.* hacer una pausa.

pave, *v. a. &* n. pavimentar.

pavement, *s.* pavimento *m.,* empedrado *m.*

pavilion, *s.* pabellón *m.*

paw, *s.* pata *f.*

pay, *v. a.* pagar; *order to* ~ orden *(f.)* de pago; ~ *a visit* hacer una visita; *— s.* paga *f.,* sueldo *m.*

payable, *adj.* pagable.

pay-day, *s.* día *(m.)* de pago.

payment, *s.* pago *m.,* pagamiento *m.*

pea, *s.* guisante *m.*

peace, *s.* paz *f.*

peaceful, *adj.* pacífico, tranquilo.

peach, *s.* melocotón *m.*

peak, *s.* cima *f.,* cúspide *f.*

pear, *s.* pera *f.*

pearl, *s.* perla *f.*

peasant, *s.* campesino *m.,* labriego *m.*

peculiar, *adj.* peculiar, raro.

peel, *s.* cáscara *f.,* pellejo *m.; — v. a.* pelar.

peer,¹ *s.* noble *m.*

peer,² *v. n.* escudriñar.

peg, *s.* clavija *f.; — v. a.* fijar.

pen, *s.* pluma *f.*

penalty, *s.* castigo *m.;* multa *f.;* ~ *area* área *(f.)* de castigo.

pencil, *s.* lápiz *m.*

penetrate, *v. a.* penetrar.

penicillin, *s.* penicilina *f.*

peninsula, *s.* península *f.*

penknife, *s.* cortaplumas *m.,* navaja *f.*

penny, *s.* penique *m.*

pension, *s.* pensión *f.; (boarding-house)* casa *(f.)* de huéspedes; — *v. a.* pensionar.

people, *s.* gente *f.,* país *m.; many* ~ mucha gente; *— v. a.* poblar.

pepper, *s.* pimienta *f.; red* ~ pimienta roja.

per, *prep.* por; ~ *annum* anualmente; ~ *cent* porciento *m.;* ~ *day* al día; ~ *person* por persona.

perceive, *v. a.* percibir.

perch,¹ *s.* percha *f.*

perch,² *s. (fish)* perca *f.*

perfect, adj. perfecto; — v. a. perfeccionar.

perfectly, adv. perfectamente.

perforate, v. a. perforar.

perform, v. a. hacer, ejecutar.

performance, s. función f., representación f.; (of a job) desempeño m.; (of a machine) rendimiento m.

perfume, s. perfume m.; — v. a. perfum(e)ar.

perhaps, adv. quizás.

peril, s. peligro m.

period, s. período m.; tiempo m.; (full stop) punto m.

periodical, adj. & s. periódico (m.).

perish, v. n. perecer.

perishable, adj. perecedero.

permanent, adj. permanente; ~ wave permanente f.

permission, s. permiso m.

permit, v. a. permitir; — s. permiso m.

Persian, adj. & s. persa.

person, s. persona f.; in ~ personalmente.

personal, adj. personal

personality, s. personalidad f.

perspiration, s. transpiración f., sudor m.

persuade, v. a. persuadir.

pessimist, s. pesimista m., f.

pet, adj. preferido; — v. a. mimar.

petition, s. petición f.; — v. a. suplicar.

petrol, s. gasolina f., nafta f.; ~ station surtidor m.

petroleum, s. petróleo m.

petticoat, s. enaguas f. pl.

petty, adj. mezquino.

phase, s. fase f.

pheasant, s. faisán m.

phial, s. redoma f.

philosopher, s. filósofo m.

philosophical, adj. filosófico.

philosophy, s. filosofía f.

phone, s. teléfono m.; — v. n. telefonear.

phosphorus, s. fósforo m.

photograph, s. fotografía f., foto f., retrato m.; — v. a. fotografiar, retratar.

phrase, s. frase f.

physical, adj. físico.

physician, s. médico m.

physicist, s. físico m.

physics, s. pl. física f.

pianist, s. pianista m., f.

piano, s. piano m.

pick, v. a. coger; (lock) abrir con ganzúa; ~ out escoger; ~ up recoger; ~ up speed ganar velocidad; — s. pico m.

pickle, s. encurtido m., pepinillo m.

picnic, s. merienda f., jira (f.) campestre; — v. n. ir de campo.

picture, s. cuadro m., fotografía f., retrato m.; (cinema) película f.; — v. a. figurar; imaginarse.

picturesque, adj. pintoresco.

pie (meat), s. pastel m., tarta f.

piece, s. pieza f.; (of paper) pedazo m., trozo m.

pier, s. muelle m.

pierce, v. a. perforar.

piety, s. piedad f.

pig, s. cerdo m., puerco m.; fig. cochino m.

pigeon, s. paloma f.

pigeon-hole, *s.* palomar *m.*; *(office)* casilla *f.*; − *v. a.* clasificar.

pile, *s.* pila *f.*, montón *m.*; − *v. a.* ~ up apilar.

pilgrim, *s.* peregrino *m.*, romero *m.*

pill, *s.* píldora *f.*

pillar, *s.* pilar *m.*, columna *f.*

pillar-box, *s.* buzón *m.*

pillow, *s.* almohada *f.*

pilot, *s.* piloto *m.*; − *v. a.* pilotear.

pin, *s.* alfiler *m.*; broche *m.*; − *v. a.* fijar; adornarse con.

pinch, *v. a.* pellizcar; − *s.* pellizco *m.*; a ~ of salt un pizco de sal.

pine, *s.* pino *m.*

pineapple, *s.* piña *f.*

pink, *adj.* rosado; − *s.* color *(m.)* de rosa; *(flower)* lave *m.*

pint, *s.* pinta *f.*

pioneer, *s.* pionero *m.*, iniciador *m.*; − *v. a.* abrir(se) paso.

pious, *adj.* piadoso.

pipe, *s.* tubo *m.*, cañería *f.*; smoke a ~ fumar en pipa.

pipe-line, *s.* cañería *f.*, tubería *f.*

pit, *s.* hoyo *m.*

pitcher, *s.* jarro *m.*

pitiful, *adj.* lastimoso.

pitiless, *adj.* despiadado.

pity, *s.* lástima *f.*, compasión *f.*; − *v. a.* compadecer.

place, *s.* sitio *m.*, lugar *m.*; take ~ *(seat)* tomar asiento; *fig.* tener lugar, ocurrir; *(post)* puesto *m.*; − *v. a.* colocar, poner.

plague, *s.* plaga *f.*

plain, *adj.* sencillo, corriente; in ~ English claramente, en buen romance; in ~ clothes en traje de paisano; − *s.* llanura *f.*, planicie *f.*

plan, *s.* plan *m.*; − *v. a.* planear, proyectar.

plane [1], *s.* aeroplano *m.*, avión *m.*; *(level)* nivel *m.*; − *adj.* plano.

plane, [2] *s.* *(tree)* plátano *m.*

planet, *s.* planeta *f.*

plank, *s.* tablón *m.*

plant, *s.* planta *f.*; fábrica *f.*; − *v. a.* plantar, sembrar.

plantation, *s.* plantación *f.*

plaster, *s.* estuco *m.*, repello *m.*; *(on wound)* parche *m.*

plastic, *adj.* plástico, sintético.

plastics, *s. pl.* materiales *(m. pl.)* plásticos.

plate, *s.* plancha *f.*, lámina *f.*; *(dish)* plate *m.*; − *v. a.* enchapar.

platform, *s.* plataforma *f.*; *(on a station)* andén *m.*

platinum, *s.* platino *m.*

platter, *s.* fuente *f.*

play, *s.* juego *m.*; *(theatre)* representación *f.*; obra *(f.)* teatral; fair ~ juego limpio; foul ~ vileza *f.*; − *v. a. & n.* jugar; ~ a part hacer un papel de; ~ a joke gastar una broma; ~ the piano tocar el piano.

player, *s.* jugador *m.*

playground, *s.* patio *(m.)* de recreo.

playmate, *s.* compañero *(m.)* de juego.

plaything, *s.* juguete *m.*

plead, *v. a. (beg)* suplicar, pedir; *(a lawsuit)* defender; ~ guilty (not guilty) declararse culpable (inocente).

pleasant, *adj.* agradable.

please, *v. a. & n.* agradar, gustar; *be ~d with* estar contento con; *shut the door ~* cierre la puerta, por favor.

pleasure, *s.* placer *m.*; *take ~ in* complacerse en; *with ~* con mucho gusto; *at ~* a gusto.

plentiful, *adj.* copioso, abundante.

plenty, *adj. & s.* mucho, abundante; *~ of books* bastantes libros; *~ more* mucho más.

plot, *s.* conspiración *f.*, complot *m.*; *(of a play)* trama *f.*; *~ of land* solar *m.*, lote *m.*; — *v. a.* conspirar.

plough, *s.* arado *m.*; — *v. a.* arar.

pluck, *v. a.* desplumar; — *s.* valor *m.*, ánimo *m.*

plug, *s.* tapón *m.*, enchufe *m.*; — *v. a.* enchufar.

plum, *s.* ciruela .

plume, *s.* pluma *f.*

plunge, *v. a.* zambullir; *v. n.* zambullirse; — *s.* zambullida *f.*

plural, *adj. & s.* plural *(m.).*

plus, más.

pocket, *s.* bolsillo *m.*; *~ dictionary* diccionario *(m.)* de bolsillo.

pocket-book, *s.* agenda *f.*, cartera *f.*

pocket-money, *s.* dinero *(m.)* de bolsillo.

poem, *s.* verso *m.*, poema *m.*

poet, *s.* poeta *m.*

poetic(al), *adj.* poético.

poetry, *s.* poesía *f.*

point, *s.* punto *m.*; *(of a pencil)* punta *f.*; *(sports)* tanto *m.*, punto *m.*; *decimal ~* coma; *three ~ six* tres coma seis; — *v. a.* señalar; *(weapon)* apuntar; *~ out* indicar, mostrar.

poison, *s.* veneno *m.*; — *v. a.* envenenar.

poisonous, *adj.* venenoso.

polar, *adj.* polar.

pole, [1] *s.* poste *m.*, palo *m.*

pole, [2] *s.* polo; *The North Pole* el. Polo Norte.

Pole, *adj. & s.* polaco.

police, *s.* policía *f.*

policeman, *s.* agente *(m.)* de policía.

police-station, *s.* comisaría *f.*

policy, *s.* política *f.*; *insurance ~* póliza *(f.)* de seguro.

polite, *adj.* cortés.

political, *adj.* político.

politician, *s.* político *m.*

politics, *s.* política *f.*

pond, *s.* estanque *m.*

pony, *s.* jaca *f.*, caballito *m.*

pool, [1] *s.* charco *m.*; *swimming ~* piscina *f.*

pool, [2] *s.* puesta *f.*; — *v. a. & n.* reunir.

poor, *adj.* pobre.

pope, *s.* papa *m.*

poplar, *s.* álamo *m.*

poppy, *s.* amapola *f.*

popular, *adj* popular.

popularity, *s.* popularidad *f.*

population *s.* población *f.*

pore, *s.* poro *m.*

pork, *s.* puerco *m.*

port, ¹ s. puerto m.; reach ~ llegar a puerto.

port, ² s. babor m.

port, ³ s (wine) vino de oporto m.

portable, adj. portátil.

porter, s. portero m.; (railway) mozo (m.) de estación; (beer) cerveza (f.) de malta.

portfolio, s. cartera f.

portion, s. porción f., parte f.

portrait, s. retrato m.

Portuguese, adj. & s. portugués (m.).

position, s. posición f.; (place) sitio m.; (employment) puesto m., empleo m.

positive, adj. positivo.

possess, v. a. poseer.

possession, s. posesión f.; take ~ of apoderarse de.

possibility, s. posibilidad f.

possible, adj. posible; as early as ~ lo antes posible.

post, ¹ s. poste m., pilar m.; (employment) puesto m., cargo m.; (military) puesto (m.) de guardia; — v. a. fijar, colocar.

post, ² s. Correos m. pl.; send by ~ enviar por correo; — v. a. llevar al correo.

postage, s. franqueo m.

poster, s. cartel m.

posterity, s. posteridad f.

postman, s. cartero m.

post-office, s. oficina (f.) de Correos, estafeta f.

postpone, v. a. aplazar.

postscript, s. posdata f.

pot, s. olla f.

potato, s. patata f.

pottery, s. cerámica f.

poultry, s. aves (f. pl.) de corral.

pound, s. libra f.; (money) libra esterlina.

pour, v. a. echar; ~ out vaciar.

poverty, s. pobreza f.

powder, s. polvos m. pl.; (gun-) pólvora f.; — v. a. pulverizar; ~ed milk leche (f.) en polvo; v. n. empolvarse.

power, s. potencia f., poder m.; the Great Powers las grandes potencias.

powerful, adj. poderoso.

power-station, s. central (f.) de energía eléctrica.

practical, adj. práctico.

practice, s. práctica f.; (of a doctor) clientela f.

practise, v. a. hacer ejercicios, practicar.

praise, v. a. alabar, elogiar; — s. alabanza f., elogio m.

pray, v. n. rezar, orar.

preach, v. a. & n. predicar.

preacher, s. predicador m.

precede, v. n. preceder.

precious, adj. valioso, precioso.

precise, adj. preciso.

precisely, adj. precisamente.

precision, s. precisión f.

predict, v. a. predecir, pronosticar.

prefabricated, adj. prefabricado.

preface, s. prefacio m.

prefer, v. a. preferir a.

preferable, adj. preferible.

preference, s. preferencia f.

pregnant, adj. preñada,

encinta, embarazada.

prejudice, *s.* *(bias)* prejuicio *m.;* *(harm)* perjuicio *m.;* — *v. a.* prejuzgar.

preliminary, *adj.* & *s.* preliminar *(m.).*

premier, *adj.* primero; — *s.* primer ministro *m.*

premises, *s. pl.* casa *(f.)* y anejos.

premium, *s.* prima *f.*

preparation, *s.* preparativo *m.;* *(product)* producto *m.,* preparación *f.*

prepare, *v. a.* preparar; *v. n.* prepararse.

preposition, *s.* preposición *f.*

presbyterian, *adj.* & *s.* presbiteriano *(m.).*

prescribe, *v. a.* prescribir; *(doctor)* recetar.

prescription, *s.* receta *f.*

presence, *s.* presencia *f.*

present,[1] *adj.* presente; *at the* ~ *time* hoy día; — *s.* presente *m.;* *at* ~ ahora; *for the* ~ por ahora.

present,[2] *v. a.* presentar; — *s.* regalo *m.*

preserve, *v. a.* preservar ; — *s.* compota *f.;* mermelada *f.; (hunting)* coto *m.,* vedado *m.*

president, *s.* presidente *m.*

press, *v. a. (button)* apretar, tocar; *(suit)* planchar; *time* ~*es* el tiempo apremia; — *s.* prensa *f.*

pressure, *s.* presión *f.;* urgencia *f.*

prestige, *s.* prestigio *m.*

pretend, *v. a.* aparentar, simular.

pretension, *s.* pretensión *f.*

pretext, *s.* pretexto *m.*

pretty, *adv.* bonito; — *adv.* ~ *well* bastante

bien.

prevail, *v. n.* prevalecer, predominar.

prevent, *v. a.* impedir, evitar.

previous, *adj.* previo.

pre-war, *adj.* de anteguerra, de preguerra.

prey, *s.* botín *m.,* presa *f.*

price, *s.* precio *m.;* premio *m.*

price-list, *s.* lista *(f.)* de precios.

pride, *s.* orgullo *m.;* — *take* ~ *in sg* enorgullecerse de.

priest, *s.* sacerdote *m.,* cura *m.*

primary, *adj.* primario, primero.

prime, *adj.* primero; — *s. in the* ~ *of life* en la flor de la vida.

Prime Minister, *s.* primer ministro *m.*

primitive, *adj.* primitivo.

prince, *s.* príncipe *m.*

princess, *s.* princesa *f.*

principal, *adj.* & *s.* principal *(m.).*

principle, *s.* principio *m.,* teoría *f.; in* ~ en principio.

print, *s.* tipo *m.,* letra *f.;* *(from negative)* copia *f.;* — *v. a.* imprimir, tirar; copiar; escribir en letras de imprenta.

printed matter, *s.* impreso *m.*

printing office, *s.* imprenta *f.*

priority, *s.* prioridad *f.*

prison, *s.* cárcel *f.,* prisión *f.*

prisoner, *s.* preso *m.;* ~ *of war* prisionero

m.; *take* ~ capturar.
private, *adj.* particular;
keep ·sg ~ tener en
secreto; — *s.* soledad
f.; in ~ en privado;
(soldier) soldado *(m.)*
raso.
privilege, *s.* privilegio *m.*;
— *v. a.* privilegiar.
prize, *s.* premio *m.*; ~
scholarship beca *f.*; —
v. a. apreciar.
probability, *s.* probabili-
dad *f.*
probable, *adj.* probable.
problem, *s.* problema *m.*
process, *s.* proceso *m.*;
— *v. a.* elaborar, transformar; *v. n.* desfilar.
procession, *s.* procesión *f.*
proclaim, *v. a.* proclamar.
proclamation, *s.* pro-
clamación *f.*
procure, *v. a.* lograr,
conseguir.
produce,¹ *v. a.* producir; *(play)* montar;
presentar.
produce,² *s.* producto *m.*
producer, *s.* producente
m., productor *m.; (of a
play)* director *(m.)* de
producción.
product, *s.* producto *m.*
production, *s.* producción *f.*; ~ *line* cadena *f.*
productive, *adj.* produc-
tivo.
profession, *s.* profesión *f.*
professional, *adj. & s.*
profesional *(m.).*
professor, *s.* profesor *m.*
profile, *s.* perfil *m.*
profit, *s.* beneficio *m.*,
ganancia *f.*; — *v. n.*
aprovechar, sacar pro-
vecho.
profitable, *adj.* provechoso.
programme, *s.* programa
m.

progress, *s.* progreso *m.*;
be in ~ estar en curso,
estar en marcha; —
v. n. progresar, mar-
char, andar.
progressive, *adj.* progre-
sivo.
prohibit, *v. a.* prohibir.
project, *v. a.* proyectar;
v. n. (protrude) so-
bresalir, resaltar; — *s.*
provecto *m.*
projectile, *s.* proyectil *m.*
projector, *s.* proyector
m.
prolong, *v. a.* prolongar.
promise, *s.* promesa *f.*;
break one's ~ faltar a
su promesa; — *v. a.*
prometer.
promising, adj. muy pro-
metedor.
promote, *v. a.* promo-
ver, fomentar.
promotion, *s.* ascenso *m.*,
promoción *f.*
prompt, *adj.* pronto; —
v. a. impulsar; *(at
school)* soplar; *(at theatre)* apuntar.
pronoun, *s.* pronombre *m.*
pronounce, *v. a.* pronunciar.
pronunciation, *s.* pronun-
ciación *f.*
proof, *s.* prueba *f.*
propagate, *v. a.* propagar;
v. n. propagarse.
propeller, *s.* hélice *f.*
proper, *adj.* propio, correcto.
property, *s.* propiedad, *f.*
prophecy, *s.* profecía *f.*
prophet, *s.* profeta *m.*
proportion, *s.* proporción
f.; out of ~ despro-
porcionado.
propose, *v. a.* proponer;
~ *sy's health* brin-
dar a la salud de;

v. n. proponerse, tener intención de.

proposition, *s.* proposición *f.*; propuesta *f.*; *(affair)* negocio *m.*

prose, *s.* prosa *f.*

prospect, *s.* perspectiva *f.* — *v. n.* hacer sondeos.

prospectus, *s.* prospecto *m.*

prosper, *v. n.* prosperar.

prosperity, *s.* prosperidad *f.*

prosperous, *adj.* próspero.

protect, *v. a.* proteger.

protection, *s.* protección *f.*

protest, *v. n.* protestar, quejarse; — *s.* protesta *f.*

Protestant, *adj. & s.* protestante *(m.).*

proud, *adj.* orgulloso.

prove, *v. a.* probar, demostrar; ~ *to be bad* resultar malo.

proverb, *s.* refrán *m.*

provide, *v. a.* proporcionar, proveer; *be* ~*d for* estar asegurado; *v. n.* ~ *for sy* cuidarse de.

province, *s.* provincia *f.*; competencia *f.*, incumbencia *f.*

provincial, *adj.* provincial.

provision, *s.* provisión *f.*; preparativos *m. pl.*

provoke, *v. a.* provocar; irritar.

prudent, *adj.* prudente.

psalm, *s.* salmo *m.*

psychological, *adj.* psicológico.

psychology, *s.* psicología *f.*

public, *adj. & s.* público.

publication, *s.* publicación *f.*

publicity, *s.* publicidad *f.*

publish, *v. a.* publicar.

publisher, *s.* editor *m.*

pudding, *s.* postre *m.*

pull, *v. a.* tirar de; *(tooth)* sacar, extraer; ~ *at* tirar de; ~ *down* bajar; *(building)* derribar, tumbar; ~ *off* sacar, quitar; ~ *up (car)* parar; — *s.* tirón *m.*; *(holder)* mango *m.*

pulse, *s.* pulso *m.*

pump, *s.* bomba *f.*; — *v. n.* bombear; ~ *up* inflar.

pumpkin, *s.* calabaza *f.*

punch, *v. a.* picar, marcar; *(beat)* dar un puñetazo; — *s.* puñetazo *m.*; *(ticket-)* perforador *m.*

punctual, *adj* puntual.

puncture, *s.* pinchazo *m.*, punzada *f.*; — *v. a.* pinchar.

punish, *v. a.* castigar.

punishment, *s.* castigo *m.*, pena *f.*

pupil, *s.* alumno *m.*, discípulo *m.*

puppy, *s.* cachorro *m.*, perrito *m.*

purchase, *s.* compra *f.*; *make* ~*s* hacer compras; — *v. a.* comprar.

pure, *adj.* puro.

purge, *v. a.* purgar; — *s.* purga *f.*

purify, *v. a.* purificar.

purity, *s.* puridad *f.*

Purple, *adj.* morado; — *s.* púrpura *f.*

Purpose, *s.* objeto *m.*, propósito *m.*; *on* ~ a propósito; *to no* ~ en vano; — *v. a.* proponerse, intentar.

Purse, *s.* bolso *m.*, portamonedas *m.*

pursue, *v. a.* perseguir; ~ *a profession* ejercer una

profesión.

pursuit, s. persecución f.; ocupación f.

push, v. a. empujar; (button) apretar, tocar; — s. empujón m.

puss(y), s. gatito m., minino m.

put, v. a. poner; (facts) exponer; ~ sg right arreglar, reparar; ~ a question hacer una pregunta; ~ an end to sg poner fin a; ~ aside ahorrar; ~ away poner de lado; ~ back poner a su lugar; ~ in order poner en orden; ~ off dejar; ~ on ponerse; ~ on speed aumentar la velocidad; ~ on the light encender la luz; ~ out (light) apagar; through ejecutar; (on the phone) poner con; ~ to bed acostar; ~ up at a hotel alojar (se).

puzzle, s. enigma m.; rompecabezas m.; — v. a. dejar perplejo.

pyjamas, s pl. pijama m

pyramid, s. pirámide f.

Q

qualification, s. calificación f.; requisito m.

qualify, v. a. calificar.

quality, s. calidad f.

quantity, s. cantidad f.

quarrel, s. riña f., disputa f., disgusto m.; — v. n. reñir, disputar.

quart, s. litro m.

quarter, s. cuarto m.; cuarta parte f.; at a ~ to three a las tres

menos cuarto; it's a ~ past six son las seis y cuarto; — v. a. (divide) cuartear; (put up) alojar.

quarterly, adj. trimestral; — s. revista (f.) trimestral.

quarters, s. pl. vivienda f., morada f.

quartz, s. cuarzo m.

quay, s. muelle m., (des)embarcadero m.

queen, s. reina f.

queer, adj. extraño, raro

quench, v. a. apagar.

query, s. pregunta f.; — v. a. interrogar; poner en duda.

quest, s. busca f., búsqueda f.; in ~ of en busca de.

question, s. pregunta f.; — v. a. interrogar; dudar.

questionnaire, s. cuestionario m.

queue, s. fila f., cola f.; stand in ~ hacer cola.

quick, adj. rápido; — adv. pronto.

quiet, adj. quieto, tranquilo; be ~ callarse, no hacer ruido; — s. tranquilidad f.; — v. a. aquietar, calmar.

quilt, s. acolchado m.; — v. a. colchar.

quit, v. a. dejar; renunciar a; — adj. we are ~s quedamos iguales.

quite, adv. completamente; ~ well bastante bien; ~ right! ¡justo! ¡exacto!

quiz, v. a. interrogar; — s. quiz m.

quotation, s. citación f; (market) curso m., cotización f.

quote, v. a. citar; (prices) cotizar.

R

rabbit, s. conejo m.

race,[1] s. carrera f.; the ~s carreras (f. pl.) de caballos; (boot-) regata f.; — v. n. ir a la carrera.

race,[2] s. raza f.

rack, s. (luggage-) red f.

racket,[1] s. (tennis) raqueta f.

racket,[2] s. (noise) bulla f., estruendo m.

radar, s. radar m.

radiate, v. a. & n. radiar.

radiator, s. radiador m.

radio, s. radio f.; ~ set aparato (m.) de radio; — v. a. radiar.

radioactive, adj. radioactivo.

radish, s. rábano m.

radius, s. radio m.

rag, s. trapo m.

rage, s. rabia f., ira f · — v. n. rabiar.

ragged, adj. andrajoso.

raid, s. correría f.; (police-) batida f., redada f.; — v. a. atracar.

rail, s. (railway) riel m.; by ~ por ferrocarril; (banister) baranda f.

railway, s. ferrocarril m.; ~ station estación (f.) de ferrocarril.

rain, s. lluvia f.; — v. n. llover.

rainbow, s. arco (m.) iris.

rainfall, s. lluvias f. pl.

rainy, adj. lluvioso.

raise, v. a. (prices) aumentar; (hat) quitarse; (glass) brindar por; (army) reclu-

tar; (family) criar; (hand) levantar; (money) recoger; — s. (of salary) aumento m; (hill) colina f.

raisin, s. pasa f.

rally, v. a. reunir; — s. reunión f., mítin m.

rampart, s. bastión m.; dique m.

ranch, s. hacienda f.

range, s. (of prices) escala f.; ~ of mountains cordillera f., cadena (f.) de montañas; be within ~ estar a tiro; — v. a. alinear.

rank, s. grado m.

ransom, s. rescate m.; — v. a. rescatar.

rapid, adj rápido.

rare, adj. raro.

rash, adj. imprudente.

raspberry, s. frambuesa f.

rat, s. rata f.

rate, s. at the ~ of six per cent a razón de seis por ciento; at any ~ en todo caso; at this ~ a este paso; first-~ de primera; (speed) velocidad f.; postage ~ tarifa (f.) postal.

rather, adv. it is ~ cold hace un poco de frío; I'd ~ have ice cream preferiría tomar helado.

ration, s. porción f., ración f.; — v. a. racionar.

raven, s. cuervo m.

raw, adj crudo; ~ material materia prima.

ray, s. rayo m.

razor, s. navaja (f.) de afeitar.

razor-blade, s. hoja (f.) de afeitar.

reach, v. a. alcanzar; ~ the city llegar a la ciudad; — s. alcance m.

react, v. n. reaccionar.

reaction, *s.* reacción *f.*

reactor, *s.* reactor *m.*

read, *v. a.* leer.

reader, *s. (person)* lector *m.; (book)* libro *(m.)* de lectura.

readiness, *s.* prontitud *f.,* diligencia *f.*

ready, *adj.* preparado, listo.

real, *adj.* verdadero.

reality, *s.* realidad *f.*

realize, *v.a.* realizar; *(profit)* ganar; obtener; *(know)* comprender; darse cuenta de.

really, *adv.* verdaderamente, en realidad, de verdad.

realm, *s.* reino *m.*

reappear, *v. n.* reaparecer.

rear,[1] *v. a.* criar; *(horse)* encabritarse.

rear,[2] *s.* parte *(f.)* posterior; — *adj.* de atrás.

reason, *s.* razón *f.; listen to* ~ ser razonable; *(motive)* motivo *m.;* — *v. a. & n.* discutir, razonar.

reasonable, *adj.* razonable, justo.

recall, *v. a.* recordar; *(ambassador)* retirar.

receipt, *s.* recibo *m.;* — *v. a.* poner el recibí.

receive, *v. a.* recibir.

receiver, *s.* receptor *m.*

recent, *adj.* reciente.

recently, *adv.* recientemente.

reception, *s. (greeting)* recibimiento *m.; (party)* recepción *f.*

receptionist, *s.* recepcionista *m.*

recipe, *s.* receta *f.*

recital, *s.* recitación *f.*

recite, *v. a.* recitar.

reckless, *adj.* imprudente, temerario.

reckon, *v. a.* calcular, contar; *(think)* creer; ~ *on* contar con.

recognize, *v. a.* reconocer.

recollect, *v. a.* recordar.

recommend, *v. a.* recomendar.

recommendation, *s.* recomendación *f.*

reconstruction, *s.* reconstrucción *f.*

record, *s.* registro *m.; (sports)* record *m.; (disk)* disco *m.; be on* ~ estar registrado; — *v. a.* registrar; *(song)* grabar.

recorder, *s.* registrador *m.*

recover, *v. a.* recobrar; ~ *oneself* recobrar la serenidad; *v. n.* restablecerse.

rector, *s.* rector *m.*

recur, *v. n.* recurrir.

red, *adj.* rojo, colorado.

red-tape, *s.* balduque *m,* burocratismo *m.*

reduce, *v. a.* reducir.

reduction, *s.* reducción *f.*

reed, *s.* juncal *m.,* caña *f.*

reel, *s.* carrete *m.,* bobina *f.;* — *v. a.* devanar.

re-elect, *v. a.* reelegir.

refer, *v. n.* referirse; ~ *to* hablar de.

referee, *s.* árbitro *m.;* — *v. a.* dirigir.

reference, *s.* referencia *f.; (information)* información *f.;* ~ *book* manual *m.*

refine, *v. a.* refinar.

reflect, *v. a.* reflejar.

reflection, *s.* reflexión *f.*

reform, *v. a.* corregir, reformar; — *s.* re-

forma *f.*
reformation, *s.* reformación *f.*
refrain, *s.* estribillo *m.*; — *v. n.* evitar, reprimir.
refresh, *v. a.* refrescar.
refreshment, *s.* refresco *m.*; ~ *room* buffet *m.*, ambigú *m.*
refrigerator, *s.* frigorífico *m.*, nevera *f.*
refuge, *s* refugio *m.*
refugee, *s.* refugiado *m.*
refusal, *s.* rechazo *m.*
refuse, *v. a.* rechazar, no querer aceptar; decir que no, negarse; — *s.* basura *f.*
refute, *v. a.* refutar.
regard, *v. a.* considerar; — *s.* consideración *f.*, respeto *m.*; *in this* ~ a este respecto.
regent, *s.* regente *m.*.
regime, *s.* régimen *m.*
regiment, *s.* regimiento *m.*
region, *s.* región *f.*, comarca *f.*
regret, *v. a. & n.* sentir; — *s.* pena *f.*
regular, *adj.* regular, corriente, normal.
regulate, *v. a.* regular.
regulation, *s.* regla *f.*, reglamento *m.*
reign, *s.* reinado *m.*; — *v. n.* reinar.
rein, *s.* rienda *f.*
relate, *v. a.* relatar, contar; *be* ~*d to* estar emparentado con.
relation, *s.* relación *f.*; (*person*) pariente *m.*
relative, *adj.* relativo; *be* ~ *to* depender de; — *s.* pariente *m.*, *f.*
relax, *v. a. & n.* relajar; descansar.
release, *v. a.* soltar, rele-

var; — *s.* liberación *f.*
reliable, *adj.* seguro, digno de confianza.
relic, *s.* reliquia *f.*
relief, *s.* alivio *m.*; descanso *m.*
religion, *s.* religión *f.*
religious, *adj.* religioso.
relish, *s.* sabor *m.*; gusto *m.*; *with* ~ con gusto; — *v. a.* tomar gusto en *or* a.
reluctant, *adj* mal dispuesto, renitente.
rely, *v. n.* ~ *on* depender de, contar con.
remain, *v. n.* quedar.
remainder, *s.* resto *m.*
remark, *v. a.* observar, hacer comentarios; — *s.* observación *f.*
remarkable, *adj.* notable.
remedy, *s.* remedio *m.*; — *v. a.* remediar.
remember, *v. a.* recordar, acordarse de.
remembrance, *s.* recuerdo *m.*
remind, *v. a.* recordar.
remit, *v. a.* remitir.
remittance, *s.* remisión *f.*, giro *m.*
remorse, *s.* remordimiento *m.*
remote, *adj.* remoto; ~ *control* telemando *m.*, mando *m.* remoto.
removal, *s.* alejamiento *m.*
remove, *v. a.* quitar.
remuneration, *s.* remuneración *f.*; premio *m.*
render, *v. a.* (*service*) prestar; ~ *an account* dar cuenta de.
renew, *v. a.* renovar.
renounce, *v. a.* renunciar a.
rent, *s.* alquiler *m.*; — *v. a.* alquilar.
reorganization, *s.* reor-

ganización *f.*

reorganize, *v. a.* reorganizar.

repair, *v. a.* reparar, remediar, componer, remendar; — *s.* reparación *f.*

repay, *v. a.* reembolsar.

repeat, *v. a.* repetir.

repent, *v. a.* arrepentirse de.

repetition, *s.* repetición *f.*

replace, *v. a.* reemplazar.

reply, *v. a.* contestar, responder; — *s.* respuesta *f.*

report, *v. a.* informar, hacer un informe, dar cuenta de; *(to the police)* denunciar; — *s.* informe *m.; weather* ~ boletín *(m.)* meteorológico; *(school)* libreta *(f.)* de calificaciones; certificado *m.; (noise)* estampido *m.*

reporter, *s.* periodista *m.,* reportero *m.*

represent, *v. a.* representar.

representation, *s.* representación *f.*

representative, *adj.* representativo; típico; — *s.* diputado *m.*

reproach, *v. a.* reprochar; — *s.* reproche *m.*

reproduce, *v. a.* reproducir.

reproduction, *s.* reproducción *f.*

reptile, *s.* reptil *m.*

republic, *s.* república *f.*

republican, *adj. & s.* republicano *(m.).*

reputation, *s.* reputación *f.,* fama *f.*

request, *s.* petición *f.;* ~ *stop* parada *(f.)* discrecional.

require, *v. a.* requerir, necesitar.

requirement, *s.* requisito *m.,* condición *f.; (claim)* exigencia *f.*

research, *s.* investigación *f.*

resemble, *v. a.* parecerse.

resent, *v. a.* resentirse por.

reserve, *v. a.* reservar; — *s.* reserva *f.*

reside, *v. n.* residir.

residence, *s.* residencia *f.,* domicilio *m.*

resident, *s.* residente *m.*

resist, *v. n.* resistir.

resistance, *s.* resistencia *f.*

resolute, *adj.* resuelto.

resolution, *s.* resolución *f.*

resolve, *v. a.* resolver.

resort, *v. n.* ~ *to* recurrir a; — *s.* recurso *m.; summer* ~ lugar *(m.)* de veraneo.

respect, *s.* respeto *m.; (standpoint)* respecto *m.; in every* ~ en todos respectos; *in many* ~s en muchos puntos; *with* ~ *to* con respecto a; — *v. a.* respetar.

espectable, *adj.* respetable.

respectful, *adj.* respetuoso.

respective, *adj.* respectivo.

respiration, *s.* respiración *f.*

responsibility, *s.* responsabilidad *f.*

responsible, *adj.* responsable; *be* ~ *for* ser causa de.

rest, *s.* descanso *m.; at* ~ parado; *set at* ~ tranquilizar; — *v. n.* des-

resume, *v. a.* recomenzar, reanudar.

retain, *v. a.* retener.

retire, *v. n.* retirarse.

retreat, *v. n.* retirarse; — *s.* retiro *m.*

return, *v. a.* devolver; *v.* cansar.

restaurant, *s.* restaurante *m.*, restorán *m.*

restless, *adj.* inquieto.

restoration, *s.* restauración *f.*

restore, *v. a.* restaurar; *be ~d to health* ser restablecido; *~to life* salvar la vida a.

result, *s.* resultado *m.;* — *v. n.* ~ *in* terminar en; ~ *from sg* resultar.

n. regresar, volver; ~ *thanks for sg* dar las gracias por; — *s.* vuelta *f.*, regreso *m.;* *by ~ of post* a vuelta de correo; *many happy ~s* feliz cumpleaños; *~s* rédito *m.;* provecho *m.*

reveal, *v. a.* revelar.

revenge, *s.* venganza *f.;* — *v. a.* vengar.

revenue, *s.* renta *s.*

reverend, *adj.* reverendo.

reverse, *adj.* contrario; ~ *gear* marcha *(f.)* atrás; — *v. a.* dar vuelta a; *(decision)* revocar; — *s.* revés *m.;* *~s* contratiempos *m. pl.*

review, *s.* revista *f.;* — *v. a.* repasar; hacer la crítica de.

revolution, *s.* revolución *f.*

reward, *s.* recompensa *f.*, gratificación *f.;* — *v. a.* recompensar, premiar.

rheumatism, *s.* reumatismo *m.*

rhyme, *s.* rima *f.;* — *v. n.* rimar.

rhythm, *s.* ritmo *m.*

rib, *s.* costilla *f.*

ribbon, *s.* cinta *f.*

rice, *s.* arroz *m.*

rich, *adj.* rico; *(land)* fértil.

rid, *v. a.* librar; *get ~ of* librarse de, quitarse.

riddle, *s.* acertijo *m.*

ride, *v. a.* montar, andar; ~ *a bicycle* montar en bicicleta; *v. n.* ir, pasear; — *s.* paseo *m.*, viaje *m.;* *give sy a ~* llevar en su coche.

ridiculous, *adj.* ridículo.

right, *adj.* derecho; *on the ~ side* a la derecha; *be ~* tener razón; *that's ~* eso es; *all ~!* bien; — *s.* derecho *m.;* *by ~* legítimamente; *with ~* con razón; *by ~ of* a causa de; *keep to the ~!* llevar la derecha; — *adv.* bien; ~ *now* en este momento; ~ *away* ahora mismo; — *v. a.* enderezar; restaurar, reparar.

rim, *s.* borde *m.;* *(hat)* ala *f.*

ring,[1] *s.* anillo *m.;* *(sports)* ring *m.*, ruedo *m.*, pista *f.*

ring,[2] *v. a.* ~ *the bell* tocar el timbre; *v. n. the bell ~s* suena el timbre; ~ *out* sonar; ~ *up* llamar por teléfono, — *s.* timbre *m.*

riot, *s.* tumulto *m.*, motín *m.*

rip, *v. a.* rasgar.

ripe, *adj.* maduro; *grow ~* madurar.

ripen, *v. a. & n.* madurar.

rise, *v. n.* levantarse, ponerse en pie; *(prices)* subir; *(river)* crecer; *(to a post)* ascender; *(sun)* salir; — *s.* subida *f.*

risk, *s.* riesgo *m.;* — *v. n.* arriesgarse.

risky, *adj.* arriesgado.

rival, *adj. & s.* rival *(m.);* — *v. a.* competir.

river, *s.* río *m.*

road, *s.* carretera *f.,* camino *m.;* ~ *map* mapa *(m.);* itinerario.

roast, *v. a.* asar; — *adj. & s.* asado *(m.);* ~ *beef* rosbif *m.,* carne *(f.)* de vaca asada; ~ *meat* asado *m.*

rob, *v. a.* robar.

robber, *s.* ladrón *m.*

robbery, *s.* robo *m.*

robe, *s.* hábito *(m.)* talar, toga *f.; (dressing gown)* bata *f.*

rock,[1] *s.* roca *f.,* escollo *m.*

rock,[2] *v. a.* mecer; *v. n.* balancearse.

rocket, *s.* cohete *m.;* ~ *plane* avión *(m.)* cohete.

rocket-range, *s.* rampa *(f.)* de lanzamiento de cohetes.

rocky, *adj.* rocoso.

rod, *s.* varilla *f.,* barra *f.; (fishing)* caña *(f.)* de pescar.

roll, *s. (coil)* rollo *m.; (list)* lista *f.;* ~ *of bills* fajo *(m.)* de billetes; *(bread)* panecillo *m.;* — *v. n. (ball)* rodar; *(ship)* balancearse; ~ *up* enrollar; *(sleeves)* remangarse.

Roman, *adj. & s.* romano *(m.);* ~ *Catholic* católico romano; ~ *type* letra *(f.)* romana.

romantic, *adj.* romántico.

romanticism, *s.* romanticismo *m.*

roof, *s.* tejado *m.;* ~ *of*

the mouth paladar *m.*

room, *s.* cuarto *m.,* habitación *f.; (place)* sitio *m.;* ~ *and board* pensión *(f.)* completa.

root, *s.* raíz *f.; fig.* origen *m.; take* ~ arraigar; — *v. a.* ~ *out* desarraigar.

rope, *s.* cuerda *f.,* soga *f.*

rose, *s.* rosa *f.*

rotten, *adj.* podrido, malo.

rough, *adj. (sea)* tempestuoso, agitado; *(ground)* quebrado; *(to the touch)* áspero; ~ *draft* borrador *m.*

round, *adj.* redondo; ~ *cheeks* mejillas *(f. pl.)* llenas; ~ *trip ticket* billete *(m.)* de ida y vuelta; — *adv.* alrededor, en círculo; *all the year* ~ todo el año; *go* ~ dar la vuelta a; — *prep.* alrededor, a la vuelta de; — *s. (daily)* recorrido *m.; (of drinks)* ronda *f.; (sports)* asalto *m.;* — *v. a.* redondear; *v. n.* redondearse.

route, *s.* ruta *f.,* vía *f.*

routine, *s.* rutina *f.,* marcha *f.;* ~ *work* trabajo *(m.)* rutinario.

row,[1] *s.* fila *f.*

row,[2] *v. n.* remar; — *s.* remar *m.*

row,[3] *s. (quarrel)* pelea *f.*

royal, *adj.* real, regio.

rub, *v. a.* frotar; *(clothes)* restregar; *v. n.* ~ *against* rozar contra; ~ *in* machacar; ~ *out* borrar; — *s.* fricción *f.*

rubber, *s.* caucho *m.,* ~*s* chanclos *m. pl.*

rubbish, *s.* basura *f.*

ruby, *s.* rubí *m.*

rude, *adj.* rudo; *fig.* des-

cortés.
rug, s. alfombra f.; (bed) manta f.
rugged, adj. accidentado, aspero.
ruin, s. ruina f.; — v. a. arruinar, dañar.
rule, s. regla f.; (domination) dominio m.; mando m.; as a ~ por regla general; — v. a. & n. regir, gobernar; ~ out excluir.
ruler, s. regla f.; (person) gobernante m.
rumour, s. rumor m.
run, v. n. correr m.; pasar; (road) andar, marchar; (law) estar en vigor; (horse) correr; (story) decir; (stocking) hacerse carreras; v. a. (machine) manejar; (rope) pasar; (shop) conducir, dirigir; ~ dry secarse; ~ away huir, escaparse; ~ down pararse; (car) atropellar; ~ for presentarse; ~ off fugarse; ~ out acabarse; ~ over derramarse; — s. carrera f.; viaje m.; (on goods) demanda f.; in the long ~ a la larga, al fin y al cabo.
runner, s. corredor m.; (of a sled) patín m.
runway, s. pista (f.) de despegue, (or) aterrizaje.
rural, adj. rural.
rush, v. n. darse prisa; ~ through hacer de prisa; — s. aglomeración f.; the ~ hours horas (f. pl.) de máxima circulación.
Russian, adj. & s. ruso.
rust, s. herrumbre f., orín m.; — v. n. oxidarse.
rustic, adj. rústico.

rye, s. centeno m.

S

sack, s. saco m.; give sy the ~ echar, despedir; — v. a. ensacar; (plunder) saquear.
sacred, adj. sagrado.
sacrifice, s. sacrificio m.; — v. a. sacrificar.
sad, adj. triste.
saddle, s. silla (f.) de montar; — v. a. ensillar.
sadness, s. tristeza f.
safe, adj. seguro; (saved) a salvo; ~ and sound sano y salvo; — s. caja (f.) fuerte, caja de caudales.
safely, adv. sin peligro, a salvo.
safety, s. seguridad f.; ~ pin imperdible m.
sail, s. vela f.; — v. n. navegar; hacerse a la mar, zarpar; ~ for Spain embarcarse para España; v. a. ~ a boat gobernar un barco.
sailor, s. marinero m.
saint, adj. & s. santo (m.).
sake, s. for my ~ por mí.
salad, s. ensalada f.
salary, s. salario m., sueldo m.
sale, s. venta f.; for ~ en venta; ~s liquidación f.
salesman, s. vendedor m.
salmon, s. salmón m.
saloon, s. salón m.
salt, s. sal f.; — adj. salado; — v. a. salar.
salt-cellar, s. salero m.
salvation, s. salvación f.
same, adj. mismo; at the ~ time al mismo tiempo; it is all the ~ to me a mí me da lo mismo; all the ~ no obstante, a pesar de todo; the ~ to you lo

mismo digo.

sample, *s.* muestra *f.;* — *v. a.* probar.

sanatorium, *s.* sanatorio *m.*

sand, *s.* arena *f.;* ~s playa *f.*

sandal, *s.* sandalia *f*

sandwich, *s.* emparedado *m.,* bocadillo *m.*

sane, *adj.* cuerdo, sano.

sanitary, *adj.* higiénico.

sardine, *s.* sardina *f.*

satellite, *s.* satélite *m.*

satin, *s.* satén *m.*

satisfaction, *s.* satisfacción *f.*

satisfactory, *adj.* satisfactorio.

satisfy, *v. a.* satisfacer; *be satisfied* estar convencido.

Saturday, *s.* sábado *m.*

sauce, *s.* salsa *f.*

saucepan, *s.* sartén *f.*

saucer, *s.* platillo *m.*

sausage, *s.* salchicha *f.*

savage, *adj.* salvaje.

save, *v.a.* salvar; *(trouble)* ahorrar, evitar; *(keep)* guardar; *(stamps)* coleccionar; *(the goal)* parar; — *prep.* salvo.

savings, *s. pl.* ahorros *m. pl.;* ~ *bank* caja *(f.)* de ahorros.

say, *v. a.* decir; *that is to* ~ es decir; *what did you* ~? ¿cómo dijo usted?; *so to* ~ para así decirlo; *let us* ~ digamos; *he is said* dicen que él; — *s.* opinión *f.*

scale,[1] *s.* escala *f.,* graduación *f.;* — *v. a.* escalar.

scale,[2] *s. (of fish)* escama *f.;* — *v. a.* escamar.

scales, *s.* balanza *f.*

scandal, *s.* escándalo *m.*

scar, *s.* cicatriz *f.;* — *v. n.* cicatrizarse.

scarce, *adj.* escaso, raro.

scarcely, *adv.* apenas.

scare, *v. a.* asustar; — *s.* susto *m.*

scarf, *s.* bufanda *f.*

scarlet, *adj.* escarlata; ~ *fever* escarlatina *f.*

scatter, *v. a.* esparcir, dispersar.

scene, *s.* escena *f.; behind the* ~s entre bastidores; *make a* ~ hacer escenas; *a beautiful* ~ una hermosa vista.

scenery, *s.* decoración *f.*

scent, *s.* olor *m.; (of dog)* olfato *m.;* — *v. a.* husmear, rastrear.

schedule, *s.* programa *m.;* plan *m.; (train)* horario *m.; according to* ~ puntualmente.

scheme, *s.* proyecto *m.,* esquema *m.;* — *v. a.* proyectar, idear.

scholar, *s.* escolar *m.,* estudiante *m.;* — *(scientist)* sabio *m.,* erudito *m.; (holder of scholarship)* becario *m.*

school, *s.* escuela *f.; primary* ~ escuela primaria; *public* ~ escuela secundaria; *trade* ~ escuela profesional.

schoolmaster, *s.* profesor *m.;* maestro *m.,* director *(m.)* de escuela.

schoolroom, *s.* sala *(f.)* de clase, aula *f.,* auditorio *m.*

science, *s.* ciencia *f.*

scientific, *adj.* científico.

scientist, *s.* hombre *(m.)* de ciencia.

scissors, *s. pl.* tijeras *f. pl.*

scooter, *s.* patinete *m.*

scope, *s.* alcance *m.; be within the* ~ *of* estar al alcance de.

scorch, v. a. chamuscar.

score, s. (cut) entalladura f.; (debt) deuda f.: (sports) tanto m.; (musical) partitura f. (twenty) veintena f.; — v. a. entallar; (game) ganar puntos, marcar; ~ a goal marcar un gol; (music) instrumentar.

scorn, s. desprecio m.; — v. a. despreciar.

Scotch, adj. & s. escocés (m.); the ~ los escoceses; (drink) whisky m.

scout, s. explorador m.; — v. a. explorar.

scramble, v. n. trepar; ~d eggs huevos (m. pl.) revueltos.

scrape, v. a. raspar; s. lío m. enredo m.; get into ~s meterse en un lío.

scratch, v. a. arañar, rasguñar; — s. rasguño m., raspadura f.

scream, v. n. gritar; — s. grito m.

screen, s. pantalla f.; (fender) biombo m.

screw, s. tornillo m.; — v. a. atornillar; ~ on enroscar.

screw-driver, s. destornillador m.

sculptor, s. escultor m.

sculpture, s. escultura f.

sea, s. mar m.; be at ~ navegar; fig. estar confuso; go to ~ zarpar, hacerse a la mar.

seal,[1] s. foca f.

seal,[1] s. sello m.; — v. a. ~ up cerrar con lacre.

seam, s. costura f.

seaman, s. marinero m.

seaport, s. puerto (m.) marítimo, (or) de mar.

search, v. a. buscar; (a person) registrar; — s. registro m.; in ~ of en busca de.

search-light, s. proyector m.

season, s. estación f.; temporada f.; — v. a. (food) sazonar, condimentar.

seat, s. asiento m.; (theatre) localidad f.; (residence) residencia f.; — v. n. sentarse, tomar asiento; be ~ed tome usted asiento.

second, adj. & s. segundo (m); — v. a. apoyar, secundar.

secondary, adj. secundario; ~ school instituto (m.) secundario.

second-hand, adj. de segunda mano, de ocasión.

secret, adj. & s. secreto (m.).

secretary, s. secretario m.; Secretary of State ministro (m.) de Estado.

section, s. sección f., parte f.; (of town) barrio m.

secure, adj. seguro; — v. a. asegurar, garantizar; (get) obtener, conseguir.

security, s. seguridad f., garantía f.; securities s. pl. títulos m., valores m., bonos m.

sedative, adj. & s. sedante (m.), sedativo (m.).

seduce, v. a. seducir.

see, v. a. ver; let me ~ ! ¡a ver!; ~ you again hasta la vista; ~ you on Tuesday hasta martes; I ~! ya lo veo, comprendo; come to ~ me venga a verme; ~ sy home acompañar a casa; ~ off despedir; ~ to encargarse de, cuidar de.

seed, s. semilla f.; — v. n. sembrar,

seek, v. a. buscar.

seem, v. n. parecer.

seize, v. a. agarrar; *(take away)* confiscar; *(opportunity)* aprovechar; *(arrest)* detener; *(understand)* comprender.

seldom, adv. raramente, rara vez.

select, v. a. elegir; — adj. selecto.

selection, s. selección f.

self, pron & s. mismo.

selfish, adj. egoísta.

selfishness, s. egoísmo m.

self-service, adj. & s. autoservicio (m.).

sell, v. a. vender; ~ off liquidar.

seller, s. vendedor m.

send, v. a. enviar, mandar; *(telegram)* mandar, poner; ~ for llamar.

sender, s. remitente m., f.; expedidor m.

senior, adj. mayor; — s. decano m.

sense, s. sentido m.

senseless, adj. insensible; insensato, sin sentido.

sensible, adj. sensato, cuerdo.

sensitive, adj. sensible.

sensual, adj. sensual.

sentence, s. sentencia f.; frase f.; — v. a. condenar, sentenciar.

sentry, s. centinela m.

separate, adj. separado; — v. a. separar; v. n. separarse.

separation, s. separación f.

September, s. septiembre m.

serenade, s. serenata f.

sergeant, s. sargento m.

serial, adj. periódico; ~ number número (m.) de orden.

series, s. serie f.

serious, adj. serio.

servant, s. criado m.; public ~ funcionario m.

serve, v. a. servir.

service, s. servicio m.; civil ~ administración (f.) pública, servicio (m.) público; be of ~ ser útil; I'm at your ~ estoy a sus órdenes.

session, s. sesión f.

set, v. a. poner, colocar; *(type)* componer; *(price)* fijar; ~ an example dar ejemplo; v. n. *(sun)* ponerse; ~ off salir; ~ up poner, establecer; — s. colección f.; *(radio)* aparato m.; — adj. terco, obstinado; ~ price precio (m.) fijo.

setting, s. disposición f., arreglo m.; *(of types)* composición f.

settle, v. a. establecer; *(claim)* satisfacer; ~ down establecerse; ~ up arreglar.

settlement, s. acuerdo m., arreglo m.; *(colony)* caserío m.

seven, adj. & s. siete.

seventeen, adj. & s. diecisiete.

seventh, adj. séptimo.

seventy, adj. & s. setenta.

several, adj. varios pl.

severe, adj. severo; *(winter)* duro.

sew, v. a. coser.

sewing-machine, s. máquina (f.) de coser.

sex, s. sexo m.

sexual, adj. sexual.

shabby, adj. raído, gastado.

shade, s. sombra f.; − v. a. sombrear.

shadow, s. sombra f.

shady, adj. sombreado; sombrío.

shaft, s. mango m.; (pit) pozo m.

shake, v. a. sacudir; (medicament) agitar.

shall, v. n. I ~ go iré; ~ I wait? ¿debo esperar?

shame, s. vergüenza f.; v. a. avergonzar.

shameful, adj. vergonzoso.

shameless, adj. descarado, desvergonzado.

shampoo, s. champú m.

shape, s. forma f.; estado m.; I'm in bad ~ me siento mal; − v. a. modelar, dar forma.

share, s. parte f.; (stock) acción f.; − v. a. compartir, repartir.

shareholder, s. accionista m., f.

sharp, adj. afilado; (mind) agudo; − adv. at five o'clock ~ a las cinco en punto.

sharpen, v. a. afilar.

shave, v. a. afeitar; v. n. afeitarse; − s. afeite m.

shawl, s. chal m.; mantón m.

she, pron. ella; − s. hembra f.

shed,[1] v. a. verter, echar.

shed,[2] s. cobertizo m.

sheep, s. oveja f.

sheet, s. (of paper) pliego m., hoja f.; (of bed) sábana f.

shelf, s. estante m.

shell, s. concha f.; cáscara f.; (bullet) proyectil m.; − v. a. (peas) desgranar; bombardear.

shelter, s. albergue m., refugio m.; − v. a. albergar.

shepherd, s. pastor m.

shield, s. escudo m.; − v. a. proteger, amparar.

shift, v. a. & n. mudar, cambiar; − s. cambio m.; (in work) turno m.

shine, v. n. brillar; − s. brillo m.

ship, s. barco m.; − v. a. embarcar; v. n. embarcarse.

shipment, s. embarque m., cargamento m.

shipwreck, s. naufragio m.

shipyard, s. astilleros m. pl.

shirt, s. camisa f.

shiver, v. n. tiritar; − s. tiritón m.

shock, s. choque m.; − v. a. chocar; be ~ed at escandalizarse de.

shocking, adj. espantoso chocante.

shoe, s. zapato m.; (horse-) herradura f.; − v. a. herrar.

shoe-cream, s. pomada (f.) para calzado.

shoe-lace, s. cordón (m.) de zapato.

shoemaker, s. zapatero m.

shoot, v. n. disparar; tirar; (car) salir disparado; v. a. (photo) tomar.

shooting, s. disparo m.; (hunting) caza f.; (film) rodaje m.

shop, s. tienda f.; − v. a. ir de compras.

shop assistant, s. dependiente m., dependienta f.

shopkeeper, s. tendero m.

shore, s. orilla f., costa f., playa f.

short, adj. corto; ~ cut atajo m.; ~ story cuento m.; in a ~ time dentro de poco; − adv. cut ~ interrumpir; run

~ of sg quedarse falto de; — s. ~s pantalones (m. pl.) cortos.

shorten, v. a. acortar, abreviar.

shorthand, s. taquigrafía f.

shortly, adv. en breve, dentro de poco.

shot, s. disparo m., tiro m.; (person) tirador m.; (photo) instantánea f.; (drink) trago m., sorbo m.; (injection) inyección f.

shoulder, s. hombro m.

shout, s. grito m.; — v. n. gritar.

show, v. a. enseñar, mostrar; indicar; (prove) probar, justificar; ~ in hacer entrar; ~ off presumir; ~ up presentarse, aparecer; — s. espectáculo m., función f.

shower, s. chubasco m., aguacero m., lluvia f.; (bath) ducha f.

shrewd, adj. astuto.

shrill, adj. agudo, penetrante.

shrine, s. relicario m.

shrink, v. n. encogerse.

shrub, s. arbusto m., mata f.

shrug, v. n. encogerse de hombros.

shudder, s. estremecimiento m.; — v. n. estremecerse.

shut, v. a. cerrar; ~ in encerrar; ~ up cerrar; (be silent) callarse.

shutter, s. persiana f.; (photo) obturador m.

shy, adj. tímido.

sick, adj. enfermo; be ~ sentirse mal, vomitar; feel ~ sentir náuseas; fall ~ caer enfermo; be

~ of estar harto de.

sicken, v. n. enfermar.

sickness, s. enfermedad f.

side, s. lado m.; on all ~s por todas partes; — adj. lateral.

sigh, s. suspiro m.; — v. n. suspirar.

sight, s. vista f.; by ~ de vista; see the ~s visitar los lugares interesantes; — v. a. notar, avistar.

sightseeing, s. el visitar los lugares interesantes.

sign, s. señal f.; (signboard) letrero m.; — v. a. firmar; ~ on contratar.

signal, s. señal f.; — v. a. hacer señales a.

signature, s. firma f.

significant, adj. significante, significativo.

signify, v. a. significar.

silence, s. silencio m.; — v. a. acallar.

silent, adj. silencioso; callado; v. n. keep ~ callarse.

silk, s. seda f.

silly, adj. tonto.

silver, s. plata f.; — v. a. azogar, platear.

silvery, adj. plateado.

similar, adj. semejante, similar.

simple, adj. sencillo; simple.

simplicity, s. sencillez f.

sin, s. pecado m.; — v. n. pecar.

since, adv. & prep. desde; ever ~ desde entonces; — conj. puesto que.

sincere, adj. sincero.

sinew, s. tendón m.

sinful, adj. pecaminoso.

sing, v. a. & n. cantar.

singer, s. cantante m., f.

single, adj. solo; (not married) soltero.

singlet, s. camiseta f.

singular, adj. singular.

sinister, adj. siniestro.

sink, v n. hundirse; — v. a. abrir, excavar; — s. fregadero m., pila f.

sip, v. a. sorber, chupar; —s. sorbo m., trago m.

sir, s. señor m.

sister, s. hermana f.

sister-in-law, s. cuñada f.

sit, v. n. sentarse; be ~ ting estar sentado; ~ down sentarse; ~ for posar; ~ up incorporarse; (all night) estarse levantado.

site, s. solar m., sitio m.

sitting-room, s. cuarto (m.) de estar.

situation, s. situación f.

six, adj. & s. seis.

sixteen, adj. &. s. dieciséis.

sixth, adj. sexto.

sixty, adj. & s. sesenta.

size, s. tamaño m., número m.

skate, s. patín m.; — v. n. patinar.

skeleton, s. esqueleto m.; ~ key ganzua f., llave (f.) maestra.

sketch, s. croquis m,; — v. a. dibujar.

ski, s. esquí m.: — v. n. esquiar.

skiff, s. bote m., canoa f

skilful, adj. hábil, diestro.

skill, s. habilidad f., destreza f.

skilled, adj. diestro, experto, especializado.

skin, s. piel f.; — v. a. desollar.

skip, v. a. & n. saltar.

skirt, s. falda f.; — v. a. orillar, orlar.

skull, s. cráneo m.

sky, s. cielo m.

slab, s. placa f.

slack, adj. flojo.

slacken, v. a. aminorar, disminuir.

slacks, s. pl. pantalones m. pl.

slander, s. calumnia f.; — v. a. calumniar.

slate, s. pizarra f.; — v. a. empizarrar.

slaughter, s. matanza f.; — v. a. matar.

slave, s. esclavo m.

slay, v. a. matar.

sledge, s. trineo m.; — v. n. ir en trineo.

sleep, v. n. dormir; — s. sueño m.

sleeping-car, s. coche-cama m.

sleepy, adj. soñoliento.

sleeve, s. manga f.

sleigh, s. trineo m.; — v. n. ir en trineo.

slender, adj. delgado.

slice, s. tajada f., rebanada f.; — v. a. cortar en tajadas, rebanar.

slide, v. n. deslizarse, resbalar.

slight, adj. leve, ligero; — v. a. desairar; — s. desprecio m., desaire m.

slim, adj. delgado.

sling, s. nudo (m.) corredizo; cabestrillo m.

slip, s. (of paper) trozo m., tira f.; (fault) imprudencia f., pata f.; (combination) combinación f.; pillow ~ funda f.; give the ~ dar esquinazo; — v n. resbalar; (escape) escapar; it ~ped my memory se me olvidó; v. a. echar; ~ away escabullirse.

slipper, s. zapatilla f., pantufla f.

slot, s. ranura f.

slow, adj. lento; (child)

retrasado; — adv. despacio; — v. a. retardar; v. n. atrasar.

slum, s. calle (f.) sucia; ~s barrios (m. pl.) bajos, tugurios m. pl.

slumber, v. n. dormitar; — s. sueño (m.) ligero.

sly, adj. astuto, taimado.

small, adj. pequeño; ~ change suelto m.; ~ talk charla f.

smallpox, s. viruelas f. pl.

smart, adj. listo; elegante.

smell, s. olfato m.; olor m.; — v. a. oler.

smile, s. sonrisa f.; — v. n. sonreír.

smoke, s. humo m.; — v. n. fumar; v. a. ahumar.

smooth, adj. llano; (sea) tranquilo; (wine) suave; (person) lisonjero; — v. a. alisar; (way) allanar.

smuggle, v. a. pasar de contrabando; v. n. hacer contrabando.

snack, s. merienda f.

snail, s. caracol m.

snake, s. serpiente f., culebra f.

snap, s. instantánea f.; — v. a. sacar una instantánea.

sneeze, s. estornudo m.; — v. n. estornudar.

snore, v. n. roncar; — s. ronquido m.

snow, s. nieve f.; — v. n. nevar.

snug, adj. cómodo, íntimo.

so, adv. así; that's not ~! ¡eso no es cierto!; — I see ya lo veo; and ~ on etcétera; ~ much tanto; ~ that a fin de que; ~ long! ¡hasta luego!

soak, v. a. empapar, re-

mojar.

soap, s. jabón m.; — v. a. enjabonar.

sober, adj. sobrio; — v. a. desembriagar.

social, adj. social.

socialism, s. socialismo m.

socialist, adj. & s. socialista (m., f.).

society, s. sociedad f.

sock, s. calcetín m.

socket, s. enchufe m.

soda, s. soda f., agua (f.) de Seltz.

sofa, s. sofá m., canapé m.

soft, adj. blando, suave; ~-boiled eggs huevos (m. pl.) pasados por agua.

soil, s. tierra f.; — v. a. ensuciar.

soldier, s. soldado m.

sole, s. suela f., (fish) lenguado m.; — v. a. poner suelas.

solemn, adj. solemne.

solicit, v. a. solicitar.

solicitor, s. abogado m.

solid, adj. & s. sólido (m.).

solidarity, s. solidaridad f.

solitude, s. soledad f.

soluble, adj. soluble.

solution, s. solución f.

solve, v. a. resolver, solucionar.

some, adj. algo, poco, algún; algunos, pocos; to ~ extent hasta cierto punto; ~ twenty boys unos veinte muchachos.

somebody, pron. alguien.

someone, pron. alguien.

something, pron. algo.

sometime, adv. algún día.

sometimes, adv. a veces; algunas veces.

somewhat, adv. algo, un poco.

somewhere, adv. en al-

guna parte.
son, s. hijo m.
song, s. canción f.
son-in-law, s. yerno m.
soon, adv. pronto; as ~ as tan pronto como; as ~ as possible lo antes posible; ~er or later tarde o temprano.
soprano, s. soprano f.
sore, adj. mal, lastimado;

I've a ~ throat me duele la garganta; get ~ ofenderse; — s. llaga f.
sorrow, s. aflicción f.; — v. n. afligirse.
sorry, adj. triste; so ~! ¡lo siento mucho!
sort, s. clase f.
soul, s. alma f.
sound,[1] s. sonido m.; — v. n. sonar.
sound,[2] adj. sano, bueno.
soup, s. sopa f.
sour, adj. agrio, ácido.
source, s. fuente f.; fig. origen m.; motivo m.
south, s. sur m.; — adj. del sur; — adv. hacia el sur.
southern, adj. meridional, al sur, del sur.
sovereign, adj. & s. soberano (m.).
sow,[1] s. puerca f., marrana f.
sow,[2] v. a. sembrar.
space, s. espacio m.; ~ vehicle nave (f.) espacial; — v. a. espaciar, separar.
space-flight, s. vuelo (m.) orbital.
spaceman, s. astronauta m., cosmonauta m.
space-ship, s. nave (f.) espacial.
space-suit, s. traje (m.) espacial.
spacious, adj. espacioso.
spade, s. pala f., azada f.;

(card) espada f.; — v. n. cavar con pala, remover la tierra.
Spaniard, s. español m.
Spanish, adj. español.
spanner, s. llave (f.) inglesa.
spare, v. a. ahorrar; sobrar; conceder; — adj. ~ parts piezas (f. pl.) de repuesto; ~ time momentos (m. pl.) libres.
spark, s. chispa f.; — v. n. chispear.
sparrow, s. gorrión m.
speak, v. a. & n. hablar.
speaker, s. orador m., conferencista m.
spear, s. lanza f.
special, adj. especial; — s. edición (f.) extra.
specialist, s. especialista m.
specially, adv. especialmente.
species, s. especie f.
specific, adj. específico.
specify, v. a. especificar.
specimen, s. muestra f., espécimen m.
speck, s. motita f.
spectacle, s. espectáculo m.
spectacles, s. gafas f. pl., anteojos m. pl.
spectator, s. espectador m.
speech, s. discurso m.
speed, s. velocidad f.; prisa f.; — v. n. apresurarse; ~ up acelerar.
speedway, s. autódromo m.; autopista f.
speedy, adj. rápido.
spell,[1] v. a. deletrear; how do you your ~ name? ¿cómo se escribe su nombre?
spell,[2] s. encanto m.
spelling, s. deletreo m., ortografía f.

spend, v. a. gastar; (night) pasar.

sphere, s. esfera f.

spice, s. especia f.; — v. a. condimentar, sazonar.

spider, araña f.

spill, v. a. derramar.

spin, v. a. & n. hilar.

spinach, espinaca f.

spine, s. columna (f.) vertebral; espinazc m.

spinster, s. solterona f.

spiral, adj. & s. espiral (f.).

spirit, s. espíritu m.; — v. a. entusiasmar; ~ away hurtar.

spirits, s. pl. alcohol m.; low ~ mal humor m.; in high ~ de buen humor.

spiritual, adj. espiritual.

spit,[1] v. a. & n. escupir; — s. saliva f.

spit,[2] s. asador m. (a rotación)

splash, v. a. salpicar; — s. salpicadura f.

splendid, adj. espléndido.

splendour, s. esplendor m.

split, v. a. dividir, repartir; ~ hairs pararse en pelillos; a ~ting headache un tremendo dolor de cabeza; — s. grieta f., hendedura f.

spoil, v. a. echar a perder; (child) mimar; — s. botín m.

spokesman, s. portavoz m.

sponge, s. esponja f.

spontaneous, adj. espontáneo.

spoon, s. cuchara f.

spoonful, s. cucharada f.

sport, s. deporte m.; he is a real ~ es un buen muchacho.

spot, s. mancha f.; (place) lugar m., punto m.; — on the ~ en el sitio; — v. a. manchar; (see) reconocer, distinguir.

spotless, adj. inmaculado.

spray, s. rociada f.; — v. a. rociar.

spread, v. a. extender; v. n. extenderse; — s. propagación f.

spring,[1] s. primavera f.

spring,[2] v. n. saltar, dar un salto; lanzarse; ~ back rebotar; ~ from proceder; — s. origen m.; (water-) manantial m.; (watch-) resorte m., muelle m.

sprinkle, v. a. rociar; v. n. (rain) lloviznar.

spur, s. espuela f.; fig. impulso m.; — v. a. estimular.

spy, s. espía m.; — v. n. espiar.

square, s. cuadrado m.; plaza f.; — adj. ~ foot pie (m.) cuadrado; (honest) honrado; a ~ meal una comida abundante; — v. a. arreglar, ajustar.

squeeze, v. a. (lemon) exprimir; (hand) apretar, estrujar.

squint, v. n. bizcar.

squire, s. terrateniente m.

squirrel, s. ardilla f.

stab, v. a. apuñalar; — s. punzada f.

stability, s. estabilidad f.

stable, s. caballeriza f.; establo m.

stack, s. pila f., montón m.; v. a. apilar, amontonar.

stadium, s. estadio m.

staff, s. báculo m.; (personnel) personal m.

stag, s. ciervo m.

stage, s. escenario m.,

teatro *m.; (period)* período *m.; — v. a.* representar.

stagger, *v. n.* tambalearse.

stain, *v. a.* manchar; — *s.* mancha *f.*

stairs, *s. pl.* escalera *f.*

staircase, *s.* escalera *f.,* escalerón *m.*

stake, *s.* estaca *f.,* palo *m.; (game)* postura *f.; — v. a.* estacar; *fig.* arriesgar.

stale, *adj.* rancio, viejo.

stall, *s.* pesebre *m.; (market)* tenderete *m.;* puesto *m.; (seat)* butaca *f.; — v. n.* atascar; *v. a.* entretener.

stammer, *v. n.* tartamudear.

stamp, *s.* sello *m.,* estampilla *f.; — v. a.* poner sello, franquear; *(mark)* marcar, sellar; *(feet)* patalear; ~ *on* pisar.

stand, *v. n.* estar de pie; estar situado; *(remain)* quedarse; *v. a.* poner; *I can't* ~ *him* no puedo soportarle; ~ *aside* apartarse; ~ *for* estar partidario de; ~ *off* mantenerse a distancia; ~ *out* destacarse; resistir; ~ *up* levantarse; — *s.* tribuna *f.,* plataforma *f.; (market)* puesto *m.*

standard, *s.* bandera *f.;* ~ *of living* nivel *(m.)* de vida; norma *f.; — adj.* corriente; ~ *weight* peso *(m.)* legal.

standstill, *s.* parada *f.,* suspensión *f.*

star, *s.* estrella *f.; — v. n.* figurar como estrella.

start, *v. n.* partir, ponerse en camino; *v. a.* empezar; *(engine)* poner en marcha; *(frighten)* asustar; — *s.* principio *m.; (fright)* susto *m.*

strarve, *v. n.* morir de hambre; *v. a.* hacer morir de hambre.

state, *s.* estado *m.,* situación *f.; (country)* Estado *m.; — v. a.* declarar.

statement, *s.* declaración *f.;* ~ *of account* estado *(m.)* de cuentas.

statesman, *s.* estadista *m.,* político *m.*

station, *s.* estación *f.; police* ~ comisaría *f.; — v. a.* apostar; *fig.* destinar.

stationer, *s.* papelero *m.*

statistical, *adj.* estadístico.

statistics, *s. pl.* estadística *f.*

statute, *s.* estatuto *m.*

stay *v. n.* permanecer, quedarse; *(in a place)* alojarse, parar; — *s.* estancia *f.,* temporada *f.*

steady, *adj.* firme; constante; — *v. a.* sostener.

steak, *s.* solomillo *m.,* biftec *m.*

steal, *v. a.* robar, hurtar.

steam, *s.* vapor *m.; — v. n.* evaporarse; ~ *out* zarpar.

steam-engine, *s.* máquina *(f.)* de vapor.

steamer, *s.* vapor *m.,* barco *m.*

steel, *s.* acero *m.; — v. a.* fortalecer; *v. n.* fortalecerse.

steep, *adj.* escarpado, empinado; *(price)* exorbitante.

steeple, s. campanario m., torre f.

steeple-chase, s. carrera (f.) de obstáculos.

steer, v. a. (ship) gobernar, dirigir; (car) conducir, manejar.

steering-gear, s. mando m.

steering-wheel, s. rueda (f.) del timón; volante m.

stem, s. tallo m.

step, v. n. poner el pie, pisar; ~ this way! ¡por aquí! ~ aside ponerse a un lado; ~ in entrar; ~ off bajarse, apearse; ~ on pisar; ~ up subir; — s. paso m.; ~ by ~ paso a paso; ~s escalones m. pl.

stepmother, s. madrastra f.

stereo, adj. estéreo-.

stereotype, s. estereotipia f.; — adj. estereotípico; — v. a. estereotipar.

sterility, s. esterilidad f.

stern,[1] adj. duro, severo.

stern,[2] s. popa f.

stew, v. a. estofar; — s. guisado m.

steward, s. administrador m.; (on ship) camarero m.

stewardess, s. camarera f.; (on plane) azafata f.

stick, s. palo m., bastón m.; — v. a. pinchar, poner; (glue) pegar; (pig) matar; ~ out sobresalir; ~ to seguir en, no abandonar.

sticky, adj. pegajoso.

stiff, adj. tieso, duro; a ~ neck torticolis m.

still,[1] adj. quieto; ~ stand ~ estarse quieto; — s. calma f.

still,[2] adv. todavía, aún.

stimulate, v. a. estimular.

sting, v. a. picar; — s. picadura f.

stink, v. n. heder, apestar; — s. hedor m.

stipulate, v. a. estipular.

stir, mover, menear; provocar, excitar; v. n. moverse; — s. conmoción f.

stock, s. surtido m.; (share) acción f.; (cattle) ganado m.; take ~ hacer inventario; — v. a. tener en existencia.

stock-exchange, s. Bolsa f.

stockholder, s. accionista m., f.

stocking, s. media f.

stomach, s. estómago m.

stone, s. piedra f.; precious ~ piedra preciosa; — v. a. apedrear.

stony, adj. pedregoso.

stool, s. taburete m.

stoop, v. n. inclinarse, doblarse.

stop, v. a. parar; (pay) suspender; (hinder) impedir, detener; v. n. pararse; — s. parada f.

store, s. provisión f.; tienda f.; ~s almacén m. — v. a. acumular.

stork, s. cigüeña f.

storm, s. tormenta f., tempestad f.; — v. a. asaltar.

stormy, adj. tempestuoso, borrascoso.

story,[1] s. cuento m., historieta f.; relato m., información f.; short ~ cuento m., novela (f.) corta.

story,[2] s. piso m.

stout, adj. gordo, corpulento.

stove, s. estufa f.; hornilla f.; fogón m.

straight, adj. (road) recto;
(honest) honrado.

straighten, v. a. poner en
orden, arreglar.

strait, adj. & s. estrecho
(m.).

strand, s. playa f.; (of
pearls) sarta f.; — v.
n. encallar(se).

strange, adj. extraño,
raro.

stranger, s. forastero m.,
extranjero m., desconocido m.

strap, correa f.; — v. a.
amarrar, sujetar.

strategy, s. estrategia f.

straw, s. paja f.

strawberry, s. fresa f.

streak, s. raya f., lista f.;
— v. a. rayar.

stream, s. corriente f.,
río m., arroyo m.; —
v. n. afluir; salir a
torrentes.

street, s. calle f.

strength, s. fuerza f.

strenghten, v. a. reforzar;
v. n. fortalecerse, cobrar fuerzas.

stress, s. énfasis m.; — v.
a. recalcar, subrayar.

stretch, v. a. tender,
extender; (shoes) ensanchar; — s. (of road)
trecho m.

stretcher, s. camilla f.

strew, v. a. esparcir.

strict, adj. estricto.

strike, v. a. pegar, golpear; ~ a match encender
un fósforo ;~ a bargain
llegar a un acuerdo; ~
work estar en huelga;
v. n. (clock) dar; —
s. golpe m.; huelga f.

striking, adj. sorprendente.

string, s. cuerda f., cordel
m.; ~ of pearls collar
(m.) de perlas; — v. a.

tender.

strip, v. a. descortezar;
v. n. desnudarse; — s.
tira f., franja f.

stripe, s. raya f., lista f.;
— s. galones m. pl.

stroke, s. golpe m.; (swimming) brazada f.;
(apoplexy) ataque m.;
~ of luck suerte f.; —
v. a. acariciar.

stroll, s. paseo m.; go
for a ~ dar un paseo;
— v. n. pasear.

strong, adj. fuerte, resistente; ~ tea té (m.)
cargado.

structure, s. estructura f.

struggle, v. n. luchar; — s.
lucha f.; ~ for life
lucha por la vida.

student, s. estudiante m.

study, s. estudio m.; —
v. n. & s. estudiar.

stupid, adj. tonto, estúpido.

stupidity s. tontería f.

sturdy, adj. fuerte, robusto.

style, manera f., estilo m.,
moda f.

subdue, v. a. dominar,
sojuzgar.

subject, adj. ~ to sujeto
a; — s. tema m.;
(person) súbdito m.;
— v. a. someter.

sublime, adj. sublime.

submarine, adj. & s.
submarino (m.).

submission, s. sumisión
f.

submit, v. a. someter.

subordinate, adj. subordinado; — v. a. subordinar.

subscribe, v. a. suscribir;
v. n. ~ to suscribirse,
abonarse a.

subscriber, s. su(b)scriptor
m.; abonado m.

subsidy, *s.* subsidio *m.*

subsist, *v. n.* subsistir.

substance, *s.* sustancia *f.*

substantial, *adj.* sustancial, sustancioso.

substitute, *s.* su(b)stituto *m.; — v. a.* su(b)stituir.

subtle, *adj.* sutil, ingenioso.

subtract, *v. a.* su(b)straer, restar.

suburb, *s.* suburbio *m.*

subway, *s.* paso *(m.)* subterráneo.; metro *m.*

succeed, *v. n.* suceder; *v. a.* lograr, tener éxito.

success, *s.* éxito *m.*

successful, *adj.* afortunado, próspero.

succession, *s.* sucesión *f.*

successive, *adj.* sucesivo.

successor, *s.* sucesor *m.*

such, *adj. & pron.* tal; así; ~ *as* tal como; ~ *is life!* ¡así es la vida!

suck, *v. a.* chupar.

sudden, *adj.* repentino, súbito; *all of a* ~ de repente.

suffer, *v. n.* sufrir.

sufficient, *adj.* suficiente.

suffocate, *v. a.* sofocar, asfixiar; *v. n.* sofocarse, asfixiarse.

sugar, *s.* azúcar *m.; — v. a.* azucarar.

suggest, *v. a.* sugerir, proponer; insinuar.

suggestion, *s.* sugestión *f.*, sugerencia *f.*

suicide, *s.* suicidio *m.; (person)* suicida *m., f.*

suit, *s. (dress)* traje *m.; (lawyer's)* pleito *m.; (cards) follow* ~ jugar el mismo palo; *— v. n.* venir bien, convenir; *this hat* ~*s me* este sombrero me va bien.

suitable, *adj.* apropiado, adecuado.

suitcase, *s.* maleta *f.*

suitor, *s.* pretendiente *m.; (law)* demandante *m.*

sulphur, *s.* azufre *m.*

sum, *s.* suma *f.; — v. a.* sumar; ~ *up* resumir.

summary, *adj.* sumario; *— s.* resumen *m.*, compendio *m.*

summer, *s.* verano *m.*

summit, *s.* cima *f.*, cumbre *f.*

summon, *v. a.* citar.

sun, *s.* sol *m.; — v. n.* tomar el sol.

Sunday, *s.* domingo *m.*

sunny, *adj.* (a)soleado.

sunrise, *s.* amanecer *m.*, salida *(f.)* del sol.

sunset, *s.* crepúsculo *m.*, puesta *(f.)* del sol.

sunshine, *s.* luz *(f.)* del sol.

sunstroke, *s.* insolación *f.*

superb, *adj.* soberbio.

superfluous, *adj.* supérfluo.

superintendent, *s.* superintendente *m.*

superior, *adj. & s.* superior *(m.).*

superiority, superioridad *f.*

supermarket, *s.* supermercado *m.*

supersonic, *adj.* supersónico.

superstition, *s.* superstición *f.*

superstitious, *adj.* supersticioso.

supper, *s.* cena *f.*

supply, *v. a.* suplir; proporcionar; *— s.* provisión *f.*, abastecimiento *m.; (store)* surtido *m.; ~ and demand* oferta *(f.)* y demanda *(f.).*

support, *v. a.* aguantar, resistir; *fig.* mantener, apoyar; — *s.* soporte *m.*; sostén *m.*; *fig.* mantenimiento *m.*, sustento *m.*

suppose, *v. a.* suponer.

suppress, *v. a.* suprimir.

suppression, *s.* supresión *f.*

supreme, *adj.* supremo.

sure, *adj.* seguro; *be ~* estar seguro; *make ~* asegurarse; — *adv.* claro, por supuesto, ciertamente.

surely, *adv.* ciertamente, sin duda.

surface, *s.* superficie *f.*

surgeon, *s.* cirujano *m.*

surpass, *v. a.* sobrepasar, superar.

surprise, *s.* sorpresa *f.*; — *v. a.* sorprender.

surprising, *adv.* sorprendente.

surrender, *v. n.* rendirse, capitular; — *s.* rendición *f.*, capitulación *f.*

surround, *v. a.* rodear.

surroundings, *s.* ambiente *m.*; alrededores *m. pl.*, cercanías *f. pl.*

survive, *v. a. & n.* sobrevivir.

survivor, *adj. & s.* sobreviviente *(m., f.).*

suspect, *v. a.* sospechar; *adj.* sospechoso.

suspenders, *s.* liga *f.*; *(braces)* tirantes *m. pl.*

suspicion, *s.* sospecha *f.*

suspicious, *adj.* sospechoso; receloso.

swallow,[1] *v. a.* tragar.

swallow,[2] *s.* golondrina *f.*

swan, *s.* cisne *m.*

swarm, *s.* enjambre *m.*; — *v. n.* enjambrar.

swear, *v. n.* jurar; *~ in* jurar, prestar juramento.

sweat, *s.* sudor *m.*; — *v. n.* sudar.

sweater, *s.* suéter *m.*, jersey *m.*

Swedish, *adj.* sueco.

sweep, *v. a.* barrar; *~ aside* derribar; — *s.* barredura *f.*; extensión *f.*, dimensión *f.*

sweet, *adj.* dulce; — *s. ~s* dulces *m. pl.*; caramelos *m. pl.*

sweetheart, *s.* enamorado *m.*, enamorada *f.*, cariño *m.*, novia *f.*

sweetness, *s.* dulzor *m.*, suavidad *f.*

swell, *v. n.* aumentar, crecer; *v. a.* hinchar; — *adj.* estupendo; elegante.

swift, *adj.* rápido, veloz.

swim, *v. n.* nadar; — *s.* nadada *f.*; natación *f.*

swindler, *s.* embustero *m.*, estafador *m.*

swine, *s.* puerco *m.*, cerdo *m.*

swing, *v. a.* mecer, balancear; *v. n.* mecerse; — *s.* columpio *m.*

Swiss, *adj.* suizo.

switch, *s. (railway)* aguja *f.*; *(electric)* conmutador *m.*; *(stick)* varita *f.*, varilla *f.* — *v. a.* cambiar (de sitio); *~ off* apagar (la luz); *~ or* encender (la luz).

swollen, *adj.* hinchado

syllable, *s.* sílaba *f.*

symbol, *s.* símbolo *m.*

symmetrical, *adj.* simétrico.

sympathy, *s.* simpatía *f.*

symphony, *s.* sinfonía *f.*

symptom, *s.* síntoma *m.*

synagogue, *s.* sinagoga *f.*

syndicate, *s.* sindicato *m.*

synthetic, *adj.* sintético.

syringe, *s.* jeringa *f.*

syrup, s. jarabe m., almíbar m.

system, s. sistema m., método m.

systematic(al), adj. sistematico, metódico.

T

table, s. mesa f.; ~ of contents sumario m., índice m.

table-cloth, s. mantel m.

tablet, s. tableta f., pastilla f.

tail, s. rabo m., cola f.; heads or ~s cara o cruz; — v. a. seguir de cerca.

tailor, s. sastre m.; — v. a. cortar.

take, v. a. tomar, coger; (to a place) llevar; (accept) aceptar; (advice) seguir; (last) durar; (pictures) sacar, tomar; ~ a bath bañarse; ~ advantage of aprovechar; ~ a seat, please tome asiento, por favor; ~ place tener lugar; ~ down bajar, descolgar; ~ off (hat) quitarse; (plane) despegar; ~ out sacar; (spot) quitar.

tale, s. cuento m.

talent, s. talento m., aptitud f.

talk, s. discurso m.; — v. n. hablar.

talkative, adj. locuaz.

tall, adj. alto.

tame, adj. domesticado; manso; — v. a. domesticar.

tank, s. tanque m. (petrol) depósito m.

tape, s. cinta f.

tape-recorder, s. magnetófono m., grabador (m.)

de sonido.

tapestry, s. tapiz m.

tariff, s. tarifa f.

task, s. tarea f.

taste, s. gusto m.; sabor m.; — v. a. probar; v. n. saber.

tasteless, adj. soso, insípido; fig. de mal gusto.

tavern, s. taberna f., posada f.

tax, s. impuesto m.; — v. a. poner impuestos.

taxi, s. taxi m.

tea, s. té m., merienda f.

teach, v. a. enseñar.

teacher, s. maestro m., profesor m.

team, s. equipo m.

tea-pot, s. tetera f.

tear,[1] s. lágrima f.

tear,[2] v. a. romper, ~ down derribar; ~ out arrancar; — s. rasgadura f., roto m.

tease, v. a. fastidiar, molestar.

teaspoon, s. cucharita f.

technical, adj. técnico.

technique, s. técnica f.

teenager, s. adolescente m., f.

telecast, s. transmisión (f.) televisiva.

telecommunication, s. telecomunicación f.

telegram, s. telegrama m.

telegraph, s. telégrafo m.; — v. n. telegrafiar.

telephone, s. teléfono m., — v. n. telefonear.

telephone-box, cabina (f.) telefónica.

telephone-exchange, s. central (f.) telefónica

telescope, s. telescopio m.

teleprinter, telex, s. teletipo m., teleimpresor m.

television, s. televisión f.

television-set, s. televisor *m.*

televise, *v. a.* transmitir por televisión, televisar.

tell, *v. a.* decir; *I was told* me han dicho; *(a story)* contar.

temper, *s.* humor *m.*

temperature, *s.* temperatura *f.*

tempest, *s.* tempestad *f.*

temporary, *adj.* provisorio.

tempt, *v. a.* tentar.

temptation, *s.* tentación *f.*

ten, *adj. & s.* diez *(m.).*

tenant, *s.* inquilino *m.*

tendency, *s.* tendencia *f.*

tender, *adj.* tierno; delicado.

tennis, *s.* tenis *m.*

tense, *adj.* tenso, nervioso; — *s.* tiempo *m.* (verb).

tension, *s.* tensión *f.*

tent, *s.* tienda (de campaña).

tenth, *adj.* décimo.

term, *s.* período *m.*, semestre *m.; (name)* nombre *m.; ~s* condiciones *f. pl.; come to ~s* llegar a un arreglo; *be on good ~s* estar en buenas relaciones.

terminate, *v. a. & n.* terminar.

terminus, *s.* estación *(f.)* terminal.

terrace, *s.* terraza *f.*

terrible, *adj.* terrible.

territory, *s.* territorio *m.*

test, *s.* examen *m.*, prueba *f.; — v. a.* examinar, analizar, probar.

testify, *v. a.* testificar, declarar.

testimony, *s.* testimonio *m.*

text, *s.* texto *m.*

text-book, *s.* libro *(m.)* de texto.

than, *conj.* que.

thank, *v. n.* dar las gracias; *~ you* gracias; *— s. ~s* gracias *f. pl.*

thankful, *adj.* agradecido.

that,[1] *adj. & pron.* ese, aquel; *~ is to say* es decir; *~'s all* eso es todo.

that,[2] *conj.* que.

thaw, *s.* deshielo *m.; — v. n.* deshelarse.

the, el, la; los, las.

theatre, *s.* teatro *m.*

their, *pron.* su, sus, de ellos *(m.),* de ellas *(f.).*

theirs, *pron.* de ellos *(m.),* de ellas *(f.).*

them, *pron.* ellos, les, los *(m.);* ellas, las *(f.).*

theme, *s.* tema *m.*

themselves, *pron.* se; ellos mismos *(m.);* ellas mismas *(f.).*

then, *adv.* entonces, luego, después.

thence, *adv.* de allí; por eso.

theology, *s.* teología *f.*

theory, *s.* teoría *f.*

there, *adv.* allí; *~ is, ~ are* hay.

thereby, *adv.* ahí, de este modo.

therefore, *conj.* por lo tanto, por eso.

thermometer, *s.* termómetro *m.*

thermo-nuclear, *adj.* termonuclear.

thermos, *s.* termos *m.*

these, *adj. & pron.* estos *(m.),* estas *(f.).*

they, *pron.* ellos *(m.),* ellas *(f.).*

thick, *adj.* grueso; *(soup)* espeso.

thief, *s.* ladrón *m.*

thigh, s. muslo m.

thimble, s. dedal m.

thin, adj. delgado, flaco; (soup) claro.

thing, s. cosa f.

think, v. a. & n. pensar, creer; I ~ so creo que sí; ~ about pensar en; ~ out inventar.

third, adj. tercero.

thirst, s. sed f.

thirsty, adj. be ~ tener sed.

thirteen, adj. & s. trece.

thirty, adj. & s. treinta.

this, adj. & pron. esto; éste; ésta; ~ far hasta aquí; ~ much tanto.

thorn, s. espina f.

thorough, adj. completo, cuidadoso.

thoroughfare, s. paso m.; no ~ prohibido el paso.

those, adj. & pron. esos, aquellos (m.); esas, aquellas (f.).

though, conj. aunque; as ~ como si.

thought, s. pensamiento m.; consideración f.

thoughtless, adj. imprudente, desatento.

thousand, adj. mil.

thrash, v. a. trillar.

thread, a. hilo m.; (of screw) rosca f.; v. a. enhebrar.

threat, s. amenaza f.

threaten, v. a. amenazar.

three, adj. & s. tre (m.).

threshold, s. umbral m.

throat, s. garganta f.

throne, s. trono m.

throng, s. muchedumbre f., — v. n. apiñarse.

through, prep. & adv. por; a través de; — adj. directo; ~ train

tren (m.) directo.

throughout, prep. & adv. durante todo; ~ the world en el mundo entero.

throw, s. tiro m., tirada f.; — v. a. tirar; ~ away tirar; ~ up renunciar.

thrust, s. empuje m.; — v. a. empujar.

thumb, s. pulgar m.

thunder, s. trueno m.; — v. n. tronar.

Thursday, s. jueves m.

thus, adv. así, de este modo.

ticket, s. billete m.

tide, s. marea f.; high ~ pleamar f., marea alta; low ~ bajamar f., marea baja.

tie, s. corbata f.; (bond) lazo m.; — v. a. atar, amarrar; ~ (score) empatar.

tiger, s. tigre m.

tight, adj. estrecho, apretado; (drunk) borracho.

till,¹ prep. hasta; — conj. hasta que.

till,² v. a. cultivar, labrar.

timber, s. tronco m., madera (f.) de construcción.

time, s. tiempo m.; what's the ~? ¿qué hora es?; (period) época f.

timetable, s. guía (f.) de ferrocarriles; horario m.

timid, adj. tímido.

tin, s. lata f., estaño m., bote m.

tin-opener, s. abrelatas m.

tint, s. matiz m., tono m.; — v. a. teñir.

tiny, adj. chiquito, menudo.

tip,¹ s. punta f.; extremo

m.; — v. a. ~ up volcar; v n. volcarse.

tip,² s. propina f.; — v. a. dar propina.

tire,¹ v. a. cansar; aburrir.

tire,² s. llanta f., cubierta f., neumático m.

tired, adj. cansado; I'm ~ estoy cansado.

tiresome, adj. pesado, aburrido.

tissue, s. tejido m.; gasa f.; toilet ~ papel (m.) higiénico.

title, s. título m.; — v. a. titular.

to, prep. a; go ~ town ir a la ciudad; what do you say ~ this? ¿qué dice de esto?; I've come ~ see you he venido para verle; it's five minutes to six son las seis menos cinco.

toast, s. (bread) tostada f.; (drink) brindis m.

tobacco, s. tabaco m.

tobacconist, s. tabaquero m.

today, adv. hoy.

toe, s. dedo (m.) del pie.

together, adv. juntos; gather ~ reunir(se).

toilet, s. tocado m.; (table) tocador m; (W. C.) excusado m., retrete m.

tomato, s. tomate m.

tomb, s. tumba f.

tomorrow, adv. mañana f.; ~ morning mañana por la mañana.

ton, s. tonelada f.

tone, s. sonido m., tono m.; — v. a. entonar.

tongs, s. pl. tenazas f. pl.

tongue, s. lengua f.

tonight, adv. esta noche.

tonnage, s. tonelaje m.

tonsil, s. amígdala f.

too, adv. demasiado; ~ bad! ¡qué lástima!; (also) también.

tool, s. herramienta f.; instrumento m.

tooth, s. diente m.; (molar) muela f.

toothache, s. dolor (m.) de muelas.

toothbrush, s. cepillo (m.) de dientes.

toothpaste, s. pasta (f.) dentífrica.

toothpick, s. mondadientes m.

top, s. cima f., cumbre f.; on ~ of encima de; — adj. máximo; último; at ~ speed a la velocidad máxima; ~ floor último piso m.

torch, s. antorcha f., lámpara f., linterna f.

torment, s. tormento m.; — v. a. atormentar.

torrent, s. torrente m.

tortoise, s. tortuga f.

total, adj. & s. total (m.); — v. a. sumar, hacer la suma.

touch, s. tacto m.; contacto m.; a ~ of salt una pizca de sal; — v. a. tocar; fig. afectar; (affect) conmover.

tough, adj. duro; ~ luck mala suerte f.

tour, s. jira f.; — v. n. viajar, hacer una jira.

tourism, s. turismo m.

tourist, s. turista m., f.

tow, s. barcaza f., remolque m.; — v. a. remolcar.

toward(s), prep. hacia.

towel, s. toalla f.

tower, s. torre f.

town, s. ciudad f.

town hall, s. municipalidad f., ayuntamiento m.

toy, s. juguete m.

trace, s. huella f., rastro m.; señal f.; — v. a. marcar, señalar.

track, s. pista f.

tractor, s. tractor m.

trade, s. comercio m.; oficio m.; — v. a. & n. comerciar.

trade-mark, s. marca (f.) de fábrica.

tradesman, s. comerciante m., negociante m.

trade(s)-union, s. sindicato m.

tradition, s. tradición f.

traditional, adj. tradicional.

traffic, s. tráfico m.; ~ lights señales f pl., luz (f.) de tráfico.

tragedy, s. tragedia f.

trail, s. sendero m., huella f.

train, s. tren m.; go by ~ ir en tren; — v. a. enseñar, entrenar; v. n. entrenarse.

trainer, s. entrenador m.

tram, s. tranvía m.

transact, v. a. ~ business hacer un negocio.

transatlantic, adj. transatlántico.

transfer, s. traslado m, traspaso m.; ~ ticket billete (m.) de trasbordo; — v. a. trasladar, transferir.

transform, v. a. transformar.

transfusion, s., transfusión f.

transistor, adj. & s. transistor (m.).

transit, s. tránsito m.; ~ visa visado (m.) de tránsito.

translate, v. a. traducir.

translation, s. traducción f., versión f.

translator, s. traductor m.

transmission, s. transmisión f.

transmit, v. a. transmitir.

transmitter, s. transmisor m.

transparent, adj. tra(n)sparente.

transport, s. transporte m.; — v. a. transportar.

travel, s. viaje m.; — v. n. viajar.

traveller, s. viajero m.

traverse, s. traversa f.; — v. a. atravesar, cruzar.

tray, s. bandeja f.

treacherous, adj. traicionero.

tread, v. a. & n. pisar.

treason, s. traición f.

treasure, s. tesoro m.

treasury, s. tesorería f.

treat, s. placer m.; (of guests) convidada f.; — v. a. tratar; (guests) convidar.

treaty, s. tratado m., pacto m.

tree, s. árbol m.

tremendous, adj. tremendo, formidable.

trench, s. trinchera f.

trespass, s. traspaso m.; — v. a. traspasar; no ~ing! ¡prohibido el paso!

trial, s. prueba f.; (law) proceso m., juicio m.; (affliction) mortificación f.

triangle, s. triángulo m.

tribe, s. tribu f., raza f.

tribute, s. tributo m.

trick, s. maña f.; (card) baza f.; — v. a. engañar.

trifle, s. bagatela f.;

— v. n. jugar con.

trim, v. a. igualar; *(hair)* cortar un poco.

trip, s. viaje m.; — v. n. brincar; *(stumble)* tropezar.

triple, adj. triple; — v. a. triplicar.

triumph, s. triunfo m.; — v. n. triunfar.

trivial, adj. trivial.

trolley, s. carreta f.; tea ~ carrito (m.) de servicio.

trolley-bus, s. trolebús m.

troop, s. tropa f.; —v. n. apiñarse.

trophy, s. trofeo m.

tropic(al), adj. tropical.

tropics, s. pl. trópicos m. pl.

trot, s. trote m.; — v. n. trotar.

trouble, s. apuro m., dificultad f.; get into ~ meterse en un lío; what's the ~? ¿qué le pasa?; — v. a. molestar, incomodar.

troublesome, adj. molesto.

trousers, s. pl. pantalones m. pl.

trout, s. trucha f.

truck, s. carreta f.; vagón(m.) de mercancías; camión m.

true, adj. verdadero; leal; *(story)* verídico.

truly, adv. sinceramente, de verdad; Yours very ~ Suyo affmo. (afectísimo).

trumpet, s. trompeta f.

trunk, s. tronco m.; *(bag)* baúl m.

trunk-call, s. conferencia *(f.)* interurbana.

trust, s. confianza f.; hold in ~ guardar en depósito; *(company)* trust m.; — v. a. & n. tener confianza en; confiar; dar crédito.

trustee, s. síndico m.

truth, s. verdad f.

try, s. intento m.; — v. a. probar, tratar de; *(case)* juzgar; ~ on probarse; ~ out hacer una prueba.

tub, s. *(bathtub)* baño m.; *(washtub)* tina f.

tube, s. tubo m.

Tuesday, s. martes m.

tug-boat, s. remolcador m.

tuition, s. enseñanza f., instrucción f.

tumble, s. tumbo m., caída f.; — v. n. caer, derribar.

tumour, s. tumor m.

tune, s. melodía f., tonada f.; out of ~ desafinado; — v. a. afinar; ~ in sintonizar.

tunnel, s. túnel m.

turbine, s. turbina f.

turbo-jet, ~ engine motor *(m.)* ,a turboreacción.

turbo-prop, s. avión *(m.)* a turbopropulsión, de turbohélices.

turf, s. césped m.; hipódromo m.

turkey, s. pavo m.

Turkish, adj. turco; ~ towel toalla *(f.)* de baño.

turn, s. vuelta f.; *(in line)* turno m.; by ~s por turno, alternativamente; — v. a. dar vuelta a; *(corner)* doblar; *(stomach)* revolver; *(ankle)* torcer; v. n. volverse: ~ away rechazar; ~ in entrar; ~ into cambiar por; ~ off *(gas,*

water) cerrar la llave
de; *(light)* apagar; ~
on abrir; *(light)* en-
cender; ~ *out* echar;
~ *to* recurrir a.

turning, *s.* bocacalle, *f.*; ángulo *m.*

turnip, *s.* nabo *m.*

tutor, *s.* instructor *m.*,
preceptor *m.*; — *v. a.*
instruir.

twelfth, *adj.* duodécimo.

twelve, *adj.* & *s.* doce.

twenty, *adj.* & *s.* veinte.

twice, *adv.* dos veces.

twig, *s.* ramita *f.*

twilight, *s.* crepúsculo
m.

twin, *s.* gemelo *m.*, mellizo *m.*; ~ *beds* camas
(f. pl.) gemelas.

twist *v. a.* torcer.

twitter, *s.* gorjeo *m.*; —
v. n. gorjear.

two, *adj.* & *s.* dos *(m.).*

two-seater, *adj.* de dos
asientos.

type, *s.* tipo *m.*; clase *f.*,
estilo *m.*; *(letter)* tipo
(m.) de letra; — *v. a.*
escribir a máquina.

type-script, *s.* escrito *(m.)*
mecanografiado.

typewriter, *s.* máquina
(f.) de escribir.

typist, *s.* mecanógrafo *m.*,
mecanógrafa *f.*

tyre, *s.* llanta *f.*, cubierta
f., neumático *m.*

tyranny, *s.* tiranía *f.*

U

ugly, *adj.* feo.

ultraviolet, *adj.* ultra-
violeta.

umbrella, *s.* paraguas *m.*

unable, *adj.* incapaz.

unaccustomed, *adj.* desacostumbrado.

unanimous, *adj.* unánime.

unauthorized, *adj.* des-
autorizado, sin auto-
rización.

unaware, *adj.* no ente-
rado; *be* ~ *of* ignorar.

unbearable, *adj.* insoportable.

uncertain, *adj.* incierto,
inseguro.

unchangeable, *adj.* inal-
terable, irrevocable.

uncle, *s.* tío *m.*

uncomfortable, *adj.* incómodo, molesto.

uncommon, *adj.* insólito,
desacostumbrado.

unconscious, *adj.* inconsciente, sin conoci-
miento.

uncover, *v. a.* descubrir.

undamaged, *adj.* intacto,
entero, sano y salvo.

undecided, *adj.* indeciso;
pendiente.

undeniable, *adj.* inne-
gable, indiscutible.

under, *prep.* bajo, debajo
de.

underclothes, *s.* ropa *(f.)*
interior.

underdeveloped, *adj.* sub-
desarrollado, atrasado.

underdone, *adj.* un poco
crudo.

undergo, *v. a.* sufrir,
padecer, experimen-
tar.

undergraduate, *s.* estudiante *(m.)* univer-
sitario no licenciado.

underground, *adj.* subterráneo; — *s.* metro
m., metropolitano *m.*;
(illegality) ilegalidad *f.*

underline, *v. a.* subrayar.

understand, *v. a.* comprender, entender; *make
oneself understood* ha-

cerse entender.

undertake, *v. a.* emprender.

underwear, *s.* ropa *(f.)* interior.

undisturbed, *adj.* imperturbado.

undo, *v. a.* desatar, deshacer.

undress, *v. n.* desnudarse; *v. a.* desnudar.

uneasy, *adj.* inquieto, molesto.

uneducated, *adj.* ineducado.

unemployed, *adj.* desocupado, sin trabajo.

unemployment, *s.* falta *(f.)* de trabajo.

unequal, *adj.* desigual.

uneven, *adj.* impar; *(surface)* escabroso, accidentado.

unexpected, *adj.* inesperado.

unfair, *adj.* incorrecto.

unfavorable, *adj.* desfavorable.

unfinished, *adj.* inacabado, sin terminar.

unfortunate, *adj.* desafortunado, infeliz, desgraciado.

unhappy, *adj.* infeliz, desdichado.

unhealthy, *adj.* malsano, insalubre; *(look)* enfermizo.

uniform, *adj. & s.* uniforme *(m.).*

union, *s.* unión *f.;* *(trade-)* sindicato *m.*

unique, *adj.* único *m.*

unit, *s.* unidad *f.*

unite, *v. a.* unir; *v. n.* unirse.

unity, *s.* unidad *f.*

universal, *adj.* universal.

universe, *s.* universo *m.*

unjust, *adj.* injusto.

unkind, *adj.* poco ama-

ble, duro.

unknown, *adj.* desconocido.

unless, *conj.* a menos que, a no ser que.

unlike, *adj.* diferente, distinto.

unload, *v. a.* descargar.

unlock, *v. a.* abrir, abrir con llave.

unmarried, *adj. & s.* soltero *(m.),* soltera *(f.).*

unnecessary, *adj.* innecesario.

unoccupied, *adj.* libre, desocupado.

unpack, *v. a. & n.* desempaquetar; deshacer las maletas.

unpaid, *adj.* impagado, no pagado.

unpleasant, *adj.* desagradable.

unpopular, *adj.* impopular.

unprecedented, *adj.* inaudito, sin precedente.

unprejudiced, *adj.* imparcial, sin prejuicios.

unprepared, *adj.* sin preparación, improvisado, improviso.

unqualified, *adj.* sin calificación; absoluto.

unreasonable, *adj.* irrazonable.

unselfish, *adj.* desinteresado.

unsettled, *adj.* indeciso, pendiente; ∼ *account* cuenta *(f.)* sin saldar.

unsolved, *adj.* no resuelto.

unsteady, *adj.* inconstante.

unsuccessful, *adj.* vano, infructuoso, sin resultado.

untidy, *adj.* desordenado, mal cuidado.

until, *prep.* hasta; — *conj.* hasta que.

unusual, *adj.* raro, extraordinario.

unwell, *adv.* no bien, mal; enfermo; *be ~* sentirse mal.

unwilling, *adj. & adv.* de mala gana, de mala voluntad.

unworthy, *adj.* indigno.

up, *adv.* arriba; *be ~* estar levantado.

uphill, *adv.* cuesta arriba.

upholsterer, *s.* tapicero *m.*

upon, *see* on; *~ my word!* ¡palabra!

upper, *adj.* superior, de arriba; *the Upper House* la Cámara Alta, el senado.

upright, *adj.* erecto, recto; *(honest)* honrado.

upset, *v. a. (person)* perturbar, contrariar, trastornar; *(thing)* volcar; desarreglar.

upside down, *adv.* patas arriba; revuelto, en desorden.

upstairs, *adv.* arriba.

up-to-date, *adj.* moderno, al día, de última moda.

urge, *v. a.* instar; *— s.* impulso *m.,* deseo *m.*

urgent, *adj.* urgente.

us, *pron.* nos; *of ~* de nosotros; *let ~ go!* ¡vámonos!

use, *s.* uso *m.; be of no ~* ser inútil, no servir para nada; *make ~ of* aprovechar; *what's the ~ of arguing?* ¿para qué sirve discutir?; *— v. a.* usar; *be ~d to* acostumbrar; *~ up* gastar.

useful, *adj.* útil.

useless, *adj.* inútil.

usher, *s.* acomodador *m.; (judiciary)* ujier *m.; — v. a.* introducir; anunciar.

usual *adj.* usual, acostumbrado.

usually, *adv.* usualmente, por lo común.

utensil, *s.* utensilio *m.*

utility, *s.* utilidad *f.*

utilize, *v. a.* utilizar.

utmost, *adj* sumo; *do one's ~* hacer lo más que pueda; *to the ~* a más no poder.

utter,[1] *adj.* completo.

utter,[2] *v. a.* proferir, declarar.

utterly, *adv.* completamente.

V

vacancy, *s.* vacante *f.*

vacant, *adj.* vacante, desocupado, vacío, libre.

vaccination, *s.* vacuna *f.*

vacuum-cleaner, *s.* aspirador *m.*

vain, *adj,* vano; *in ~* en vano, en balde.

valid, *adj.* válido, valedero.

validity, *s.* validez *f.*

valley, *s.* valle *m.*

valuable, *adj.* valioso; *— s. ~s* objetos *(m.)* de valor.

value, *s.* valor *m.; — v. a.* valuar; *fig.* estimar, apreciar.

valve, *s.* válvula *f.*

van, *s.* vagón *(m.)* de mercancías; camion *m.*

vanity, *s.* vanidad *f.*

vapour, *s.* vapor *m.*

various, *adj.* varios *pl.,* diversos *pl.*

varnish, *s.* barniz *m.; — v. a.* barnizar.

vary, *v. a. & n.* variar, cambiar.

vase, *s.* florero *m.*

vast, *adj.* vasto.

vault, s. bóveda f.

veal, s. carne (f.) de ternera.

vegetable, adv. vegetal; — s. legumbre f., verdura f., hortaliza f.

vehicle, s. vehículo m.

veil, s. velo m.; — v. a. velar.

vein, s. vena f.

velvet, s. terciopelo m.

vengeance, s. venganza f.

venison, s. venado m.

ventilation, s. ventilación f.

ventilator, s. ventilador m.

verb, s. verbo m.

verdict, s. veredicto m., fallo m., sentencia f.; opinión f.

verge, s. borde m.

verify, v. a. verificar, comprobar.

vermicelli, s. tallarines m. pl., fideos m. pl.

verse, s. verso m.

vertical, adj. vertical.

very, adv. muy; — adv. mismo; the ~ day el mismo día.

vessel, s. (container) vasija f.; (ship) barco m.

vest, s. camiseta f.

vestry, s. sacristía f.

veteran, veterano m.

vex, v. a. irritar, molestar.

via, adv. & prep. por, por la vía de.

vibrate, v. a. & n. vibrar.

vice, s. vicio m.

vice-president, s. vicepresidente m.

vicinity, s. vecindad f.

victim, s. víctima f.

victorious, adj. victorioso.

victory, s. victoria f.

victuals, s. pl. comestibles m. pl., víveres m. pl.

view, s. vista; opinión f.

vigorous, adj. vigoroso.

vigour, s. vigor m.

vile, adj. bajo, vil.

village, s. aldea f., pueblo m.

villain, s. malvado m.

vine, s. vid f., parra f.

vinegar, s. vinagre m.

vineyard, s. viña f., viñedo m.

vintage, s. vendimia f.

violate, v. a. violar.

violent, adj. violento.

violet, s. violeta f.

violin, s. violín m.

violinist, s. violinista m., f.

violoncello, s. violoncelo m.

virgin, adj. & s. virgen (f.)

virtue, s. virtud f.

virtuous, adj. virtuoso.

visible, adj. visible.

visibility, s. visibilidad f.

vision, s. visión f.

visit, s. visita f.; — v. a. visitar.

visitor, s. visitante m., f.

vitamin, s. vitamina f.

vivid, adj. vivo, brillante.

vocabulary, s. vocabulario m.

vocation, s. ocupación f., profesión f., oficio m.

voice, s. voz f.

void, adj. nulo, sin efecto; be ~ of sg faltar; — s. (emptiness) vacío m.; — v. a. anular.

volcano, s. volcán m.

volume, s. volumen m.

voluntary, adj. ;voluntario.

volunteer, s. voluntario m.; — v. n. ofrecerse a hacer algo.

vomit, v. a. & n. vomitar.

vote, s. voto m.; votación

f.; – v. n. votar.

voter, s. votante m., f., votador m.

voucher, s. recibo m.

vow, s. voto m., promesa f.; – v. n. hacer voto.

voyage, s. viaje (m.) por mar.

vulgar, adj. vulgar, ordinario, soez; (joke) verde.

W

wage, s. sueldo m., salario m.; daily ~ jornal m.; living ~ mínimo (m.) vital.

wag(g)on, s. carro (m.) de cuatro ruedas; vagón m.

waist, s. cintura f.

waistcoat, s. chaleco m.

wait, v. n. esperar; ~ on sy atender a.

waiter, s. camarero m., mozo m.

waiting-room, s. sala (f.) de espera.

wake,[1] v. a. despertar; v. n. despertarse.

wake,[2] s. estela f.

walk, s. paseo m.; take a ~ dar un paseo; (way) camino m.; (gait) modo (m.) de andar; – v. n. caminar, andar, ir a pie.

walkie-talkie, s. radio-receptor (m.) portátil.

walking-tour, s. excursión (f.) a pie; caminata f.

wall, s. pared f.; tapia f.; muralla f.

wallet, s. cartera f.

wall-paper, s. papel (m.) pintado.

wall-socket, s. enchufe m.

walnut, s. (nut) nuez f.; (tree) nogal m.

waltz, s. vals m.

wander, v. n. vagar, extraviarse.

want, s. necesidad f.; for ~ of sg a falta de; – v. a. querer.

war, s. guerra f.

ward, s. tutela f.; (hospital) sala f.; – v. a. defender, parar.

wardrobe, s. armario m.; (clothes) ropero m., guardarropa m.

ware, s. mercancía f.

warehouse, s. almacén m., depósito m.

warm, adj. caliente; cálido; (greetings) caluroso, afectuoso, cariñoso; it's ~ hace calor; I'm ~ tengo calor; s. calor m.; – v. a. ~ up calentar; v. n. calentarse.

warn, v. a. advertir, avisar.

warning, s. advertencia f., aviso m.

warrant, s. autorización f.; – a. garantizar.

warrior, s. combatiente m., soldado m., guerrero m.

wash, v. a. lavar; v. n. lavarse; – s. lavado m., lavadura f.; ropa (f.) lavada.

wash-basin, s. jofaina f., palangana f., lavamanos m.

washing-machine, s. lavaropas m., máquina (f.) de lavar; lavadora f.

washing-up, s. fregado m.

wash-stand, s. lavabo m.

was , s. avispa f.

waste, s. desperdicio m., desechos m. pl.; —v. a. perder.

watch, v. a. observar; ~ your step! ¡tenga cuidado!; v. n. tener cuidado, velar; — s. servicio m., guardia f.; (clock) reloj m.; my ~ is fast tengo el reloj adelantado.

watch-maker, s. relojero m.

watchman, s. vigilante m., sereno m.

water, s. agua f.; by ~ por barco; — v. a. (flowers) regar; (horses) dar ᴄe beber; (wine) aguar.

watercolour, s. acuarela f.

waterfall, s. ascada f., catarata f.

watering-place, s. estación (f.) balnearia.

waterproof, adj. & s. impermeable (m.).

wave, s. ola f., onda f.; ~ length longitud (f.) de onda; — v. a. & n. ondear; (hand) agitar las manos, hacer señas.

wax, s. cera f.

way, s. camino m.; fig. módo m., manera f.; a long ~ muy lejos; by the ~ a propósito.

we, pron. nosotros m., nosotras f.

weak, adj. débil.

weaken, v. a. debilitar, extenuar; — v. n. debilitarse.

weakness, s. debilidad f.

wealth, s. riqueza f.

wealthy, adj. rico.

weapon, s. arma f.

wear, s. ropa f., trajes m. pl.; — v. a. llevar,

usar; (last) durar.

weather, s. tiempo m.

weather-forecast, s. pronóstico (m.) del tiempo.

weave, v. a. tejer.

weaver, s. tejedor m.

web, s. (cloth) tela f.; (spider) tela de araña.

wedding, s. matrimonio m., boda f.

wedding-ring, s. anillo (m.) de boda.

Wednesday, s. miércoles m.

weed, s. maleza f., mala hierba f.; — v. a. escardar, desherbar.

week, s. semana f.

week-day, s. día (m.) de semana, día laborable.

weekly, adj. semanal; — s. revista (f.) semanal.

weep, v. n. llorar.

weigh, v. a. & n. pesar; ~ anchor llevar anclas.

weight, s. peso m.; fig. importancia f.

welcome, adj. & int. ~! ¡bienvenido!

welfare, s. bienestar m.

well, adv. bien; very ~! ¡muy bien!

wellbeing, s. bienestar m.

wellbred, adj. bien educado.

well-informed, adj. bien informado.

well-to-do, adj. acomodado, adinerado.

west, s. oeste m., poniente m.; — adj. occidental.

western, adj. occidental, oeste.

wet, adj. mojado; (paint) fresco; get ~ mojarse; v. a. mojar.

whale, s. ballena f.

wharf, s. muelle m.

what, pron qué; ~ time is it? ¿qué hora es?; ~'s the news? ¿qué hay de nuevo?; ~ for? ¿por qué?; — int. ~! ¡cómo!

whatever, pron. do ~ you want haga usted lo que quiera; he has no money ~ no tiene ningún dinero.

wheat, s. trigo m.

wheel, s. rueda f.; — v. a. conducir, llevar.

when, adv. cuando; ~? ¿cuándo?

whence, adv. de donde; ~? ¿de dónde?

whenever, conj. siempre que.

where, adv. donde, por donde; ~? ¿dónde?

wherefore, adv. por esto; ~? ¿por qué?

wherein, adv. en que; ~? ¿en qué?

wherever, adv. Jonde-quiera que.

whether, conj. si.

which, pron. que, el cual; ~? ¿cuál?; ~ book? ¿qué libro?; ~ way? ¿por dónde?

whichever, pron. cualquiera.

while, conj. mientras que; — s. rato m.

whirlwind, s. torbellino m., remolino m.

whisper, v. a. cuchichear.

whistle, s. silbido m.; pito m; — v. n. silbar.

white, adj. blanco.

Whitsun, s. Pentecostés m.

who, pron. quien, que; ~? ¿quién?

whoever, pron. quienquiera.

whole, adj. todo, entero;

~ lot gran cantidad f.; — s. totalidad f.; on the ~ en general.

wholesale, adj. & adv. al por mayor.

wholesome, adj. sano, saludable.

wholly, adv. enteramente.

whom, pron. a quien; ~? ¿a quién?

whose, pron. de quien, cuyo; ~? ¿de quién?

why, adv. & conj. ¿por qué?; — int. ~! ¡cómo!

wicked, adj. malo, malvado.

wide, adj. ancho.

widow, s. viuda f.

widower, s. viudo m.

wife, s. mujer f., esposa f., señora f.

wig, s. peluca f.

wild, adj. salvaje; (flower) silvestre; fig. bárbaro.

wilful, adj. premeditado.

will, s. voluntad f.; (testament) testamento m.; at ~ a voluntad; — v. n. querer; he ~ come today vendrá hoy.

willing, adj. be ~ estar dispuesto.

willingly, adv. con placer; voluntariamente.

willow, s. sauce m.

win, v. a. ganar; vencer.

wind,[1] s. viento m.

wind,[2] v. n. (road) torcer; ~ oneself enroscarse; v. a. (watch) dar cuerda a.

windmill, s. molino (m.) de viento.

window, s. ventana f., ventanilla f.

windscreen, s. parabrisas

m.
windy, *adj.* ventoso.
wine, *s.* vino *m*
wing, *s.* ala *f.;* *(theatre)*
bastidor *m.; (football)*
exterior *m.,* ala *f.;* —
v. n. volar.
wink, *v. n.* guiñar; — *s.*
guiño *m.*
winner, *s.* vencedor *m.,*
ganador *m.*
winter, *s.* invierno *m.*
wipe, *v. a. (dry)* secar;
(clean) limpiar.
wire, *s.* alambre *m.;* hilo
m.; (telegram) tele-
grama *m.;* — *v. n.*
telegrafiar.
wireless, *s.* telégrafo *(m.)*
sin hilos; radio *f.*
wisdom, *s.* sabiduría *f.;*
(judgment) juicio *m.*
wise, *adj.* sensato, juicioso; listo, sabio, serio.
wish, *s.* deseo *m.,* voto *m.;*
— *v. a.* gustar, desear.
wit, *s.* agudeza *f.,* ingenio *m.*
with, *prep.* con; ~ *you*
contigo; ~ *me* con-
migo; ~ *him* con él.
withdraw, *v. a.* retirar;
v. n. retirarse.
within, *prep.* dentro de.
without, *prep.* sin; —
adv. por fuera.
withstand, *v. n.* resistir,
aguantar.
witness, *s.* testigo *m.*
witty, *adj.* ingenioso, agudo.
wolf, *s.* lobo *m.*
woman, *s.* mujer *f.;*
~ *doctor* doctora *f.*
wonder, *s.* maravilla *f.,*
admiración *f.;* — *v. n.*
preguntarse; *I* ~! no
lo sé; estoy curioso
de saberlo.
wonderful, *adj.* maravilloso, estupendo.

wood, *s.* madera *f.;*
(forest) bosque *m.;*
(fire) leña *f.*
wooden, *adj.* de madera.
wool, *s.* lana *f.*
woollen, *adj.* de lana.
word, *s.* palabra *f.;*
(news) noticia *f.*
work, *s.* trabajo *m.;*
(composition) obra *f.;*
set to ~ poner manos
a la obra; ~s fábrica *f.,*
planta *(f.)* industrial;
public ~s servicios *(m.*
pl.) públicos; — *v. n.*
trabajar; ~ *out* pre-
parar; resolver.
worker, *s.* trabajador *m.,*
obrero *m.*
workshop, *s.* taller *m.*
world, *s.* mundo *m.;*
all the ~ *over* en el
mundo entero.
worldly, *adj.* terrestre.
world-politics, *s.* política
(f.) mundial.
world-war, *s.* guerra *(f.)*
mundial.
worm, *s.* gusano *m.,*
lombriz *f.*
worn, *adj. (tired)* ago-
tado; *(used)* usado.
worry, *s.* preocupación
f. — *v. n.* preocupar-
se; *don't* ~! ¡descuide

usted!; *v. n.* moles-
tar.
worse, *adj.* peor; *get* ~
empeorar.
worst, *adj. & adv.* peor;
at ~ a lo peor.
worth, *s,* valor *m.,* mérito
m.; — *adj. what is*
it ~ *?* ¿cuánto vale?;
it is ~ *while* vale la
pena.
worthless, *adj.* sin valor.
worthy, *adj.* digno.
wound, *s.* herida *f.;*
— *v. a.* herir.

wounded, *adj. & s.* herido.

woven, *adj.* tejido, textil.

wrap, *v. a.* envolver.

wrapper, *s.* envoltura *f.*, embalaje *m.*, faja *f.*

wrath, *s.* cólera *f.*, ira *f.*

wreath, *s. (funeral)* corona *f.; (decoration)* guirnalda *f.*

wreck, *s.* destrucción *f.*, ruina *f.*; restos *(m. pl.)* de un naufragio; — *v. a.* destrozar.

wrench, *s.* llave *(f.)* para tuercas.

wrestle, *v. n.* luchar.

wrestler, *s.* luchador *m.*

wretched, *adj.* miserable, desdichado.

wring, *v. a.* retorcer.

wrinkle, *s.* arruga *f.;* — *v. a.* arrugar.

wrist, *s.* muñeca *f.*

write, *v. a.* escribir.

writer, *s.* escritor *m.*

writing-desk, *s.* escritorio *m.*

written, *adj.* escrito.

wrong, *adj.* equivocado, incorrecto; *be* ~ no tener razón, estar equivocado; — *adv.* mal; — *v. a.* ofender, agraviar.

X

Xmas, *s.* Navidad *f.*

X-ray, *s. (ray)* rayo *(m.)* X; *(picture)* radiografía *f.;* — *v. a.* radiografiar.

Y

yacht, *s.* yate *m.*

yard *s.* yarda *(court-)* patio *m.*

year, *s.* año *m.*

yearly, *adj.* anual; — *adv.* anualmente, cada año.

yeast, *s.* levadura *f.*

yell, *s.* grito *m.*, alarido *m.;* — *v. n.* gritar, dar alaridos.

yellow, *adj.* amarillo; ~ *fever* fiebre *(f.)* amarilla.

yes, sí.

yesterday, *adv.* ayer.

yet, *adv.* todavía, aún, sin embargo; *as* ~ hasta ahora, todavía; *not* ~ todavía no, aún no.

yield, *v. a.* producir; ~ *to* sy rendirse.

yolk, *s.* yema *f.*

you, *pron.* usted; ustedes *pl.; let me help* ~ permítame que le ayude; *I love* ~ yo te quiero.

young, *adj.* joven; ~ *girl* chica *f.*, muchacha *f.;* ~ *lady* señorita *f.;* — *s.* cachorros *m. pl.*, crías *f. pl.*

youngster, *s.* mozo *m.*, muchacho *m.*

your, *pron.* su, sus; tu, tus; vuestro, vuestros.

yours, *pron.* el suyo, el de usted; el tuyo; el vuestro; *a friend of* ~ uno de sus amigos.

yourself, usted mismo, tú mismo.

youth, *s.* juventud *f.; (person)* joven *m.*, muchacho *m.*

Z

zeal, *s.* celo *m.*

zealous, *adj.* celoso.

zero, *s.* cero *m.*

zigzag, *s.* zigzag *m.;* — *v. n.* zigzaguear.

zinc, *s.* zinc *m.*

zipper, *s.* cremallera *f.*

zone, *s.* zona *f.*, región *f.*

zoo, *s.* jardín *(m.)* zoológico, zoo *m.*

zoology, *s.* zoología *f.*

SPANISH-ENGLISH
DICTIONARY

A

a, *prep.* at, on, to; by; *a la mesa* at table; *a las diez* at ten o'clock; *a caballo* on horseback; *a pie* on foot; *poço a poco* little by little; *voy a la ciudad* I go to town; *voy a verle* I'll go to see him.

abad, *s. m.* abbot.

abajo, *adv.* below, down, downstairs.

abandonado, *adj.* negligent, untidy.

abandonar, *v. a.* abandon, leave.

abandono, *s. m.* abandonment.

abanico, *s. m.* fan.

abedul, *s. m.* birch(-tree).

abeja, *s. f.* bee.

abertura, *s. f.* opening, aperture.

abeto, *s. m.* fir(-tree).

abierto, *adj.* open.

abogado, *s. m.* lawyer, solicitor.

abolición, *s. f.* abolition.

abolir, *v. a.* abolish.

abominable, *adj.* abominable.

abominar *de,* *v. n.* abhor.

abonado, *s. m.* subscriber.

abonar, *v. a.* pay, settle; improve; fertilize; *v. n.* ~*se* a subscribe.

abono, *s. m.* subscription; fertilizer; *(theatre)* seasonticket.

abordar, *v. n.* go aboard; reach port.

aborrecer, *v. a.* abhor.

abotonar, *v. a.* button.

abrazar, *v. a.* embrace, hug.

abrazo, *s. m.* embrace, hug.

abrelatas, *s. m.* tin-opener

abreviar, *v. a.* abbreviate.

abrigar, *v. a.* warm; shelter, protect; *v. n.* ~*se* dress warmly.

abrigo, *s. m.* overcoat; shelter.

abril, *s. m.* April.

abrir, *v. a.* open, unlock.

absolutamente, *adv.* absolutely.

absoluto, *adj.* absolute; *en* ~ (not) at all.

absorbente, *adj.* absorbent.

absorber, *v. a.* absorb.

abstenerse, *v. n.* abstain.

abstinencia, *s. f.* abstinence.

abstinente, *adj.* abstinent, teetotal.

abstracto, *adj.* abstract.

absurdo, *adj.* absurd; — *s. m.* absurdity.

abuela, *s. f.* grandmother.

abuelo, *s. m.* grandfather.

abuelos, *pl. m.* grandparents.

abundancia, *s. f.* abundance.

abundante, *adj.* abundant.

aburrido, *adj.* boring, dull, bored.

aburrir, *v. a.* bore, tire; *v. n.* ~*se* be bored.

abusar *de,* *v. n.* abuse.

abuso, *s. m.* abuse.

acá, *adv.* here, this way; *por* ~ around here.

acabado, *adj.* finished; exhausted, worn out.

acabar, *v. a.* finish, end, terminate; put an end to; ~ *con* exhaust; ~ *de* have just (done sg); *acabo de llegar* I've just arrived; ~ *por* end by; *v. n.* ~*se* run out.

academia, *s. f.* academy.

acaecer, *v. n.* happen.

acalorar, *v. a.* warm (up); incite; *v. n.* ∼se become heated or excited.

acampar, *v. n.* camp, be encamped; ∼se pitch camp.

acariciar, *v. a.* caress, pet.

acaso, *s. m.* coincidence, chance; − *adv.* perhaps, maybe.

acatarrarse, *v. n.* catch cold.

acaudalado, *adj.* well-to-do, well-off.

acceder *a,* *v. n.* assent, agree; fulfil, comply.

accesorio, *adj. & s. m.* accessory.

accidentado, *adj.* uneven.

accidental, *adj.* accidental.

accidente, *s. m.* accident, mishap, chance.

acción, *s. f.* action; plot (of a drama); share.

accionamiento, *s. m.* drive, propulsion.

accionista, *s. m.* shareholder.

acedía, *s. f.* gastric acid.

aceitar, *v. a.* oil, grease.

aceite, *s. m.* oil; ∼ *de higado de bacalao* codliver oil; ∼ *mineral* crude oil.

aceleración, *s. f.* acceleration.

acelerado, *adj.* accelerated.

acelerador, *s. m.* accelerator.

acelerar, *v. a.* accelerate.

acento, *s. m.* stress, accent, pronunciation.

acentuar, *v. a.* accent.

aceptación, *s. f.* acceptance.

aceptar, *v. a.* accept.

acera, *s. f.* pavement.

acerca de, *prep.* concerning.

acercar, *v. a.* bring near; *v. n.* ∼se a approach.

acero, *s. m.* steel.

acertado, *adj.* skilful, clever.

acertar, *v. a.* guess right; ∼ con locate, find; ∼ en hit the mark.

acertijo, *s. m.* riddle.

ácido, *adj.* sour; − *s. m.* sourness, acid.

aclamación, *s. f.* acclamation, cheers.

aclamar, *v. a.* acclaim, applaud.

aclarar, *v. a.* make clear, clarify; *v. n.* brighten, clear up.

aclimatar, *v. n.* acclimatize.

acoger, *v. a.* lodge, receive.

acogida, *s. f.* reception.

acometer, *v. a.* attack.

acometida, *s. f.* attack.

acomodado, *adj.* well-to-do.

acomodador, *s. m.* usher.

acomodar, *v. a.* put, place; *v. n.* ∼se adapt oneself, make oneself comfortable.

acompañamiento, *s. m.* accompaniment.

acompañar, *v. a.* accompany, see off.

acondicionar, *v. a.* form, shape; prepare, dress (dish).

aconsejar, *v. a.* advise; *v. n.* ∼se de consult sy.

acontecer, *v. n.* happen, occur.

acontecimiento, *s. m.* event, ocurrence.

acorazado, *s. m.* battleship.

acordar, *v. a.* agree to, on; *v. n.* ∼se de remember, recollect.

acostar, *v. a.* put to bed;

lay; v. n. ~se go to bed.
acostumbrar, v. a. accustom, be accustomed; v. n. ~se get accustomed, get used.
acre, adj. acrid, pungent.
acrecer, v. a. augment.
acreditado, adj. accredited; reliable; of good reputation; solvent.
acreditar, v. a. accredit.
acreedor, s. m. creditor.
acróbata, s. m. acrobat.
acta, s. f. protocol, record; levantar ~ protocol, record.
actitud, s. f. attitude.
activar, v. a. promote; set in motion.
actividad, s. f. activity.
activo, adj. active; — s. m. assets.
acto, s. m. act; ceremony; en el ~ right away.
actor, s. m. actor; plaintiff.
actriz, s. f. actress.
actual, adj. present, current; real, true.
actualidad, s. f. present time; en la ~ at present.
actualmente, adv. at present.
actuar, v. n. act.
acuarela, s. f. watercolour.
acuario, s. m. aquarium.
acuático, adj. water-.
acudir, v. n. rush; ~ a la cita keep an appointment.
acueducto, s. m. water-conduit.
acuerdo, s. m. agreement; estar de ~ be of the same opinion; de ~ con in accordance with.
acumulador, s. m. accumulator.
acumular, v. a. accumulate.

acuoso, adj. watery; juicy.
acusación, s. f. accusation.
acusado, s. m. defendant.
acusar, v. a. accuse; ~ recibo acknowledge receipt.
acusativo, s. m. accusative.
adelantado, adj. progressive; por ~ in advance; ir ~ be fast.
adelantar, v. a. surpass, take the lead; nos adelantaron they passed us; v. n. gain time, be fast; improve, advance; ~se beat sy to.
adelante, adv. forward; ¡~! come in!.
adelgazar, v. a. make thin; v. n. lose weight.
ademán, s. m. bearing; gesture.
además, adv. moreover, besides; ~ de in addition to.
adentro, adv. within, inside.
adición, s. f. addition.
adicional, adj. additional.
adicionar, v. a. add.
adiestrar, v. a. train; (horse) break in.
adinerado, adj. well-to-do.
adiós s. m. good-bye; so long!
adivinanza, s. f. riddle, puzzle.
adivinar, v. a. foresee; guess.
adivino, s. m. fortune-teller.
adjetivo, m. adjective.
adjudicar, v. a. adjudicate.
adjunto, adv. & adj. enclosed.
administración, s. f. administration, manage-

ment.

administrador, *s. m.* manager; superintendent.

administrar, *v. a.* manage, administer.

administrativo, *adj.* administrative..

admirable, *adj.* admirable, excellent, wonderful.

admiración, *s. f.* admiration, wonder.

admirador, *s. m.* admirer.

admirar, *v. a.* admire, amaze.

admisión, *s. f.* admission.

admitir, *v. a.* admit; let, allow; accept.

adobar, *v. a.* prepare, cook.

adolescencia, *s. f.* adolescence, youth.

adolescente, *adj. & s. m.* adolescent.

adonde, *conj.* where, to what place; — *pron.* ¿adónde? where to?

adorable, *adj.* adorable.

adorar, *v. a.* adore, worship.

adormitarse, *v. n.* fall into a slumber.

adornar, *v. a.* decorate, trim.

adorno, *s. m.* ornament, trimming.

adquirir, *v. a.* acquire.

adquisición, *s. f.* acquisition.

adrede, *adv.* deliberately.

aduana, *s. f.* customhouse; customs.

aduanero, *s. m.* customs officer.

adulterar, *v. a.* adulterate.

adulto, *adj. & s.* adult.

adunar, *v. a.* unite, join.

adverbio, *s. m.* adverb.

adversario, *s. m.* opponent.

adversidad, *s. f.* adversity,

misfortune.

adverso, *adj.* adverse.

advertencia, *s. f.* warning.

advertir, *v. a.* notice, observe; advise, warn.

aeración, *s. f.* airing, ventilation.

aéreo, *adj.* aerial; *correo ∼* air mail.

aerodinámico, *adj.* streamlined.

aeródromo, *s. m.* airport.

aeronauta, *s. m.* aeronaut.

aeronáutica, *s. f.* aeronautics.

aeronáutico, *adj.* aeronautic.

aeronave, *s. f.* airship.

aeroplano, *s. m.* airplane.

aeropuerto, *s. m.* air-port.

afabilidad, *s. f.* affability.

afamado, *adj.* famous.

afanoso, *adj.* industrious.

afección, *s. f.* affection.

afectación, *s. f.* affectation.

afectado, *adj.* affected, unnatural.

afectar, *v. a.* affect.

afecto, *s. m.* affection, regard.

afectuoso, *adj.* affectionate.

afeitar, *v. a.* shave; *v. n.* *∼se* shave (oneself).

afición, *s. f.* fondness, inclination.

aficionado, *adj.* attached, devoted; — *s. m.* fan; amateur.

aficionarse *a,* *v. n.* become fond of.

afilado, *adj.* sharp.

afilalápices, *s. m.* pencil-sharpener.

afilar, *v. a.* sharpen.

afinar, *v. a.* refine; tune.

afinidad, *s. f.* relationship (by marriage).

afirmación, s. f. affirmation.

afirmar, v. a. affirm, assert, maintain.

afirmativo, adj. affirmative.

aflicción, s. f. affliction, sorrow, grief.

afligir, v. a. grieve sy; v. n. ~se grieve.

afluir, v. n. flow into.

aforrar, v. a. line, fur.

afortunadamente, adv. fortunately.

afortunado, adj. fortunate, lucky.

afrenta, s. f. affront, insult.

africano, adj. & s. African.

afuera, adv. out, outside; ¡~! get out!

afueras, pl. f. suburbs, outskirts.

agencia, s. f. agency; ~ de informaciones inquiry-agency; ~ de viajes, ~ de turismo tourist office.

agenda, s. f. note-book; agenda.

agente, s. m. agent, representative; ~ de policía policeman; ~ de transportes forwarding agent.

ágil, adj. quick, agile.

agilidad, s. f. quickness, agility.

agitación, s. f. agitation, excitement.

agitar, v. a. shake; stir up, excite; v. n. ~se become excited.

agonía, s. f. agony.

agonizar, v. n. agonize.

agosto, s. m. August.

agotar, v. a. use up, exhaust; v. n. ~se wear oneself out, give out.

agraciado, adj. graceful, charming.

agradable, adj. agreeable, pleasant.

agradar, v. n. be pleasing.

agradecer, v. a. appreciate; Le agradezco mucho su ayuda I thank you very much for your help.

agradecido, adj. thankful, grateful; estoy muy ~ a usted I'm very grateful.

agradecimiento, s. m. gratitude.

agrandar, v. a. enlarge; let out (garment).

agrario, adj. agricultural.

agravar, v. a. aggravate, make worse; v. n. ~se get worse.

agregado, s. m. attaché.

agregar, v. a. add; v. n. se a join, follow.

agresión, s. f. aggression.

agresivo, adj. aggressive.

agresor, s. m. aggressor.

agrícola, adj. agricultural.

agricultor, s, m. farmer.

agricultura, s. f. agriculture.

agrio, adj. sour.

agrupar, v. a. group.

agua, s. f. water; ~s termales hot springs.

aguador, s. m. watercarrier.

aguafuerte, s. f. etching.

aguanieve, s. f. sleet.

aguantar, v. a. bear, endure, stand; hang on, not give up; v. n. ~se be patient, take it.

aguar, v. a. add water to sg.

aguardar, v. a. expect, wait for.

aguardiente, s. m. brandy,

whisky.

agudeza, *s. f.* sagacity; wit.

agudo, *adj.* sharp, keen; clever; high-pitched; witty; *ángulo ~* acute angle.

águila, *s. f.* eagle.

aguja, *s. f.* needle; switch (railway); hand (of watch); *~ de hacer media* knitting-needle.

agujero, *s. m.* hole.

aguzar, *v. a.* sharpen to a point; *~ el oído* prick up one's ears.

¡ah! *int.* oh!

ahí *adv.* there; *por ~* that way; around here.

ahogar, *v. a.* choke; — *v. n. ~se* drown, be drowned; be suffocated.

ahondar, *v. a.* deepen; *v. n.* plunge.

ahora, *adv.* now; *~ bien* now then; *~ mismo* at once, right away, just now; *de ~ en adelante* from now on; *hasta ~* up to now, so far; *por ~* for the present.

ahorrar, *v. a.* save (money).

ahorro, *s. m.* saving; *caja (s. f.) de ~s* savings-bank.

ahumado, *adj.* smoked; — *s. m.* smoked meat.

ahumar, *v. a.* smoke.

aire¹, *s. m.* air; wind; look, appearance; *al ~ libre* in the open air; *tomar el ~* get some fresh air.

aire², *s. m.* melody; time.

airear, *v. a.* air, ventilate; *v. n. ~se* get some fresh air; catch cold.

airoso, *adj.* smart; handsome.

aislado, *adj.* isolated.

aislador, *s. m.* insulator.

aislamiento, *s. m.* isolation.

aislar, *v. a.* isolate, cut off.

¡ajá! *int.* so that's it!

ajedrecista, *s. m.* chess-player.

ajedrez, *s. m.* chess; *jugar al ~* play chess.

ajenjo, *s. m.* absinthe.

ajeno, *adj.* another's, someone else's.

ajo, *s. m.* garlic.

ajustar, *v. a.* settle, agree about, adjust; tighten (screw); *v. n.* fit.

al (a + el) *see* **a.**

ala, *s. f.* wing; brim (of hat).

alabar, *v. a.* praise; *v. n. ~se* boast.

alacena, *s. f.* wall-cupboard.

alado, *adj.* winged.

alambicar, *v. a.* distil.

alambique, *s. m.* retort.

alambre, *s. m.* wire.

alameda, *s. f.* alley, public walk (lined with poplars).

álamo, *s. m.* poplar.

alargar, *v. a.* lenghten, extend; hand; *~ el paso* force one's pace.

alarma, *s. f.* alarm; *freno de ~* emergency brake.

alarmar, *v. a.* alarm; *v. n. ~se* get anxious.

alba, *s. f.* dawn.

albañil, *s. m.* mason, bricklayer.

albaricoque, *s. m.* apricot.

albergar, *v. a.* harbour, lodge.

albergue, *s. m.* lodgings; shelter.

albóndiga, *s. f.* meat ball.

albornoz, *s. m.* bathing-gown.

alborotar, *v. a. & n.* disturb, make noise.

alboroto, *s. m.* tumult, uproar.

álbum, *s. m.* album.

alcachofa, *s. f.* artichoke.

alcalde, *s. m.* mayor.

alcance, *s. m.* reach.

alcanfor, *s. m.* camphor.

alcantarilla, *s. f.* canal; duct.

alcanzar, *v. a.* cath up with, overtake; reach, attain.

alcázar, *s. m.* fortress; Royal Palace.

alción, *s. m.* kingfisher.

alcoba, *s. f.* bedroom.

alcohol, *s. f.* alcohol.

alcohólico *adj. & s.* alcoholic.

aldaba, *s. f.* knocker.

aldea, *s. f.* village.

aldeana, *s. f.* countrywoman.

aldeano, *s. m.* countryman.

alegrar, *v. a.* cheer up brighten; *v. n.* ~*se de* rejoice, be glad.

alegre, *adj.* glad, happy; cheerful; bright (colour); drunk, tipsy.

alegría, *s. f.* delight, joy, pleasure.

alejar, *v. a.* remove, send away; *v. n.* ~*se* withdraw, go away.

alemán, *adj. & s.* German.

alerta, *adj. & adv.* (on the) alert.

aleta, *s. f.* fin.

aletear, *v. n.* flutter.

alfabético, *adj.* alphabetical.

alfabeto, *s. m.* alphabet.

alféizar, *s. m.* windowsill.

alférez, *s. m.* cadet.

alfil, *s. m.* bishop (chess).

alfiler, *s. m.* pin.

alfombra, *s. f.* carpet, rug.

algo, *pron.* something; — *adv.* rather, somewhat; ~ *de dinero* some money; *por* ~ for some reason; *servir para* ~ be good for something.

algodón, *s. m.* cotton; ~ *en rama* cotton-wool.

alguacil, *s. m.* usher (in court).

alguien, *pron.* somebody, someone; anybody, anyone.

algún, *adj.* some; ~ *día* some day.

alguno, *adj.* some, any; *alguna cosa más* anything else; *alguna vez* now and then, ever; ~*s* some people.

alhaja, *s. f.* jewel.

aliado, *adj.* allied; — *s.* ally.

alianza, *s. f.* union, alliance.

aliarse, *v. n.* form an alliance, ally oneself.

alienar, *v. a.* alienate.

aliento, *s. m.* breath.

aligerar, *v. a.* lighten; *v. n.* hasten, hurry.

alimentar, *v. a.* feed, nourish.

alimento, *s. m.* food, nourishment.

alistar, *v. a.* enlist; *v. n.* ~*se* enlist; get ready.

aliviar, *v. n.* relieve, alleviate; *v. n.* recover.

alivio, *s. m.* relief; recovery.

alma, *s. f.* soul; *lo siento en el* ~ I'm terribly sorry; *¡hijo de mi* ~! my dear child!

almacén, *s. m.* warehouse; store(s).

almendra, *s. f.* almond.
almendro, *s. m.* almond-tree.
almíbar, *s. m.* syrup.
almidonar, *v. a.* starch.
alminar, *s. m.* minaret.
almirante, *s. m.* admiral.
almohada, *s. f.* pillow; *consultar con la ~* sleep on it.
almorzar, *v. n.* lunch, breakfast.
almuerzo, *s. m.* lunch, noon meal; breakfast.
alojamiento, *s. m.* dwelling, lodgings.
alojar, *v. a.* put up, lodge, quarter; *v. n. ~se* stay.
alquilar, *v. a.* rent, hire; let.
alquiler, *s. m.* (price of) rent.
alrededor, *adv.* around; *– prep. ~ de* around, about; *– s. pl. m. ~es* outskirts, surroundings.
altar, *s. m.* altar.
altavoz, *s. m.* loud speaker.
alterar, *v. a.* change, transform; *– v. n. ~se* get excited.
alternar, *v. n.* alternate; take turns.
alternativa, *s. f.* alternative.
alternativamente, *adv.* by turns.
alternativo, *adj.* alternate.
alto¹, *adj.* high, tall; *hablar ~* talk loud; *a altas horas de la noche* very late at night; *pasar por ~* overlook, forget.
alto², *s. m.* stop, halt; *hacer ~* stop; *¡~!* halt! stop!.
altura, *s. f.* height, altitude, elevation.

aludir *a, v. n.* allude to, refer to.
alumbrado, *s. m.* lighting.
alumbrar, *v. a.* give light, light, illuminate.
alumbre, *s. m.* alum.
aluminio, *s. m.* aluminium.
alumno, *s. m.* pupil, student.
alusión, *s. f.* allusion; reference; hint.
aluvión, *s. f.* inundation, flood.
alzar, *v. a.* lift, raise; cut (cards); *v. n. ~se* rise; revolt.
allá, *adv.* there; *por ~* over there.
allegado, *adj.* related, kindred.
allende, *adv.* beyond.
allí, *adv.* there; *de ~* from there; *por ~* that way.
ama, *s. f.* mistress of the house; hostess; *~ de llaves* housekeeper.
amabilidad, *s. f.* kindness.
amable, *adj.* kind, amiable.
amador, *s. m.* lover.
amaestrar, *v. a.* train, instruct.
amanecer, *v. n.* dawn; *– s. m.* daybreak, dawn.
amansar, *v. a.* tame, domesticate.
amante, *adj.* loving; *– s. m.* lover; *s. f.* mistress.
amapola, *s. f.* poppy.
amar, *v. a.* love; *hacerse ~* win sy's affection.
amargar, *v. n.* be bitter; *v. a.* make bitter, make miserable.
amargo, *adj.* bitter.
amargura, *s. f.* bitterness.
amarillento, *adj.* yellowish.
amarillo, *adj.* yellow.

amarrar, v. a. tie, fasten.

amasar, v. a. massage; knead.

amatista, s. f. amethyst.

ámbar, s. m. amber.

ambición, s. f. ambition.

amblcionar, v. a. strive after.

ambicioso, adj. overambitious.

ambiente, s. m. atmosphere, environment.

ambigú, s. m. bar, buffet.

ambigüedad, s. f. ambiguity.

ambiguo, adj. ambiguous.

ambos, adj. pl. both.

ambulancia, s. f. ambulance.

ambulante, adj. migrant, wandering.

amén, s. m. amen; — prep. ~ de besides.

amenazar, v. a. threaten, menace.

ameno, adj. lovely, charming.

americana, s. f. coat (of a man's suit), jacket.

americano, adj. & s. American.

amianto, s. m. asbestos.

amiga, s. f. (girl)friend.

amígdala, s. f. tonsil.

amigdalitis, s. f. tonsillitis.

amigo, adj. friendly; — s. m. friend.

aminorar, v. a. diminish.

amistad, s. f. friendship; hacer ~ become friends; hacer ~es get acquainted.

amistoso, adj. friendly.

amo, s. m. master of the house; host; owner, proprietor; boss.

amontonar, v. a. heap, pile up.

amor, s. m. love; darling; ~ propio self-esteem, pride; por ~ de Dios

for goodness sake.

amortiguar, v. a. weaken, diminish.

amortizar, v. a. amortize.

amotinarse, v. n. mutiny.

amparar, v. a. protect, defend.

amparo, s. m. protection; aid.

ampliar, v. a. enlarge, amplify, extend.

amplio, adj. ample, roomy, large.

amputar, v. a. amputate.

amueblado, adj. furnished.

amueblar, v. a. furnish.

ánade, s. m. duck.

analfabeto, adj. & s. illiterate.

análisis, s. m. analysis.

analizar, v. a. analyse.

ananá, s. m. pineapple.

anaquel, s. m. shelf.

anaranjado, adj. orange-coloured.

anarquía, s. f. anarchy.

anciano, adj. aged, very old.

ancla, s. f. anchor; echar ~s cast anchor; levar ~s weigh anchor.

anclaje, s. m. berth.

anclar, v. n. anchor.

ancho, adj. wide, broad.

anchoa, s. f. anchovy.

andar, v. n. walk, go on foot; run, work (clock).

andén, s. m. (railway) platform.

anfiteatro, s. m. dress-circle.

ángel, s. m. angel.

anglosajón, adj. Anglo-Saxon.

angosto, adj. narrow.

anguila, s. f. eel.

ángulo, s. m. angle.

angustia, s. f. fear, anxiety.

angustiar, v. a. alarm.

anhelar, v. n. pant, gasp;

v. a. long for.

anhelo, *s. m.* longing.

anidar, *v. n.* nest.

anillo, *s. m.* ring.

animación, *s. f.* animation, liveliness.

animado, *adj.* animated, lively.

animal, *adj.&s. m.* animal.

animar, *v. a.* cheer, encourage.

ánimo. *s. m.* (state of) mind, spirits; courage; *dar* ~s cheer up, encourage.

animosidad, *s. f.* grudge; courage.

animoso, *adj.* courageous.

aniñado, *adj.* childish.

aniquilar, *v. a.* annihilate.

aniversario, *s. m.* anniversary.

anoche, *adv.* last night.

anochecer, *v. n.* grow dark; — *s. m.* dusk, nightfall.

ánodo, *s. m.* anode.

anómalo, *adj.* anomalous.

anónimo, *adj.* anonymous; *sociedad* ~a joint-stock company.

ansia, *s. f.* fear, anxiety; desire, eagerness.

ansiar, *v. a.* long for, crave for.

ansiedad, *s. f.* anxiety.

ansioso, *adj.* anxious, eager, impatient.

antaño, *adv.* formerly.

ante, *prep.* in front of; ~ *todo* first of all.

anteanoche, *adv.* night before last.

anteayer, *adv.* day before yesterday.

antecedente, *adj. & s. m.* antecedent; ~s past, police-record.

anteceder, *v. n.* precede.

antedatar, *v. a.* date back.

antedicho, *adj.* aforementioned.

anteguerra, *s. f.; período (s. m.) de* ~ pre-war time.

antemano, *adv.; de* ~ in advance, beforehand.

antena, *s. f.* feeler; aerial.

anteojo, *s. f.* field-glass; ~s eyeglasses, spectacles.

anterior, *adj.* previous, last.

anterioridad, *s. f.* antecedence; *con* ~ previously.

antes, *adv.* before, formerly; — *prep.* ~ *de*, *conj.* ~ *que* before; *cuanto* ~ as soon as possible; *poco* ~ not long ago; *el día* ~ the day before.

antesala, *s. f.* waiting-room.

anticipación, *s. f.* anticipation.

anticipar, *v. a.* advance; lend; get ahead of; *v. n.* ~se arrive ahead of time.

anticipo, *s. m.* advanced money.

anticuado, *adj.* antiquated.

antigüedad, *s. f.* antiquity.

antiguo, *adj.* former; old, ancient; *a la antigua* in an old-fashioned way.

antipatía, *s. f.* dislike.

antipático, *adj.* disagreeable.

antiséptico, *adj. & s. m.* antiseptic.

antorcha, *s. f.* torch.

antro, *s. m.* cave; den.

anual, *adj.* annual, yearly.

anuario, *s. m.* annual.

anublar, *v. a.* cloud.

anudar, *v. a.* tie.

anular[1], *v. a.* annul.

anular[2], *adj.* annular; *dedo* ~ ring-finger.

anunciar, *v. a.* announce, advertise.

anuncio, *s. m.* advertisement, announcement; notice.

anzuelo, *s. m.* fishing-hook

añadir, *v. a.* add to.

año, *s. m.* year; ~ *bisiesto* leap year; *feliz ~ nuevo* Happy New Year; *tengo cuarenta* ~*s* I'm forty years old.

añoso, *adj.* aged.

apagar, *v. a.* put out, extinguish; *v. n.* ~*se* go out (lights).

aparador, *s. m.* sideboard; dresser.

aparato, *s. m.* apparatus; set.

aparecer, *v. n.* show up, appear.

aparentar, *v. a.* pretend.

aparente, *adj.* apparent.

aparición, *s. f.* appearance; apparition.

apariencia, *s. f.* appearance, looks.

apartar, *v. a.* separate, divide.

aparte, *adj.* separate; — *adv.* aside, separately.

apasionado, *adj.* passionate; ~ *por* partial to.

apeadero, *s. m.* halt.

apearse, *v. n.* get off.

apelación, *s. f.* appeal.

apelar, *v. n.* appeal.

apellidar, *v. a.* name, call.

apellido, *s. m.* (family) name.

apenas, *adv.* scarcely, hardly; *conj.* as soon as.

apéndice, *s. m.* appendix.

apendicitis, *s. f.* appendicitis.

aperitivo, *adj.* appetizing; — *s. m.* appetizer; aperient.

apertura, *s. f.* opening.

apestar, *v. a.* infect, poison.

apetecer, *v. a.* desire, crave for.

apetito, *s. m.* appetite.

apilar, *v. a.* pile up, stack.

apio, *s. m.* celery.

aplastar, *v. a.* crush; flatten.

aplaudir, *v. n.* applaud.

aplauso, *s. m.* applause.

aplazar, *v. a.* adjourn.

aplicado, *adj.* studious, industrious.

aplicar, *v. a.* apply.

apoplejía, *s. f.* apoplexy.

aposento, *s. m.* room, apartment.

apostar, *v. n.* bet.

apóstol, *s. m.* apostle.

apoyar, *v. a.* rest, prop; back, support, second; *v. n.* ~*se* support oneself, lean.

apoyo, *s. m.* prop, support.

apreciar, *v. a.* appreciate.

aprender, *v. a.* learn.

aprendiz, *s. m.* apprentice.

aprendizaje, *s. m.* apprenticeship.

aprestar, *v. a.* prepare, dress.

apresurar, *v. a.* hasten, hurry; *v. n.* ~*se* hurry up.

apretar, *v. a.* tighten, press down, compress; grip; clench; *v. n.* be too tight; go faster, sprint.

aprieto, *s. m.* jam, tight spot.

aprisa, *adv.* swiftly, fast, quickly.

aprisionar, *v. a.* arrest.

aprobar, *v. a.* approve of; pass (an examination).

aprovechar, *v. a.* profit by, make use of; — *v. n.* ~*se de* take advantage of.

aprovisionar, *v. a.* supply, provision.

aproximarse, *v. n.* approach, move near.

aptitud, *s. f.* aptitude.

apto, *adj.* apt.

apuesta, *s. f.* bet, wager.

apuesto, *adj.* well-shaped.

apuntar, *v. a.* aim; make a note, jot down; prompt.

apurado, *adj.* difficult, hard.

apurar, *v. a.* drain, drink up, consume; *v. n.* ~*se* worry; hurry.

apuro, *s. m.* jam, tight spot, fix.

aquel, aquella *adj.* that.

aquí, *adv.* here; ~ *dentro* in here; *de* ~ *en adelante* from now on; *por* ~ here, this way.

árabe, *adj. & s. m.* Arab(ian).

arado, *s. m.* plough.

arancel, *s. m.* tariff.

araña, *s. f.* spider.

arañar, *v. a. & n.* scratch.

arañazo, *s. m.* scratch.

arar, *v. a.* plow.

arbitrar, *v. n.* arbitrate.

arbitrario, *adj.* arbitrary.

árbitro, *s. m.* arbiter, umpire, referee.

arbol, *s. m.* tree.

arbusto, *s. m.* bush, shrub.

arca, *s. f.* trunk, chest; safe.

arcilla, *s. f.* clay.

arco, *s. m.* arch; bow (for arrows); ~ *iris* rainbow.

archiduque, *s. m.* archduke.

archiduquesa, *s. f.* archduchess.

archipiélago, *s. m.* archipelago.

archivo, *s. m.* archives.

arder, *v. n.* burn.

ardid, *s. m.* ruse; trick.

ardiente, *adj.* burning.

ardilla, *s. f.* squirrel.

ardor, *s. m.* heat; ardour.

arena, *s. f.* sand; arena.

arenque, *s. m.* herring.

argentino, *adj. & s. m.* Argentine.

argüir, *v. n.* argue.

argumentar, *v. a.* deduce, conclude.

argumento, *s. m.* argument, logic, premises; plot, story.

árido, *adj.* arid, dry, barren.

arma, *s. f.* weapon.

armada, *s. f.* navy.

armadura, *s. f.* armour; framework.

armar, *v.* arm; put together; ~ *jaleo* make a racket; — *v. n.* ~*se de* provide oneself with.

armario, *s. m.* closet, wardrobe.

armonía, *s. f.* harmony.

arpa, *s. f.* harp.

arquitecto, *s. m.* architect.

arquitectura, *s. f.* architecture.

arrancar, *v. a.* root out, pull out; *v. n.* start.

arranque, *s. m.* sudden impulse; starter.

arrastrar, *v. a.* drag along; *v. n.* ~*se* crawl, creep, drag oneself.

arreglar, *v. a.* arrange, adjust, settle; fix; *v. n.* ~*se* tidy up, dress.

arreglo, *s. m.* arrangement, settlement, agreement; *con* ~ according to, in accordance with.

arrendar, *v. a.* rent, let; hire.

arrepentirse, *v. n.* be sorry for, regret.

arrestar, *v. a.* arrest, imprison.

arresto, *s. m.* arrest, imprisonment.

arriba, *adv.* up, above; upstairs.

arribar, *v. n.* land; arrive.

arriero, *s. m.* mule-driver.

arriesgar, *v. a.* risk, hazard; *v. n.* ~se take risk.

arrodillarse, *v. n.* kneel down.

arrogante, *adj.* arrogant, haughty, proud.

arrojar, *v. a.* throw, hurl, cast; *v. n.* ~se rush, plunge.

arroyo, *s. m.* brook; stream.

arroz, *s. m.* rice.

arruinar, *v. a.* destroy, ruin.

arte, *s. m. (s. pl. f.)* art; skill; craft, cunning.

artefacto, *s.m.* machinery, mechanism.

arteria, *s. f.* artery.

artesano, *s. m.* artisan, craftsman.

articulación, *s. f.* joint; articulation.

articular, *v. a.* articulate.

artículo, *s. m.* joint; article; news article; ~s things, goods.

artificial, *adj.* artificial.

artificio, *s. m.* artifice, trick, knack.

artillería, *s. f.* artillery.

artista, *s. m., f.* artist.

artístico, *adj.* artistic.

arzobispo, *s. m.* archbishop.

as, *s. m.* ace, star; ace (cards).

asa, *s. f.* handle.

asado, *s. m.* roast.

asalto, *s. m.* assault, attack.

asamblea, *s. f.* assembly, convention.

asar, *v. a.* roast.

ascender, *v. a.* ascend, go up; be promoted; ~ *a* amount to.

ascensor, *s. m.* lift.

asco, *s. m.* nausea, disgust.

asegurar, *v. a.* secure, fasten; assure, affirm, maintain; insure; *v. n.* ~se. make sure; get insured.

asenso, *s. n.* consent.

asentir, *v. n.* assent, agree.

aseo, *s. m.* care of the body.

aseverar, *v. a.* affirm.

asfalto, *s. m.* asphalt.

así, *adv.* so, that way; in this manner, this way; therefore, and so; ~ ~ so so; ~ *como* any way; ~ *que* as soon as, after.

asiduidad, *s. f.* assiduity.

asiduo, *adj.* assiduous, industrious.

asiento, *s. m.* seat, chair; *tome usted* ~ take a seat.

asignar, *v. a.* assign.

asilo, *s. m.* orphanage; home (for aged).

asimilar, *v. a.* assimilate.

asimismo, *adv.* likewise, in the same way.

asistencia, *s. f.* attendance, presence; assistance, help.

asistenta, *s. f.* charwoman.

asistente, *s. m.* assistant, help.

asistir, *v. a. & n.* assist, help, take care of; ~ *a* attend, be present at.

asma, *s. f.* asthma.

asno, *s. m.* ass, donkey.

asociación, *s. f.* association, club.

asociado, *s. m.* associate, partner.

asociar, *v. a. & n.* associate.

asomar, *v. a.* put out (one's head); *v. n.* ~*se* lean out of.

asombrar, *v. a.* astonish, amaze; *v. n.* ~*se* wonder at; be astonished by, be amazed at.

asordar, *v. a.* deafen; stun.

aspecto, *s. m.* appearance, look; sight, aspect.

áspero, *adj.* rough, rash.

aspiración, *s. f.* respiration; ambition.

aspirador (*s. m.*) *de polvo* vacuum cleaner.

aspirante, *s. m.* aspirant.

aspirar, *v. a. & n.* aspire.

aspirina, *s. f.* aspirin.

asqueroso, *adj.* filthy, nasty, mean, low.

asta, *s. f.* shaft; horn (of a bull).

astil, *s. m.* handle, haft; quill.

astilla, *s. f.* chip; splinter.

astillero, *s. m.* dockyard.

astro, *s. m.* star; constellation.

astrología, *s. f.* astrology.

astrólogo, *s. m.* astrologer.

astronomía, *s. f.* astronomy.

astrónomo, *s. m.* astronomer.

astucia, *s. f.* cunning.

astuto, *adj.* astute, crafty.

asunto, *s. m.* subject; affair, business.

asustar, *v. a.* frighten; *v. n.* ~*se* be frightened.

atacar, *v. a.* attack.

atajar, *v. a.* take a short cut; overtake, catch up with; interrupt, cut short.

atajo, *s. m.* short cut, shorter road.

atañer, *v. a.* concern; affect.

ataque, *s. m.* attack, assault; fit.

atar, *v. a.* tie, bind, lace; ~ *cabos* put two and two together.

atardecer, *v. n.* night is falling; — *s. m.* evening.

atareado, *adj.* busy.

ataúd, *s. m.* coffin.

atemperar, *v. a.* moderate, mitigate.

atención, *s. f.* attention; kindness; *llamar la* ~ attract attention.

atender, *v. a. & n.* attend, wait on; pay attention to; look after, take care of.

atenerse *a*, *v. n.* depend on.

atentado, *s. m.* attempt (on the life of sy).

atento, *adj* polite, courteous; attentive; *su* ~ *y seguro servidor* yours faithfully.

aterrar¹, *v. a.* terrify.

aterrar², *v. n.* land.

aterrizaje, *s. m.* landing.

aterrizar, *v. n.* land.

aterrorizar, *v. a.* terrorize.

atestación, *s. f.* testimony, statement.

atestado, *adj.* obstinate; overfilled, crammed; — *s. m.* attestation, certificate.

atestiguar, *v. a.* testify.

atlántico, *adj.* Atlantic.

atleta, *s. m.*, *f.* athlete.

atlético, *adj.* athletic.

atmósfera, *s. f.* atmosphere.

atolladero, *s. m.* pool, puddle.

atomico, *adj.* atomic; *bomba~a* atomic bomb; *energia ~a* atomic energy; *pila ~a* atomic pile.

atomo, *s. m.* atom.

atormentar, *v. a.* torment, torture.

atornillar, *v. a. & n.* screw; turn a screw.

atracción, *s. f.* attraction.

atraco, *s. m.* robbery, hold-up.

atractivo, *adj.* attractive, charming; — *s. m.* charm, appeal.

atraer, *v. a.* attract, charm.

atrás, *adv.* back; *dar marcha ~* go into reverse, back; *hacia ~* backward; *quedarse ~* stay behind.

atrasado, *adj. & adv.* backward, behind.

atrasar, *v. a.* delay, detain; put back (watch); *v. n.* go *or* be slow, lose time; *~se* remain behind; be late.

atraso, *s. m.* backwardness; delay.

atravesar, *v. a.* pierce; cross.

atreverse, *v. n.* dare, venture.

atribuir, *v. a.* attribute.

atrocidad, *s. f.* atrocity, horrible thing.

atropellar, *v. a.* run over, knock down.

atropello, *s. m.* accident; abuse, outrage.

atroz, *adj.* terrible, atrocious.

atún, *s. m.* tunny.

aturdir, *v. a.* rattle; *v. n. ~se* be stunned.

audaz, *adj.* bold, daring.

audición, *s. f.* (radio) reception; *~ musical* radio concert.

audiencia, *s. f.* audience; courtroom.

auditorio, *s. m.* audience, listeners.

aula, *s. f.* auditorium, lecture-room, hall.

aumentar, *v. a.* increase.

aumento, *s. m.* increase.

aun, aún, *adv.* still; even; yet; *~ cuando* even though, even if.

aunque, *conj.* although, even if.

áureo, *adj.* golden.

auricular, *s. m.* ear-piece.

aurora, *s. f.* dawn.

auscultar, *v. a.* examine by auscultation.

ausencia, *s. f.* absence.

ausente, *adj.* absent.

austral, *adj.* austral.

austriaco, *adj. & s.* Austrian.

auténtico, *adj.* authentic.

auto, *s. m.* auto, car.

autobús, *s. m.* bus.

autocar, *s. m.* sightseeing car.

autogiro, *s. m.* gyroplane, autogiro.

automación, *s. f.* automation.

automático, *adj.* automatic.

automóvil, *s. m.* automobile.

automovilismo, *s. m.* motoring.

automovilista, *s. m.*, *f.* motorist.

autopista, *s. f.* motorway.
autopsia, *s. f.* autopsy.
autor, *s. m.* author.
autora, *s. f.* authoress.
autoridad, *s. f.* authority; ~es authorities, government.
autorización, *s. f.* authorization.
autorizar, *v. s.* authorize.
auxilio, *s. m.* aid, help.
avalancha, *s. f.* avalanche.
avance, *s. m.* advance; advance payment.
avanzado, *adj.* advanced, progressive.
avanzar, *v. n.* move forward; advance.
avaricia, *s. f.* avarice.
avaricioso, avariento *adj.* avaricious.
avaro, *adj.* &. *s. m.* miser(ly).
ave, *s. f.* bird, fowl.
avellana, *s. f.* hazel-nut.
avena, *s. f.* oats.

avenida, *s. f.* avenue, flood.
aventura, *s. f.* adventure.
aventurar, *v. a.* risk, hazard.
aventurero, *s. m.* adventurer.
avergonzar, *v. a.* shame, make ashamed; *v. n.* ~se be ashamed.
avería, *s. f.* average, damage.
averiarse, *v. n.* be damaged, be spoiled.
averiguar, *v. a.* find out.
aversión, *s.. f.* aversion, dislike.
avestruz, *s. m.* ostrich.
aviación, *s. f.* aviation.
aviador, *s. m.* aviator.
ávido, *adj.* eager, anxious.
avión, *s. m.* (air)plane.
avisar, *v. a.* notify, inform; warn, advise, counsel.

aviso, *s. m.* announcement, notice; warning.
¡ay! oh! ouch!
ayer, *adv.* yesterday.
ayuda, *s. f.* help, aid, assistance.
ayudar, *v. a.* help, aid, assist.
ayunar, *v. n.* fast.
ayuntamiento, *s. m.* town-hall.
azafata, *s. f.* stewardess, air-hostess.
azar, *s. m.* chance, risk; al ~ at random.
azorar, *v. a.* frighten; embarras, confuse; *v. n.* ~se be embarrassed.
azúcar, *s. m.* sugar.
azucarar, *v. a.* sugar.
azucarera, *s. f.* sugar-basin.
azufre, *s. m.* sulphur.
azul, *adj.* blue.

B

babucha, *s. f.* slipper.
bacalao, *s. m.* codfish.
bacilo, *s. m.* microbe.
bacteria, *s. f.* bacterium.
bache, *s. m.* pot-hole.
bachiller, *s. m.* graduate.
bagaje, *s. m.* luggage.
bagatela, *s. f.* trifle.
bahía, *s. f.* bay (arm of sea).
bailador, *adj.* dancing; — *s. m.* dancer.
bailar, *v. a. & n.* dance.
bailarín, *s. m.* dancer.
bailarina, *s. f.* dancer.
baile, *s. m.* dance, ball.
bailete, *s. m.* ballet.
baja, *s. f.* drop, fall (in price); (military) casualty; dar de ~ drop out; darse de ~ resign, withdraw.
bajar, *v. n.* go down, descend; fall, drop;

~se bend over; get down, get off; — v. a. bring down, take down, lower.

bajo, adj. low; short (not tall); soft (voice); bass (instrument); — s. m. groundfloor; — adv. below; — prep. below.

bala[1], s. f. bullet.

bala[2], s. f. bale.

balance, s. m. swaying, wobbling; balance; balance sheet.

balancear, v. a. balance; v. n. (~se) sway, rock, swing.

balanza, s. f. scales, balance.

balcánico, adj. Balkan.

balcón, s. m. balcony.

balde, s. m. bucket, pail; de ~ gratis, free; en ~ in vain, without success.

balneario, s. m. bathing-resort.

balompié, s. m. football.

balón, s. m. football.

baloncesto, s. m. basketball.

balonmano, s. m. handball.

balonvolea, s. m. volleyball.

balsa, s. f. raft; ferry.

baluarte, s. m. bulwark.

ballena, s. f. whale.

bambú, s. m. bamboo (cane).

banal, adj. banal, trite, commonplace.

banana, s. f. banana.

banca, s. f. stand, stall; bank(ing).

banco, s. m. bank; bench.

banda[1], s. f. sash, band (wide strip); side (of a ship).

banda[2], s. f. (music) band; gang.

bandeja, s. f. tray.

bandera, s. f. flag.

banderola, s. f. pennon.

bandido, s. m. bandit.

bando, s. m. party, sect.

banquero, s. m. banker.

banqueta, s. f. stool.

banquete, s. m. banquet.

banquetear, v. n. banquet.

banquillo, s. m. dock, prisoner's box.

bañador, adj. & s. m. bather.

bañar, v. a. bathe; v. n. ~se take a bath.

bañera, s. f. bathtub; bath attendant.

bañero, s. m. swimming master.

bañista, s. m., f. visitor at a spa.

baño, s. m. bath; bathroom; bathtub; ~s wateringplace, spa.

bar, s. m. bar; taproom.

baraja, s. f. pack of cards.

barajar, v. a. shuffle (cards).

barato, adj. cheap; — adj. cheaply; — s. m. sale.

barba, s. f. beard; chin.

bárbaro, adj. & s. m. barbarian.

barbero, s. m. barber.

barbudo, adj. bearded.

barca, s. f. (small) boat.

barcaza, s. f. barge; launch.

barco, s. m. boat, ship; ~ de vapor steamship; ~ de vela sailing-vessel.

barómetro, s. m. barometer.

barón, s. m. baron.

baronesa, s. f. baroness.

barquero, s. m. boatman.

barra, s. f. bar, rod; ~*de labios* lipstick.

barraca, s. f. hut, peasant-cottage.

barrena, s. f. borer, gimlet.

barrer, v. a. sweep.

barrera, s. f. barrier, gate.

barrica, s. f. tun.

barriga, s. f. belly, paunch.

barril, s. m. barrel, cask.

barrilero, s. m. cooper.

barrio, s. m. quarter, district.

barro, s. m. mud; clay.

barroco, adj. & s. m. baroque.

bártulos, s. m. pl. bag and baggage.

basa, s. f. base of a column.

basar, v. a. & n. base.

báscula, s. f. platform-balance.

base, s. f. base; basis; *punto de* ~ starting-point; *a* ~ *de* on the basis of.

básico, adj. basic; *inglés* ~ Basic-English.

¡basta! enough! stop!

bastante, adj. & adv. enough, sufficient; rather.

bastar, v. n. be enough.

bastardilla, s. f. italics.

bastidores, s. m. pl. scenes; *entre* ~ behind the scenes, backstage.

bastión, s. m. bastion.

bastón, s. m. cane, walking stick.

basura, s. f. garbage, refuse.

bata, s. f. robe, bathrobe; house coat.

batalla, s. f. battle.

batata, s. f. sweet potato.

batel, s. m. boat.

batería, s. f. battery; ~ *de cocina* kitchen utensils.

batida, s. f. battue; raid.

batir, v. a. beat; defeat; v. n. ~*se* fight (a duel).

batuta, s. f. baton.

baúl, s. m. trunk.

bautismo, s. m. baptism.

bautizar, v. a. baptize.

baya, s. f. berry.

baza, s. f. trick (cards).

bazar, s. m. bazaar.

beatitud, s. f. happiness, bliss.

beato, adj. pious, religious.

bebé, s. m. baby.

bebedor, s. m. drinker, drunkard.

beber, v. a. drink.

bebida, s. f. drink, beverage.

beca, s. f. scholarship.

becerro, s. m. calf; calf-skin.

beldad, s. f. beauty.

belga, adj. & s. m., f. Belgian.

beligerante, adj. & s. m. belligerent.

belleza, s. f. beauty.

bello, adj. beautiful; *el* ~ *sexo* the fair sex; *las bellas letras* polite letters; *las bellas artes* the fine arts.

bencina, s. f. benzine; petrol.

bendecir, v. a. bless; *¡que Dios le bendiga!* God bless you!

bendición, s. f. blessing.

bendito, adj. blessed, holy.

beneficencia, s. f. charity.

beneficio, s. m. favour; profit.

benéfico, adj. beneficent.

benemérito, adj. meritorious.

benevolencia, s. f. kindness, good will.

benévolo, adj. benevolent.

benigno, adj. good, kind.

bermejo, adj. bright red, vermilion.

berza, s. f. cabbage.

besar, v. a. kiss.

beso, s. m. kiss.

bestia, s. f. beast; blockhead.

bestial, adj. bestial, brutal.

Biblia, s. f. Bible.

biblioteca, s. f. library.

bibliotecario, s. m. librarian.

bicicleta, s. f. bicycle; *ir en ~* ride a bicycle.

bicho, s. m. vermin; *~ raro* funny person.

bidón, s. m. can, container.

bien, adv. well; very; *muy~* very well; *está ~* all right; *no~* scarcely; *si ~* although; *ahora ~* now then; *— s. m.* good; welfare; benefit; *~es* property, estate.

bienal, adj. biennial.

bienestar, s. m. well-being, comfort.

bienvenida, s. f. safe arrival; *dar la ~* welcome.

bienvenido, adj. welcome.

biftec, s. m. beefsteak.

bigote, s. m. moustache.

bilis, s. f. bile.

billar, s. m. billiards, pool.

billete, s. m. ticket; *~ de andén* platform ticket; *~ de banco* banknote; *~ de ida y vuelta* return ticket; *~ de correspondencia* transfer ticket.

billón, s. m. a million millions.

bimestral, adj. bimensal.

biografía, s. f. biography.

biología, s. f. biology.

biombo, s. m. screen.

bis adv. once more; *— int.* encore!

bisemanal, adj. biweekly.

bisonte, s. m. bison.

bistec, s. m. beefsteak.

bizarro, adj. courageous; noble-minded.

bizcocho, s. m. (ship's) biscuit, sponge-cake.

blanco, adj. white; *en ~* blank; *— s. m.* white person; target; *hacer ~* hit the mark; *tirar al ~* shoot at the target.

biando, adj. soft, tender.

blanquear, v. a. bleach; whitewash.

blasón, s. m. (coat of) arms; glory, fame.

blindado, adj. armoured, iron-clad.

blindaje, s. m. armourplating.

blindar, v. a. armour.

bloque, s. m. block, piece.

bloquear, v. a. block, brake.

biusa, s. f. blouse.

bobina, s. f. spool, reel.

bobo, adj. foolish.

boca, s. f. mouth; entrance; *~ de riego* hydrant, fire-plug.

bocacalle, s. f. streetcrossing, turning.

bocadillo, s. m. sandwich.

bocallave, s. f. keyhole.

bocina, s. f. horn.

bocha, s. f. skittle-ball; *~s* ninepin, skittles.

bochorno, s. m. sultry weather; embarrassment.

bochornoso, adj. sultry;

embarrassing; shameful.

boda, *s. f.* wedding.

bodega, *s. f.* (wine) cellar; (ship's) hold.

bofetada, *s. f.* slap.

boina, *s. f.* beret.

bola, *s. f.* ball; round body or mass; shoe-polish; false report, hoax.

bolero¹, *s. m.* swindler; liar.

bolero², *s. m.* bolerodancer.

boletín, *s. m.* slip (of paper); ~ *meteorológico* weather report; ~ *oficial* official gazette; ~ *de equipaje* luggage-ticket.

bolsa, *s. f.* purse; bag; stock exchange.

bolsillo, *s. m.* pocket.

bolso, *s. m.* (woman's) handbag.

bollo, *s. m.* (French) roll.

bomba¹, *s. f.* pump; ~ *de incendios* fire engine.

bomba², *s. f.* bomb; *a prueba de* ~ shellproof.

bombardear, *v. a.* bombard, shell.

bombero, *s. m.* fireman.

bombilla, *s. f.* (incandescent) bulb.

bombón, *s. m.* bonbon, sweet.

bonachón, *adj.* good-natured.

bondad, *s. f.* kindness, goodness; *tenga la* ~ please.

bondadoso, *adj.* kind.

bonificación, *s. f.* compensation; amelioration.

bonito, *adj.* pretty.

bono, *s. m.* credit note.

boquilla, *s. f.* cigarette holder.

bordado, *s. m.* embroidery.

borde, *s. m.* edge, border.

bordo, *s. m.* (ship)board; *a* ~ aboard.

boreal, *adj.* northerly; *aurora* ~ northern lights.

borla, *s. f.* tassel; powder-puff.

borracho, *adj.* drunk; — *s. m.* drunkard.

borrador, *s. m.* (rough) sketch.

borrar, *v. a.* rub out, erase.

borrasca, *s. f.* storm; ~ *de nieve* snow-storm.

bosque, *s. m.* forest, woods.

bostezar, *v. n.* yawn.

bota, *s. f.* boot; wine bag.

botánica, *s. f.* botany.

botánico, *adj.* botanic(al).

bote, *s. m.* boat; tin, box; stab; jump.

botella, *s. f.* bottle.

botica, *s. f.* pharmacy.

boticario, *s. m.* chemist.

botín, *s. m.* lace-shoe; booty, prey.

botiquín, *s. m.* portable medicine-case.

botón, *s. m.* button; bud.

botones, *s. m.* (hotel) page-boy.

bóveda, *s. f.* vault.

boxear, *v. n.* box.

boxeo, *s.m.* boxing-match.

boya, *s. f.* buoy.

brasero, *s. m.* brazier, fire-pan.

brasileño, *adj. &. s. m.* Brasilian.

bravo, *adj.* fierce, wild; angry, mad; courageous; *¡*~*!* Bravo!

brazalete, *s. m.* bracelet.

brazo, *s. m.* arm (of body); foreleg; branch, bough; manpower; might, strength; force.

brea, *s. f.* pitch, tar.

breve, *adj.* brief, short; en ~ in a little while, shortly.

bribón, *s. m.* rascal, rogue.

brillante, *adj.* shiny, bright; – *s.m.* diamond.

brillar, *v. n.* shine.

brillo, *s. m.* shine, gloss.

brindar, *v. n.* drink to a person's health.

brindis, *s. m.* toast.

brío, *s. m.* vigour, energy.

brisa, *s. f.* breeze.

brocha, *s. f.* paint-brush, shaving-brush.

broche, *s. m.* hook; brooch.

broma, *s. f.* joke, jest.

bromear, *v. n.* joke.

bromista, *s. m.* joker, wag.

bronquitis, *s. f.* bronchitis.

brotar, *v. n.* bud, sprout.

brote, *s. m.* bud, sprout.

bruja, *s. f.* witch.

brújula, *s. f.* (mariner's) compass.

brumoso, *adj.* foggy.

brusco, *adj.* abrupt, rough.

brutalidad, *s. f.* brutality.

bruto, *adj.* brutish; stupid.

bucle, *s. m.* curl, ringlet.

budín, *s. m.* pudding.

bueno, *adj.* good; *no estoy muy* ~ I'm not feeling very well; ¡~! all right!; ~s días good morning; *por las buenas* willingly.

buey, *s. m.* ox, bullock.

bufanda, *s. f.* muffler, scarf.

bufón, *adj.* foolish; – *s. m.* court-fool.

buho, *s. m.* owl.

buitre, *s. m.* vulture.

bujía, *s. f.* candle; sparking-plug.

bulto, *s. m.* bundle; *sacar el* ~ duck out.

bulla, *s. f.* noise, racket.

buque, *s. m.* ship, steamer; ~ *de guerra* man-of-war; ~ *de vela* sailing-vessel.

burgués, *s. m.* bourgeois; citizen.

burla, *s. f.* mockery, jest; *por* ~ in jest, for fun.

burlador, *s. m.* rogue.

burlesco, *adj.* burlesque.

burocracia, *s. f.* red tape.

burro, *s. m.* donkey, ass; jackass, dope.

busca, *s. f.* search; *en* ~ *de* in search of.

buscar, *v. a.* look for, seek.

busto, *s. m.* bust (body).

butaca, *s. f.* armchair; orchestra stall seat.

buzo, *s. m.* diver.

buzón, *s. m.* letter-box.

C

¡ca!, *int.* oh no! no indeed.

cabal, *adj.* complete.

cábala, *s. f.* cabal, intrigue.

caballa, *s. f.* mackerel.

caballeresco, *adj.* chivalrous.

caballería, *s. f.* cavalry; saddle-horse.

caballeriza, *s. f.* stable.

caballero, *s. m.* knight; nobleman; gentleman; ¡~! sir!

caballo, *s. m.* horse; (chess) knight; *a ~* on horseback.

cabaña, *s. f.* cabin, hut.

cabaret, *s. m.* cabaret, night-club.

cabecear, *v. n.*, shake (head); doze off; pitch (boat).

cabecera, *s. f.* head (of a bed, table); seat of honour; *médico de ~* family doctor.

cabello, *s. m.* hair (of the head).

caber, *v. n.* fit, be contained in; go through; *no cabe duda* there is no doubt.

cabeza, *s. f.* head; mind, brains; *s. m.* chief, leader, head.

cabezudo, *adj.* stubborn, obstinate.

cabildo, *s. m.* municipal council.

cable, *s. m.* cable; cablegram.

cabo, *s. m.* end; cape; corporal; *al ~* at the end; *al ~ de* after; *de ~ a rabo* from beginning to end; *dar ~ a* end, put an end to; *llevar a ~* carry out.

cabotaje, *s. m.* coasting.

cabra, *s. f.* goat.

cabrilla, *s. f.* kid (glove).

cacahuete, *s. m.* peanut.

cacao, *s. m.* cacao tree, cocoa bean.

cacería, *s. f.* hunting.

cacerola, *s. f.* casserole.

cacharro, *s. m.* old rickety vehicle.

cachear, *v. a.* search sy.

cada, *adj.* every, each; *~ día* every day; *~ cual*, *~ uno* every one;

~ vez que whenever.

cadáver, *s. m.* corpse.

cadena, *s. f.* chain; range (of mountains).

cadena-oruga, *s. f.* caterpillar tread.

cadera, *s. f.* hip.

cadete, *s. m.* cadet.

caer, *v. n.* fall; *~ enfermo* fall ill; *~ en la cuenta* realize, notice, think of; *dejar ~* drop.

café, *s. m.* coffee; café.

cafetera, *s. f.* coffeepot.

caída, *s. f.* fall, drop; collapse; *a la ~ del sol* at sunset.

caja, *s. f.* box, case; cash desk; *~ de ahorros* savingsbank; *~ de caudales* safe; *~ registradora* cash register.

cajero, *s. m.* cashier.

cajón, *s. m.* box; drawer.

cajetilla, *s. f.* pack of cigarettes.

cal, *s. f.* lime.

calabaza, *s. f.* pumpkin; *dar ~s* plough (at an examination); refuse, reject (a declaration of love).

calamar, *s. m.* cuttlefish, squid.

calambre, *s. m.* cramp.

calamidad, *s. f.* calamity disaster, misfortune.

calamitoso, *adj.* disastrous.

calar, *v. a. & n.* pierce, penetrate; *~se* get drenched.

calavera, *s. f.* skull; madcap.

calcañar, *s. m.* heel.

calcetín, s. m. sock.

calculación, s. f. calculation.

calculadora, s. f. calculating machine.

calcular, v. a. calculate, figure out.

cálculo, s. m. calculation.

calda, s. f. heating.

caldear, v. a. heat.

caldera, s. f. kettle, boiler.

caldo, s. m. broth, beef-tea.

calefacción, s. f. heating (system).

calendario, s. m. calendar.

calentador, s. m. boiler.

calentar, v. a. & n. heat, warm; ~se get warm.

calentura, s. f. fever.

calidad, s. f. quality.

cálido, adj. warm, hot.

caliente, adj. hot; ardent.

calificable, adj. qualifiable.

calificación, s. f. qualification.

calificar, v. a. qualify.

cáliz, s. m. cup.

calma, s. f. calm, quiet.

calmante, adj. & s. m. anodyne, analgesic, sedative.

calmar, v. a. calm, soothe; v. n. ~se calm down.

calor, s. m. heat; hace ~ it's warm; tengo ~ I'm warm.

calumnia, s. f. slander.

calumniar, v. a. slander.

calumnioso, adj. slanderous.

caluroso, adj. warm, hot.

calva, s. f. bald head; baldness.

calvo, adj. bald.

calzada, s. f. paved highway.

calzado, s. m. footwear.

calzador, s. m. shoe-horn.

calzar, v. a. put on or wear (shoes).

calzones, s. m. pl. breeches; ~ de baño bathing-drawers.

calzoncillos, s. m. pl. drawers, shorts.

callado, adj. silent.

callar, v. a. conceal; v. n. keep quiet; ~se shut up, stop talking.

calle, s. f. street: echar a la ~ throw out, fire.

callejón, s. m. alley, lane.

callo, s. m. corn (on the foot).

cama, s. f. bed; guardar ~ be confined to bed.

cámara, s. f. camera; ~ de comercio chamber of commerce.

camarada, s. m., f. comrade; pal.

camarera, s. f. (chamber)maid; waitress.

camarero, s. m. waiter; valet, steward.

camarote, s. m. cabin, stateroom.

cambiar, v. a. change.

cambio, s. m. change; small change, coins; ~ del dia rate of the day; a ~ de in exchange for.

cambista, s. m. money changer.

camello, s. m. camel.

camilla, s. f. stretcher, litter.

caminador, s. m. walker.

caminar, v. n. walk.

caminata, s. f. long walk, hike.

camino, s. m. road, way; method; *ponerse en* ~ set out.

camión, s. m. (motor) lorry.

camioneta, s. f. delivery-van.

camisa, s. f. shirt.

camisería, s. f. gentlemen's outfitting.

camiseta, s. c. under-vest.

camisón, s. m. night-dress.

campamento, s. m. camp.

campana, s. f. bell; ~ *de chimenea* chimney-hood.

campanada, s. f. stroke of a bell *or* clock.

campanario, s. m. bell-tower, belfry.

campanilla, s. f. small bell, hand-bell.

campaña, s. f. campaign.

campeón, s. m. champion.

campeonato, s. m. championship.

campesino, s. m. peasant.

campestre, adj. rural.

campo, s. m. country; field; *en el* ~ in the country.

caña, s. f. leg (of a boot); reed, cane; walking stick; ~ *de azúcar* sugar-cane; ~ *de pescar* fishing-rod; ~ *de la pierna* shin-bone.

canal, s. m. canal; strait, channel.

canalizar, v. a. canalize; sewer.

canalla, s. f. mob; scamp.

canalón, s. m. eaves.

canapé, s. m. sofa.

canario, s. m. canary; /~/ the deuce!

canasta, s. f. wide basket.

cañaveral, s. m. reeds; sugar-cane plantation.

cancelar, v. a. cancel.

cáncer, s. m. cancer.

cancha, s. f. sports ground.

canciller, s. m. chancellor.

canción, s. f. song.

candado, s padlock.

candela, s. f. candle.

candelero, s. m. candle-stick.

candidato, s. m. candidate, applicant.

canela, s. f. cinnamon.

cañería, s. f. water-pipe, pipeline.

cangrejo, s. m. crab (snelifish).

canilla, s. f. shin-bone; tap.

canjear, v. a. exchange.

canoa, s. f. canoe.

canónigo, s. m. canon.

canoso, adj. grey-haired.

cansado, adj. tired; tiresome, boring.

cansancio, s. m. tiredness, fatigue.

cansar, v. a. tire; v. n. ~*se* get tired.

cantante, s. m., f. singer.

cantar, v. a. sing.

cántara, s. f. jug.

cantatriz, s. f. singer.

cántico, s. m. choral, sacred song.

cantidad, s. f. amount, quantity.

cantimplora, s. f. canteen, water-bottle.

cantina, s. f. canteen; wine-cellar.

canto[1], s. m. singing, song.

canto[2], s. m. edge.

cantor[1], adj. singing; *ave* ~*a* singing bird.

cantor[2], s. m. singer.

canturrear, v. a. & n. hum (a tune).

cañón, *s. m.* barrel (of a gun); cannon, gun; canyon, gorge.

cañonazo, *s. m.* cannon-shot.

caoba, *s. f.* mahogany.

caos, *s. m.* chaos.

caótico, *adj.* chaotic.

capa, *s. f.* cape (clothing); coat (of paint); (social) class, rank.

capacidad, *s. f.* capacity; capability.

capataz, *s. m.* foreman.

capaz, *adj.* capable; able, competent; large.

capilla, *s. f.* chapel; hood.

capital, *adj.* capital· *pena* ~ capital punishment; — *s. m.* capital (money) *s. f.* capital (city).

capitán, *s. m.* captain.

capó, *s. m.* (engine) bonnet.

capote, *s. m.* cloak, over-coat.

capricho, *s. m.* whim, fancy.

caprichoso, *adj.* capricious.

captar, *v. a.* get, pick up (broadcasting station).

captura, *s. f.* capture.

capturar, *v. a.* capture.

cara, *s. f.* face.

carabina, *s. f.* carabine.

caracol, *s. m.* snail; *escalera (s. f.) de* ~ winding staircase.

carácter, *s. m.* character; firmness.

característica, *s. f.* characteristic.

caracterizar, *v. a.* characterize; act, play (a part).

¡caramba! *int.* gosh! heavens!

caramelo, *s. m.* candy, sweet.

carbón, *s. m.* coal.

carbonera, *s. f.* coal-scuttle.

carburador, *s. m.* carburetter.

carcajada, *s. f.* burst of laughter, loud laughter.

cárcel, *s. f.* jail, prison.

carcelero, *s. m.* jailer.

carda, *s. f.* teasel.

cardenal¹, *s. m.* cardinal.

cardenal², *s. m.* bruise, contusion.

cardinal, *adj.* cardinal; *los puntos* ~*es* the cardinal points.

cardiograma, *s. m.* cardiogram.

cardo, *s. m.* thistle.

carecer *de,* *v. n.* lack, not to have.

carestía, *s. f.* famine, starvation; rise in prices.

careta, *s. f.* mask; ~ *antigas* gas-mask.

carga, *s. f.* load, freight.

cargamento, *s. m.* ship-load; cargo, freight.

cargar, *v. a.* load; charge.

cargo, *s. m.* load; burden; debit; post, charge; *hacerse* ~ *de* assume.

caricatura, *s. f.* caricature.

caricia, *s. f.* caress.

caridad, *s. f.* charity.

caries, *s. f.* (dental) caries.

cariño, *s. m.* affection, love.

cariñoso, *adj.* affectionate.

carlinga, *s. f.* cockpit.

carnaval, *s. m.* carnival.

carne, *s. f.* meat; ~ *de vaca* beef.

carnero, *s. m.* ram; mutton.

carnicería, *s. f.* butcher's shop.

carnicero, *s. m.* butcher.

caro, *adj.* dear; expensive.

carpa, *s. f.* carp.

carpeta *s. f.* letter-file, folder; writing-case; table-cover.

carpintero, *s. m.* carpenter.

carrera, *s. f.* race; sprint; highway; career.

carreta, *s. f.* cart.

carretera, *s. f.* road, highway.

carro, *s. m.* cart.

carroza, *s. f.* coach.

carruaje, *s. m.* carriage (vehicle).

carta, *s. f.* letter; (play) card; ~ *blanca* full discretionary power; ~ *certificada* registered letter; *jugar a las* ~s play cards.

cartel, *s. m.* placard, bill, poster; ~ *de teatro* play-bill.

cartera, *s. f.* letter-case, wallet; document-case, brief-case.

cartero, *s. m.* postman.

cartón, *s. m.* cardboard.

cartucho, *s. m.* cartridge.

casa, *s. f.* house; home; *voy a* ~ I go home; *en* ~ at home; ~ *de banco* banking-house; ~ *de comercio* commercial firm; ~ *de empeños* pawnshop; ~ *de huéspedes* boarding house; ~ *de socorro* emergency hospital.

casado, *adj.* married.

casamiento, *s. m.* wedding, marriage.

casar, *v. a.* marry; *v. n.* ~se get married; ~se *con* marry sy.

cascabel, *s. m.* little bell.

cascada, *s. f.* cascade, waterfall.

cascar, *v. a.* crack.

cáscara, *s. f.* rind, peel; shell (of nuts, eggs).

casco, *s. m.* helmet; hull (of ship); fragment; ~ *de caballo* horse's hoof.

caserío, *s. m.* small village, settlement.

casero, *adj.* home-made; — *s. m.* landlord.

casi, *adv.* almost, nearly.

casilla, *s. f.* hut; pigeon-hole; square.

caso, *s. m.* case; occurrence, event; *en tal* ~ in such a case; *en todo* ~ at all events, anyway; *hacer* ~ *a* pay attention to, heed.

¡**cáspita**! *int.* good gracious! the deuce!

castaña, *s. f.* chestnut.

castañeta, *s. f.* castanet.

castaño, *adj.* brown; — *s. m.* chestnut-tree.

castillo, *s. m.* castle.

castizo, *adj.* correct, pure; genuine, real.

casto, *adj.* chaste; pure.

casual, *adj.* accidental.

casualidad, *s. f.* coincidence; *por* ~ by chance.

catálogo, *s. m.* catalogue, list.

catarro, *s. m.* cold, catarrh.

catástrofe, *s. f.* catastrophe.

cátedra, *s. f.* lecturing desk.

catedral, *s. f.* cathedral.

catedrático, *s. m.* professor.

categoría, *s. f.* category, class; rank; *de* ~ of importance.

católico, *adj. & s. m.* Catholic.

catorce, *adj. & s. m.* fourteen.

catre, *s. m.* campbed.

caución, *s. f.* guarantee,

bail.

caucho, *s. m.* rubber
(material).

caudal, *s. m.* fortune,
wealth, means; vol-
ume (of water).

caudillo, *s. m.* leader,
chief.

causa, *s. f.* cause; case,
trial, lawsuit; *a ~ de*
because of.

causar, *v. a.* cause,
occasion.

cautela, *s. f.* (pre)cau-
tion; reserve.

cautivar, *v. a.* capture.

cauto, *adj.* cautious,
careful.

cavar, *v. a.* dig.

caverna, *s. f.* cavern, cave.

cavial, caviar, *s. m.*
caviar.

caza, *s. f.* hunt, hunting;
game; *andar a ~ de*
go in search of.

cazador, *s. m.* hunter.

cazar, *v. a. & n.* hunt.

cebada, *s. f.* barley.

cebar, *v. a.* feed; nourish.

cebo, *s. m.* bait.

cebolla, *s. f.* onion; bulb.

ceder, *v. a.* transfer, turn
over, cede; *v. n.* yield,
give in.

cédula, *s. f.; ~ personal*
identity card.

ceja, *s f.* eyebrow.

celda, *s. f.* cell.

celebración, *s. f.* celebration.

celebrar, *v. a.* celebrate,
commemorate; praise,
applaud, approve; be
glad, rejoice; hold (a
session).

célebre, *adj.* famous.

celebridad, *s. f.* celeb-
rity.

celeridad, *s. f.* swiftness,
speed.

celo, *s. m.* zeal, enthusi-

asm; *~s pl.* jealousy;
tener ~s be jealous.

celosía, *s. f.* Venetian
blind, jealousy.

celoso, *adj.* jealous; zealous.

celulosa, *s. f.* cellulose.

cementerio, *s. m.* cemetery, graveyard.

cemento, *s. m.* cement,
concrete; *~ armado*
ferro-concrete.

cena, *s. f.* dinner, supper.

cenar, *v. n.* dine, eat; *v. a.*
have for supper.

cenicero, *s. m.* ash-tray.

ceniza, *s. f.* ashes, cinders.

censura, *s. f.* censorship;
reproach, criticism.

censurar, *v. a.* blame,
criticize.

centavo, *s. m.* a hundredth; centavo (money
of South America).

centella, *s. f.* spark.

centenar, *s. m.* a hundred.

centenario, *adj. & s. m.*
centenary.

centeno, *s. m.* rye.

centésimo, *adj.* hundredth.

centímetro, *s. m.* centi-
metre.

céntimo, *s. m.* cent,
céntimo (Spanish mon-
ey).

centinela, *s. m.* sentry,
guard; *estar de ~* be on
guard.

central, *adj. & s. f.* central;
~ eléctrica electric
power plant.

céntrico, *adj.* central.

centrifugador, *s. m.* sepa-
rator, centrifuge.

centro, *s. m.* centre; city.

cepillar, *v. a.* brush; plane,
make smooth.

cepillo, *s. m.* brush;
~ de cabeza hairbrush;
~ de carpintero car-

penter's plane; ~ de dientes toothbrush; ~ de ropa clothes brush.

cera, s. f. wax.

cerámica, s. f. ceramics.

cerca¹, s. f. fence.

cerca², adv. near; nearly, about, almost; por aquí ~ near here; — prep. ~ de near (in place).

cercanía, s. f. nearness, proximity.

cercano, adj. near, close.

cercar, v. a. surround, fence in.

cerciorarse, v. n.: ~ de make sure of sg.

cerdo, s. m. pig; pork.

cereal, adj. & s. m. cereal.

cerebro, s. m. brain(s).

ceremonia, s. f. ceremony.

ceremonioso, adj. formal, ceremonial.

cereza, s. f. cherry.

cerilla, s. f. match.

cero, s. m. zero; nought.

cerradura, s. f. lock.

cerrar, v. a. close, shut.

cerro, s. m. hill.

cerrojo, s. m. bolt, latch.

certero, adj. well-aimed.

certeza, s. f. assurance, certainty.

certificado, adj.; carta ~a registered letter; — s. m. certificate.

certificar, v. a. attest, certify; register (a letter).

cervecería, s. f. brewery; beer-saloon.

cerveza, s. f. beer, ale.

cesar, v. a. stop, cease; sin ~ without interruption.

cesión, s. f. cession.

césped, s. m. lawn, grass.

cesta, s. f. basket.

cesto, s. m. large basket.

ciática, s. f. sciatica.

cicatriz, s. f. scar.

cicatrizar, v. n. cicatrize, scar.

ciclismo, s. m. cycling.

ciclista, s. m., f. cyclist.

ciclón, s. m. cyclone.

ciego, adj. & s. m. blind (person); a ciegas in the dark, blindly.

cielo, s. m. sky; paradise, heaven; llovido del ~ out of a clear sky.

cien, adj. & s. m. one hundred; ~ mil a hundred thousand.

ciencia, s. f. science.

científico, adj. scientific.

ciento, adv & s. m. one hundred; por ~ per cent.

cierre, s. m. closing, closure; ~ metálico rolling shutter; ~ de cremallera zip fastener.

cierto, adj. sure, certain, true; — adv. certainly.

ciervo, s. m. deer.

cifra, s. f. figure, digit; code; en ~ in code.

cifrar, v. a. figure; code.

cigarrera, s. f. woman cigar maker; cigar-box.

cigarrillo, s. m. cigarette.

cigarro, s. m. cigar.

cigüeña, s. f. stork.

cilindro, s. m. cylinder.

cima, s. f. summit, peak.

cinco, adj. & s. m. five.

cincuenta, adj. & s. m. fifty.

cine, s. m. cinema, the pictures.

cínico, adj. cynic(al).

cinta, s. f. ribbon; ~ (cinematográfica) film, moving picture; ~ magnetofónica recording tape.

cintura, s. f. waist.

cinturón, s. m. belt.

circo, s. m. circus.

circuito, s. m. (electric)

circuit; *corto* ~ short circuit.

circulación, *s. f.* circulation; traffic.

circular[1], *v. n.* move about, get around, circulate.

circular[2], *adj.* circular; — *s. f.* circular (letter).

círculo, *s. m.* circle; club.

ciruela, *s. f.* plum.

cirugía, *s. f.* surgery.

cirujano, *s. m.* surgeon.

cisne, *s. m.* swan.

cisterna, *s. f.* cistern.

cita, *s. f.* appointment, date; quotation.

citación, *s. f.* summons; citation; quotation.

ciudad, *s. f.* city; town.

ciudadanía, *s. f.* citizenship.

ciudadano, *s. m.*; **-a,** *s. f.* citizen; towns(wo)man.

cívico, *adj.* civic.

civil, *adj.* civil; *guardia* ~ constabulary; *guerra* ~ civil war; *derechos* ~es civil rights.

civilización, *s. f.* civilization, culture.

civilizar, *v. a.* civilize.

clara, *s. f.* white of egg.

claramente, *adv.* clearly, openly, frankly.

clarear, *v. n.* dawn; grow light.

claridad, *s. f.* clearness, distinctness.

clarín, *s. m.* trumpet.

claro, *adj.* clear; plain; transparent; thin (hair); fair, cloudless (day); light (suit).

clase, *s. f.* class, kind, sort; classroom; *dar* ~ give a lesson, teach.

clásico, *adj.* classical; — *s. m.* classic.

clasificar, *v. a.* sort out, classify.

claustro, *s. m.* cloister.

clavar, *v. a.* nail; stick, pin.

clave, *s. f.* key (of a code); key (in music).

clavel, *s. m.* carnation, pink.

clavo, *s. m.* nail; clove; *dar en el* ~ hit the nail on the head.

clérigo, *s. m.* clergyman.

clero, *s. m.* clergy.

cliente, *s. m.* client, customer.

clientela, *s. f.* clientèle.

clima, *s. m.* climate.

clínica, *s. f.* clinic.

cloaca, *s. f.* sewer, sink.

clorosis, *s. f.* greensickness, chlorosis.

clorótico, *adj.* chlorotic.

club, *s. m.* club.

cobarde, *adj.* cowardly; — *s. m.*, *f.* coward.

cobardía, *s. f.* cowardice.

cobertizo, *s. m.* shed.

cobrador, *s. m.* collector (of bills, taxes); conductor (of bus, trolley).

cobrar, *v. a.* collect, receive; cash; *v. n.* charge.

cobre, *s. m.* copper.

cobro, *s. m.* collection (of money due).

cocer, *v. a. & n.* boil; bake.

cocina, *s. f.* kitchen; cuisine, cooking.

cocinar, *v. a. & n.* cook.

cocinera, *s. f.*; **cocinero,** *s. m.* cook.

coche, *s. m.* carriage, coach; car; ~-*cama* sleeping-car; ~-*comedor* dining-car.

cochero, *s. m.* coachman.

código, *s. m.* code (of laws).

codo, *s. m.* elbow.

cofre, *s. m.* trunk; chest.

coger, *v. a.* catch; pick, gather .

coincidencia, *s. f.* coincidence.

coincidir, *v. n.* coincide, agree.

cojín, *s. m.* pad, cushion.

cojo, *adj.* lame, limping.

col, *s. f.* cabbage.

cola[1], *s. f.* tail; train (of dress); line of people, queue; *hacer* ~ stand in line, queue.

cola[2], *s. f.* glue.

colaboración, *s. f.* collaboration, working together.

colaborador, *s. m.* collaborator, co-worker.

colaborar, *v. n.* collaborate, cooperate; contribute.

colación, *s. f.* snack; comparison.

colador, *s. m.* colander, strainer.

colar, *v. a.* strain.

colcha, *s. f.* bedspread.

colchón, *s. m.* mattress.

colección, *s. f.* collection (of things).

coleccionar, *v. a.* collect (stamps, coins).

colecta, *s. f.* collection (charity).

colectivo, *adj.* collective.

colega, *s. m.* fellow-worker, colleague.

colegio, *s. m.* school; association, college.

cólera[1], *s. f.* anger, rage, fury.

cólera[2], *s. f.* cholera.

colgadero, *s. m.* hook.

colgar, *v. a.* hang.

coliflor, *s. f.* cauliflower.

colina, *s. f.* hill.

colindante, *adj.* adjacent, contiguous.

colisión, *s. f.* collision.

colmena, *s. f.* bee-hive.

colmo, *s. f.* excess; *fig.* top.

colocación, *s. f.* arrangement; job, position.

colocar, *v. a.* put arrange; take on; ~' *dinero* invest (money); *v. n.* ~*se* take a job.

colonia, *s. f.* colony; settlement; *(agua de) Colonia* eau-de-Cologne.

color, *s. m.* colour; complexion; *de* ~ coloured.

colorar, *v. a.* colour.

colorido, *s. m.* colours, colouring.

columna, *s. f.* column.

columpio, *s. m.* swing.

comadre, *s. f.* godmother; midwife; old woman; gossip.

comadrear, *v. n.* gossip.

comandante, *s. m.* commander; major.

comandita, *s. f.* sociedad *(s. f.) en* ~ limited partnership.

comarca, *s. f.* tract of land, region.

combatir, *v. a.* combat, fight; attack; oppose.

combinar, *v. a.* combine, join, unite.

combustible, *s. m.* fuel.

comedia, *s. f.* comedy; play.

comediante, *s. m.* actor.

comedor, *s. m.* dining-room.

comentar *v. a. & n.* comment on.

comentario, *s. m.* remark, comment, commentary.

comenzar, *v. a. & n.* begin, commence.

comer, *v. a.* eat; dine. ~*se* eat up.

comercial, *adj.* commercial.

comerciante, *s. m.* merchant.

comerciar, v. n. trade, deal.

comercio, s. m. commerce, trade, business; store, shop.

comestible, adj. edible, good to eat; — ~s s. m. pl. eatables, victuals; tienda (s. f.) de ~s provision stores.

cometa, s. m. comet; kite.

cometer, v. a. commit.

cómico, adj. comic, funny, amusing; — s. m. actor.

comida, s. f. food; dinner.

comienzo, s. m. beginning; start.

comillas, s. f. pl. quotation mark, inverted comma.

comisaría, s. f. police-station.

comisario, s. m.; ~ de policía chief of police.

comisión, s. f. assignment; committee, delegation.

comité, s. m. board, committee.

comitiva, s. f. suite, retinue.

como, conj. & adv. how; as; since; like; if.

¿cómo? adv. & conj. how? why?

cómoda, s. f. chest of drawers.

comodidad, s. f. convenience, ease, comfort.

cómodo, adj. convenient, handy; comfortable.

compadecer, v. a. pity, sympathize with.

compadre, s. m. godfather, gossip.

compañero, s. m. companion, pal, schoolmate.

compañía, s. f. company; hacer ~ a keep company with sy.

comparable, adj. comparable.

comparación, s. f. comparison.

comparar, v. a. compare.

comparecer, v. n. appear (in answer to summons).

comparsa, s. f. suite; (theatre) extra.

compartimiento, s. m. compartment.

compartir, v. a. share.

compás, s. m. compass; rhythm, time; (music) bar.

compasión, s. f. compassion, pity, sympathy.

compasivo, adj. pitiful, compassionate.

compatriota, s. m., f. (fellow) countryman, fellow citizen.

compendiar, v. a. abridge.

compendio, s. m. extract, summary; compendium.

compensar, v. a. balance, compensate.

competencia, s. f. competition, rivalry.

competidor, s. m. competitor, rival.

competir, v. n. compete.

complacer, v. a. please, accommodate; v. n. ~se en take pleasure in sg.

completar, v. a. complete, finish.

completo, adj. complete; full; por ~ completely.

cómplice, s. m., f. accomplice.

componente, s. m. component (part).

componer, v. a. repair, fix; compose; v. n. ~se de be composed of, consist of.

comportar, v. a. tolerate;
v. n. ~se behave one-
self.

composición, s. f. com-
position.

compositor, s. m. com-
poser.

compota, s. f. stewed
fruit.

compotera, s. f. compote
dish.

compra, s. f. purchase,
buy; ir de ~s go shop-
ping.

comprador, s. m. pur-
chaser, buyer.

comprar, v. a. purchase,
buy.

comprender, v. a. under-
stand, comprehend; in-
clude, comprise.

comprimir, v. a. compress.

comprobar, v. a. verify,
confirm; check.

comprometer, v. a. risk;
expose, jeopardize, en-
danger; v. n. ~se get
involved; become en-
gaged.

compromiso, s. m. obliga-
tion, engagement; pre-
dicament, plight, fix.

computar, v. a. compute,
calculate.

común, adj. common,
usual, general; por lo ~
as a rule, in general.

comunicación, s. f. com-
munication.

comunicar, v. a. communi-
cate, transmit, issue;
v. n. ~se tell one
another.

con, prep. with; ~ tal que
provided that.

concebir, v. a. imagine.

conceder, v. a. give, grant.

concentrar, v. a. & n.
concentrate.

concepto, s. m. judge-
ment, opinion.

concertar, v. a. close,
settle; agree.

concesión, s. f. concession,
grant.

conciencia, s. f. con-
science; consciousness;
scruples; a ~ con-
scientiously; painstak-
ingly.

concienzudo, adj. con-
scientious.

concierto, s. m. concert;
agreement.

conciliar, v. a. conciliate,
reconcile; ~ el sueño
fall asleep; v. n. ~se
be reconciled with sy.

concilio, s. m. council.

conciudadano, s. m. fel-
low-citizen.

concluir, v. a. conclude,
end, close, finish.

concluyente, adj. con-
clusive.

concordar, v. a. & n.
concord.

concretar, v. a. express
concretely.

concreto, adj. definite,
concrete; en ~ con-
cretely.

concurrencia, s. f. con-
currence, participants,
public.

concurrente, adj. con-
current; — s. m. com-
petitor.

concurrido, adj. much
frequented, well-at-
tended.

concurrir, v. n. attend.

concurso, s. m. competi-
tion, contest.

concha, s. f. shell; prom-
pter's box.

condado, s. m. county.

conde, s. m. count (title).

condecoracón, s. f. decoration; order, medal.

condecorar, v. a. decorate

(with a medal).

condena, s. f. sentence, term of imprisonment, penalty.

condenar, v. a. sentence; declare guilty; condemn, blame.

condensar, v. a. condense.

condición, s. f. condition; character; quality, state; *condiciones* s. f. pl. terms; *a ~ de que* on condition that, provided that.

condiscípulo, s. m. schoolmate, fellow-student.

condolerse, v. n. condole.

condonar, v. a. condone.

conducir, v. a. lead; drive; take, accompany; v. n. *~se* act, behave.

conducta, s. f. behaviour; conduct.

conducto, s. m. pipe, duct.

conductor, s. m. guard; conductor; driver.

conectar, v. a. connect.

conejo, s. m. rabbit.

conexión, s. f. connection.

confección, s. f. confection.

confeccionar, v. a. make, manufacture.

conferencia, s. f. conference, meeting; public lecture; (telephone) trunk call.

conferenciar, v. n. confer, consult together.

confesar, v. a. admit, confess.

confesión, s. f. confession, acknowledgment.

confiado, adj. trusting, unsuspecting.

confianza, s. f. confidence, faith; *de ~* informal, intimate; *en ~* confidentially; in confidence; *tener ~ con* be on intimate terms with; *tener ~ en* trust sy.

confiar, v. a. & n. entrust to; *~ en* rely on, trust in, count on.

confidencial, adj. confidential.

confidente, s. m. intimate friend.

confirmar, v. a. confirm, corroborate.

confitería, s. f. confectioner's shop.

confitero, s. m. confectioner.

confitura, s. f. preserves.

conflicto, s. m. conflict, struggle.

confluencia, s. f. confluence.

conformar, v. a. conform; v. n. *~se con* content oneself with.

conforme, adj. conformable; *estar ~ con* be resigned to, be in agreement with; — *conj.* as; — *prep.* *~ a* in accordance with;¡*~*! agreed!

confortante, s. m. restorative, tonic.

confundir, v. a. confound, mix up; v. n. *~se* make a mistake.

confusión, s. f. confusion, disorder; embarrassment.

confuso, adj. confusing, not clear; confused, mixed up; hazy, vague.

confutar, v. a. confute.

congelación, s. f. congelation, freezing.

congelarse, v. n. congeal.

congestionado, adj. congested (traffic).

congraciarse con, v. n. get into one's good graces.

congratulación, *s. f.* congratulation, good wishes.

congratular, *v. a.* congratulate.

congregar, *v. a.* congregate, assemble; *v. n.* ~se gather, assemble.

congreso, *s. m.* congress, convention; *Congreso de los Diputados* House of Representatives.

cónico, *adj.* cone-shaped.

conjeturar, *v. a.* conjecture.

conjunto, *adj.* joint, unified; — *s. m.* whole, entirety; *en* ~ as a whole.

conmemoración, *s. f.* commemoration.

conmemorativo, *adj.* commemorative.

conmigo, *prep.* & *pron.* with me.

conmover, *v. a* move, shock.

conmutador, *s. m.* switch.

conmutar, *v. a.* switch over; commute.

cono, *s. m.* cone.

conocer, *v. a.* know, understand; be acquainted with; *v. n.* ~se meet, become acquainted; know each other.

conocido, *adj.* prominent, well-known; — *s. m.* acquaintance.

conocimiento, *s. m.* knowledge, understanding; consciousness.

conque, *conj.* thus; well then.

conquista, *s. f.* conquest.

conquistador, *s. m.* conqueror; lady-killer.

conquistar, *v. a.* conquer, subdue; win.

consciente, *adj.* conscious.

consecuencia, *s. f.* consequence.

consecuente, *adj* consequential.

consecutivo, *adj.* consecutive.

conseguir, *v. a.* attain, obtain, get; succeed in.

consejero, *s. m.* councillor.

consejo, *s. m.* advice, counsel; council; ~ *de ministros* Cabinet Meeting.

consentir, *v. a.* allow, permit, tolerate; spoil, coddle.

conserje, *s. m.* porter, janitor; care-taker.

conserva, *s. f.* preserves.

conservador, *s. m.* conservative.

conservar, *v. a.* conserve, preserve, keep; *v. n.* ~se be well preserved.

consideración, *s. f.* consideration, account; respect; *tomar en* ~ take into consideration.

considerar, *v. a.* consider, think over; esteem highly.

consigna, *s. f.* password; slogan.

consignar, *v. a.* consign.

consigo, *prep.* & *pron.* with himself, (herself, yourself, themselves); *hablar* ~ *mismo* talk to himself.

consiguiente, *adj.* consistent, logical; *por* ~ consequently, therefore.

consistir *en,* *v. n.* consist of.

consolación, *s. f.* comfort, consolation.

consolar, *v. a.* comfort, console.

consolidar, v. a. consolidate, strengthen.

consorcio, s. m. syndicate.

consorte, s. m., f. partner.

constancia, s. f. perseverance.

constante, adj. firm, faithful, constant.

constar, v. n. be evident, be clear, be certain; be recorded, be registered; ~ de consist of, be composed of.

constipado, s. m. cold (in the head); catarrh.

constiparse, v. n. catch cold.

constitución, s. f. constitution.

constituir, v. a. constitute; establish, organize.

construcción, s. f. construction; structure, building.

constructor, s. m. builder.

construir, v. a. build, construct.

consuelo, s. m. consolation, comfort.

cónsul, s. m. consul.

consulado, s. m. consulate.

consulta, s. f. consultation, conference; office hours.

consultar, v. a. consult.

consumado, adj. complete, perfect, accomplished.

consumar, v. a. carry out, commit.

consumidor, s. m. consumer.

consumir, v. a. consume, use up.

consumo, s. m. consumption.

contabilidad, s. f. bookkeeping, accounting.

contable, s. m. bookkeeper, accountant.

contacto, s. m. contact, touch; ignition.

contado; al ~ (for) cash.

contador, s. m. accountant, book-keeper; meter (for gas, water etc.).

contaduría, s. f. bookkeeping department; en ~ booking in advance.

contagiar, v. a. infect.

contagio, s. m. contagion.

contagioso, adj. contagious.

contante, adj. cash (money).

contar, v. a. count; relate, tell; ~ con depend upon, count on.

contemporáneo, adj. & s. m. contemporary.

contener, v. n. contain; check; control; v. n; ~se contain oneself.

contenido, s. m. contents.

contentar, v. a. satisfy, please; v. n. ~se con be satisfied with.

contento, adj. happy, glad.

contestación, s. f. reply, answer.

contestar, v. a. & n. reply, answer.

contigo, prep. & pron. with you.

contiguo, adj. adjacent, next.

continental, adj. continental.

continente, s. m. continent.

continuación, s. f. continuation; sequence; a ~ immediately, right away.

continuar, v. a. & n. continue, carry on; go on, keep on; remain.

continuo, *adj.* continuous, uninterrupted.

contorno, *s. m.* contour, outline; neighbourhood.

contra, *prep.* against; *llevar la* ~ oppose.

contrabando, *s. m.* contraband, smuggling.

contraer, *v. a.* contract (illness); incur, run into (debt); ~ *matrimonio* marry, get married.

contrariar, *v. a.* annoy.

contrariedad, *s. f.* disappointment.

contrario, *adj.* contrary; *al* ~, *por el* ~ on the contrary; *de lo* ~ otherwise, if not; *todo lo* ~ just the opposite.

contrasentido, *s. m.* nonsense.

contraseña, *s. f.* countersign; check (for readmittance).

contrastar, *v. n.* contrast, be opposed; ~ *bien* harmonize; ~ *mal* clash.

contraste, *s. m.* contrast.

contratar, *v. a.* engage, hire.

contrato, *s. m.* contract.

contravención, *s. f.* transgression, infringement.

contribución, *s. f.* contribution; tax.

contribuir, *v. n.* contribute.

contribuyente, *s. m.* taxpayer.

control, *s. m.* control.

controlar, *v. a.* control.

contusión, *s. f.* contusion.

convalecer, *v. n.* convalesce.

convencer, *v. a.* convince.

convención, *s. f.* agreement, arrangement.

convencional, *adj.* conventional.

conveniencia, *s. f.* decency; self-interest, advantage.

conveniente, *adj.* convenient, suitable; desirable, advisable.

convenir, *v. n.* agree; be advisable; suit.

convento, *s. m.* convent.

conversación, *s. f.* conversation, talk.

conversar, *v. n.* converse, talk.

convertir, *v. a.* convert, turn.

convicción, *s. f.* conviction, belief.

convidado, *s. m.* invited guest.

convidar, *v. a.* invite.

convite, *s. m.* treat, invitation.

convocar, *v. a.* convoke, call.

cooperación, *s. f.* co-operation.

cooperar, *v. n.* co-operate.

copa, *s. f.* (stem)glass, goblet; drink; treetop; crown (of hat); hearts(of playing cards); *sombrero (s. m.) de* ~ tophat.

copia, *s. f.* copy.

copiar, *v. a.* copy, make a copy of.

copioso, *adj.* copious.

copla, *s. f.* popular song.

copo, *s. m.* flake (of snow).

coque, *s. m.* coke.

corazón, *s. m.* heart; core (of fruits); *de buen* ~ kind-hearted; *de (todo)* ~ heartily, sincerely.

corbata, *s. f.* necktie.

corcho, *s. m.* cork.

cordel, *s. m.* thin rope,

cord.

cordero, *s. m.* lamb.

cordial, *adj.* cordial, hearty; — *s. m.* cordial.

cordillera, *s. f.* mountain range.

cordón, *s. m.* cord, lace; cordon (of police).

corneja, *s. f.* crow.

corneta, *s. f.* bugle; cornet.

coro, *s. m.* chorus, choir.

corona, *s. f.* crown; wreath.

coronar, *v. a.* crown.

coronel, *s. m.* colonel.

corral, *s. m.* corral; *aves (s. f. pl.) de* ~ domestic fowls.

correa, *s. f.* strap, belt.

corrección, *s. f.* correction; blame, censure; *casa de* ~ penitentiary.

correcto, *adj.* correct, right; irreproachable.

corredor, *s. m.* runner, racer; corridor.

corregir, *v. a.* correct.

correo, *s. m.* mail; post-office; *echar al* ~ mail; *lista (s. f.) de* ~s general delivery.

correr, *v. n.* run, race; flow (river); *v. a.* move, push; draw (the curtain); go over, travel over.

correspondencia, *s. f.* correspondence; mail.

corresponder, *v. a.* return; *v. n.* correspond, match; concern, be up to; ~*se* carry on correspondence.

corresponsal, *s. m.* correspondent.

corrida *(s. f.) de toros* bullfight.

corriente, *adj.* current, common; ordinary; running, flowing (water); instant, present (month, year); — *s. f.* current (of electricity, air, river); *al* ~ informed; *contra* ~ upstream, against the tide.

corromper *v. a.* corrupt.

corrupto, *adj.* corrupt.

cortaplumas, *s. m.* pocket-knife.

cortar, *v. a.* cut; cut short, interrupt; cut off; cut out.

cortauñas, *s. m.* nail-scissors.

corte¹, *s. m.* cut.

corte², *s. f.* court; *hacer la* ~ court sy; *las* ~s the Spanish parliament.

cortés, *adj.* polite, courteous.

cortesía, *s. f.* courtesy.

corteza, *s. f.* bark (of tree) crust (of bread).

cortina, *s. f.* curtain.

corto, *adj.* short; ~ *de vista* near-sighted.

corzo, *s. m.* roe, doe.

cosa, *s. f.* thing.

cosecha, *s. f.* crop, harvest.

cosechar, *v. a.* reap, harvest.

coser, *v. a. & n.* sew; *máquina (s. f.) de* ~ sewing-machine.

cosmético, *s. m.* cosmetics.

costa¹, *s. f.* expenses, cost; *a* ~ *de* at the expense of; *a poca* ~ with little effort; *a toda* ~ at any cost.

costa², *s. f.* coast.

costado, *s. m.* side, flank.

costar, *v. n.* cost.

coste, *s. m.* cost, price.

costilla, *s. f.* rib.

costo, *s. m.* cost, price.

costoso, *adj.* costly, expensive.

costumbre, *s. f.* custom; habit.

costura, *s. f.* sewing; seam.

costurera, *s. f.* seamstress.

cotidiano, *adj.* daily.

cráneo, *s. m.* skull.

creación, *s. f.* creation.

creador, *s. m.* creator.

crear, *v. a.* create.

crecer, *v. n.* increase, grow.

crédito, *s. m.* credit; *dar* ~ *a* believe.

creencia, *s. f.* belief.

creer, *v. a.* believe; think.

crema, *s. f.* cream (of milk); (cosmetic) cream.

cremallera, *s. f.* cog; zip-fastener.

crepúsculo, *s. m.* nightfall, dusk.

crespo, *adj.* curly.

cría, *s. f.* breeding; the young (of animals).

criada, *s. f.* maid, servant.

criado, *s. m.* man-servant.

criar, *v. a.* raise, bring up.

criatura, *s. f.* baby, infant.

crimen, *s. m.* crime.

criminal, *adj. & s. m.* criminal.

crisis, *s. f.* crisis.

cristal, *s. m.* crystal, glass; window-pane; lens.

cristianismo, *s. m.* Christianity.

cristiano, *adj. & s. m.* Christian.

criterio, *s. m.* criterion, judgment.

crítica, *s. f.* criticism.

criticar, *v. a.* criticize.

crítico, *adj.* critical; — *s. m.* critic.

cruce, *s. m.* crossing, crossroads.

crudo, *adj.* raw; crude.

cruel, *adj.* cruel.

cruz, *s. f.* cross.

cruzar, *v. a.* cross, go across.

cuaderno, *s. m.* exercise-book, notebook.

cuadra, *s. f.* stable.

cuadro, *s. m.* painting; scene; *a* ~s checked.

cual, *pron.* which; ~ *si* as if; *por lo* ~ for that reason; that's why.

¿cuál? *pron.* which? which one? what?

cualidad, *s. f.* quality.

cualquier(a), *pron.* any, whatever; anyone.

cuando, *conj.* when; if; ~ *más* at most; ~ *quiera* when you please; *de* ~ *en* ~ from time to time.

¿cuándo? *ad'.* when?

cuanto, *conj. & pron.* as much as, all that; ~ *antes* as soon as possible.

¿cuánto? *pron.* how much?; *¿*~s*?* how many?; *¡cuánto me alegro!* how glad I am!

cuarenta, *adj. & s. m.* forty.

cuaresma, *s. f.* Lent.

cuartel, *s. m.* barracks.

cuarto, *adj.* fourth; — *s. m.* quarter; room; *son las dos y* ~ it's a quarter past two; ~ *de baño* bathroom.

cuatro, *adj. & s. m.* four.

cuba, *s. f.* barrel, cask.

cubierta, *s. f.* wrapping; cover (of book); deck (of ship).

cubierto, *adj.* covered; cloudy; — *s. m.* place (at table); ~s *pl.* set of silver.

cubo, *s. m.* die; cube; bucket, pail.

cubrir, *v. a.* cover; *v. n.* ~se put on one's hat.

cucaracha, *s. f.* cockroach.

cucurucho, *s. m.* (paper-)bag.

cuchara, *s. f.* spoon.

cucharada, *s. f.* spoonful.

cucharadita, *s. f.* teaspoonful.

cucharita, *s. f.* teaspoon.

cucharón, *s. m.* ladle.

cuchillo, *s. m.* knife.

cuello, *s. m.* neck; collar.

cuenca, *s. f.* deep valley.

cuenta, *s. f.* account; bill.

cuento, *s. m.* story, tale.

cuerda, *s. f.* cord; string; spring (of a watch); *dar* ~ *a* wind up (a clock).

cuerdo, *adj.* wise, sensible.

cuerno, *s. m.* horn; bugle.

cuero, *s. m.* skin; leather.

cuerpo, *s. m.* body; corps.

cuervo, *s. m.* crow.

cuesta, *s. f.* slope, hill.

cuestión, *s. f.* question, problem; argument.

cuestionario, *s. m.* questionnaire.

cueva, *s. f.* cave; cellar.

cuidado, *s. m.* care; *tener* ~ be careful; *¡*~*!* look out!

cuidadoso, *adj.* careful.

cuidar, *v. a.* take care of, mind; *v. n.* ~se de take care of.

culpa, *s. m.* fault, blame; *sin; tener la* ~ be to blame.

culpable, *adj.* guilty.

culpar, *v. a.* blame, accuse.

cultivar, *v a.* cultivate.

cultivo, *s. m.* cultivation, cultivated field.

culto, *adj.* cultured, educated; — *s. m.* worship.

cultura, *s. f.* culture (of the mind).

cumbre, *s. f.* top, summit.

cumpleaños, *s. m.* birthday.

cumplido, *adj.* polite.

cumplimiento, *s. m.* performance, fulfilment; compliment.

cumplir, *v. a.* carry out, execute; ~ *los veinte años* reach one's twentieth birthday.

cuna, *s. f.* cradle.

cuneta, *s. f.* ditch, gutter (along highway).

cuña, *s. f.* wedge.

cuñada, *s. f.* sister-in-law.

cuñado, *s. m.* brother-in-law.

cuota, *s. f.* share; quota.

cúpula, *s. f.* dome.

cura,[1] *s. m.* priest, minister.

cura,[2] *s. f.* cure, treatment; ~ *de urgencia* first aid.

curación, *s. f.* healing, recovery.

curar, *v. a.* cure, treat; *v. n.* ~se recover.

curiosidad, *s. f.* curiosity.

curioso, *adj.* curious, inquisitive; odd, strange, quaint, rare.

cursar, *v. a. & n.* study.

curso, *s. m.* course.

curva, *s. f.* curve.

curvo, *adj.* curved, bent.

custodia, *s. f.* custody.

custodiar, *v. a.* guard, watch.

cutaneo, *adj.* cutaneous.

cúter, *s. m.* cutter.

cutis, *s. m.* complexion, skin.

cuyo, *pron.* whose.

Ch

chacal, *s. m.* jackal.

chal, *s. m.* shawl.

chaleco, *s. m.* waistcoat.

chalupa, *s. f.* sloop.

champaña, *s. m.* champagne.

champú, *s. m.* shampoo.

chamuscar, *v. a.* singe.

chancleta, *s. f.* slipper.

chanclo, *s. m.* rubbershoe, galosh.

chantaje, *s. m.* blackmail.

chanza, *s. f.* joke, jest.

chapa, *s. f.* plate, sheet (of metal).

chaparrón, *s. m.* heavy shower, downpour.

chapurrear, *v. a.* speak (a language) brokenly.

chaqueta, *s. f.* jacket, coat.

charco, *s. m.* puddle, pond.

charla, *s. f.* chat.

chelín, *s. m.* shilling

cheque, *s. m.* check (money); *talonario (s. m.) de* ~s chequebook.

chica, *s. f.* little girl.

chico, *adj.* little, small; — *s. m.* little boy, kid.

chicle, *s. m.* chewing gum.

chiflado, *adj.* eccentric, stupid.

chillar, *v. n.* screech, scream.

chimenea, *s. f.* chimney; fire-place; (ship) funnel.

china, *s. f.* pebble, small stone.

chinche, *s. f.* bedbug; drawing-pin.

chino, *adj. & s. m.* Chinese.

chiquillo, *s. m.* small child.

chisme, *s. m.* gossip, malicious remark.

chispa, *s. f.* spark; *echar* ~s rage, be furious.

chiste, *s. m.* joke.

chistoso, *adj.* funny, witty.

chivo, *s. m.* kid.

chocante, *adj.* surprising, witty; annoying.

chocar, *v. n.* collide, crash.

chocolate, *s. m.* chocolate.

chófer, *s. m.* chauffeur, driver.

choque, *s. m.* collision, crash.

chorizo, *s. m.* Spanish sausage.

chorro, *s. m.* jet; spurt; *a* ~s abundantly; *llover a* ~s pour (rain).

choza, *s. f.* hut, cabin.

chuleta, *s. f.* chop, cutlet.

chulo, *adj.* good-loking; pretty, handsome; — *s. m.* a tough (in Madrid).

chupar, *v. a.* suck.

churro, *s. m.* a kind of doughnut.

chuzo, *s. m.* spear, pike; spit.

D

dado, *s. m.* die; *jugar a los* ~s play at dice.

dama, *s. f.* lady.

danza, *s. f.* dance.

danzar, *v. n.* dance (as a performance).

dañar, *v. a.* damage; *v. n.*

~se go wrong; break down.

daño, *s. m.* damage; *hacerse* ~ get hurt, hurt oneself.

dar, *v. a.* give; *la ventana da a la calle* the window faces the street; ~ *las gracias* thank; ~ *parte* report; ~ *por cierto* feel sure; ~ *recuerdos* give regards; ~se *la mano* shake hands; ~se *prisa* hurry.

datar, *v. a.* date.

dátil, *s. m.* date (fruit).

datos, *s. m. pl.* data.

de, *prep.* of, 's; from; about; *la casa* ~ *mi padre* my father's house; *él es* ~ *Madrid* he is from Madrid; *he llegado* ~ *Paris* I've come from Paris; *adv.* ~ *memoria* by heart; ~ *niño* as a child; ~ *noche* at night.

debajo, *adv.* below; downstairs; — *prep.* ~ *de* beneath, under.

debate, *s. m.* debate.

deber[1], *v. a. & n.* owe; to have to; *debemos irnos* we have to go; *debe de hacer frío* it must be cold.

deber[2], *s. m.* duty, obligation; homework.

débil, *adj.* weak.

década, *s. f.* decade.

decano, *s. m.* dean.

decena, *s. f.* ten (pieces of sg).

decenio, *s. m.* decennium.

decente, *adj.* decent, nice; honest.

decepcionar, *v. a.* disappoint.

decidido, *adj.* determined.

decidir, *v. a.* decide; *v. n.* ~se make up one's mind.

décima, *s. f.* tenth (part).

décimo, *adj.* tenth.

decir, *v. a.* tell, say; *es* ~ that is to say; *decir para sí* say to oneself; *¿qué quiere* ~ *eso?* what does that mean?

decisión, *s. f.* decision; determination.

declamar, *v. a.* declaim.

declaración, *s. f.* declaration, statement; ~ *de aduana* customs declaration.

declarar, *v. a.* declare; testify; *v. n.* ~se declare one's love.

declinar, *v. a.* decline.

declive, *s. m.* declivity.

decoración, *s. f.* decoration; (stage) setting.

decorar, *v. a.* decorate.

decoro, *s. m.* dignity, decorum.

decretar, *v. a.* decree.

decreto, *s. m.* decree.

dedicar, *v. a.* dedicate; devote; inscribe, autograph.

dedillo, *s. m.* little finger; *saber al* ~ know perfectly.

dedo, *s. m.* finger; toe.

deducir, *v. a.* deduce, imagine; subtract.

defectivo, *adj.* defective.

defecto, *s. m.* defect, imperfection, shortcoming.

defender, *v. a.* defend; protect.

defensa, *s. f.* defence; protection; — *s. m.* (football) back.

defensor, *s. m.* defender; legal adviser.

deficiencia, *s. f.* deficiency.

deficiente, *adj.* deficient.

definitivo, *adj.* final,

definite.

defuera, *adv.* outside.

defunción, *s. f.* death, decease.

degenerar, *v. n.* degenerate.

dejar, *v. a.* let; leave, abandon; permit, allow; ~ *caer* drop; ~ *dicho* leave word; *déjeme en paz* leave me alone; *dejó de comer* he stopped eating.

del *(de* + *el),* see de.

delantal, *s. m.* apron.

delante, *adv.* in front; — *prep.* ~ *de* before, in front of; in the presence of.

delantera, *s. f.* start, lead; *tomar la* ~ take the lead; front row (of seats); front (of building).

delantero, *s. m.* (football) forward.

delegación, *s. f.* delegation; substitution, proxy.

delegado, *adj.* delegated; — *s. m.* delegate.

delegar, *v. a.* delegate.

deleitar, *v. a.* delight.

deletrear, *v. a.* spell.

delfín, *s. m.* dolphin.

delgado, *adj.* thin, slim; light (coat).

deliberar, *v. a. & n.* deliberate.

delicadeza, *s. f.* delicacy.

delicado, *adj.* delicate.

delicia, *s. f.* delight.

delicioso, *adj.* delightful; delicious.

delineante, *s. m.* draftsman.

delito, *s. m.* crime.

demanda, *s. f.* claim, request; demand, call; legal proceeding, court action; *oferta y* ~ supply and demand.

demandado, *s. m.* defendant.

demandante, *s. m.* plaintiff, claimant.

demandar, *v. a.* claim, demand, request.

demás, *pron. lo* ~ the rest; *los* ~ the others.

demasiado, *adv.* too much; — *adj.* too many.

democracia, *s. f.* democracy.

demócrata, *s. m., f.* democrat.

democrático, *adj.* democratic.

demoler, *v. a.* demolish.

demonio, *s. m.* devil; *¡~!* damn it!

demostración, *s. f.* demonstration; proof.

demostrar, *v. a.* show; prove.

denegar, *v. a.* deny, refuse.

densidad, *s. f.* density.

denso, *adj.* dense, thick.

dentadura, *s. f.* set of teeth.

dentífrico, *s. m.* dentifrice.

dentista, *s. m.* dentist.

dentro, *adv.* inside, within; *por* ~ on the inside; — *prep.* ~ *de* inside (of); ~ *de poco* soon, in a little while.

denunciar, *v. a.* denounce.

departamento, *s. m.* section, department; compartment.

depender *de, v. n.* depend on, be dependent; *depende* it depends.

dependiente, *s. m.* subordinate; shop-assistant.

deplorar, *v. a.* deplore, regret, lament.

deponer, *v. a.* depose.

deportar, *v. a.* deport,

exile.

deporte, *s. m.* sport.

deportista, *s. m.,* *f.* sports(wo)man.

deportivo, *adj.* sport, athletic.

depositar, *v. a.* deposit, put.

depósito, *s. m.* deposit, bond; warehouse; ~ *de equipajes* cloak-room.

depresión, *s. f.* depression.

deprimir, *v. a.* depress.

derecha, *s. f.* right hand, right side; *a* ~*s* right, well; *a la* ~ to the right.

derecho¹, *adj.* right (opposed to left); straight; – *adv. siga usted todo* ~ go straight ahead.

derecho², *s. m.* right; law; tax, duty; ~*s de aduana* customs duties; ~*s de autor* copyright.

derivar, *v. a.* divert; derive.

derramar, *v. a.* spill.

derretir, *v. a. & n.* (~*se*) melt.

derribar, *v. a.* demolish, tear down; knock down; overthrow; shoot down (a plane).

derrota, *s. f.* defeat.

derrotar, *v. a.* defeat.

derrumbar, *v. a.* throw down, fell; *v. n.* ~*se* collapse, tumble down.

desabotonar, *v. a.* unbutton.

desabrigarse, *v. n.* take off the outer clothing.

desacostumbrar *de,* *v. a.* disaccustom to sg.

desacreditar, *v. a.* discredit.

desacuerdo, *s. m.* disagreement.

desafiar, *v. a.* challenge,

defy.

desafío, *s. m.* duel; challenge.

desafortunado, *adj.* unlucky.

desagradable, *adj.* disagreeable, unpleasant.

desagradar, *v. n.* displease.

desaguar, *v. a.* drain.

desagüe, *s. m.* drainage.

desairar, *v. a.* scorn, disregard.

desalentar, *v. a.* discourage.

desaliento, *s. m.* discouragement.

desalojar, *v. a.* expel, evict, eject; *v. n.* move (from dwelling).

desalquilado, *adj.* unrented, vacant.

desalquilarse, *v. n.* become vacant.

desamueblado, *adj.* unfurnished.

desanimado, *adj.* lowspirited, dull, flat.

desanimar, *v. a.* discourage, dishearten; *v. n.* ~*se* become discouraged.

desanudar, *v. a.* untie.

desapacible, *adv.* grim, raw; dismal.

desaparecer, *v. n.* disappear.

desaparición, *s. f.* disappearance.

desapercibido, *adj.* unprepared.

desapreciar, *v. a.* despise.

desaprobar, *v. a.* disapprove.

desarmar, *v. a.* disarm; take to pieces.

desarme, *s. m.* disarmament.

desarraigar, *v. a.* uproot; eradicate.

desarreglar, *v. a.* disarrange.

desarreglo, s. m. disorder.

desarrollar, v. a. & n. (~se) develop.

desarrollo, s. m. development.

desaseado, adj. slovenly, not clean.

desastre, s. m. disaster, catastrophe.

desastroso, adj. disastrous, unfortunate.

desatar, v. a. untie.

desatento, adj. inattentive; discourteous.

desaviar, v. a. mislead.

desayunar, v. n. have breakfast.

desayuno, s. m. breakfast.

desbaratar, v. a. destroy, ruin; v. n. ~se fall to pieces.

desbordar(se), v. a. & n. overflow.

descalificar, v. a. disqualify.

descalzarse, v. n. take off one's shoes.

descalzo, adj. barefoot.

descansar, v. n. rest.

descanso, s. m. rest; interval; landing (of staircase).

descargar, v. a. unload; free (from obligation or debt).

descargo, s. m. unloading.

descartar, v. a. discard, eliminate.

descendencia, s. f. descendants.

descender, v. n. descend, go down, come down; drop, decrease.

descendiente, s. m., f. descendant.

descenso, s. m. descent, going down; fall, decrease.

descifrar, v. a. decipher, make out.

descolgar, v. a. take down.

descolorido, adj. faded, pale.

descomponer, v. a. decompose, take to pieces; upset (plans); v. n. ~se get out of order; dislocate; spoil; get angry.

descompuesto, adj. out of order; spoiled.

desconcertar, v. a. disturb, confuse.

desconectar, v. a. switch off, disconnect.

desconfiar de, v. n. distrust, suspect.

desconocer, v. a. disregard, ignore.

desconocido, adj. unknown, strange; — s. m. stranger.

desconsolado, adj. disconsolate.

descontar, v. a. discount, deduct.

descontento, adj. dissatisfied, displeased; — s. m. dissatisfaction.

descorchar, v. a. uncork.

descortés, adj. discourteous, rude.

describir, v. a. describe.

descubrimiento, s. m. discovery.

descubrir, v. a. discover; disclose, show; v. n. ~se take off one's hat.

descuento, s. m. discount, deduction.

descuidado, adj. slovenly, unclean; careless, negligent; unaware.

descuidar, v. a. neglect; v. n. descuide don't worry.

descuido, *s. m.* carelessness, negligence; *al* ~ carelessly; *por* ~ through carelessness.

desde, *prep.* from; since; ~ *ahora* from now on; ~ *entonces* since then.

desdeñoso, *adj.* contemptuous.

desdicha, *s. f.* misfortune.

desdichado, *adj.* unhappy, unfortunate.

desdoblar, *v. a.* unfold.

desear, *v. a.* desire, want, like.

desecar, *v. a.* dry up.

desembalar, *v. a.* unpack.

desembarcar, *v. a.* unload, put ashore; *v. n.* land, disembark.

desembarco, *s. m.* landing, disembarkation.

desembocar, *v. n.* flow into (river); end, lead (street).

desembolsar, *v. a. & n.* pay out.

desembragar, *v. a.* disconnect, uncouple; declutch.

desempeñar, *v. a.* redeem (pawn); carry out (duty, office).

desencantar, *v. a.* disenchant, dissappoint.

desengañar, *v. a.* undeceive, set right; *v. n.* ~*se* be disillusioned.

desengaño, *s. m.* disillusion, disappointment.

desenvuelto, *adj.* forward; free and easy.

deseo, *s. m.* desire, wish; *tengo* ~ *de* I'm eager to.

deseoso *de,* *adj.* desirous, eager.

desertar, *v. n.* desert.

desertor, *s. m.* deserter.

desesperación, *s. f.* desperation.

desesperar, *v. n.* despair, lose hope.

desfavorable, *adj.* unfavourable.

desfilar, *v. n.* march past, parade.

desfile, *s. m.* parade.

desgana, *s. f.* dislike; lack of appetite.

desgarrar, *v. a.* tear, rip.

desgracia, *s. f.* misfortune; sorrow, grief; *por* ~ unfortunately.

desgraciado, *adj.* unfortunate.

deshabitado, *adj.* uninhabited.

deshacer, *v. a.* undo; untie, unwrap; dissolve; solve, upset; *v. n.* ~*se* wear oneself out; ~*se de* dispose of, get rid of.

deshecho, *adj.* undone, not made; worn out, exhausted.

deshielo, *s. m.* thaw.

deshonesto, *adj.* dishonest.

desierto, *adj.* deserted; uninhabited; — *s. m.* desert.

designar, *v. a.* name, appoint.

desigual, *adj.* unequal; uneven.

desilusión, *s. f.* disillusionment.

desinfectante, *s. m. & adj.* disinfectant.

desinfectar, *v. a.* disinfect.

desinteresado, *adj.* disinterested; impartial.

desistir *de,* *v. n.* give up; call off.

desleal, *adj.* disloyal.

deslizarse, *v. n.* slip, slide, glide.

deslumbrar, *v. a.* dazzle.

desmayarse, *v. n.* faint.

desmayo, *s. m.* swoon.

desmentir, *v. a.* disprove; *v. n.* ~se take back, retract.

desnudar, *v. a.* undress; *v. n.* ~se take off one's clothes, get undressed.

desnudo, *adj. & s. m.* naked, bare, nude.

desobedecer, *v. a.* disobey.

desocupación, *s. f.* unemployment.

desocupado, *adj.* unoccupied, vacant; not occupied.

desocupar, *v. a.* vacate, empty.

desolación, *s. f.* desolation.

desolado, *adj.* desolate, disconsolate; disappointed.

desorden, *s. m.* disorder, confusion, mess.

desordenado, *adj.* disorderly.

desordenar, *v. a.* upset.

desorientar, *v. a.* confuse; *v. n.* ~se get confused.

despacio, *adv* slowly.

despachar, *v. a.* ship, send out; attend to, take care of; wait on; dismiss, fire.

despacho, *s. m.* dispatch; office; ~ de billetes booking-office.

despedida, *s. f.* farewell.

despedir, *v. a.* see sy off; dismiss, discharge; *v. n.* ~se take leave, say good-bye.

despegar, *v. a.* unglue; take off; *v. n.* rise, start (plane).

despejado, *adj.* bright (boy); cloudless (sky).

despejar, *v. a.* clear.

despensa, *s. f.* pantry, larder.

desperdiciar, *v. a.* waste.

desperdicio, *s. m.* waste; ~s pl. refuse, garbage.

desperezarse, *v. n.* stretch oneself.

despertador, *s. m.* alarm-clock.

despertar, *v. a.* wake up; arouse, excite; *v. n.* ~se wake up.

despierto, *adj.* awake; smart.

despojar, *v. a.* strip, despoil; *v. n.* ~se de take off (clothing).

despreciar, *v. a.* despise; scorn, reject.

desprecio, *s. m.* contempt.

después, *adv.* later, then, afterwards; — *prep.* ~ de after; ~ de todo after all.

desquitarse, *v. n.* get even.

destacado, *adj.* distinguished, famous.

destapar, *v. a.* open (bottle); take off (lid, cover).

destinar, *v. a.* appoint, assign.

destinatario, *s. m.* addressee.

destino, *s. m.* destiny, fate; destination; job; con ~ a bound for, going to.

destornillador, *s. m.* screw-driver.

destornillar, *v. a.* unscrew.

destreza, *s. f.* skill.

destrucción, *s. f.* destruction.

destruir, *v. a.* destroy.

desván, *s. m.* attic.

desventaja, *s. f.* disadvantage; handicap.

desventura, *s. f.* misfortune, mishap.

desvergonzado, *adj.* impudent, insolent.

detallar, v. a. detail, tell in detail.

detalle, s. m. detail.

detener, v. a. detain, stop; arrest; v. n. ~se stop.

determinar, v. a. determine, fix; decide; v. n. ~se make up one's mind.

detrás, adv. behind; — prep. ~ de behind, at the back of.

deuda, s. f. debt; estar en ~ be indebted.

deudor, s. m. debtor.

devolver, v. a. return, give back; pay back; restore.

día, s. m. day; al ~ a day, per day; ocho ~s a week; quince ~s two weeks; todos los ~s daily, every day.

diablo, s. m. devil.

diálogo, s. m. dialogue.

diamante, s. m. diamond.

¡diantre! int. the deuce! the devil!

diario, adj. daily; — s. m. diary, journal; newspaper.

dibujar, v.a. draw, sketch.

dibujo, s. m. drawing.

diccionario, s. m. dictionary.

diciembre, s.m. December.

dictar, v. a. dictate; issue (by decree).

dicha, s. f. happiness.

dicho, s. m. saying; witty remark.

diente, s. m. tooth cog.

diez, adj. & s. m. en.

diferencia, s. f. difference.

diferenciar, v. a. distinguish.

diferente, adj. different.

diferir, v. a. postpone, differ.

difícil, adj. difficult, hard.

dificultad, s. f. difficulty.

difunto, adj. dead, deceased.

difusora, s. f. broadcasting station.

digerir, v. a. digest.

digestión, s. f. digestion.

dignidad, s. f. dignity; high rank.

digno, adj. dignified; worthy.

diligencia, s. f. diligence.

diligente, adj. industrious.

diluvio, s. m. flood, deluge.

dinamarqués, adj. Danish; — s. m. Dane.

dineral, s. m. large sum of money.

dinero, s. m. money.

Dios, s. m. God; ¡a ~! goodbye!; gracias a ~ thank God.

dique, s. m. dam; dock.

dirección, s. f. direction; address; board of directors; management; calle (s. f.) de ~ única one-way street.

directo, adj. direct.

director, s. m. director; manager; ~ de escena stage manager; ~ de escuela headmaster; ~ de orquesta conductor.

dirigible, s. m. dirigible.

dirigir, v. a. direct; address; lead; steer; manage; v. n. ~se a to go to.

discípulo, s. m. student, pupil.

disco, s. m. disk; (gramophone) record.

discreto, adj. discreet; fair.

disculpa, s. f. excuse.

disculpar, v. a. excuse, pardon; v. n. ~se apologize.

discurso, s. m. speech.

discusión, s. f. discussion.

discutir, v. a. discuss; argue.

disgustar, v. a. grieve, displease; v. n. ~se be hurt or displeased.

disgusto, s. m. quarrel; grief, sorrow.

disimular, v. a. conceal, dissimulate.

disminuir, v. a. decrease; v. n. decline, lessen, diminish.

disolver, v. a. dissolve.

disparar, v. n. shoot, fire.

disparate, s. m. nonsense; mistake.

dispensar, v. a. excuse; dispénseme excuse me.

disponer, v. a. place; arrange; order, decree; v. n. ~se a get ready to.

disponible, adj. availal

disposición, s. f. disposu., service; order; arrangement.

dispuesto, adj. disposed, ready.

distancia, s. f. distance.

distante, adj. far, distant.

distar, v. n. be distant, be far.

distinción, s. f. distinction, difference.

distinguir, v. a. distinguish; esteem, show regard for.

distintivo, s. m. badge.

distinto, adj. different.

distracción, s. f. absent-mindedness; diversion, pastime, amusement.

distraer, v. a. distract; entertain, divert; v. n. ~se be distracted; amuse oneself.

distribución, s. f. distribution.

distribuir, v. a. distribute.

distrito, s. m. district.

disturbar, v. a. disturb.

diurno, adj. daily. ,

divagar, v. n. digress.

diván, s. m. couch.

diverso, adj. different.

divertir, v. a. amuse. entertain, divert; v. n. ~se be entertained, have a good time.

dividir, v. a. divide.

divino, adj. divine.

división, s. f. division.

divorciarse, v. n. get a divorce.

divulgar, v. a. reveal, let out; popularize.

doblar, v. a. fold; double.

doble, adj. double; thick, heavy; deceitful.

doce, adj. & s. m. twelve.

docena, s. f. dozen.

dócil, adj. docile, obedient.

doctor, s. m. doctor.

documento, s. m. document, paper.

dólar, s. m. dollar.

doler, v. n. hurt, pain.

dolor, s. m. pain, ache; sorrow, grief.

domar, v. a. tame; subdue.

doméstico, adj. domestic; — s. m. domestic, servant.

domicilio, s. m. residence.

dominar, v. a. & n. dominate, predominate; overlook, command a view; v. n. ~se control oneself.

domingo, s. m. Sunday.

doncella, s. f. maid, servant; girl.

donde, conj. & adv. where.

¿**dónde**? adv. where?; ¿a ~? where to?; ¿de ~? where from ?; ¿por ~? which way ?

dondequiera, pron. wherever, anywhere.

dorado, *adj.* gold, gilded.

dormilón, *s. m.* lie-abed.

dormir, *v. n.* sleep; *v. n.* ~se fall asleep.

dormitorio, *s. m.* bedroom.

dos, *adj. & s. m.* two; *el* ~ *de enero* the second of January; *de* ~ *en* ~ in pairs, by twos.

doscientos, *pl.* two hundred. .

dote, *a. f.* dowry; talent.

drama, *s. m.* play, drama.

droga, *s. f.* drug.

droguería, *s. f.* druggist's shop.

ducha, *s. f.* shower (bath).

duda, *s. f.* doubt; *sin* ~ certainly, without doubt.

dudar, *v. a.* doubt; hesitate.

duelo[1]**,** *s. m.* mourning; sorrow.

duelo[2]**,** *s. m.* duel.

dueño, *s. m.* owner, landlord; master.

dulce, *adj.* sweet; — *s. m.* (a piece of) candy.

duodécimo, *adj.* twelfth.

duplicado, *s. m.* duplicate.

duplicar, *v. a.* double, duplicate, repeat.

duque, *s. m.* duke.

duquesa, *s. f.* duchess.

duradero, *adj.* lasting, durable.

durante, *prep.* during.

durar, *v. n.* last.

duro, *adj.* hard; rough; stubborn; — *adv. trabaja muy* ~ he works very hard; *a duras penas* with difficulty; hardly.

E

e *conj.* and (before *i* or

hi); *padre e hijo* father and son.

ebanista, *s. m.* cabinetmaker. |

ébano, *s. m.* ebony.

eco, *s. m.* echo.

economía, *s. m.* economy; ~ *política* economics; ~s *pl.* savings.

económico, *adj.* economical.

economizar, *v. a.* save.

ecuador, *s. m.* equator.

echar, *v. a.* throw; discharge, dismiss, fire; pour; ~ *a correr* begin to run; ~ *a perder* spoil, ruin; ~ *de menos* miss; ~ *la llave* lock the door; *v. n.* ~se lie down; ~se *a perder* spoil.

edad, *s. f.* age.

edificar, *v. a.* build.

edificio, *s. m.* building.

editor, *s. m.* publisher.

educación, *s. f.* education, breeding, upbringing.

educar, *v. a.* educate; train.

efecto, *s. m.* effect; impression; *en* ~ in fact; ~s *pl.* securities; commodities.

efectuar, *v. a.* carry out, put into effect.

eficaz, *adj.* efficient, effective.

egipcio, *adj. & s. m.* Egyptian.

egoísta, *adj.* selfish.

eje, *s. m.* axle, axis.

ejecución, *s. f.* execution; performance.

ejecutar, *v. a.* execute, carry out.

ejemplar, *adj.* exemplary; — *s. m.* copy.

ejemplo, *s. m.* example; *por* ~ for instance.

ejercer, v. a. practise; handle, hold.

ejercicio, s. m. exercise, drill.

ejército, s. m. army.

el, m. (definite article) the.

él, m. pron. he.

elástico, s. m. & adj. elastic.

elección, s. f. election; choice.

electricidad, s. f. electricity.

electricista, s. m. electrician.

eléctrico, adj. electric.

elefante, s. m. elephant.

elegancia, s. f. elegance.

elegante, adj. elegant, stylish, smart.

elegir, v. a. choose, select, elect.

elemento, s. m. element, factor.

elevar, v. a. erect; v. n. ~se climb, ascend.

eliminar, v. a. eliminate.

elogiar, v. a. praise.

elogio, s. m. praise.

ella, f. pron. she.

ellas, f. pl. pron. they.

ello, pron. it, that.

ellos, pl. m. pron. they.

embajada, s. f. embassy; delegation.

embajador, s. m. ambassador.

embarcación, s. f. shipment; ship.

embarcar, v. a. ship, send by boat; v. n. (~se) embark.

embargo, s. m. seizure, confiscation; sin ~ however, nevertheless.

embellecer, v. a. embellish.

emblema, s. m. emblem; insignia.

embolsar, v. a. put in, pocket.

embragar, v. a. couple, put clutch in.

embrague, s. m. clutch (car).

embromar, v. a. make jokes on.

embuchado, s. m. sausage.

embuste, s. m. lie.

embustero, s. m. liar.

emergencia, s. f. emergency.

emigración, s. f. emigration.

emigrante, adj. & s. m., f. emigrant.

emigrar, v. n. emigrate.

eminente, adj. eminent, famous.

emisión, s. f. emission; issue; transmission.

emisora, s. f. broadcasting station.

emitir, v. a. emit; transmit, broadcast.

emocionarse, v. n. be moved.

empacar, v. a. pack.

empalmar, v. n. make connexions with a train.

empalme, s. m. junction; connexion.

empanada, s. f. pie.

empapar, v. a. soak; v. n. ~se be soaked, be drenched.

emparedado, s. m. sandwich.

empastar, v. a. stop, fill (tooth).

empate, s. m. draw.

empeñar, v. a. pledge, give; pawn; v. n. ~se be bent on.

empeño, s. m. determination, firmness; pawn, pawning; con ~ emphatically.

empeorarse, v. n. grow worse.

emperador, s. m. emperor.

empezar, *v. a. & n.* begin.

empleado, *s. m.* employee.

emplear, *v. a.* employ, use; hire; invest.

empleo, *s. m.* employment, use.

empolvarse, *v. n.* powder oneself; get dusty.

emprender, *v. a.* undertake.

empresa, *s. f.* undertaking; enterprise; project; company.

empresario, *s. m.* (theatrical) manager; promoter.

empujar, *v. a.* push.

empujón, *s. m.* push.

en, *prep.* in; on; at; ~ *vano* in vain.

enamorado, *adj. & s. m.* in love; sweetheart.

enamorar, *v. a.* make love to, flirt with; *v. n.* ~se de fall in love with.

enano, *s. m.* dwarf.

encadenar, *v. a.* chain.

encajar, *v. n.* fit (in).

encaje, *s. m.* lace.

encaminar, *v. a.* direct; *v. n.* ~se make one's way, go.

encanecer, *v. n.* become gray.

encantador, *adj.* charming.

encantar, *v. a.* charm, delight.

encanto, *s. m.* charm.

encargado, *adj.* in charge; — *s. m.* person in charge, manager.

encargar, *v. a.* entrust; urge, ask; *v. n.* ~se take charge of sg.

encargo, *s. m.* errand; job, assignment.

encarnado, *adj.* red.

encendedor, *s. m.* lighter.

encender, *v. a.* light, put on; *v. n.* ~se light up, go on.

encendido, *adj.* bright-coloured; *ponerse* ~ blush.

encerado, *s. m.* oilcloth; blackboard.

encerrar, *v. a.* lock up; include, contain.

encima, *adv.* above; *por* ~ superficially; — *prep.* ~ *de* above.

encinta, *adj. f.* pregnant.

encoger, *v. n.* shrink; *v. n.* ~se de hombros shrug one's shoulders.

encogido, *adj.* bashful.

encolerizar, *v. a.* anger; *v. n.* ~se become angry.

encomendar, *v. a.* entrust to, charge with.

encontrar, *v. a.* find; meet; *v. n.* ~se meet; collide; be (somewhere); feel.

encrucijada, *s. f.* street intersection.

encuadernar, *v. a.* bind (book).

encubridor, *s. m.* receiver (of stolen goods).

encuentro, *s. m.* meeting; match; *salir al* ~ *de* go to meet sy.

enchufar, *v. a.* join, link up, plug in.

enderezar, *v. a.* straighten; *v. n.* ~se straighten up, sit up.

endosar, *v. a.* endorse.

endulzar, *v. a.* sweeten.

enemigo, *s. m.* enemy.

enemistad, *s. f.* enmity.

energia, *s. f.* energy;

~ *eléctrica* electric power-er.

enérgico, *adj.* energetic.

enero, *s. m.* January.

enfadar, *v. a.* anger, annoy; *v. n.* ~*se* get angry.

énfasis, *s. m.* emphasis.

enfermar(se), *v. a. & n.* fall ill, get sick.

enfermedad, *s. f.* illness, sickness, disease.

enfermera, *s. f.* nurse.

enfermería, *s. f.* sick-room, infirmary.

enfermero, *s. m.* hospital attendant.

enfermo, *adj.* sick; — *s. m.* patient.

enfocar, *v. a.* focus.

enfrenar, *v. a.* rein, check; brake.

enfrente, *adv.* opposite, across; — *prep.* ~ *de* opposite.

enfriar, *v. a.* cool; *v. n.* ~*se* cool off, become cold; get chilled.

enfurecerse, *v. n.* rage.

enganchar, *v. a.* hook on.

engañar, *v. a.* deceive; *v. n.* ~*se* make a mistake, be wrong.

engaño, *s. m.* deceit.

engordar, *v. a.* fatten; *v. n.* get fat.

engrandecer, *v. a.* enlarge, magnify.

engrasar, *v. a.* grease.

enhorabuena, *s f.* congratulations.

enigma, *s. m.* riddle, enigma, puzzle.

enjabonar, *v. a.* soap; lather.

enjuagar, *v. a.* rinse.

enlace, *s. m.* connection; marriage.

enlazar, *v. a. & n.* connect.

enojar, *v. a.* anger; *v. n.* ~*se* get angry.

enojo, *s. m.* anger, trouble.

enorme, *adj.* enormous.

enrabiar, *v. a.* enrage.

enriquecer, *v. a. & n.* enrich; get rich.

enrojecerse, *v. n.* blush.

enrollar, *v. a.* roll up.

enronquecer, *v. n.* get hoarse.

ensalada, *s. f.* salad.

ensanchar, *v. a.* widen; let out, enlarge.

ensayar, *v. a.* try, test; rehearse.

enseñanza, *s. f.* instruction, teaching.

enseñar, *v. a.* teach; show, point out.

ensillar, *v. a.* saddle.

ensordecer, *v. a.* deafen.

ensuciar, *v. a.* soil, dirty.

ensueño, *s. m.* dream.

entablar, *v. a.* board up; begin, start.

ente, *s. m.* being.

entender, *v. a.* understand; be good at, be familiar with, *a mi* ~ in my opinion.

entendido, *adj.* informed; skilled; *está* ~ it is understood.

entendimiento, *s. m.* understanding; mind.

enteramente, *adv.* entirely, wholly.

enterar, *v. a.* inform, report; *v. n.* ~*se* pay attention; find out, inquire; learn.

entero, *adj.* entire, whole.

enterrar, *v. a.* bury.

entierro, *s. m.* burial.

entonces, *adv.* then, at the time; *desde* ~ since that time.

entrada, *s. f.* entrance;

admission; attendance; ticket, seat; beginning.

entrar, v. n. enter, come in, go in; fit; join.

entre, prep. between; among.

entreabierto, adj. & adv. ajar, half-open.

entreacto, s. m. interval.

entrega, s. f. delivery.

entregar, v. a. deliver; hand (over); give up; surrender; v. n. ~se give in, yield; surrender.

entrenador, s. m. trainer, coach.

entrenamiento, s. m. training, coaching.

entrenar v. a. train.

entresuelo, s. m. intermediate storey.

entretanto, adv. meanwhile.

entretener, v. a. entertain, amuse; delay; v. n. ~se amuse oneself; be delayed.

entretenido, adj. entertaining, amusing.

entretenimiento, s. m. pastime.

entrevista, s. f. interview.

entusiasmo, s. m. enthusiasm.

envenenar, v. a. poison.

enviado, s. m. envoy.

enviar, v. a. send.

envidia, s. f. envy.

envidiar, v. a. envy.

envidioso, adj. envious, invidious.

envío, s. m. s nding; consignment.

envolver, v. a. wrap.

episodio, s. m. episode.

época, s. f. epoch; period, time.

equilibrio, s. m. balance.

equipaje, s. m. luggage.

equipo, s. m. team; equipment.

equivocación, s. f. mistake.

equivocar, v. a. mistake, confuse; v. n. ~se make a mistake, be wrong.

equívoco, adj. ambiguous.

era, s. f. age; threshing-floor.

erario, s. m. treasury.

errar, v. a. miss.

error, s. m. mistake.

esbelto, adj. slender, slim.

esbozo, s. m. sketch.

escala, s. f. ladder; scale; *hacer* ~ make a stop, (ship) call at.

escalera, s. f. ladder· staircase, stairs.

escalofrío, s. m. shivering fit.

escalopa, s. f. veal scallop.

escama, s. f. scale (of fish).

escandalizar, v. a. shock, scandalize.

escándalo, s. m. scandal.

escapar(se), v. n. escape; run away; slip out.

escaparate, s. m. shop-window.

escape, s. m. escape, exhaust (car).

escarlata, s. f. scarlet.

escarlata, s. f. scarlet.

escasear, v. n. be scarce.

escasez, s. f. shortage.

escaso, adj. scarce, short.

escena, s. f. scene; stage.

escenario, s. m. stage (of a theatre).

esclavo, s. m. slave.

escocés, adj. Scotch; — s. m. Scotchman.

escoger, v. a. choose, select.

esconder, v. a. hide.

escopeta, *s. f.* shotgun.

escorpión, *s. m.* scorpion.

escribir, *v. a.* write; ~ *a máquina* type, typewrite.

escrito, *adj.* written; — *s. m.* writing; *por* ~ in writing.

escritor, *s. m.* writer, author.

escritorio, *s. m.* office; desk.

escuadra, *s. f.* (naval) fleet; carpenter's square.

escuchar, *v. a.* listen to.

escudo, *s. m.* shield.

escuela, *s. f.* school.

escultura, *s. f.* sculpture.

ese, *m.*; esa, *f. adj.* that; *esos, esas pl.* those.

ése, *m.*; ésa, *f. pron.* that one; *ésos, ésas pl.* those.

esencia, *s. f.* essence.

esencial, *adj.* essential.

esfera, *s. f.* sphere.

esfuerzo, *s. m.* effort.

esmeralda, *s. f.* emerald.

espacio, *s. m.* space; blank; line.

espada, *s. f.* sword; spade (cards); *s. m.* bullfighter.

espalda, *s. f.* back (of the body); *a ~s de* behind one's back.

espantar, *v. a.* scare, frighten.

espanto, *s. m.* fear, fright.

español, *adj. & s. m.* Spanish; Spaniard.

espárrago, *s. m.* asparagus.

especial, *adj.* special.

especialista, *s. m., f.* expert, specialist.

espectáculo, *s. m.* spectacle, show; scene.

espejo, *s. m.* mirror.

espera, *s. f.* wait; *sala de* ~ waiting-room.

esperanza, *s. f.* hope.

esperar, *v. a.* hope, expect; wait for.

espeso, *adj.* thick.

espía, *s. m., f.* spy.

espina, *s. f.* thorn; (fish) bone.

espinacas, *s. f. pl.* spinach.

espinazo, *s. m.* spine.

espíritu, *s. m.* spirit, soul.

espléndido, *adj.* splendid, wonderful; generous.

esponja, *s. f.* sponge.

esposa, *s. f.* wife.

esposo, *s. m.* husband.

espuma, *s. f.* foam; lather.

esqueleto, *s. m.* skeleton.

esquema, *s. m.* scheme.

esquí, *s. m.* ski.

esquiar, *v. n.* ski.

esquina, *s. f.* corner (outer).

establecer, *v. a.* establish; *v. n.* ~se settle.

establecimiento, *s. m.* establishment.

establo, *s. m.* stable.

estación¹, *s. f.* season.

estación², *s. f.* station; stop.

estacionar, *v. a.* park (car).

estadio, *s. m.* stadium.

estado, *s. m.* condition; status; state; government.

estanco, *s. m.* tobacconist's shop.

estanque, *s. m.* pond.

estante, *s. m.* shelf.

estar, *v. n.* be (in a place); look, seem; ¿*a cuántos estamos? estamos a 2 de mayo* what's the date? it's the second of May; ~ *de acuerdo* agree; ~ *de viaje* be travelling; *estoy para salir* I'm about to leave: *estoy leyendo* I'm reading; *está bien* all right.

estatua, *s. f.* statue.

estatura, *s. f.* stature; height.

este¹, *s. m.* east.

este², *m.,* **esta** *f. adj.* this.

estos, *m. pl.,* **estas,** *f. pl. adj.* these.

éste, *m.,* **ésta,** *f. pron.* this one.

estéril, *adj.* sterile.

esterlina; *libra (s. f.)* ~ pound sterling.

estilo, *s. m.* style.

estilográfica, *s. m.* fountain-pen.

estimar, *v. a.* value, respect.

estimular, *v. a.* stimulate.

estirar, *v. a.* stretch, pull.

esto, *pron.* this.

estofado, *s. m.* stew.

estómago, *s. m.* stomach.

estornudar, *v. n.* sneeze.

estrechar, *v. a.* make narrower, take in; ~ *la mano a* shake hands with.

estrecho, *adj.* narrow; tight; close; — *s. m.* strait.

estrella, *s. f.* star.

estrenar, *v. a.* open, represent for the first time (a play).

estropear, *v. a.* ruin, damage; spoil.

estruendo, *s. m.* noise, din.

estuche *s. m.* case, box.

estudiante, *s. m.* student.

estudio, *s. m.* study.

estufa, *s. f.* stove.

estupendo, *adj.* wonderful.

estúpido, *adj.* stupid.

etapa, *s. f.* stage.

etcétera, and so on.

éter, *s. m.* ether.

etiqueta, *s. f.* label; *de* ~ formal.

europeo, *adj. & s. m.* European.

evangelio, *s. m.* gospel.

evento, *s. m.* event.

evitar, *v. a.* avoid; prevent.

exactitud, *s. f.* accuracy; punctuality.

exacto, *adj.* exact, correct; accurate.

exagerar, *v. a.* exaggerate.

examen, *s. m.* examination, test.

examinar, *v. a.* examine; inspect; observe.

excelente, *adj.* excellent; fine.

excepción, *s. f.* exception.

exceso, *s. m.* excess.

excursión, *s. f.* excursion.

excusa, *s. f.* excuse.

excusado, *s. m.* lavatory.

excusar, *v. a.* excuse, pardon; decline; *v. n.* ~*se* apologize.

exhibir, *v. a.* exhibit, show.

exigir, *v. a.* require; demand.

existencia, *s. f.* existence, life; stock.

éxito, *s. m.* success.

expedir, *v. a.* dispatch.

experiencia, *s. f.* experience, experiment.

experto, *adj.* expert, skilled.

expirar, *v. n.* expire.

explicar, *v. a.* explain.

explorador, *s. m.* explorer; boy scout.

explosión, *s. f.* explosion, blast.

explotar, *v. a.* exploit, work; use.

exponer, v. a. expose; explain.

exportación, s. f. export.

exportar, v. a. export.

exposición, s. f. exhibition.

expresar, v. a. express; v. n. ~se express oneself, speak.

expresión, s. f. expression.

expresivo, adj. expressive; affectionate.

expreso, adj. express, explicit; tren ~ fast train, express.

exprimir, v. a. squeeze out.

expuesto, adj. exhibited; in danger.

expulsar, v. a. expel.

exquisito, adj. delicious; exquisite.

externo, adj. external.

extracto, s. m. extract.

extranjero, adj. foreign; — s. m. foreigner; en el ~ abroad.

extraño, adj. strange; — s. m. stranger.

extraordinario, adj. extraordinary.

extraviarse, v. n. lose one's way.

extremo, adj. extreme; — s. m. end.

F

fábrica, s. f. factory

fabricación, s. f. manufacture.

fabricante, s. m. manufacturer, maker.

fabricar, v. a. manufacture, make.

fábula, s. f. fable.

fabuloso, adj. fabulous.

facción, s. f. faction; faciones pl. features (of the face).

fácil, adj. easy.

facilidad, s. f. facility, ease; aptitude.

facilitar, v. a. facilitate, make easier; supply.

factura, s. f. bill, invoice.

facultad, s. f. faculty.

fachada, s. f. front (of a building).

faja, s. f. sash; girdle; (postal) wrapper.

falda, s. f. skirt; lap; slope, (mountain) side.

falsedad, s. f. falsehood, lie.

falsificar, v. a. forge, counterfeit.

falso, adj. false, untrue; forged; — s. m. padding, wadding.

falta, s. f. error, mistake; fault; misdemeanour; a ~ de for lack of; hacer ~ be necessary, be needed; miss; me hace falta un tenedor I need a fork; sin ~ without fail.

faltar, v. n. lack, be missing, be needed; faltan tres minutos para las seis it's three minutes to six; ~ a la clase be absent from class; ¡no faltaba más! of course! by all means!

fallecer, v. n. die.

fama, s. f. fame; reputation.

familia, s. f. family.

familiar, adj. familiar; — s. m. relative.

famoso, adj. famous.

fanático, adj. & s. m. fanatic.

fanfarronear, v. n. brag, exaggerate.

fango, s. m. mud.

fantasía, s. f. imagination; whim; fantasy.

fantasma, s. m. ghost.

fantástico, adj. fantastic, unbelievable; extravagant.

fardo, s. m. big bundle, bale.

faringe, s. f. throat, gullet.

farmacéutico, s. m. chemist.

farmacia, s. f. chemist's shop.

faro, s. m. beacon, lighthouse; headlight.

farol, s. m. lantern; street-lamp.

farsa, s. f. farce.

fase, s. f. phase.

fastidiar, v. a. annoy, bother.

fastidioso, adj. annoying, tiresome.

fatal, adj. fatal.

fatalidad, s. f. fate.

fatigar, v. a. tire; v. n. ~se get tired.

favor, s. m. favour; a ~ de with, aided by; in favour of; ¿ me hace el ~ de pasarme la sal? will you please pass me the salt?; por ~ please.

favorable, adj. favourable.

fe, s. f. faith; de buena ~ in good faith.

fealdad, s. f. ugliness.

febrero, s. m. February.

febril, adj. feverish.

fecundo, adj. prolific, fruitful.

fecha, s. f. date.

federación, s. f. federation.

felicidad, s. f. happiness.

felicitación, s. f. congratulations.

felicitar, v. a. congratulate.

feliz, adj. happy.

femenino, adj. feminine.

fenómeno, s. m. phenomenon; prodigy.

feo, adj. ugly.

feraz, adj. fertile.

féretro, s. m. coffin.

feria, s. f. country-market; fair.

ferretería. s. f. ironmonger's shop.

ferrocarril, s. m. railway.

fértil, adj. fertile.

festivo, adj. humorous; gay; dia ~ holiday.

fiambres, s. m. pl. cold meat, cold cuts.

fidelidad, s. f. fidelity; faithfulness; exactness.

fideos, s. m. pl. vermicelli.

fiebre, s. f. fever.

fiel, adj. faithful; accurate.

fieltro, s. m. felt (material).

fiera, s. f. wild animal, beast.

fiesta, s. f. holiday; party.

figura, s. f. figure, build.

figurar, v. n. figure; be conspicuous; ~se imagine, think.

fijar, v. a. fix, set; post; establish; ~ los ojos en stare at; v. n. ~se imagine; ~se en pay attention to.

fijo, adj. permanent; fixed, set; fast; de ~ surely.

fila, s. f. row; line, rank; en ~ in line.

filete, s. m. steak.

film, s. m. film.

filtrar, v. a. filter.

fin, s. m. end; aim, purpose; a ~ de que so that; a ~es de toward the end of; al ~ at last, finally; al ~ y al cabo after all; por ~ at last.

final, *adj.* final; — *s. m.* end, conclusion.

finca, *s. f.* piece of land, estate, farm.

fineza, *s. f.* politeness, kindness, courtesy.

fino, *adj.* fine; delicate; refined; thin, sharp; courteous.

firma, *s.f.* signature; firm, commercial house.

firmar, *v. a.* sign.

firme, *adj.* firm, steady.

firmeza, *s. f.* firmness.

fiscal, *adj.* fiscal; — *s. m.* Attorney General.

física, *s. f.* physics.

físico, *adj.* physical; — *s. m.* physicist.

flaco, *adj.* thin, lean; weak.

flan, *s. m.* caramel custard.

flaqueza, *s. f.* weakness.

flauta, *s. f.* flute.

flecha, *s. f.* arrow.

flexible, *adj.* flexible; — *s. m.* electric cord.

flirtear, *v. n.* flirt.

flojo, *adj.* loose; slack; lazy.

flor, *s. f.* flower.

florecer, *v. n.* bloom.

florero, *s. m.* florist; flower-vase.

florido, *adj.* florid, flowery; in bloom.

flota, *s. f.* fleet (of ships).

flotar, *v. n.* float.

flúido, *adj. & s. m.* fluid.

foco, *s. m.* focus.

fogón, *s. m.* cooking-stove, range.

follaje, *s. m.* foliage.

folleto, *s. m.* booklet, pamphlet.

fonda, *s. f.* inn.

fondo, *s. m.* bottom; back, background; ~s *pl.* funds; a ~ thoroughly; artículo (s. m.) de ~ editorial; en el ~ at heart, at bottom.

forma, *s. f.* shape, form; way, manner.

formal, *adj.* reliable; serious, settled.

formalidad, *s. f.* red tape; earnestness, seriousness.

formalizar, *v. a.* arrange, legalize.

formar, *v. a.* form, make.

fórmula, *s. f.* formula; solution.

formular, *v. a.* draw up, formulate.

foro, *s. m.* law-court; background (stage).

forraje, *s. m.* feed.

forro, *s. m.* lining (in clothing).

fortaleza, *s. f.* fortress; fortitude, strength.

fortuna, *s. f.* fortune; luck; por ~ fortunately.

forzar, *v. a.* force, compel.

forzoso, *adj.* compulsory; unavoidable; paro ~ unemployment.

fosa, *s. f.* grave.

foso, *s. m.* pit; trap-door.

fósforo, *s. m.* match.

fotografía, *s. f.* photography.

fotografiar, *v. a.* photograph.

fotógrafo, *s. m.* photographer.

fractura, *s. f.* fracture.

fragancia, *s. f.* fragrance.

frágil, *adj.* fragile.

fragmento, *s. m.* fragment.

fraile, *s. m.* monk, friar.

francés, *adj.* French; — *s. m.* Frenchman.

franco, *adj.* frank; free; exempt; ~ *de porte* prepaid.

franela, *s. f.* flannel.

franja, *s. f.* fringe.

franquear *v. a.* prepay, stamp.

franqueo, *s. m.* postage, amount of postage.

franqueza, *s. f.* frankness; *con* ~ frankly.

frasco, *s. m.* bottle, flask.

frase, *s. f.* phrase.

fraternidad, *s. f.* brotherliness, fraternity.

fray, *s. m.* monk, friar.

frecuentar, *v. a.* frequent.

frecuente, *adj.* frequent.

fregadero, *s. m.* kitchensink.

freír, *v. a.* fry.

frenar, *v. a.* (put on the) brake; restrain.

frenesí, *s. m.* madness; frenzy.

frenético, *adj.* very angry; frenzied.

freno, *s. m.* brake; bit (for horses).

frente, *s. f.* forehead; *s. m.* front, battle-field.

fresa, *s. f.* strawberry.

fresco, *adj.* cool; fresh; cheeky; — *s. m.* fresco (painting); *tomar el* ~ get some fresh air.

frescura, *s. f.* coolness; nerve, cheek.

frialdad, *s. f.* coldness; coolness, unconcern.

frigorífico, *s. m.* coldstorage plant, fridge.

frío, *adj.* cold; *hace* ~ it's cold; *tengo* ~ I'm cold.

frito, *adj.* fried; *estar* ~ be annoyed.

fritura, *s. f.* fritter.

frontera, *s. f.* frontier, boundary.

frotar, *v. a.* rub.

fructuoso, *adj.* useful, profitable, fruitful.

fruta, *s. f.* (edible) fruit.

frutal: *adj.* *árbol (s. m.)* ~ fruit-tree.

frutero, *s. m.* fruiterer.

fruto, *s. m.* fruit; reward; profit.

fuego, *s. m.* fire; *hacer* ~ fire (a weapon).

fuente, *s. f.* fountain; source; dish.

fuera, *adv.* out, outside; *desde* ~ from the outside; *por* ~ on the outside; — *prep.* ~ *de* out of; ~ *de sí* beside oneself; ~ *de eso* besides, moreover; *¡*~*!* get out!

fuerte, *adj.* strong; intense (cold); heavy (rain); — *adv. hablar* ~ speak loud; — *s. m.* fort; strong point.

fuerza, *s. f.* power; *a la* ~ forcibly.

fuga, *s. f.* flight, escape.

fulano, *s. m.* Mr. so-and-so.

fulminar, *v. n.* flash.

fumador, *s. m.* smoker.

fumar, *v. a. & n.* smoke.

función, *s. f.* function, duty, position; show, performance.

funcionamiento, *s. m.* working, functioning.

funcionar, *v. n.* work, function, run.

funcionario, *s. m.* official; functionary.

funda, *s. f.* case, pillowcase.

fundación, *s. f.* foundation, founding.

fundador, *s. m.* founder.

fundamento, *s. m.* basis.

fundar, *v. a.* found, establish; *v. n.* ~*se* base oneself.

funeral *adj.* funeral; — *s. m.* funeral service.

funicular, *s. m.* cable railway.

furgón, *s. m.* luggage-van.

furia, *s. f.* fury.

furioso, *adj.* furious.

furor, *s. m.* fury, anger; rage, fashion.

fusible, *adj.* fusible; — *s. m.* fuse, cut-out.

fusil, *s. m.* (shot)gun.

fusión, *s. f.* fusion.

fútbol, *s. m.* soccer, football (game).

futuro, *adj.* & *s. m.* future; *en lo* ~ in the future, hereafter.

G

gabán, *s. m.* overcoat.

gabinete, *s. m.* cabinet; study, small living-room.

gafas, *s. f. pl.* eye-glasses, spectacles.

gala, *s. f.* gala; *función (s. f.) de* ~ gala performance; *traje (s. m.) de* ~ dress-suit.

galante, *adj.* attentive.

galantería, *s. f.* compliment; courtesy.

galera, *s. f.* galley; tophat.

galería, *s. f.* (art) gallery; (theatre) gallery; passageway (underground).

galgo, *s. m.* greyhound.

galopar, *v. n.* gallop.

galope, *s. m.* gallop, canter.

galleta, *s. f.* ship's biscuit; slap.

gallina, *s. f.* hen; coward.

gallinero, *s. m.* hen-house; (theatre) top-gallery.

gallo, *s. m.* cock; bully.

gamuza, *s. f.* chamois; yellow duster.

gana, *s. f.* desire, mind; *de buena* ~ willingly; *de mala* ~ unwillingly; *tener* ~s *de* feel like.

ganado, *s. m.* cattle.

ganador, *s. m.* winner.

ganar, *v. a.* win; gain; earn; ~ *tiempo* save time; *v. n.* ~*se la vida* earn a living.

gancho, *s. m.* hook.

ganso, *s. m.* & *f.* goose, gander.

garaje, *s. m.* garage.

garantía, *s. f.* security.

garantizar, *v. a.* guarantee, vouch for.

garbanzo, *s. m.* chick-pea.

garbo, *s. m.* grace.

garganta, *s. f.* throat.

gárgara, *s. f.* gargle; *hacer* ~s gargle.

garrafa, *s. f.* decanter.

gas, *s. m.* gas.

gasa, *s. f.* gauze.

gaseosa, *s. f.* soda-water.

gasolina, *s. f.* petrol.

gasolinera, *s. f.* motor-boat.

gastar, *v. a.* spend; waste; wear, use; ~ *bromas* joke, jest.

gasto, *s. m.* expense; wear and tear; *pagar los* ~s foot the bill.

gata, *s. f.* (she-)cat.

gato, *s. m.* cat, tom-cat; jack (car).

gemelo, *s. m.* twin; ~s *pl.*cuff-links; binoculars, opera-glasses.

gemir, *v. n.* moan, whine, groan.

general, *adj.* general; *en* ~, *por lo* ~ usually,

generally; *por regla* ~ as a general rule; — *s. m.* general.

generalizar, *v. a.* generalize; *v. n.* ~se become general.

género, *s. m.* kind; gender; ~ *humano* mankind.

generosidad, *s. f.* generosity.

generoso, *adj.* generous.

genial, *adj.* brilliant.

genio, *s. m.* genius; temper, nature; *buen* ~ good nature; *mal* ~ bad temper.

gente, *s. f.* people; folks.

gentil, *adj.* gracious, kind.

gentileza, *s. f.* graciousness, kindness.

geografía, *s. f.* geography.

geográfico, *adj.* geographical.

gerente, *s. m.* manager.

gesticular, *v. n.* gesticulate.

gesto, *s. m.* gesture; *hacer* ~s make gestures, signal.

gigante, *s. m.* giant.

gimnasia, *s. f.* gymnastics; *hacer* ~ practise gymnastics.

ginebra, *s. f.* gin.

girar, *v. n.* revolve, turn; draw (of money).

giro, *s. m.* turn; draft; ~ *postal* money-order.

gitana, *s. f.,* **gitano,** *s. m.* gipsy.

glacial, *adj.* icy.

glándula, *s. f.* gland.

globo, *s. m.* globe; sphere; balloon.

gloria, *s. f.* glory; heaven.

gloriarse, *v. n.* boast.

glorificar, *v. a.* glorify.

glorioso, *adj.* glorious.

glotón, *s. m.* glutton.

gobernación, *s. f.* government; *Ministerio de la Gobernación* Ministry of the Interior; Home Office.

gobernador, *s. m.* governor.

gobernar, *v. a.* govern.

gobierno, *s. m.* government; cabinet (of ministers); control.

golfo, *s. m.* gulf.

golondrina, *s. f.* swallow.

golosina, *s. f.* dainty, delicacy.

golpe, *s. m.* blow; *de* ~ suddenly; ~ *de Estado* coup d'état; *dar* ~s knock, pound.

golpear, *v. n.* pound.

goma, *s. f.* glue; rubber, eraser.

gordo, *adj.* fat; *premio* ~ first prize in lottery.

gorra, *s. f.* cap.

gorrión, *s. m.* sparrow.

gorro, *s. m* cap.

gota, *s. f.* drop; gout.

gotear, *v. n.* drizzle; leak.

gótico, *adj.* Gothic.

gozar, *v. a. & n.* enjoy; enjoy oneself, have a good time.

grabado, *s. m.* engraving; etching; picture (illustration).

grabar, *v. a.* engrave; cut (a record).

gracia, *s. f.* charm, grace; mercy; wit, joke; name; *tiene* ~ it's funny; *gracias* pl. thanks.

grado, *s. m.* degree; *de mal* ~ unwillingly; reluctantly.

graduar, *v. a.* gauge; *v. n.* ~se graduate.

gráfica, *s. f.* graph, diagram.

gráfico, *adj.* graphic.

gramática, *s. f.* grammar.

gramo, *s. m.* gram(me) (weight).

gramófono, *s. m.* gramophone.

gran, grande, *adj.* large; tall; great; **en ~** on a large scale.

grandeza, *s. f.* greatness.

grandioso, *adj.* grandiose, magnificent.

granero, *s. m.* granary.

granizar, *v. n.* hail.

granizo, *s. m.* hail.

granja, *s. m.* farm.

grano, *s. m.* grain; **~s** *pl.* cereals; **ir al ~** get to the point.

grasa, *s. f.* fat; grease.

grasiento, *adj.* greasy, oily.

gratificación, *s. f.* gratification, tip.

gratificar, *v. a.* reward.

gratis, *adv.* gratis, free.

gratitud, *s. f.* gratitude.

grato, *adj.* pleasant.

gratuito, *adj.* free.

gratulación, *s. f.* congratulation. good wishes.

gratular, *v. a.* congratulate.

grave, *adj.* grave, serious; deep (voice).

griego, *adj.* & *s. m.* Greek.

grieta, *s. f.* crack.

grifo, *s. m.* water-tap.

grillo, *s. m.* cricket (insect).

gripe, *s. f.* grippe, influenza.

gris, *adj.* gray.

gritar, *v. n.* shout, scream.

grito, scream, shout.

grosero *adj.* rude, coarse.

grúa, *s. f.* crane.

gruesa, *s. f.* gross (twelve dozen).

grueso, *adj.* stout, thick; **~** *s. m.* main body (of troops).

gruñido, *s.m.* growl, grunt.

grupo, *s. m.* group; clump.

guante, *s. m.* glove.

guapo, *adj.* handsome, pretty.

guarda, *s. m.* guard.

guardabarrera, *s. m.* gatekeeper.

guardabosque, *s. m.* forest ranger.

guardacostas, *s. m.* coastguard.

guardar, *v. a.* keep, guard; **~ silencio** keep quiet; *v. n.* **~se de** avoid.

guardarropa, *s. m.* wardrobe; cloakroom.

guardia, *s. f.* guard; **en ~** on guard; *estar de* **~** be on (guard) duty; *s. m.* policeman; **~ civil** member of the civil guard.

guardián, *s. m.* watchman.

guarnición, *s. f.* trimming, edging; garrison.

guerra, *s. f.* war; *Gran Guerra* World War.

guerrero, *s. m.* warrior.

guía, *s. m.,* *f.* guide; *s. f.* guide-book, directory; **~ de ferrocarriles** railway guide; **~ telefónica** telephone directory.

guiar, *v. a.* guide; drive (a car); *v. n.* **~se por** follow.

guisante, *s. m.* pea.

guisar, *v. a.* & *n.* cook.

guitarra, *s. f.* guitar.

gusano, *s. m.* worm; **~ de luz** glow-worm; **~ de seda** silkworm.

gustar, *v. a.* please; *m e gusta eer* I like reading; *nos gustan los deportes* we like sports.

gusto, *s. m.* taste; liking; *a* ~ comfortable; *con mucho* ~ with much pleasure, gladly, willingly; *dar* ~ *a* please; *tengo mucho* ~ *en conocerle* I'm very glad to meet you.

gustoso, *aoj.* savoury.

H

haba, *s. f.* broad bean.

haber, *(auxiliary verb) he leido que* I have read that; *he de hacerlo* I have to do it; *hay there is, there are; hay que comer* it's necessary to eat; *no hay de que* don't mention it; you're welcome; — *s. m.* credit; ~*es,* pl. incomings, revenues.

hábil, *adj.* skilful, clever.

habilidad, *s. f.* ability.

habitación, *s. f.* dwelling; room.

habitante, *s. m., f.* inhabitant.

habitar, *v. a. & n.* inhabit.

habitual, *adj.* habitual; — *s. m.* customer.

habituar, *v. a.* accustom; *v. n.* ~*se* get accustomed.

habitud, *s. f.* habit, custom.

habla, *s. f.* speech; language.

hablador, *adj.* talkative.

hablar, *v. a. & n.* speak, talk.

hacer, *v. a.* make; do; *hace frio* it's cold; *hace*

calor it's hot; ~ *caso a* pay attention to; ~ *el favor* please; ~ *el honor de* do the honour of; ~ *los honores* act as host(ess); ~ *furor* make a hit; ~ *el sueco* pretend not to understand; ~*se* become; *hace una semana* a week ago.

hacia, *prep.* toward; ~ *adelante* forward; ~ *allá* that way; ~ *atrás* backwards.

hacienda, *s. f.* country seat, estate; fortune; *Ministro de Hacienda* Minister of Finance.

hacha, *s. f.* axe.

hallar, *v. a.* find; *v. n.* ~*se* be.

hamaca, *s. f.* hammock.

hambre, *s. f.* hunger; *tengo mucha* ~ I'm very hungry.

hambriento, *adj.* hungry, starved.

harina, *s. f.* flour, meal.

harinoso, *adj.* mealy.

hartar, *v. a.* satiate, satisfy, *v. n.* ~*se* gorge, stuff oneself.

harto, *adj.* full, stuffed; fed up.

hasta, *prep.* until; ~ *aqui* so far; ~ *la vista,* ~ *luego* so long; ~ *las seis* till six o'clock; — *adv.* even.

hay, see **haber.**

hazaña, *s. f.* feat, exploit, deed.

hectárea, *s. f.* hectare.

hectolitro, *s. m.* hectolitre.

hecho, *adj.* done; readymade; — *s. m.* deed; fact.

heder, *v. n.* stink.

helada, *s. f.* white frost.

helado, *adj.* frozen; — *s. m.* ice-cream.

helar, *v. a.* freeze; *v. n.* ~se freeze up.

hélice, *s. f.* propeller (of ship).

hembra, *s. f.* female.

hemisferio, *s. m.* hemisphere.

hemorragia, *s. f.* haemorrhage.

hemorroide, *s. f.* haemorrhoids, piles.

heno, *s. m.* hay.

heredar, *v. a.* inherit.

heredero, *s. m.* heir.

hereditario, *adj.* hereditary.

herencia, *s. f.* inheritance

herida, *s. f.* wound.

herido, *s. m.* wounded man.

herir, *v. a.* wound, hurt.

hermana, *s. f.* sister; nun.

hermano, *s. m.* brother.

hermoso, *adj.* beautiful, handsome.

héroe, *s. m.* hero.

heroína, *s. f.* heroine.

herradura, *s. f.* horseshoe.

herramienta, *s. f.* tool; set of tools.

herrería, *s. f.* forge, smithy; blacksmith's shop; ironworks.

herrero, *s. m.* blacksmith.

herrumbre. *s. m.* rust.

hervir, *v. n.* boil.

hidráulica, *s. f.* hydraulics.

hidroavión, *s. m.* hydroplane.

hidrógeno, *s. m.* hydrogen.

hiel, *s. f.* gall; bitterness.

hielo, *s. m.* ice.

hierba, *s. f.* grass; *mala ~* weed.

hierro, *s. m.* iron.

hígado, *s. m.* liver.

higiene, *s. f.* hygiene.

higiénico, *adj.* hygienic.

higo, *s. m.* fig.

higuera, *s. f.* fig-tree.

hija, *s. f.* daughter.

hijastra, *s. f.* stepdaughter.

hijastro, *s. m.* stepson.

hijo, *s. m.* son.

hila, *s. f.* row, line

hilar, *v. a.* spin.

hilera, *s. f.* row, line.

hilo, *s. m.* thread; wire.

himno, *s. m.* hymn.

hincha, *s. f.* fan.

hinchado, *adj.* swollen; haughty.

hinchar, *v. n.* swell.

hipocresía, *s. f.* hypocrisy.

hipócrita, *adj.* hypocritical; — *s. m.* hypocrite.

hipódromo, *s. m.* racecourse, racetrack.

hipoteca, *s. f.* mortgage.

hipotecar, *v. a.* mortgage.

hipótesis, *s. f.* hypothesis.

historia, *s. f.* history, story, tale.

histórico, *adj.* historic.

historieta, *s. f.* short story; comics.

hogar, *s. m.* fireplace; home, hearth.

hoguera, *s. f.* bonfire.

hoja, *s. f.* leaf, page; blade; ~ *de lata* tinplate; *doblar la ~* charge the subject.

hojalata, *s. f.* tin.

hojalatero, *s. m.* tinsmith; plumber.

hojear, *v. a.* thumb through, glance through (a book).

¡hola! *int.* hello!

holgazán, *adj.* lazy.

hollín, *s. m.* soot.

hombre, *s. m.* man; ~ *de Estado* statesman.

hombrecillo, *s. m.* little man.

hombro, *s. m.* shoulder.

homenaje, *s. m.* homage.

hondo, *adj.* deep.

honesto, *adj.* decent, honest.

hongo, *s. m.* fungus; mushroom.

honor, *s. m.* honour.

honra, *s. f.* honour; ~s *pl.* obsequies.

honradez, *s. f.* honesty, integrity.

honrado, *adj.* honest.

honrar, *v. a.* honour.

hora, *s. f.* hour; time; *¿qué ~ es?* what time is it?; *a última ~* at the last moment.

horario, *adj.* hourly; — *s. m.* time-table.

horizontal, *adj.* horizontal.

horizonte, *s. m.* horizon.

hormiga, *s. f.* ant.

hormigón, *s. m.* concrete; ~ *armado* reinforced concrete.

hormiguero, *s. m.* anthill; crowd, throng.

hornillo, *s. m.* cooking-range.

horno, *s. m.* baking-oven; *alto ~* blast-furnace.

horquilla, *s. f.* hairpin.

horrible, *adj.* horrible, horrid.

horror, *s. m.* horror.

hortaliza, *s. f.* vegetable.

hospedar, *v. a.* lodge, accommodate, shelter.

hospicio, *s. m.* hospice.

hospital, *s. m.* hospital.

hospitalario, *adj.* hospitable.

hospitalidad, *s. f.* hospitality.

hostil, *adj.* hostile.

hotel, *s. m.* hotel.

hoy, *adv.* today; *por ~* for the present.

hoyo, *s. m.* hole; ditch.

hueco, *adj.* hollow, empty; — *s. m.* hole.

huelga, *s. f.* strike (of workers).

huelguista, *s. m.* striker.

huella, *s. f.* track; footprint, fingerprint; trace, sign.

huérfano, *adj. & s. m.* orphan.

huerta, *s. f.* large vegetable garden.

huerto. *s. m.* orchard.

hueso, *s. m.* bone; stone (of fruit).

huésped, *s. m.* guest; *casa de ~es* boarding-house.

huevera, *s. f.* egg-cup.

huevo, *s. m.* egg.

huir, *v. n.* flee.

hule, *s. m.* oilcloth.

hulla, *s. f.* pit-coal.

humanidad, *s. f.* humanity; humaneness.

humear, *v. n.* smoke.

humedad, *s. f.* dampness, humidity, moisture.

humedecer, *v. a.* moisten.

húmedo, *adj.* damp, humid.

humilde, *adj.* humble.

humillar, *v. a.* humiliate.

humo, *s. m.* smoke;

~s pl. airs. affected manner.

humor, s. m. humour, mood; wit.

humorismo, s. m. humour.

humorista, s. m. humorist.

hundir, v. a. sink; destroy; v. n. ~se sink; fall off, diminish.

huracán, s. m. hurricane.

hurtar, v. a. steal, pilfer.

hurto, s. m. theft, larceny.

huso, s. m. spindle.

I

iberoamericano, adj. & s. m. Latin American.

ida, s. f. leaving, going; billete (s. m.) de ~ y vuelta return ticket.

idea, s. f. idea.

ideal, adj. ideal, perfect; — s. m. ideal, principle.

idear, v. a. plan, invent.

identidad, s. f. identity.

idioma, s. m. language.

ídolo, s. m. idol.

iglesia, s. f. church; clergy.

ignición, s. f. ignition.

ignorante, adj. ignorant.

ignorar, v. a. not to know, lack knowledge; ignore.

ignoto, adj. unknown.

igual, adj. same; similar; ~ a equal to; pienso ~ que usted I think the same as you.

igualar, v. a. equal; level (road); v. n. ~se be equal, be tied (score).

igualdad, s. f. equality; evenness, smoothness.

ilegalidad, s. f. illegality.

ilegible, adj. illegible.

ilimitado, adj. boundless, unlimited.

iluminación, s. f. illumination.

iluminar, v. a. light, illuminate.

ilusión, s. f. illusion, delusion; hacerse ilusiones chase after rainbows.

ilusionar, v. a. thrill; v. n. ~se get thrilled or excited.

ilusorio, adj. illusory.

ilustración, s. f. illustration, picture; learning.

ilustrado, adj. illustrated, with pictures; learned.

ilustrar, v. a. illustrate.

ilustre, adj. illustrious, distinguished.

imagen, s. f. image.

imaginación, s. f. imagination.

imaginar, v. a. think of, devise, figure out; v. n. ~se imagine, suspect.

imán, s. m. magnet.

imitar, v. a. imitate.

impaciencia, s. f. impatience.

impacientarse, v. n. be impatient.

impaciente, adj. impatient.

impacto, s. m. impact.

impar, adj. unlike; odd.

impecable, adj. blameless.

impedir, v. a. prevent; ~ el paso block the way.

imperativo, adj. imperative.

imperdible, s. m. safety-pin.

imperdonable, *adj.* unpardonable.

imperfecto, *adj.* imperfect.

imperio, *s. m.* empire; command; spell.

impermeable, *adj.* waterproof; — *s. m.* raincoat.

impertinente, *adj.* impertinent.

impertinentes, *s. m. pl.* lorgnette.

ímpetu, *s. m.* impetus, impulse.

impetuoso, *adj.* impetuous.

implicar, *v. a.* involve, implicate.

implorar, *v. a.* beg, implore.

imponente, *adj.* imposing.

imponer, *v. a.* impose, levy; *v. n.* ~se assert oneself; dominate; get one's way.

importación, *s. f.* import, importation.

importador, *s. m.* importer.

importancia, *s. f.* importance.

importante, *adj.* important.

importar, *v. a.* import; *v. n.* ¿cuánto importa? what does it amount to?; no importa it doesn't matter, never mind.

importe, *s. m.* amount.

importuno, *adj.* importunate, annoying.

imposibilidad, *s. f.* impossibility.

imposible, *adj.* impossible.

impotencia, *s. f.* impotence, weakness.

impotente, *adj.* impotent.

impregnar, *v. a.* impregnate.

imprenta, *s. f.* press; print; *error (s. m.) de* ~ printer's error.

impresión, *s. f.* impression; imprint; printing.

impresionar, *v. a.* impress; expose (photo); make *or* cut (a record); *v. n.* ~se be moved.

impreso, *s. m.* printed matter; blank (to be filled).

imprevisto, *adj.* unforeseen, unexpected.

imprimir, *v.a.* print.

improductivo, *adj.* unfruitful.

improperio, *s. m.* abuse, invective.

impropio, *adj.* inappropriate, unfitting.

improvisado, *adj.* makeshift.

improvisar, *v. a.* improvise.

improviso, *adj.* unforeseen.

imprudente, *adj.* imprudent, unwise.

impuesto, *s. m.* tax.

inaceptable, *adj.* unacceptable.

inadvertido, *adj.* inattentive, careless.

inagotable, *adj.* inexhaustible.

inaudito, *adj.* unheard of, strange, unexpected.

inauguración, *s. f.* inauguration, opening (ceremony).

inaugurar, *v. a.* inaugurate, open.

incansable, *adj.* untiring.

incapaz, *adj.* incompetent, incapable.

incendiar, *v. a.* set on fire.

incendio, *s. m.* fire (conflagration).

incidente, *s. m.* incident, disturbance.

incierto, *adj.* uncertain, doubtful.

inclinación, *s. f.* inclination; bent; slope.

inclinar, *v. a.* bend, bow; *v. n.* ~se bow; yield, give in; ~se a be inclined to.

incluir, *v. a.* include; enclose.

inclusión, *s. f.* inclusion.

inclusivo, *adj.* inclusive.

incomodar, *v. a.* disturb, inconvenience, bother; *v. n.* ~se become angry, be upset.

incomodidad, *s. f.* inconvenience.

incómodo, *adj.* uncomfortable.

incompleto, *adj.* incomplete.

inconsciente, *adj.* unconscious.

inconsecuente, *adj.* contradictory, inconsequential.

inconveniente, *adj.* unbecoming, improper; — *s. m.* disadvantage; objection.

incorporar, *v. a.* incorporate, unite; add; *v. n.* ~se sit up (in bed); join (a military unit).

increíble, *adj.* incredible, unbelievable.

incubadora, *s. f.* incubator.

inculpar, *v. a.* inculpate.

inculto, *adj.* uncultivated.

incumplido, *adj.* unful-filled.

incurrir, *v. n.* incur.

indagar, *v. a.* investigate.

indecente, *adj.* indecent, obscene.

indeciso, *adj.* vacillating, hesitant; indefinite.

indefenso, *adj.* defenceless.

indefinido, *adj.* indefinite.

indemnización, *s. f.* indemnity, compensation.

indemnizar, *v. a.* indemnify.

independencia, *s. f.* independence.

indescriptible, *adj.* indescribable.

indeterminado, *adj.* indeterminate, indefinite.

indicación, *s. f.* hint, suggestion; instruction.

indicar, *v. a.* indicate, hint, show.

indicativo, *s. m.* & *adj.* indicative.

índice, *s. m.* index; table of contents; forefinger.

indicio, *s. m.* indication, clue; evidence.

indiferente, *adj.* indifferent.

indígena, *adj.* native, aboriginal; — *s. m.* native, aborigine.

indigestión, *s. f.* indigestion.

indignar, *v. a.* fill with indignation; *v. n.* ~se become indignant.

indigno, *adj.* despicable, unworthy.

indio, *adj.* & *s. m.* Indian; Hindu.

indirecta, *s. f.* insinuation, hint; *echar* ~s make insinuations.

indisciplinado, *adj.* undisciplined.

indiscreto, *adj.* indiscreet.

indiscutible, *adj.* unquestionable.

indisoluble, *adj.* indissoluble.

indisponer, *v. a.* prejudice, set against; *v. n.* ~se become ill.

indispuesto, *adj.* indisposed, ill.

individual, *adj.* individual, separate; — *s. m.* single (tennis).

individuo, *s. m.* individual, person.

índole, *s. f.* nature, character; class, kind.

indomable, *adj.* indomitable.

indudable, *adj.* indubitable, certain, evident.

indulto, *s. m.* pardon; amnesty.

industria, *s. f.* industry.

industrial, *adj.* industrial; — *s. m.* manufacturer.

ineficaz, *adj.* inefficient.

inesperado, *adj.* unexpected.

inestimable, *adj.* invaluable.

inexperto, *adj.* inexperienced.

infame, *adj.* infamous; — *s. m.* scoundrel.

infancia, *s. f.* infancy, childhood.

infantería, *s. f.* infantry.

infantil, *adj.* infantile, childlike.

infatigable, *adj.* untiring.

infección, *s. f.* infection.

infeccioso, *adj.* infectious.

infeliz, *adj.* unhappy; poor.

inferior, *adj.* inferior, lower; — *s. m.* inferior.

inferioridad, *s. f.* inferiority.

infiel, *adj.* unfaithful.

infierno, *s. m.* hell; pain.

ínfimo, *adj.* lowest.

infinidad, *s. f.* endless number, a lot.

infinito, *adj.* infinite; — *s. m.* infinity.

inflación, *s. f.* inflation.

inflamar, *v. a.* set on fire; *v. n.* ~se catch fire.

influencia, *s. f.* influence.

influir *en,* *v. n.* (have) influence on sy.

influyente, *adj.* influential.

información, *s. f.* information.

informar, *v. a.* inform, tell; *v. n.* ~se get information; find out.

informativo, *adj.* informative.

informe, *s. m.* report; information.

infortunio, *s. m.* great misfortune; ill-luck.

ingeniero, *s. m.* engineer.

ingenio, *s. m.* talent, genius; wit.

ingenioso, *adj.* ingenious.

ingenuo, *adj.* ingenuous; candid, innocent.

inglés, *adj.* English; — *s. m.* Englishman.

ingrato, *adj.* ungrateful, thankless.

ingrediente, *s. m.* ingredient.

ingresar, *v. a.* deposit; *v. n.* enter, join.

ingreso, *s. m.* entrance (joining); ~s *pl.* income, earnings.

inhalar, *v. a.* inhale.

inhibir, *v. a.* inhibit.

inhumanidad, *s. f.* inhumanity.

inicial, *adj. & s. f.* initial.

iniciar, *v. a.* initiate, begin.

iniciativa, *s. f.* initiative.

injuria, *s. f.* insult.

injuriar, *v. a.* injure, insult.

injusticia, *s. f.* injustice.

inmediato, *adj.* immediate; adjoining, next.

inmenso, *adj.* immense.

inmigración, *s. f.* immigration.

inmigrante, *s. m. f.* immigrant.

inmigrar, *v. n.* immigrate.

inmóvil, *adj.* motionless.

inmueble, *s. m.* real estate.

innecesario, *adj.* unnecessary, needless.

inocente, *adj.* innocent; not guilty; simple.

inocular, *v. a.* inoculate.

inodoro, *adj.* inodorous.

inolvidable, *adj.* unforgettable.

inquietar, *v. a.* worry, trouble; *v. n.* ~se become restless *or* worried.

inquilino, *s. m.* tenant.

inquirir, *v. n.* inquire, investigate.

insaciable, *adj.* insatiable, greedy.

insano, *adj.* insane; unhealthy, unsanitary.

inscribir, *v. a.* register, enroll.

inscripción, *s. f.* inscription; registration.

insecto, *s. m.* insect.

inseguro, *adj.* insecure, unsafe, unsteady.

insensato, *adj.* senseless, stupid, foolish.

insensible, *adj.* insensitive; heartless.

inserción, *s. f.* insertion.

insertar, *v. a.* insert.

insípido, *adj.* insipid, tasteless.

insistir *en,* *v. n.* insist on.

insolencia, *s. f.* insolence.

insolente, *adj.* insolent.

inspección, *s. f.* inspection, examination.

inspeccionar, *v. a.* inspect, examine.

inspector, *s. m.* inspector.

inspirar, *v. a.* inspire.

instalar, *v. a.* install, set up; *v. n.* ~se establish oneself; take quarters.

instancia, *s. f.* petition, application; *a* ~ *de* at the request of.

instantánea, *s. f.* snapshot.

instante, *s. m.* instant, moment; *al* ~ instantly, at once.

instinto, *s. m.* instinct.

institución, *s. f.* institution.

instituto, *s. m.* institute; school.

instrucción, *s. f.* instruction, direction; education.

instructivo, *adj.* instructive.

instructor, *s. m.* instructor; *juez* ~ examining magistrate.

instruir, *v. a.* teach, instruct.

instrumento, *s. m.* instrument.

insurrección, *s. f.* insurrection; rebellion.

insurrecto, *adj. & s. m.* insurgent.

integridad, *s. f.* integrity; entirety.

íntegro, *adj.* complete, whole; honest, righteous.

intelectual, *adj. & s. m.*

intellectual.

inteligente, *adj.* intelligent.

intención, *s. f.* intention, purpose.

intensidad, *s. f.* intensity.

intenso, *adj.* intense.

intentar, *v. a.* attempt, try.

intento, *s. m.* intent.

interés, *s. m.* interest; rate of interest.

interesado, *adj.* interested; selfish.

interesante, *adj.* interesting.

interesar, *v. a.* interest; *v. n.* ~se be interested.

interino, *adj.* temporary.

interior, *adj.* interior; domestic; — *s. m.* inside.

intermediario, *s. n.* mediator.

intermedio, *adj.* intermediate; — *s. m.* interval; *en el* ~ in the meantime; *por* ~ *de* through (the intervention of).

interminable, *adj.* endless.

internacional, *adj.* international.

interno, *adj.* internal; — *s. m.* boarding student.

interpretar, *v. a.* interpret.

intérprete, *s m.* interpreter.

interrogación, *s. f.* interrogation; question-mark.

interrogar, *v. a.* question, interrogate.

intervalo, *s. m.* interval.

intervención, *s. f.* intervention; mediation.

intervenir, *v. n.* intervene.

intestino, *adj.* intestinal;

— *s. m.* intestine.

intimar, *v. n.* become an intimate friend.

intimidad, *s. f.* intimity.

intimidar, *v. a.* frighten, intimidate.

íntimo, *adj.* & *s. m.* intimate (friend).

intoxicar, *v. a.* poison; drug.

intranquilo, *adj.* restless, worried.

intransitable, *adj.* impassable.

intratable, *adj.* unsociable.

intrépido, *adj.* brave, fearless.

introducir, *v. a.* put in, insert; present (a person).

intuición, *s. f.* intuition.

inundación, *s. f.* flood, inundation.

inun ar, *v. a.* flood.

inútil, *adj.* useless.

inválido, *adj.* &. *s. m.* invalid; useless.

invasión, *s. f.* invasion.

invencible, *adj.* invincible, unconquerable.

invención, *s. f.* inv n-tion.

inventar, *v. a.* invent.

inventario, *s. m.* inventory.

invento, *s. m.* invention; lie.

inventor, *s. m.* inventor.

invernadero, *s. m.* hothouse.

invernal, *adj.* wintry.

inverosímil, *adj.* unlikely, improbable.

invertir, *v. a.* reverse, turn upside down; invest; spend (time).

investigación, *s. f.* investigation, inquiry; research.

investigar, *v. a.* investigate; do research work.

invierno, *s. m.* winter.

invitación, *s. f.* invitation.

invitado, *s. m.* guest.

invitar, *v. a.* invite.

involuntario, *adj.* involuntary.

inyectar, *v. a.* inject.

ir, *v. n.* go; lead (play); ¿*cómo le va?* how are you? *ese color le va muy bien* that colour is very becoming to you; ~ *a caballo* ride on horseback; ~ *a pie* walk, go on foot; ~ *del brazo* walk arm in arm; ~ *de paseo* go for a walk; ~*se* leave, go away.

ira, *s. f.* anger.

iris, *s. m.* iris; *arco* ~ rainbow.

irónico, *adj.* ironical, sarcastic.

irregularidad, *s. f.* irregularity.

irremediable, *adj.* irreparable, hopeless.

irritar, *v. a.* irritate.

isla, *s. f.* island, isle.

isleño, *s. m.* islander.

istmo, *s. m.* isthmus.

itinerario, *s. m.* itinerary.

izar, *v. a.* hoist (up).

izquierda, *s. f.* left hand; *a la* ~ on the left.

izquierdo, *adj.* left.

J

jabón, *s. m.* soap.

jabonar, *v. a.* soap; lather.

jabonera, *s. f.* soap-dish.

jadear, *v. n.* pant, gasp.

jalea, *s. f.* jelly.

jaleo, *s. m.* revels, uproar.

jamás, *adv.* never, ever.

jamón, *s. m.* ham.

jaque, *s. m.* check; *dar* ~ (give) check; *tener en* ~ keep in check.

jaquear, *v. a.* (give) check.

jaqueca, *s. f.* headache, migraine.

jarabe, *s. m.* syrup.

jardín, *s. m.* garden.

jardinero, *s. m.* gardener.

jarra, *s. f.* water-jug, pitcher.

jarro, *s. m.* jug, pitcher.

jaula, *s. f.* cage, prison.

jefatura, *s. f.* chief's office; headquarters.

jefe, *s. m.* chief, leader, head; boss; ~ *de tren* guard.

jerga, *s. f.* slang.

jeringa, *s. f.* syringe.

jícara, *s. f.* small cup.

jinete, *s. m.* horseman.

jofaina, *s. f.* wash-basin.

jornada, *s. f.* journey; day's work; day's walk.

jornal, *s. m.* day's wages.

jornalero, *s. m.* day-labourer.

jota, *s. f.* the letter „j"; Aragonese folk-dance.

joven, *adj.* young; — *s. m., f.* young person.

jovial, *adj.* jovial; merry, gay.

joya, *s. f.* gem.

joyería, *s. f.* jeweller's shop.

jubilar, *v. a.* pension off.

jubileo, *s. m.* jubilee.

júbilo, *s. m.* jubilation; glee.

judía, *s. f.* bean; ~*s verdes* French beans.

judío, *adj.* Jewish; — *s. m.* Jew.

juego, *s. m.* game; play,

playing; gambling; *un ~ de mesa* table-service; *~ de palabras* play on words, pun; *hacer ~* match.

jueves, *s. m.* Thursday.

juez, *s. m.* judge.

jugada, *s. f.* move (chess); trick, prank.

jugador, *s. m.* player; gambler.

jugar, *v. a. & n.* play; gamble.

jugo, *s. m.* juice.

jugoso, *adj.* juicy, succulent.

juguete, *s. m.* toy.

juguetería, *s. f.* toy-shop.

juicio, *s. m.* judgment; trial (law).

juicioso, *adj.* judicious.

julio, *s. m.* July.

junio, *s. m.* June.

junta, *s. f.* meeting; board; joint, joining (carpentry).

juntar, *v. a.* join, connect; *v. n. ~se* meet, gather.

junto, *adj. & adv.* together; *vamos ~s* let's go together; — *prep.* *~ a* next to, beside; *~ con* with.

juntura, *s. f.* hinge; joint.

jurado, *s. m.* juryman; jury.

juramento, *s. m.* oath; swearing.

jurar, *v. n.* swear; curse.

jurídico, *adj.* juridical.

jurisconsulto, *s. m.* counsel, legal adviser.

justicia, *s. f.* justice.

justificar, *v. a.* justify.

justo, *adj.* right, just; correct, exact; tight (clothes).

juvenil, *adj.* juvenile.

juventud, *s. f.* youth; youthfulness.

juzgado, *s. m.* law-court; district court.

juzgar, *v. a.* judge; try.

K

kermesse, *s. f.* kermess.

kilo, *s. m.* kilogram.

kilociclo, *s. m.* kilocycle.

kilogramo, *s. m.* kilogram.

kilómetro, *s. m.* kilometre.

kilovatio, *s. m.* kilowatt.

kiosco, *see* quiosco.

kirsch, *s. m.* cherry-brandy.

kodak, *s. m.* camera.

kummel, *s. m.* cumin brandy.

L

la, *f. (definite article)* *~ mesa* the table; — *pron.* her, it; *las,* pl. them.

labio, *s. m.* lip.

labor, *s. f.* work, task.

laborable, *adj.; dia (s. m.)* *~* workday.

laboratorio, *s. m.* laboratory.

labrador, *s. m.* countryman, farmer.

lacrar, *v. a.* seal (up).

lacre, *s. m.* sealing-wax.

lado, *s. m.* side; edge, margin; *al ~ de* by the side of, next door to; *de ~* sideways, on its side.

ladrillo, *s. m.* brick.

ladrón, *s. m.* thief, robber.

lagarto, *s. m.* lizard.

lago, *s. m.* lake.

lágrima, *s. f.* tear.

laguna, *s. f.* lagoon.

lamentar, *v. n.* be sorry;

~se lament, wail, moan.
lamento, *s. m.* moan.
lamer, *v. a.* lick, lap.
lámina, *s. f.* sheet, plate.
lámpara, *s. f.* lamp; bulb.
lana, *s. f.* wool.
lance, *s. m.* throwing; occurrence; **de ~** secondhand.
lanceta, *s. f.* lancet.
lancha, *s. f.* (small) boat.
langosta, *s. f.* lobster; locust (insect).
lanzar, *v. a.* throw, hurl; *v. n.* **~se** throw oneself, rush.
lápida, *s. f.* commemorative tablet; headstone.
lápiz, *s. m.* pencil.
largar, *v. a.* let loose; *v. n.* **~se** leave, go away.
largo, *adj.* long; — *s. m.* length; *a lo* **~** de along.
laringe, *s. f.* larynx.
lástima, *s. f.* pity; *¡qué ~!* what a pity!; *dar* **~** inspire pity.
lastimarse, *v. n.* hurt oneself.
lata, *s. f.* tin (plate); tin box; *hoja (s. f.) de* **~** sheet metal; *dar la* **~** annoy, bother, pester.
latín, *s. m.* Latin (language).
latino, *adj. & s. m.* Latin.
latón, *s. m.* brass.
lavabo, *s. m.* washstand; washroom.
lavadero, *s. m.* washtub.
lavamanos, *s. m.* washbasin.
lavandera, *s. f.* laundress.
lavandería, *s. f.* laundry.
lavar, *v. a.* wash; *v. n.* **~se** wash.
laxante, *adj. & s. m.* laxative.
le, *pron.* him; to him, to her, to you; *les,* pl.

them, to them, to you.
leal, *adj.* loyal.
lección, *s. f.* lesson.
lectura, *s. f.* reading; *salón (s. m.) de* **~** reading-room.
leche, *s. f.* milk.
lechera, *s. f.* milk-woman.
lechería, *s. f.* dairy.
lechero, *s. m.* milk-man.
lecho, *s. m.* bed, couch.
lechuga, *s. f.* lettuce.
leer, *v. a.* read.
legación, *s. f.* legation.
legal, *adj.* legal, lawful.
legalidad, *s. f.* legality.
legalizar, *v. a.* legalize.
legendario, *adj.* legendary.
legible, *adj.* legible, readable.
legitimar, *v. a.* legitimate; *v. n.* **~se** prove one's identity.
legítimo, *adj.* lawful, legitimate.
legua, *s. f.* league (measure of length).
legumbre, *s. f.* vegetable.
lejano, *adj.* distant, far.
lejos, *adv.* far; *a lo* **~** in the distance; *desde* **~** from a distance; — *prep.* **~** *de* far from.
lengua, *s. f.* tongue; language.
lenguado, *s. m.* sole, flounder (fish).
lenguaje, *s. m.* language, speech.
lenitivo, *adj. & s. m.* lenitive.
lente, *s. m.* (optical) lens; **~s,** pl. eyeglasses; **~** *de aumento* magnifying glass.
lenteja, *s. f.* lentil.
lento, *adj.* slow.
leña, *s. f.* firewood.

leñador, s. m. wood-cutter.

león, s. m. lion.

les, pron., see **le**.

lesión, s. f. lesion.

lesionar, v. a. hurt, injure.

letra, s. f. letter (of alphabet); handwriting; ~ de cambio draft; ~ de imprenta type: escribir cuatro ~s write a few lines.

letrero, s. m. sign (-board), signpost.

levadura, s. f. yeast.

levantar, v. a. raise, lift; pick up; rise up; build; v. n. ~se get up.

levante, s. m. East.

levantino, adj. Eastern; Oriental.

leve, adj. light, slight.

ley, s. f. law.

leyenda, s. f. legend.

liar, v. a. bind; wind, roll.

liberación, s. f. liberation.

liberar, v. a. liberate, free.

libertad, s. f. liberty, freedom.

libertador, s. m. liberator.

libertar, v. a. free.

libra, s. f. pound (weight).

librar, v. a. free, deliver; v. n. ~se de get rid of.

libre, adj. free; disengaged.

librería, s. f. bookshop.

librero, s. m. bookseller.

libreta, s. f. savings book; notebook.

libro, s. m. book; ~ de apuntes notebook; ~ de cuentas account book.

licencia, s. f. licence; permit; furlough.

licenciado, s. m. ;~ del

ejército veteran; ~ en filosofía Master of Arts.

licenciar, v. a. discharge; v. n. ~se get a degree.

licitar, v. a. bid (auction).

licor, s. m. liqueur; cordial.

liebre, s. f. hare.

lienzo, s. m. canvas, picture.

liga, s. f. union, league; garter.

ligar, v. a. tie, bind, join.

ligero, adj. light, thin (coat); fast; unimportant; a la ligera quickly, superficially.

lima, s. f. file.

limar, v. a. file.

limitado, adj. limited.

limitar, v. a. restrict, limit.

límite, s. m. limit, boundary.

limón, s. m. lemon.

limonada, s. f. lemonade.

limosna, s. f. alms.

limpiabotas, s. m. bootblack.

limpiar, v. a. clean.

limpieza, s. f. cleanliness.

limpio, adj. clean; clear (sky); poner en ~ make a fair copy.

lindar con, v. n. border on.

lindo, adj. lovely, pretty; de lo ~ very much.

línea, s. f. line; figure; en ~ in a row; entre ~s between the lines.

lino, s. m. flax; linen.

linterna, s. f. lantern; flashlight.

lío, s. m. bundle; trouble, mess, jam.

liquidación, s. f. liquidation, clearance sale.

liquidar, v. a. liquidate; sell out; pay up.

líquido, *adj.* liquid; just; net (balance); — *s. m.* liquid.

lirio, *s. m.* lily.

lisiado, *s. m.;* ~ *de guerra* war-disabled.

liso, *adj.* smooth; plain.

lista, *s. f.* stripe; list; ~ *de platos* bill of fare.

listo, *adj.* ready; clever.

literario, *adj.* literary.

literato, *s. m.* author, writer.

literatura, *s. f.* literature.

litro, *s. m.* litre.

lo, *(neuter article)* lo *mejor* the best; — *pron.* him, it.

lobo, *s. m.* wolf; ~ *marino* seal.

local, *adj.* local; — *s. m.* place (indoors).

localidad, *s. f.* locality, place; seat (in a theatre).

localizar, *v. a.* locate; localize; find out.

loco, *adj.* insane, crazy; — *s. m.* madman, lunatic.

locomotora, *s. f.* locomotive.

locura, *s. f.* insanity, madness; folly.

locutor, *s. m.;* **-a,** *s. f.* announcer.

locutorio, *s. m.* telephone box.

lodo, *s. m.* mud.

lógica, *s. f.* logic.

lógico, *adj.* logical.

lograr, *v. a.* get, obtain; succeed in.

lomo, *s. m.* loin.

lona, *s. f.* canvas.

lonja, *s. f.* cut, slice.

loro, *s. m.* parrot.

los, *pron. m. pl.* them.

lote, *s. m.* share.

lotería, *s. f.* lottery.

lubrificar, *v. a.* lubricate.

lucido, *adj.* magnificent.

luciente, *adj.* shining, brilliant.

lucir, *v. n.* shine, glitter, sparkle; ~ *un traje nuevo* wear a new dress; ~ *bien* look well; ~*se* do splendidly.

lucha, *s. f.* struggle, fight.

luchar, *v. n.* struggle, fight.

luego, *adv.* afterwards; next; then; immediately, right away; *desde* ~ naturally, of course; *¡hasta* ~*!* so long!

lugar, *s. m.* place; room, space; position, office; *en* ~ *de* instead of; *en primer* ~ in the first place; *dar* ~ cause; *tener* ~ take place.

lujo, *s. m.* luxury.

lujoso, *adj.* luxurious.

lujuria, *s. f.* luxuriance.

lumbre, *s. f.* fire (in stove); *¿quiere usted darme* ~*?* will you give me a light?

luna, *s. f.* moon; ~ *de miel* honeymoon.

lunes, *s. m* Monday.

lustrar, *v. a.* polish, shine.

luto, *s. m.* mourning; grief; *estar de* ~ be in mourning.

luz, *s. f.* light; *luces* intelligence; *a todas luces* any way you look at it; *entre dos luces* in the twilight; *dar a* ~ give birth (to a child); *dar a la* ~ publish.

Ll

llaga, s. f. open sore.
llama, s. f. flame.
llamada, s. f. call.
llamar, v. a. call; knock; ring (a bell); ~ a call upon, summon; ~ por teléfono phone; v. n. ~se be called or named; ¿cómo se llama usted? what's your name?; ¿cómo se llama esto? what's the name of this?
llamativo, adj. striking, conspicuous.
llano, adj. level, even; simple, plain; frank, unaffected; — s. m. plain.
llanta, s. f. tire.
llanura, s. f. plain.
llave, s. f. key; switch; tap; ~ inglesa monkey-wrench; echar la ~ lock the door.
llavero, s. m. key-ring.
llegada, s. f. arrival.
llegar, v. n. arrive; come; reach; extend, go as far as; amount; ~ a succeed in; ~ a ser get to be, become; ~ a saber come to know.
llenar, v. a. fill (up); fill out; satisfy.
lleno, adj. full; de ~ fully; ~ de full of, — s. m. full house (theatre).
llevar, v. a. take, carry; wear (dress); take, guide, lead; conduct; ¿adónde lleva este camino? where does this road lead?; ¿cuánto tiempo lleva usted en España? how long have you been in Spain?; llevo mucho tiempo esperando I have been waiting for a long time; ~ a cabo carry through; accomplish; ~ la delantera be ahead; ~ mala vida lead a bad life; v. n. ~se carry away, take; ~se bien get along well; ~se el premio win the prize; ~se un chasco be disappointed.
llorar, v. n. weep, cry.
llover, v. n. rain; ~ a cántaros pour (rain); como llovido del cielo like manna from heaven.
lloviznar, v. n. drizzle.
lluvia, s. f. rain.
lluvioso, adj. rainy.

M

macarrones, m. pl. macaroni.
maceta, s. f. flowerpot.
macizo, adj. solid; — s. m. masonry.
mácula, s. f. spot, blemish.
machete, s. m. long and broad knife.
macho, adj. & s. m. male (animal).
madeja, s. f. clue, ball.
madera, s. f. wood; lumber, timber; talent, qualities.
madero, s. m. beam; timber.
madrastra, s. f. stepmother.
madre, s. f. mother; origin, source; ~ política mother-in-law; salirse de ~ overflow (river).
madreperla, s. f. mother-of-pearl, nacre.

madrileño, *adj. & s. m.* from *or* of Madrid.

madrina, *s. f.* godmother.

madrugada, *s. f.* dawn; *de ~* at dawn.

madrugar, *v. n.* rise early; think out, develop (an idea); mature.

madurar, *v. n.* ripen.

maduro, *adj.* ripe; mature.

maestra, *s. f.* teacher.

maestral, *adj.* masterly.

maestría, *s. f.* mastery.

maestro, *s. m.* teacher; master, craftsman; composer.

mágico, *adj.* magical.

magistrado, *s. m.* magistrate; judge.

magnético, *adj.* magnetic.

magnífico, *adj.* magnificent; excellent, grand.

mago, *s. m.* wizard.

magro, *adj.* meagre, lean.

maíz, *s. m.* maize, Indian corn.

maizal, *s. m.* maizefield.

majestad, *s. f.* majesty.

majestuoso, *adj.* grand, majestic.

mal, *adj.* bad; — *adv.* badly; — *s. m.* illness; harm; wrong; *de ~ en peor* from bad to worse.

malacostumbrado, *adj.* ill-bred.

malandante, *adj.* unlucky.

malaventura, *s. f.* misfortune.

malcomido, *adj.* undernourished.

malcontento, *adj.* dissatisfied.

malcriado, *adj.* ill-bred, spoiled.

maldad, *s. f.* wickedness.

maldecir, *v. a. & n.* damn, curse.

maldiciente, *adj.* slanderous.

maldición, *s. f.* curse.

maldispuesto, *adj.* reluctant.

maldito, *adj.* cursed, damned.

maleante, *adj.* malicious.

malecón, *s. m.* dike, dam; promenade.

maléfico, *adj.* maleficent.

malestar, *s. m.* indisposition; discontent.

maleta, *s. f.* suitcase.

maletín, *s. m.* small case.

maleza, *s. f.* underwood, scrub.

malgastar, *v. a.* waste, lavish.

malhadado, *adj.* unhappy.

malhechor, *s. m.* evildoer.

malhumorado, *adj.* ill-humoured.

malicia, *s. f.* malice; *tener ~* be malicious.

malintencionado, *adj.* wicked.

malo, *adj.* bad, unpleasant; difficult, hard; ill.

malograr, *v. a.* miss, fail; *v. n. ~se* fail.

malquerer, *v. a.* wish ill to sy.

malsano, *adj.* unhealthy, unwholesome.

maltratar, *v. a.* mistreat, abuse.

maltrato, *s. m.* mistreat, abuse.

maltrecho, *adj.* maltreated.

malucho, *adj.* sickly.

malvado, *adj.* wicked; — *s. m.* wicked person, villain.

malla, *s. f.* mesh; stitch.

mamá, *s. f.* mamma, mummy.

mamar, *v. a. & n.* suck; *dar de ~* suckle, nurse.

mamífero, *s. m.* mammal.

manantial, *s. m.* spring, source of stream.

manco, *adj.* one-armed.

mancha, *s. f.* spot, stain; patch.

manchado, *adj.* spotted, mottled.

manchar, *v. a.* stain, soil.

mandadero, *s. m.* messenger; errand-boy.

mandado, *s. m.* errand; message.

mandamiento, *s m.* order, command(ment).

mandar, *v. a.* send, transmit; order, direct.

mandatario, *s. m.* proxy; deputy.

mandato, *s. m.* order, command; mandate.

mandíbula, *s. f.* jaw.

mando, *s. m.* order; leadership; control; *cuadro de ~* dashboard, control panel.

manejar, *v. a.* manage, handle; drive; *v. n.* *~se* manage, succeed in.

manejo, *s. m.* handling; management, control; intrigue.

manera, *s. f.* way, manner; *de esta ~* in this manner; *de mala ~* rudely; *de ~ que so,* as a result; *de ninguna ~* by no means; *de otra ~* in another way, otherwise; *de todas ~s* at any rate.

manga, *s. f.* sleeve; hose; *en ~s de camisa* in shirt-sleeves.

mango, *s. m.* handle.

manía, *s. f.* madness; mania; hobby.

manicomio, *s. m.* lunatic asylum.

manifestación, *s. f.* demonstration.

manifestante, *s. m.,* *f.* demonstrator.

manifestar, *v. a.* express, show.

manifiesto, *adj.* manifest, plain, obvious; — *s. m.* manifesto.

manija, *s. f.* handle.

maniobra, *s. f.* handling; manoeuvre; trick, knack.

maniobrar, *v. n.* manoeuvre.

manipular, *v. a.* manipulate.

manivela, *s. f.* crank, winch.

mano, *s. f.* hand; coat (of paint); first player (next to dealer).

manojo, *s. m.* bunch (of flowers, vegetables).

mansión, *s. f.* stay; residence.

manso, *adj.* tame; meek; calm.

manta, *s. f.* blanket.

manteca, *s. f.* lard, fat.

mantel, *s. m.* table-cloth.

mantener, *v. a.* support, provide for; hold; maintain, defend (an opinion); keep up (a conversation); *v. n.~se* support oneself.

mantequilla, *s. f.* butter.

mantilla, *s. f.* mantilla; — *pl.* baby-clothes.

manto, *s. m.* overcoat.

manual, *adj.* manual, physical; *trabajo ~* manual labour, handwork; — *s. m.* manual, handbook.

manubrio, *s. m.* handle, crank.

manufactura, *s. f.* manufacture.

manufacturar, *v. a.* manufacture.

manuscrito, *adj.* handwritten: — *s. m.* manuscript.

manzana, *s. f.* apple; block (of houses).

manzano, *s. m.* appletree.

mañana, *s. f.* morning; *s. m.* future; — *adv.* tomorrow: *por la ~* tomorrow morning; *de ~* early in the morning; *¡hasta ~!* see you tomorrow.

mapa, *s. m.* map.

mapamundi, *s. m.* map of the world.

máquina, *s. f.* machine; *~ de escribir* typewriter; *a toda ~* at full speed.

maquinaria, *s. f.* machinery.

maquinista, *s. m.* enginedriver.

mar, *s. m., f.* sea; *alta ~* high sea, open sea; *la ~ de gente* a lot of people.

maravilla, *s. f.* wonder, marvel.

maravillar, *v. a.* amaze; *v. n. ~se* be astonished.

maravilloso, *adj.* wonderful.

marca, *s. f.* mark; characteristic; *~ de fábrica* trademark, brand.

marcar, *v. a.* mark.

marco, *s. m.* frame (of door, picture); mark (German money).

marcha, *s. f.* march; speed; *apresurar la ~* hurry; speed up.

marchar, *v. n.* run; progress, go along; go (watch); *~se* leave, go away.

marchito, *adj.* faded, withered.

marea, *s. f.* tide.

marear, *v. a.* bother; *v. n. ~se* get seasick; get dizzy.

mareo, *s. m.* seasickness; dizziness.

marfil, *s. m.* ivory.

margarita, *s. f.* daisy.

margen, *s. m., f.* margin; edge, border.

marido, *s. m.* husband.

marina, *s. f.* seascape, marine painting; navy; *~ de guerra* navy; *~ mercante* merchant marine.

marinero, *s. m.* sailor, seaman.

marino, *adj.* marine, of the sea, maritime; — *s. m.* seaman.

mariposa, *s. f.* butterfly.

mariscal, *s. m.* marshal.

marítimo, *adj.* maritime.

mármol, *s. m.* marble.

marquesina, *s. f.* sunshine roof; lean-to.

marrón, *adj.* brown.

marta, *s. f.* marten.

martes, *s. m.* Tuesday.

martillar, *v. a. & n.* hammer.

martillo, *s. m.* hammer.

mártir, *s. m., f.* martyr.

martirio, *s. m.* martyrdom; torture.

marzo, *s. m.* March.

más, *adv.* more; longer; plus; *a lo ~* at most; *a ~ tardar* at the latest; *de ~* too much, too many; *estar de ~* be unnecessary; *~ adelante* later on; *~ allá* farther on; *~ bien* rather; *~ que* more than; *no ~ que* only.

mas, *adv.* but.

masa, *s. f.* dough; mass

(of people); *con las manos en la* ~ red-handed.

masaje, *s. m.* massage.

mascar, *v. a.* chew.

máscara, *s. f.* mask; *baile (s. m.) de* ~s masquerade ball; ~ *contra gases* gas-mask; *vestido de* ~ in costume.

masculino, *adj.* masculine.

masticar, *v. a.* chew.

mástil, *s. m.* mast, pole, post.

mata, *s. f.* plant, bush; shrub.

matadero, *s. m.* slaughterhouse.

matafuego, *s. m.* fire-extinguisher.

matar, *v. a.* kill; trump; ~ *la sed* quench one's thirst; ~ *de aburrimiento* bore to death; ~ *el tiempo* kill time; *v. n.* ~*se* kill oneself, get killed.

matasellos, *s. m.* postmark.

mate, *s. m.* maté (South American tea); mate (chess); — *adj.* mat, dim, dull.

matemáticas, *s. f.* mathematics.

materia, *s. f.* material; substance; matter, topic, subject; ~ *prima* raw material; *entrar en* ~ come to the point.

material, *adj.* material; — *s. m.* material; equipment.

maternidad, *s. f.* maternity.

matinal, *adj.* morning.

matiz, *s. m.* shade, tint.

matizar, *v. a.* shade, tint.

matorral, *s. m.* thicket, bush.

matrícula, *s. f.* register; registration number.

matricular, *v. a.* matriculate.

matrimonio, *s. m.* matrimony, marriage; married couple.

matriz, *s. f.* matrix.

máxima, *s. f.* maxim; proverb.

máxime, *adv.* chiefly, mainly.

máximo, *adj. & s. m.* maximum.

mayo, *s. m.* May.

mayonesa, *s. f.* mayonnaise.

mayor¹, *adj.* larger, largest; bigger, biggest; older, oldest; *calle* ~ main street; *Estado* ~ General Staff; *al por* ~ wholesale; *ser* ~ *de edad* be of age.

mayor², *s. m.* major.

mayordomo, *s. m.* butler; administrator.

mayoría, *s. f.* majority, greater part.

mayúscula, *s. f.* large letter; bold type.

maza, *s. f.* club.

mazapán, *s. m.* marzipan.

mazo, *s. m.* mallet.

me, *pron.* me, to me.

mecánica, *s. f.* mechanics.

mecánico, *adj.* mechanical; — *s. m.* mechanic.

mecanismo, *s. m.* mechanism.

mecanógrafa, *s. f.* typist.

mecanografiar, *v. a.* typewrite.

mecer, *v. a.* rock.

medalla, *s. f.* medal.

media, *s. f.* stocking.

mediación, *s. f.* mediation.

mediado, *adj.* half-filled,

half-full; *a* ~s *de mayo* in the middle of May.

mediador, *s. m.* mediator.

mediano, *adj.* medium; mediocre.

medianoche, *s. f.* midnight.

mediante, *prep.* through, by means of.

mediar, *v. a. & n.* mediate.

medicina, *s. f.* medicine.

médico, *adj.* medical; — *s. m.* physician.

medida, *s. f.* measure; rule; number, size; *a la* ~ (made) to measure; *tomar* ~s take measures or steps.

medio, *adj.* half; middle of; *a* ~ *camino* halfway to a place; *a* ~ *hacer* half-done; — *s. m.* middle; means; *por* ~ *de* by means of.-

mediodía, *s. m.* noon, midday.

medir, *v. a.* measure.

médula, *s. f.* marrow.

mejilla, *s. f.* cheek.

mejor, *adj. & adv.* better, best; *a lo* ~ perhaps; maybe; ~ *dicho* or rather, or better; *tanto* ~ so much the better.

mejorar, *v. a.* improve.

melocotón, *s. m.* peach.

melodía, *s. f.* melody.

melón, *s. m.* melon.

meloso, *adj.* honeylike, very sweet.

mellizo, *adj. & s. m.* twin.

memoria *s. f.* memory; memorandum, report; *de* ~ by heart.

mención, *s. f.* mention.

mencionar, *v. a.* mention.

mendigo, *s. m.* beggar.

menester, *s. m.* necessity; *es* ~ it's necessary.

menor, *adj.* smaller, small

est; younger, youngest; less, least; slightest; *a l por* ~ at retail; minutely; ~ *de edad*, under age, minor.

menos, *adv.* less, least; — *prep.* except; but; *al* ~ at least, *a* ~ *que* unless; *echar de* ~ miss; ~ *de* less than; *por lo* ~ at least.

mensaje, *s. m.* dispatch.

mensajero, *s. m.* courier.

mensual, *adj.* monthly.

menta, *s. f.* mint, peppermint.

mente, *s. f.* mind.

mentir, *v. n.* lie, tell lies.

mentira, *s. f.* lie.

menudo, *adj.* tiny, very small; *a* ~ often.

meñique, *s. m.* little finger.

mercado, *s. m.* market.

mercancía, *s. f.* merchandise, goods.

mercantil, *adj.* commercial, mercantile.

merced, *s.f.* favour; mercy.

mercería, *s. f.* haberdashery.

mercurio, *s. m.* mercury.

merecer, *v. a.* deserve; *no merece la pena* it isn't worth while.

merendar, *v. n.* have a snack in the afternoon; picnic.

meridional, *adj.* southern.

merienda, *s. f.* afternoon snack, picnic.

mérito, *s. m.* merit, worth.

mermelada, *s. f.* jam; marmalade.

mes, *s. m.* month.

mesa, *s. f.* table; *poner la* ~ set the table.

meseta, *s. f.* plateau.

meta, *s. f.* aim, goal.

metal, *s. m.* metal; brass.

metálico, *adj.* metallic;
— *s. m.* coin(s).

meteorología, *s. f.* meteorology.

meter, *v. a.* put; ~ *miedo* frighten; ~ *ruido* make noise; *v. n.* ~*se en* get into; be nosy.

metódico, *adj.* systematic, methodical.

método, *s. m.* method.

metro, *s. m.* metre; underground railway.

mezclar, *v. a.* mix; blend; *v. n.* ~*se* get mixed up.

mezquita, *s. f.* mosque.

mi, *adj.* my; ~ *sombrero* my hat; *mis hijos* my sons.

mí, *pron.* me; ¿ *hay cartas para* ~? are there letters for me?

microbio, *s. m.* microbe.

micrófono, *s. m.* microphone.

microscopio, *s. m.* microscope.

miedo, *s. m.* fear; *tener* ~ be afraid.

miel, *s. f.* honey.

miembro, *s. m.* limb; member.

mientras, *conj.* while; ~ *t anto* meanwhile.

miércoles, *s. m.* Wednesday.

miga, *s. f.* crumb.

mil, *adj. & s. m.* thousand.

milagro, *s. m.* miracle, marvel.

militar, *adj.* military; — *s. m.* military man.

milla, *s. f.* mile.

millar, *s. m.* one thousand.

millón, *s. m.* million.

millonario, *s. m.* millionaire.

mimar, *v. a.* spoil (a child).

mina, *s. f.* mine (excavation and explosive).

mineral, *adj. & s. m.* mineral.

minero, *s. m.* miner.

mínimo, *adj. & s. m.* minimum.

ministerio, *s. m.* ministry.

ministro, *s. m.* minister.

minoría, *s. f.* minority.

minúscula, *s. f.* small letter.

minuta, *s. f.* draft; memorandum.

minuto, *adj.* minute; — *s. m.* minute.

mío, *adj. & pron.* (of) mine; *estos lápices son mios* these pencils are mine.

miope, *adj.* short-sighted.

mirada, *s. f.* look, glance.

mirar, *v. a.* look at; glance; regard; consider, think; watch, be careful; ~ *alrededor* look around; ~*se* look at each other.

misa, *s. f.* Mass.

miseria, *s. f.* poverty, trifle, pittance.

misericordia, *s. f.* mercy, compassion.

misión, *s. f.* mission.

misionero, *s. m.* missionary.

mismo, *adj. & pron.* same, identical; *yo* ~ I myself; *aquí mismo* right here; *me da lo* ~ it's all the same to me.

misterio, *s. m.* mistery.

mitad, *s. f.* half; *a* ~ *de camino* half-way.

mitin, *s. m.* meeting, rally.

mixto, *adj.* mixed.

mobiliario, *s. m.* furniture.

mochila, *s. f.* knapsack.

moda, *s. f.* fashion, style; *a la* ~ fashionable; *pasado de* ~ out of style.

modelo, *adj.* model, perfect; — s. m. model; pattern.

moderar, v. a. restrain, moderate; v. n. ~se control oneself.

moderno, adj. modern.

modestia, s. f. modesty, humbleness.

modesto, adj. simple.

modificar, v. a. modify.

modista, s. m., f. dressmaker.

modo, s. m. method, way; de este ~ in this way; de ~ que so, therefore; de ningún ~ by no means; de todos ~s anyhow.

mojar, v. a. wet, moisten; drench.

moler, v. a. grind, mill.

molestar, v. a. disturb; annoy; bother, inconvenience; hurt; v. n. ~se be ennoyed; bother.

molestia, s. f. trouble, discomfort.

molesto, adj. uncomfortable; annoyed.

molinero, s. m. miller.

molinillo, s. m. coffeemill.

molino, s. m. mill.

momento, s. m. moment; al ~ immediately.

momia, s. f. mummy.

mona, s. f. female monkey; drunkenness; — adj. pretty.

monarquía, s.f. monarchy.

mondar, v. a. peel, clean.

moneda, s. f. coin; currency.

monja, s. f. nun.

monje, s. m. monk.

mono, adj. cute; — s. m. monkey; overalls.

monstruoso, adj. monstrous.

montador, s. m. fitter,

assembler (of machinery).

montaje, s. m. assembling.

montaña, s. f. mountain.

montañoso, adj. mountainous.

montar, v. a. ride (horseback); set up, assemble, install; v. n. ~ a amount to (in money); ~ en cólera get furious.

monte, s. m. mountain; woods, forest.

montón, s. m. heap; pile.

montuoso, adj. mountainous.

monumento, s. m. monument.

mora, s. f. blackberry.

morada, s. f. dwelling, stay.

moral, adj. moral; — s. m. morale; black mulberry tree.

morder, v. a. & n. bite.

moreno, adj. darkskinned, brunette.

morir, v. n. die; v. n. ~se de hambre starve to death.

moro, a dj. Moorish; — s. m. Moor.

mortal, adj. deadly, terrible, mortal; — s. m. mortal being.

mosaico, s. m. mosaic.

mosca, s. f. fly.

mosquito, s. m. mosquito.

mostaza, s. f. mustard.

mosto, s. m. must.

mostrador, s. m. counter (in a shop).

mostrar, v. a. show, display; v. n. ~se appear, show oneself.

motivar, v. a. cause.

motivo, s. m. motive, reason; con ~ de on the occasion of.

motocicleta, s. f. motor-cycle.

motolancha, *s. f.* motor boat.

motor, *s. m.* motor.

mover, *v. a.* move; stir; *v. n.* ~*se* move.

móvil, *adj.* mobile; — *s. m.* motive.

movilizar, *v. a.* mobilize.

movimiento, *s. m.* movement, move; traffic; animation.

mozo, *s. m.* waiter; porter; lad, young man.

muchacha, *s. f.* young girl; maid.

muchacho, *s. m.* boy.

muchedumbre, *s. f.* crowd (of people); multitude.

mucho, *adj.* much; ~s *pl.* many; — *adv.* much, a lot; long; *sentir* ~ be very sorry.

mudanza, *s. f.* change of residence.

mudar, *v. a.* change; *v. n.* ~*se* change (clothes); ~*se de casa* change residence.

mudo, *adj.* dumb, mute.

mueble, *adj.* movable; *s. m.* piece of furniture.

muela, *s. f.* molar (tooth); millstone; *dolor* (*s. m.*) *de* ~*s* toothache.

muelle, *adj.* soft; — *s. m.* spring (wire); pier.

muerte, *s. f.* death.

muerto, *adj. & s. m.* dead; dummy (bridge).

muestra, *s. f.* sample.

mujer, *s. f.* woman; wife.

mula, *s. f.* female mule.

mulato, *adj. & s. m.* mulatto.

muleta, *s. f.* crutch.

mulo, *s. m.* mule.

multa, *s. f.* fine (punishment).

multicolor. *adj.* coloured.

múltiple, *adj.* manifold.

multiplicar, *v. a.* multiply.

multitud, *s. f.* crowd, masses.

mundano, *adj.* worldly.

mundial, *adj.* universal; *guerra* ~ World War.

mundo, *s. m.* world; *gran* ~ high society; *todo el* ~ everybody.

munición, *s. f.* ammunition.

municipal, *adj.* municipal; — *s. m.* constable.

municipalidad, *s. f.* citizens, municipality.

municipio, *s. m.* municipal council.

munífico, *adj.* liberal, generous.

muñeca, *s. f.* wrist; doll.

muralla, *s. f.* wall (of a city).

murciélago, *s. m.* bat.

muro, *s. m.* outside wall.

músculo, *s. m.* muscle.

musculoso, *adj.* muscular.

museo, *s. m.* museum.

musgo, *s. m.* moss.

música, *s. f.* music; band (of musicians).

musical, *adj.* musical.

músico, *adj.* musical; — *s. m.* musician.

muslo, *s. m.* thigh.

mustio, *adj.* withered; depressed.

mutilar, *v. a.* mutilate.

mutis, *s. m.* (theatre) exit.

mutuo, *adj.* mutual, reciprocal.

muy, *adv.* very.

N

nabo, *s. m.* turnip.

nacer, *v. n.* be born; rise, spring, have its

source; sprout.

nación, *s. f.* nation.

nacional, *adj.* national.

nacionalidad, *s. f.* nationality.

nada, *s. f.* nothing; — *adv.* not at all; ~ *más* nothing else; *de* ~ don't mention it.

nadador, *s. m.* swimmer.

nadar, *v. n.* swim.

nadie, *pron.* nobody, no one, not anybody.

naipe, *s. m.* (playing) card.

naranja, *s. f.* orange.

naranjada, *s. f.* orangeade.

naranjero, *s. m.* orangeseller.

naranjo, *s. m.* orange tree.

narcótico, *adj.* narcotic; — *s. m.* narcotic, dope.

nariz, *s. f.* nose.

narrar, *v. a.* narrate.

nata, *s. f.* cream; ~ *batida* whipped cream.

natación, *s. f.* (art of) swimming.

natal, *adj.* native; *pais* ~ native country.

natalicio, *s. m.* birthday.

natural, *adj.* natural; — *s. m.* native; nature, disposition.

naturaleza, *s. f.* nature, constitution; temperament.

naturalidad, *s. f.* naturalness.

naturalizar, *v. a.* naturalize.

naufragar, *v. n.* be shipwrecked; fail, fall through.

naufragio, *s. m.* shipwreck.

náusea, *s. f.* nausea.

náutica, *s. f.* navigation.

náutico, *adj.* nautical; *deporte* ~ aquatic sports.

navaja, *s. f.* penknife; razor.

nave, *s. f.* ship; nave.

navegación, *s. f.* navigation; voyage.

navegar, *v. n.* navigate, sail.

Navidad, *s. f.* Christmas.

neblina, *s. f.* mist, fog.

necesario, *adj.* necessary.

necesidad, *s. f.* need, necessity.

necesitar, *v. a.* need.

negación, *s. f.* negation.

negar, *v. a.* deny; refuse; *v. n.* ~*se a* refuse to do sg.

negativa, *s. f.* negative.

negativo, *adj.* negative.

negligente, *adj.* negligent.

negociación, *s. f.* negotiation.

negociante, *s. m.* business man.

negociar, *v. a. & n.* negotiate; do business.

negocio, *s. m.* business; interest.

negro, *adj.* black; dark; — *s. m.* Negro; black colour.

nena, *s. f.*, **nene**, *s. m.* baby.

neoyorquino, *adj. & s. m.* New Yorker.

nervio, *s. m.* nerve.

nervioso, *adj.* nervous.

neto, *adj.* net.

neumático, *adj.* pneumatic; — *s. m.* tire.

neumonía, *s. f.* pneumonia.

neuralgia, *s. f.* neuralgia.

neutralidad, *s. f.* neutrality.

nevada, *s. f.* snowfall.

nevar, *v. n.* snow.

nevera, *s. f.* refrigerator.

ni, *conj.* neither, nor.

nido, *s. m.* nest.

niebla, *s. f.* fog, mist, haze.

nieta, *s. f.* granddaughter.

nieto, *s. m.* grandson

nieve, *s. f.* snow.

ningun, *adj.* not a, not one.

ninguno, *adj.* not any, none; *de ninguna manera* by no means.

niña, *s. f.* girl; ~ *del ojo* pupil (of the eye); apple of the eye.

niñera, *s. f.* nurse(-maid).

niñez, *s. f.* childhood.

niño, *adj.* young; childish; — *s. m.* boy; ~s *pl.* children.

nivel, *s. m.* level; *a* ~ horizontal, level.

nivelar, *v. a.* level; balance.

no, no, not; ~ *más* only, no more.

noche, *s. f.* evening; night; *esta* ~ tonight

Nochebuena, *s. f.* Christmas Eve.

nogal, *s. m.* walnut-tree.

nombramiento, *s. m.* nomination; appointment.

nombrar, *v. a.* name, mention; appoint.

nombre, *s. m.* name; fame; reputation; noun; ~ *de familia* familyname, surname; ~ *de pila* first or Christian name.

nordeste, *s. m.* northeast.

norma, *s. f.* norm.

normal, *adj.* normal; standard.

noroeste, *s. m.* northwest.

norte, *s. m.* north.

norteamericano, *adj.* & *s. m.* North American.

noruego, *adj.* & *s. m.* Norwegian.

nos, *pron.* us, to us.

nosotros, *pron.* we.

nota, *s. f.* note; (school) mark; footnote, marginal note.

notar, *v. a.* notice, note.

notario, *s. m.* notary public.

noticia, *s. f.* news; notice.

notificar, *v. a.* notify, inform.

novedad, *s. f.* novelty; news; surprise; *sin* ~ as usual; nothing new.

novela, *s. f.* novel.

noveno, *adj.* ninth.

noventa, *adj.* & *s. m.* ninety.

novia, *s. f.* fiancée; bride.

noviembre, *s. m.* November.

novio, *s. m.* fiancé; bridegroom.

nube, *s. f.* cloud.

nublado, *adj.* cloudy, overcast.

nuca, *s. f.* (nape of the) neck.

nudo, *s. m.* knot.

nuera, *s. f.* daughter-in-law.

nuestro, *adj.* & *pron.* our, of ours.

nueve, *adj.* & *s. m.* nine.

nuevo, *adj.* new; *de* ~ again.

nuez, *s. f.* walnut.

numerar, *v. a.* number.

número, *s. m.* number; size; edition.

numeroso, *adj.* numerous.

nunca, *adv.* never, not ever; ~ *jamás* nevermore.

nutrir, *v. a.* nourish.

Ñ

ñandú, *s. m.* (South American) ostrich.

ñato, *adj.* pug-nosed.

ñoñería, *s. f.* silliness.

ñoño, *adj.* silly.

ñu, *s. m.* gnu.

O

o, *conj.* or; *o...o* either...or; *o sea* that is.
obedecer, *v. a.* obey.
obediente, *adj.* obedient.
obispo, *s. m.* bishop.
objetivo, *adj.* & *s. m.* objective.
objeto, *s. m.* object; purpose.
oblea, *s. f.* wafer.
oblicuo, *adj.* oblique.
obligación, *s. f.* obligation, responsibility; duty.
obligar, *v. a.* oblige, compel, force.
obligatorio, *adj.* obligatory, compulsory.
obra, *s. f.* work, books, works; show, performance; ~ *maestra* masterpiece.
obrar, *v. n.* do, act; behave.
obrero, *s. m.* worker, labourer.
obsequiar, *v. a.* present with; be very kind.
obsequio, *s. m.* gift, present.
observar, *v. a.* watch, observe; notice; ~ *buena conducta* behave well.
observatorio, *s. m.* observatory.
obstáculo, *s. m.* obstacle, hindrance.
obstante, *adv.*; *no* ~ notwithstanding.
obstinado, *adj.* stubborn.
obstinarse en, *v. n.* insist on.
obtener, *v. a.* get, obtain.
ocasión, *s. f.* occasion, time; chance, opportunity; *de* ~ secondhand.
ocasionar, *v. a.* cause.
occidental, *adj.* western, Occidental.
occidente, *s. m.* west; occident.

océano, *s. m.* ocean.
octavo, *adj.* eighth.
octubre, *s. m.* October.
oculista, *s. m.*, *f.* oculist.
ocultar, *v. a.* hide.
ocupación, *s. f.* occupation; business.
ocupado, *adj.* occupied, taken; busy.
ocupar, *v. a.* occupy, take possession of; *v. n.* ~*se de* take care of, pay attention to.
ocurrencia, *s. f.* incident, witticism.
ocurrir, *v. n.* occur, happen; *se me ocurre* it comes to my mind.
ochenta, *adj.* & *s. m.* eighty.
ocho, *adj.* & *s. m.* eight.
odiar, *v. a.* hate.
odio, *s. m.* hatred.
oeste, *s. m.* west.
ofender, *v. a.* offend; *v. n.* ~*se* take offense.
ofensa, *s. f.* insult, offence.
ofensiva, *s. f.* offensive.
oferta, *s. f.* offer.
oficial, *adj.* official; — *s. m.* officer, clerk.
oficina, *s. f.* office (room).
oficio, *s. m.* manual work, occupation, trade; ~ *divino* church service.
ofrecer, *v. a.* offer.
ofrecimiento, *s. m.* offer, offering.
oída, *s. f.* hearing; *de* ~*s, por* ~*s* by hearsay.
oído, *s. m.* (inner) ear; hearing; *dar* ~*s* listen, lend an ear.
oír, *v. a.* hear; listen; *¡oiga!* hello! (telephone).
ojal, *s. m.* buttonhole.
ojalá! *int.; ¡*~ *fuera posible!* if only it were

possible!

ojeada, s. f. glance; echar una ~ cast a glance.

ojear, v. a. glance through.

ojo, s. m. eye; ~ de la llave keyhole; cuesta un ~ de la cara it costs plenty.

ola, s. f. wave (of water).

¡olé! int. bravo!; well done!

óleo, s. m. oil (-colour).

oler, v. a. & n. smell.

olfato, s. m. sense of smell.

olímpico, adj. Olympic.

oliva, s. f. olive.

olivo, s. m. olive tree.

olmo, s. m. elm.

olor, s. m. smell, odour.

oloroso, adj. fragrant.

olvidar, v. a. forget.

olla, s. f. pot.

omisión, s. f. omission.

omitir, v. a. omit.

once, adj. & s. m. eleven.

onda, s. f. wave; ripple (of water); ~ corta short wave; ~ larga long wave (radio).

ondulación, s. f. wave; ~ permanente permanent *wave.

ondulado, adj. wavy; — s. m. wave, waving.

ondular, v. a. & n. wave; ripple.

onza, s. f. ounce.

opera, s. f. opera.

operación, s. f. operation.

operador, s. m. operator.

operar, v. a. operate on.

operario, s. m. skilled worker.

opereta, s. f. operetta; musical (comedy).

opinión, s. f. opinion.

oponer, v. a. set up; —

v. n. ~se a oppose.

oportunidad, s. f. opportunity.

oportuno, adj. opportune, appropriate, fitting.

oprimir, v. a. oppress.

óptica, s. f. optics.

óptico, s. m. optician.

optimista, adj. & s. m. f. optimist(ic).

óptimo, adj. excellent.

opuesto, adj. opposite.

oración, s. f. sentence; prayer.

orador, s. m. orator.

orden, s. m. order; — s. f. command, instruction; (commercial) order; (religious) order; a sus órdenes at your service; en ~ in order; ~ del día agenda, order of the day.

ordenar, v. a. put in order; order.

ordeñar, v. a. milk.

ordinario, adj. usual; ordinary, vulgar; de ~ usually.

oreja, s. f. ear.

orfanato, s. m. orphanage.

orgánico, adj. organic.

organillo, s. m. barrel-organ.

organismo, s. m. organism.

organización, s. f. organization.

organizador, s. m. organizer.

organizar, v. a. organize; arrange.

órgano, s. m. organ.

orgullo, s. m. pride.

orgulloso, adj. proud, haughty.

oriental, adj. eastern; Oriental; — s. m. Oriental.

orientar, *v. a.* orientate; *v n.* ~se orient oneself.

oriente, *s. m.* east; Orient.

origen, *s. m.* origin; descent, extraction.

original, *adj.* original; eccentric, odd; — *s. m.* original.

originalidad, *s. f.* originality; eccentricity, oddity.

originar, *v. a.* start.

orilla, *s. f.* bank; edge, rim; ~ *del mar* seashore; *a* ~s *de* on the shore of.

orla, *s. f.* seam, hem.

orlar, *v. a.* hem, border.

oro, *s. m.* gold.

orquesta, *s. f.* orchestra.

ortiga, *s. f.* stinging nettle.

ortografía. *s. f.* orthography.

oruga, *s. f.* caterpillar; *cadena-*~ caterpillar track.

os, *pron.* you, to you.

oscurecer, *v. n.* get dark.

oscuridad, *s. f.* obscurity, darkness.

oscuro, *adj.* dark; obscure.

oso, *s. m.* bear.

ostra, *s. f.* oyster.

otoñal, *adj.* autumnal.

otoño, *s. m.* autumn.

otorgar, *v. a.* grant, allow; issue.

otro, *adj.* another, other; *alguna otra cosa* something else; *uno a* ~ each other; *otra vez* again; *por otra parte* on the other hand; *el* ~ *día* lately, of late; ~ *tanto* just as much; *¡otra!* da capo! encore!

ovación, *s. f.* ovation, cheering.

oveja, *s. f.* sheep.

ovillo, *s. m.* clue, ball.

oxidar, *v. a.* oxidize.

óxido, *s. m.* oxide.

oxígeno, *s. m.* oxygen.

oyente, *s. m.*, *f.* hearer, listener.

P

pabellón, *s. m.* pavilion.

paciencia, *s f.* patience; forbearance.

paciente, *adj. & s. m.*, *f.* patient.

pacífico, *adj.* pacific.

pacto, *s. m.* agreement, pact.

padecer, *v. n.* suffer from.

padrastro, *s. m.* stepfather.

padre, *s. m.* father; priest; ~s *pl.* parents.

padrino, *s. m.* godfather; patron, sponsor.

paella, *s. f.* dish of rice with meat or chicken.

paga, *s. f.* wages, pay.

pagar, *v. a.* pay.

página, *s. f.* page (of a book).

pago, *s. m.* payment.

país, *s. m.* country; *del* ~ domestic, local.

paisaje, *s. m.* landscape, scenery.

paisano, *s. m.* person from the same country or city; civilian.

paja, *s. f.* straw.

pájaro, *s. m.* bird.

pala, *s. f.* spade, shovel.

palabra, *s. f.* word; *¡*~*!* honestly! no fooling!

palacio, *s. m.* palace.

paladar, *s. m.* palate.

palanca, *s. f.* lever.

palangana, *s. f.* washbasin.

palco, *s. m.* (theatre) box.

paliativo, adj. & s. m. palliative.

palidecer, v. n. turn pale.

palidez, s. f. pallor.

pálido, adj. pale.

paliza, s. f. beating, spanking.

palma, s. f. palm (leaf, tree, hand); llevar la ~ win the prize.

palmada, s. f. clapping; pat (on the back); dar ~s clap; applaud.

palmera, s. f. palmtree.

palmo, s. m. span.

palmotear, v. n. applaud.

palo, s. m. stick; pole; wood; suit (in cards); dar de ~s club, beat.

paloma, s. f. pigeon, dove.

palomar, s. m. dovecot.

palpar, v. a. touch, finger.

pan, s. m. bread; ~ integral whole-wheat bread; ~ tierno fresh bread.

pana, s. f. plush.

panadería, s. f. bakery.

panadero, s. m. baker.

panecillo, s. m. roll (bread).

pantalones, s. m. pl. trousers, pants.

pantalla, s. f. lampshade; screen; film.

pantano, s. m. swamp, marsh, bog.

pantorrilla, s. f. calf (of the leg).

panza, s. f. belly, paunch.

paño, s. m. cloth.

pañuelo, s. m. handkerchief.

Papa, s. m. Pope.

papa, s. f. potato.

papá, s. m. papa, dad.

papagayo, s. m. parrot.

papel, s. m. paper; docu-ment; role, part; ~ pintado wallpaper; ~ secante blotting-paper; ~ de cartas stationery; ~ de seda tissue paper; ~ moneda paper money, bills.

papelería, s. f. stationer's shop.

paquete, s. m. parcel; package.

par, adj. even (of numbers); — s. m. pair; couple; equal; sin ~ incomparable.

para, prep. & conj. ¿~ qué? why?; what for?; ~ (que) to, in order to; so that; ¿~ dónde? where to?; salgo ~ Barcelona I leave for Barcelona; taza ~ té tea-cup.

parabrisas, s. m. windscreen.

paracaídas, s. m. parachute.

parada, s. f. stop; (military) parade.

paradero, s. m. whereabouts.

parado, adj. shut down; unemployed; standing.

parador, s. m. inn, hostelry.

paraguas, s. m. umbrella.

paraíso, s. m. paradise, heaven; (theatre) gallery.

parar, v. n. stop; stay (in a hotel); end up, turn out; ~se stop.

parcial, adj. partial.

parche, s. m. plaster, patch.

pardo, adj. brown; darkgray.

parecer, v. n. look, appear; seem; según parece as it seems, apparently;

~se be alike; − s. m. opinion; al ~ apparently.

parecido, adj. like, similar; − s. m. resemblance; bien ~ good-looking.

pared, s. f. wall.

pareja, s. f. pair, couple; team; dancing partner.

parejo, adj. equal, the same.

parentela, s. f. relations.

parentesco, s. m. relationship.

paréntesis, s. m. bracket, parenthesis.

paridad, s. f. parity.

pariente, s. m., f. relative.

parlamento, s. m. parliament.

paro, s m. stoppage; unemployment; strike.

párpado, s. m. eyelid.

parque, s. m. park.

párrafo, s. m. paragraph.

parrilla, s. f. grate; grill.

parroquiano, s. m. parishioner, customer.

parte, s. m. report; − s. f. part; share; (legal) party; dar ~ inform, notify; de mi ~ on my behalf; en todas ~s everywhere; tomar ~ take part.

participante, s. m., f. participant.

participar, v. a. announce; v. n. ~ en take part in.

particular, adj. special, particular; private; odd, peculiar.

partida, s. f. departure; item (in an account); game; certificate.

partidario, s. m. follower.

partido, s. m. party, faction; match, game; sacar ~ de profit by.

partir, v. a. split; cut; divide: v. n. leave for; ~se break.

parto, s. m. birth.

pasa, s. f raisin.

pasado, adj. last; la semana ~a last week; ~ mañana day after tomorrow; − s. m. past.

pasaje, s. m. crossing; journey, voyage; fare; arcade; passage (from book).

pasajero, adj. passing, transitory; − s. m. passenger.

pasaporte, s. m. passport.

pasar, v. a. pass, overtake; hand; go through; cross; move, transfer; spend (time); tolerate, overlook; v. n. happen; come in; get along, make out; pass (at cards); stop (of rain); ~ de moda go out of style; ~ el rato kill time; ~ lista call the roll; ~ por alto skip, overlook; ~se sin do without.

pasarela, s. f. gangway.

pasatiempo, s. m. pastime, amusement.

Pascua, s. f.; ~ de Navidad Christmas; ~ florida, ~ de Resurrección Easter; ¡ Felices Pascuas! Merry Christmas!

pase, s. m. pass, permit.

pasear, v. n. stroll, take a walk.

paseo, s. m. walk; dar un ~ take a walk.

pasillo, s. m. passage,

corridor.

pasión, *s. f.* emotion, passion.

paso, *s. m.* step; gait; (mountain) pass; progress; *de ~* in passing; *~ a nivel* railway crossing.

pasta, *s. f.* paste; binding, cover; tea-cake; plastic; dough (money); *de buena ~* good-natured; *~ de dientes* toothpaste; *sopa de ~* noodle-soup.

pastel, *s. m.* pie; cake; pastel.

pastelería, *s. f.* confectioner's shop.

pastilla, *s. f.* tablet; drop.

pastor, *s. m.* shepherd.

pata, *s. f.* foot, leg (of an animal).

patata, *s. f.* potato.

patente, *adj.* evident; — *s. f.* patent.

patín, *s. m.* skate; *~ de ruedas* roller-skate.

patinar, *v. n.* skate; skid, slip.

patio, *s. m.* patio, courtyard; *~ de butacas* (theatre) orchestra-stalls.

pato, *s. m.* duck.

patria, *s. f.* fatherland, native land.

patrimonio, *s. m.* patrimony.

patriota, *s. m., f.* patriot.

patriótico, *adj.* patriotic.

patrón, *s. m.* patron saint; employer; boss; pattern.

pausa, *s. f.* rest; brake.

pausar, *v. n.* pause; hesitate.

pava, *s. f.* turkey-hen.

pavimento, *s. m.* pavement.

pavo, *s. m.* turkey-cock;

~ real peacock.

pavaso, *s. m.* clown.

paz. *s. f.* peace; *hacer las paces* become reconciled.

peatón, *s. m.* pedestrian.

pecado, *s. m.* sin.

pecar, *v. n.* sin.

pecho, *s. m.* chest; bosom.

pedazo, *s. m.* piece, bit.

pedicura, *s. f.* pedicure.

pedido, *s. m.* order, commission.

pedir, *v. a.* ask, request; order; *~ limosna* beg for alms; *a ~ de boca* according to desire.

pegar, *v. a.* stick; glue; sew on; hit, beat, strike; infect with; *~ fuego* set fire; *v. n.* *~se* adhere, stick.

peinado, *s. m.* hair-style.

peinar, *v. a.* comb.

peine, *s. m.* comb.

pelar, *v. a.* pick, pluck (fowl); skin.

peldaño, *s. m.* stair, step.

pelea, *s. f.* fight, quarrel.

pelear, *v. n.* fight, quarrel.

peletería, *s. f.* furrier's shop.

película, *s. f.* film; picture.

peligro, *s. m.* danger; *correr ~* run a risk.

peligroso, *adj.* dangerous.

pelo, *s. m.* hair; *tomar el ~* pull one's leg.

pelota, *s. f.* ball (for games).

peluca, *s. f.* wig.

peludo, *adj.* hairy.

peluquería, *s. f.* hairdresser's shop.

peluquero, *s. m.* hairdresser.

pellizcar, *v. a.* pinch.

pena, *s. f.* penalty; pain, sorrow; trouble; *a duras* ~s with great difficulty; *vale la* ~ it's worth while.

pendiente, *adj.* pending; — *s. m.* earring; — *s. f.* slope.

penetrar, *v. a.* penetrate; determine, make out.

península, *s. f.* peninsula.

pensamiento, *s. m.* thought, idea; pansy (flower).

pensar, *v. n.* think; intend; ~ *en* think of *or* about.

pensión, *s. f.* pension; boarding-house.

Pentecostés, *s. m.* Whitsuntide.

peón, *s. m.* workman; (chess) pawn.

peor, *adj. & adv.* worse, worst.

pepino, *s. m.* cucumber.

pequeño, *adj.* small, little.

pera, *s. f.* pear.

peral, *s. m.* pear-tree.

percha, *s. f.* rack (for clothes); hanger.

perder, *v. a.* lose; miss (the train); ruin; ~ *de vista* lose sight of; *echar a* ~ ruin, spoil; *v. n.* ~*se* get lost; become spoiled.

pérdida, *s. f.* loss.

perdiz, *s. f.* partridge.

perdón, *s. m.* forgiveness; pardon.

perdonar, *v. a.* pardon; forgive; excuse.

perecer, *v. n.* perish.

peregrino, *adj.* exotic, strange; — *s. m.* pilgrim.

perejil, *s. m.* parsley.

pereza, *s. f.* laziness.

perezoso, *adj.* lazy.

perfecto, *adj.* perfect.

perfil, *s. m.* profile; outline.

perfumar, *v. a.* perfume

perfume, *s. m.* perfume.

periódico, *adj.* periodical; — *s. m.* newspaper.

periodista, *s. m. f.* journalist.

perito, *adj. & s. m.* expert.

perjudicar, *v. a.* damage, hurt, injure.

perjuicio, *s. m.* prejudice; damage, injury, harm.

perla, *s. f.* pearl.

permanecer, *v. n.* stay, remain.

permanente, *adj. & s. f.* permanent (wave).

permiso, *s. m.* permission, licence; permit; *con* ~ excuse me.

permitir, *v. a.* permit, allow.

pero, *conj.* but.

perra, *s. f.* bitch.

perro, *s. m.* dog.

persiana, *s. f.* Venetian blind.

persona, *s. f.* person.

personaje, *s. m.* personage; character.

personal, *adj.* personal; — *s. m.* personnel.

persuadir, *v. a.* persuade, convince.

pertenecer, *v. n.* belong to; pertain to, concern.

pesadilla, *s. f.* nightmare.

pesado, *adj.* heavy; boring, dull, tiresome; sultry (weather); sound (sleep); stuffy.

pesadumbre, *s. f.* grief.

pésame, *s. m.* condolence.

pesar,¹ *v. a. & n.* weigh; be important, count;

me pesa I regret it.

pesar², *s. m.* sorrow; remorse; *a ~ de* in spite of.

pesca, *s. f.* fishing; *ir de ~* go fishing.

pescado, *s. m.* (caught) fish.

pescador, *s. m.* fisherman.

pescar, *v. a. & n.* fish; catch, get.

peseta, *s. f.* peseta (monetary unit of Spain).

pésimo, *adj.* the very worst

peso, *s. m.* weight; load; burden; peso (monetary unit); *de ~* weighty, important.

petición, *s. f.* petition, request.

petróleo, *s. m.* mineral oil, petroleum.

pez, *s. m.* fish (in the water); — *s. f.* tar.

picadillo, *s. m.* minced meat, hash.

picadura, *s. f.* sting; smoking tobacco.

picante, *adj.* spiced.

picar, *v. a.* sting, bite, (of insects); chop (meat); nibble; *v. n.* itch; burn.

pícaro, *adj.* mischievous; — *s. m.* rascal, rogue.

pico, *s. m.* beak; sharp point, corner; pickaxe; summit, peak.

pie, *s. m.* foot; base; *a ~* on foot; *de ~* standing.

piedad, *s. f.* piety; pity.

piedra, *s. f.* stone.

piel, *s. f.* skin; leather; fur; peel; *abrigo de ~es* fur coat.

pierna, *s. f.* leg.

pieza, *s. f.* part (of a machine); play; piece (of music); piece in games; room.

pila, *s. f.* basin; sink; electrical battery; pile; *~ de bautismo* baptismal font.

píldora, *s. f.* pill, pellet.

piloto, *s. m.* pilot.

pimentón, *s. m.* red pepper, paprika.

pimienta, *s. f.* pepper (spice).

pimiento, *s. m.* pepper (vegetable).

pino, *s. m.* pine (tree).

pintar, *v. a.* paint; *v. n. ~se* make up.

pintor, *s. m.* painter.

pintoresco, *adj.* picturesque.

pintura, *s. f.* painting; picture; paint.

piña, *s. f.* pineapple.

piojo, *s. m.* louse.

pipa, *s. f.* (smoking) pipe.

pique, *s. m.* resentment.

piropo, *s. m.* compliment, flattery.

pisar, *v. a.* step on, tread on.

piscina, *s. f.* swimming pool.

piso, *s. m.* floor; storey; *~ bajo* ground-floor.

pista, *s. f.* trace, track; manoeuvring area.

pistola, *s. f.* pistol.

pitar, *v. n.* whistle.

pitillo, *s. m.* cigarette.

pito, *s. m.* whistle.

pizarra, *s. f.* slate; blackboard.

placa, *s. f.* plaque.

placer, *s. m.* pleasure.

plaga, *s. f.* plague, epidemic.

plan, *s. m.* plan.

plancha, *s. f.* plate; flat-iron; *hacer una ~*

make a fool of oneself.

planchar, v. a. iron, press.

plano, adj. flat; — s. m. plan, drawing.

planta, s. f. sole; plant; floor, storey.

plantar, v. a. plant.

plástico, adj. plastic, pliable.

plata, s. f. silver.

plataforma, s. f. platform.

plátano, s. m. banana.

platea, s. f. orchestra (in the theatre).

platillo, s. m. saucer.

plato, s. m. plate; dish; course.

playa, s. f. beach, shore.

plaza, s. f. square; market; job, position; seat (taxi); ~ de toros bull ring.

plazo, s. m. (space of) time, term; instalment.

plegar, v. a. fold.

pleito, s. m. lawsuit; dispute.

pleno, adj. full, complete.

pliego, s. m. sheet (of folded paper).

plomero, s. m. plumber.

plomo, s. m. lead (metal); fuse.

pluma, s. f. feather; pen; ~ fuente fountain-pen.

población, s. f. population; town; village.

pobre, adj. poor; humble; — s. m. poor person; beggar.

pobreza, s. f. poverty.

poco, adj. & adv. little; dentro de ~ soon, in a short time; ~ a ~ little by little, gradually; por ~ almost nearly; un ~ de a small amount of.

poder[1], v. n. be able; a más no ~ to the utmost: no ~ más exhausted; no ~ menos de not to be able to help.

poder[2], s. m. power; influence.

poema, s. m. poem.

poesía, s. f. poetry.

poeta, s. m. poet.

policía, s. f. police; — s. m. policeman.

político, adj. political; in-law; — s. m. politician.

polo, s. m. pole; polo.

polvo, s. m. dust; -s pl. powder.

pólvora, s. f. gunpowder.

polvoriento, adj dusty.

pollo, s. m. chicken.

pompa, s. f. pomp, display.

poner, v. a. put, place, lay; suppose, assume; put on, wear; v. n. ~se get, become; ~se a begin, start; ~se, en camino set out; ~se en pie get up, rise.

poniente, s. m. west.

popular, adj. popular.

poquito, adj. little.

por, prep. by; through; for; in order to; across, over; ~ escrito in writing; ~ eso therefore; ¿~ qué? why?; ~ supuesto of course.

porcelana, s. f. china; porcelain.

porción, s. f. portion, part.

porque, conj. because, for, as.

porqué, s. m. reason.

porquería, s. f. dirty trick.

portaaviones, s. m. aircraft carrier.

portamonedas, *s. m.* purse.

portarse, *v. n.* behave oneself.

porte, *s. m.* postage; bearing (of a person).

portero, *s. m.* goal-keeper; porter.

portugués, *adj.* & *s. m.* Portuguese.

porvenir, *s. m.* future.

posada, *s. f.* lodging-house, inn.

poseer, *v. a.* possess, own.

posesión, *s. f.* possession, property.

posibilidad, *s. f.* possibility.

posible, *adj.* possible.

posición, *s. f.* position; place.

postal, *adj.* postal; — *s. f.* postcard.

posterior, *adj.* rear, back; later.

postizo, *adj.* artificial, false.

postre, *s. m.* dessert, pudding.

potable, *adj.* drinkable.

pote, *s. m.* pot, jar.

potente, *adj.* powerful, strong, potent.

pozo, *s. m.* well (for water).

práctica, *s. f.* practice.

practicar, *v. a.* practise; carry out.

práctico, *adj.* practical; — *s. m.* harbour pilot.

prado, *s. m.* lawn, field, meadow.

precio, *s. m.* price; ∼s fijos fixed prices.

precioso, *adj.* beautiful; precious.

precisar, *v. a.* fix, set; make clear; *v. n.* be necessary, must.

preciso, *adj.* accurate, exact; *es* ∼ it's necessary.

preferible, *adj.* preferable.

preferir, *v. a.* prefer.

pregunta, *s. f.* question.

preguntar, *v. a.* ask; inquire.

premiar, *v. a.* reward, give a prize.

premio, *s. m.* prize, reward.

prenda, *s. f.* security; ∼ *de vestir* garment.

prender, *v. a.* fix, pin, catch; ∼ *fuego a* set on fire.

prensa, *s. f.* press; newspapers.

preocupar, *v. a.* preoccupy, worry; *v. n.* ∼*se de* care for.

preparar, *v. a.* prepare; arrange.

preparativos, *s. m. pl.* preparations.

presa, *s. f.* prey; dam (for water).

prescribir, *v. a.* prescribe.

presencia, *s. f.* presence; appearance.

presenciar, *v. a.* see, witness.

presentar, *v. a.* present, introduce; put on (programme); *v. n.* ∼*se* present oneself.

presente, *adj.* present; *al* ∼ at present; *tener* ∼ bear in mind.

presidente, *s. m.* president, chairman.

presión, *s. f.* pressure.

préstamo, *s. m.* loan.

prestar, *v. a.* lend, loan; ∼ *atención* pay attention; ∼ *ayuda* help.

pretender, *v. a.* pretend; intend, try.

pretensión, *s. f.* pretension; claim.

pretexto, *s. m.* pretext; excuse.

prevenir, v. a. prevent, avoid; prepare; forewarn.

previo, adj. previous.

prima, s. f. female cousin.

primavera, s. f. spring (season).

primero, adj. first.

primo, s. m. male cousin.

princesa, s. f. princess.

principal, adj. main, principal; — s. m. principal.

príncipe, s. m. prince.

principiante, s. m., f. beginner.

principiar, v. a. & n. begin, start.

principio, s. m. beginning; main dish; principle.

prisa, s. f. hurry; a toda ~ at full speed; de ~ quickly.

prisión, s. f. prison.

prisionero, s. m. prisoner.

privar, v. a. deprive.

probable, adj. probable.

probar, v. a. try, test; taste; prove; v. n. ~se try on.

problema, s. m. problem.

proceder, v. n. proceed; come, be the result; act; behave; — s. m. conduct, behaviour.

procedimiento, s. m. method, procedure.

proceso, s. m. process; trial (court).

procurar, v. a. try; v. n. ~se get, obtain.

producir, v. a. produce, give.

producto, s. m. product.

profesión, s. f. profession.

profesional, adj. professional.

profesor, s. m. teacher, professor.

profeta, s. m. prophet.

profundo, adj. deep, profound.

programa, s. m. programme.

progresar, v. n. (make) progress, advance.

progreso, s. m. progress.

prohibir, v. a. forbid; se prohíbe fumar no smoking.

promesa, s. f. promise.

prometer, v. a. promise.

prometido, adj. engaged.

pronto, adj. ready; de ~ suddenly; tan ~ como as soon as; — adv. quickly; soon.

pronunciar, v. a. pronounce.

propiedad, s. f. property.

propietario, s. m. owner, proprietor.

propina, s. f. tip; gratuity.

propio, adj. own; proper, right.

proponer, v. a. propose; v. n. ~se plan, intend.

proposición, s. f. proposition.

propósito, s. m. purpose, intention; a ~ on purpose; a ~ de in connection with.

propuesta, s. f. proposal.

prosperar, v. n. prosper.

proteger, v. a. protect.

protesta, s. f. protest.

protestar, v. a. protest.

provecho, s. m. profit; de ~ useful; buen ~ enjoy your meal.

provechoso, adj. profitable.

provincia, s. f. province.

provocar, v. a. provoke.

proximidad, s. f. vicinity.

próximo, adj. next; close.

proyectar, v. a. plan; project, show.

proyecto, *s. m.* project, plan.

prudente, *adj.* prudent, wise.

prueba, *s. f.* proof, evidence; test.

pua, *s. f.* prick, sting, barb.

publicar, *v. a.* publish.

publicidad, *s. f.* publicity.

público, *adj.* public; — *s. m.* public, audience.

puchero, *s. m.* cooking-pot, stew.

pudín, *s. m.* pudding.

pueblo, *s. m.* town, village; people.

puente, *s. m.* bridge.

puerco, *s. m.* pig; pork.

puerta, *s. f.* door; gate.

puerto, *s. m.* port, pass (mountain).

pues, *adv. & conj.* because, as, since; anyhow; well; ~ *bien* all right then.

puesta, *s. f.* stake.

puesto, *s. m.* place; position, job; stall, stand, booth.

púgil, *s. m.* boxer.

pulga, *s. f.* flea.

pulgada, *s. f.* inch.

pulgar, *s. m.* thumb.

pulmón, *s. m.* lung.

pulmonía, *s. f.* pneumonia.

pulsera, *s. f.* bracelet; *reloj (s. m.) de* ~ wrist watch.

pulso, *s. m.* pulse.

punta, *s. f.* point; end, tip; top.

punto, *s. m.* point, dot; place, spot; *al* ~ instantly; *a tal* ~ that far; *coche (s. m.) de* ~

taxi, car for hire; *dar en el* ~ hit the nail; *estar a* ~ *de* be about to; ~ *de vista* point of view; ~ *y coma* semicolon; *géneros (s. m. pl.) de* ~ knitted goods.

puntual, *adj.* punctual.

puntualidad, *s. f.* punctuality.

puñado, *s. m.* handful.

puñal, *s. m.* dagger.

puño, *s. m.* fist; handle; cuff.

pupila, *s. f.* pupil (of eye).

pupitre, *s. m.* (school) desk.

pureza, *s. f.* purity.

purgante, *adj. & s. m.* purgative.

puro, *adj.* pure; clear; — *s. m.* cigar.

puya, *s. f.* lance.

Q

que, *pron.* that, wich; who, whom; what; — *conj.* that; *de manera* ~ so that; *esta habitación es mejor* ~ *la otra* this room is better than the other.

¿qué? *pron.* which?

¿ por ~ ? why?; *para* ~? what for?; *¡~!* what!; *¿~ más da?* what's the difference?; *¡* ~ *va!* go on! come on! how come?; *un no sé* ~ a certain something.

quebrado, *adj.* rough, rugged; broken; *número* ~ fraction.

quebrar, *v. a.* break; fail; *v. n.* ~*se* break.

quedar(se), *v. a. & n.* remain, be left; ~ *bien con* get along well with; ~ en agree, have an understanding; ~se atrás stay behind; me quedo con esto I'll take this.

quehaceres, s. m. pl.; ~ de casa household chores.

queja, s. f. complaint.

quejarse, v. n. complain.

quemado, adj. burnt; ~ por el sol sunburned.

quemadura, s. f. burn, scald.

quemar, v. a. burn; v. n. ~se burn oneself.

querer, v. a. want, wish; love; quisiera I should like.

querido, adj. dear, beloved.

queso, s. m. cheese.

quien, pron. who; whoever, anyone.

¿quién? pron. who?; ¿a ~? whom?; con ~ (es)? with whom?

quienquiera, pron. whoever.

quieto, adj. still; calm; quiet.

química, s. f. chemistry.

químico, adj. chemical; — s. m. chemist.

quince, adj. & s. m. fifteen.

quincena, s. f. two weeks.

quinientos, adj. & s. m. pl. five hundred.

quinina, s. f. quinine.

quinta, s. f. country house.

quintal, s. m. a hundred pounds (weight).

quinto, adj. fifth.

quiosco, s. m. newsstall.

quitar, v. a. take away, substract; v. n. ~se take off (clothing).

quizá(s), adv. perhaps, maybe.

R

rábano, s. m. radish.

rabia, s. f. rage, fury; rabies.

rabiar, v. n. be mad, rage.

rabioso, adj. furious, enraged; rabid.

rabo, s. m. tail.

racimo, s. m. cluster, bunch.

ración, s. f. ration.

racionar, v. a. ration.

radiador, s. m. radiator.

radiar, v. a. radiate.

radio, s. m. radius; radium; ~ de acción range; — s. f. radio, wireless.

radioactivo, adj. radioactive.

redioescucha, s., m., f. listener (of radio).

radiografía, s. f. radiography.

radiorreceptor, s. m. receiver.

rad otransmisor, s. m. transmitter, broadcasting station.

radioyente, s. m., f. listener (of radio).

raíz, s. f. root.

rama, s. f. branch, twig, bough.

ramillete, s. m. bunch of flowers.

ramo, s. m. bough (cut off tree); bouquet, bunch; branch, line of business.

rana, s. f. frog.

rancio, adj. rancid; old-fashioned, antiquated.

rancho, s. m. mess (dining-room); hut (South

America).

rápido, *adj.* rapid, quick; — *s. m.* express (train).

raro, *adj.* rare, unusual; odd, strange.

rascacielos, *s. m.* skyscraper.

rascar, *v. a.* scratch.

rasgar, *v. a.* tear.

rasgo, *s. m.* stroke; flourish; ~s *pl.* features; characteristics.

raspar, *v. a.* scrape, scratch.

rata, *s. f.* rat.

ratero, *s. m.* pickpocket.

ratificar, *v. a.* ratify.

rato, *s. m.* while; *al poco* ~ very soon; *a* ~*s perdidos* in one's spare time; *pasar el* ~ pass the time away; *pasar un buen* ~ have a good time.

ratón, *s. m.* mouse.

ratonera, *s. f.* mousetrap.

raya, *s. f.* dash, line; parting (in hair); ray fish.

rayado, *adj.* striped.

rayo, *s. m.* ray; flash of lightning.

raza, *s. f.* (anthropological) race.

razón, *s. f.* reason; cause! explanation; ~ *social* commercial house, firm; *a* ~ *de* at the rate of; *tengo* ~ I'm right; *n tiene* ~ he's wrong.

razonable, *adj.* reasonable.

real, *adj.* real, actual; royal.

realidad, *s. f.* reality, fact.

realizar, *v. a.* accomplish; carry out; sell out.

rebaja, *s. f.* reduction.

rebajar, *v. a.* reduce, lower.

rebanada, *s. f.* slice of bread.

rebaño, *s. m.* herd, flock.

recado, *s. m.* message; errand.

recaída, *s. f.* relapse.

recambio, *s. m.* exchange; *pieza (s. f.) de* ~ spare (part).

recelo, *s. m.* suspicion.

recepción, *s. f.* reception; formal gathering.

receta, *s. f.* prescription (medicine); ~ *de cocina* recipe.

recibir, *v. a.* receive.

recibo, *s. m.* receipt.

recién, *adv.* recently, newly; just; ~ *llegado* newcomer.

reciente, *adj.* new, fresh; recent.

recipiente, *s. m.* container; bin; tank.

reclamación, *s. f.* reclamation, complaint; claim.

reclamar, *v. a.* claim.

recobrar, *v. a.* recover, regain.

recoger, *v. a.* get; collect; gather up, pick up; take in, shelter.

recomendar, *v. a.* recommend; advise.

reconocer, *v. a.* inspect, examine; recognize; acknowledge, admit; *estoy reconocido* I'm grateful.

reconquista, *s. f.* reconquest.

reconstruir, *v. a.* rebuild, reconstruct.

recordar, *v. a.* remember; remind.

recorrer, *v. a. & n.* cover (distance); travel.

recorrido, *s. m.* route, course, run.

recreo, *s. m.* recreation.

recto, *adj.* straight; just, fair.

recuerdo, *s. m.* remembrance, memory; souvenir, memento.

recurso, s. m. argument; ~s pl. means, resources.

red, s. f. net; trap, snare.

redactar, v. a. compose.

redondo, adj. round; a la redonda around.

reducción, s. f. reduction, decrease.

reducir, v. a. reduce.

reembolso, s. m. repayment; cash on delivery.

reemplazar, v. a. replace.

referencia, s. f. reference; dar ~s inform.

referir, v. a. relate; v. n. ~se refer to.

reflujo, s. m. ebb, low tide.

reforma, s. f. alteration.

refran, s. m. proverb, saying.

refrescar, v. a. cool, refresh; v. n. ~se cool off.

refresco, s. m. refreshment; cold drink.

refrigerador, s. m. refrigerator.

refugio, s. m. refuge; shelter.

regalar, v. a. present, give (gift).

regalo, s. m. present, gift.

regar, v. a. water, irrigate.

regata, s. f. regatta.

regateo, s. m. bargaining, haggling.

régimen, s. m. regime, political system; diet.

región, s. f. region.

registrar, v. a. search; examine (luggage); record, keep a record.

regla, s. f. rule, regulation; ruler (for drawing lines); en ~ in order.

regresar, v. n. return.

regreso, s. m. return, coming or going back.

regular, adj. regular, orderly; moderate; so-so.

reina, s. f. queen.

reinar, v. n. reign.

reino, s. m. kingdom.

reir(se), v. n. laugh.

relación, s. f. story, account; relaciones pl. relations, connections.

relacionar, v. a. relate, connect.

relámpago, s. m. lightning.

relampaguear, v. n. lighten.

relatar, v. a. relate, tell.

religión, s. f. religion.

religioso, adj. religious.

reloj, s. m. clock, watch.

relojería, s. f. watchmaker's shop.

relojero, s. m. watchmaker.

relleno, adj. stuffed, filled; — s. m. stuffing.

remar, v. n. row (a boat).

remedio, s. m. remedy, medicine.

remendar, v. a. mend, patch, repair.

remitente, s. m., f. sender.

remitir, v. a. remit, send.

remo, s. m. oar.

remolacha, s. f. beet.

remolcador, s. m. tugboat.

remolcar, v. a. tow.

remordimiento, s. m. remorse.

remoto, adj. remote, distant, out-of-the-way.

remover, v. a. dig up; stir; shake; dismiss (from a post).

remunerar, v. a. remunerate.

rendido, adj. exhausted.

rendir, v. a. surrender; yield, produce; v. n. ~se surrender, yield, give in.

renglón, s. m. line; row.

renombrado, *adj.* famous, renowned.

renovar, *v. a.* renovate.

renta, *s. f.* rent; income.

renunciar, *v. a.* renounce, give up; resign; refuse, reject.

reo, *s. m.* accused.

reparar, *v. a.* repair; ~ en consider; notice.

reparo, *s. m.* objection, help.

repartir, *v. a.* distribute.

repasar, *v. a.* check (account); revise (lesson); mend (clothes).

repaso, *s. m.* revision; mending.

repente, *s. n.* sudden impulse; de ~ suddenly, unexpectedly.

repentino, *adj.* sudden.

repetición, *s. f.* repetition.

repetir, *v. a.* repeat.

replicar, *v. n.* reply, answer back; argue.

repollo, *s. m.* (head of) cabbage.

reponer, *v. a.* replace; repair; *v. n.* ~se recover (health).

reposar, *v. n.* rest.

reposo, *s. m.* rest.

representación, *s. f.* performance.

representante, *adj.* representing; — *s. m.* travelling salesman, agent.

representar, *v. a.* represent, perform.

reproducir, *v. a.* reproduce.

reptil, *s. m.* reptile.

república, *s. f.* republic.

republicano, *adj. & s. m.* republican.

repuesto, *s. m.* store. stock; supply; de ~ extra, spare.

reputación, *s. f.* reputation, repute.

resbaladizo, *adj.* slippery.

resbalar(se), *v. n.* slip.

reserva, *s. f.* reserve; secrecy, discretion; guardar ~ use discretion.

reservar, *v. a.* reserve; ~se keep for oneself.

resfriado, *s. m.* cold (illness).

resfriarse, *v. n.* catch cold.

resignarse, *v. n.* be resigned.

resistente, *adj.* strong, resistant.

resistir, *v. n.* resist; *v. n.* ~se refuse to.

resolución, *s. f.* decision, resolution; resoluteness.

resolver, *v. a.* decide; solve; *v. n.* ~se decide, make up one's mind to.

resorte, *s. m.* (elastic) spring.

respecto, *s. m.* respect; con ~ a with regard to.

respetable, *adj.* respectable; considerable.

respeto, *s. m.* respect.

respiración, *s. f.* respiration.

respirar, *v. n.* breathe.

responder, *v. a. & n.* answer, respond; react.

responsable, *adj.* responsible.

respuesta, *s. f.* answer, reply.

restablecerse, *v. n.* recover.

restaurante, *s. m.* restaurant.

resto, *s. m.* rest, remainder.

resultado, *s. m.* result.

resumen, *s. m.* summary.

retardar, *v. a.* retard.

retener, *v. a.* withhold; remember, retain; hold, keep.

retirar, *v. a.* withdraw;

retire; pull back, put aside; — v. n. ~se withdraw, retire.

retiro, s. m. retirement.

retrasar, v. a. postpone; delay; set back; v. n. ~se be late; run slow.

retraso, s. m. delay; lateness.

retratar, v. a. portray.

retrato, s. m. portrait, painting, photograph.

retrete, s. m. lavatory.

reunión, s. f. meeting, assembly, party.

reunir, v. a. unite, bring together; collect; v. n. ~se meet, unite.

revelar, v. a. reveal, show; develop.

reventa, s. f. retail, resale.

reventar, v. n. burst.

revés, s. m. wrong side, reverse side.

revisar, v. a. revise; review; examine.

revisor, s. m. guard (on train).

revista, s. f. review; magazine.

revocar, v. a. revoke.

revolución, s. f. revolution; revolt; turn.

revolucionario, adj. & s. m. revolutionary.

revólver, s.m. revolver.

revolver, v. a. revolve; stir; turn upside down.

rey, s. m. king.

rezar, v. a. & n. pray, say (prayers).

rezo, s.m. praying.

riachuelo, s. m. rivulet.

ribera, s. f. coast; beach.

rico, adj. rich, wealthy; delicious; cute.

ridículo, adj. ridículous.

riego, s. m. watering; irrigation.

riel, s. m. rail.

riesgo, s. m. danger, risk.

rígido, adj. stiff, rigid; severe, stern.

riguroso, adj. rigorous.

rincón, s. m. (inside) corner.

riña, s. f. quarrel.

riñón, s. m. kidney.

río, s. m. river.

riqueza, s. f. wealth; abundance.

risa, s. f. laugh, laughter.

rizar, v. a. curl.

rizo, s. m. curl.

robar, v. a. rob; steal.

roble, s. m. oak.

robo, s. m. robbery, theft.

robusto, adj. robust.

roca, s. f. rock; cliff.

rodar, v. n. roll; v. a. ~ una película shoot a film.

rodear, v. a. surround, encircle.

rodeo, s.m. turn winding.

rodilla, s. f. knee.

rogar, v. a. request, beg.

rojo, adj. red.

rollo, s. m. roll.

romper, v. a. break.

roncar, v. n. snore.

ronco, adj. hoarse.

ropa, s. f. clothes; ~ blanca linen; ~ de cama bedding.

ropero, s. m. wardrobe.

rosa, s. f. rose; color de ~ pink.

rosario, s. m. rosary.

rosbif, s. m. roast beef.

rosca, s. f. thread (screw); spiral; ring (bread or cake).

rostro, s. m. face.

roto, adj. broken; — s. m. tear.

rótulo, s. m. sign; label.

rozar, v. a. clear; graze, rub.

rubia, s. f. blonde.

rubio, adj. blond(e), fair.

rudo, adj: rude, rough.

rueda, s. f. wheel.

ruego, s. m. request, plea.

ruido, s. m. noise; comment, discussion.

ruidoso, adj. noisy.

ruina, s. f. ruin, decline.

ruiseñor, s. m. nightingale.

rumano, adj. & s. m. Rumanian.

rumbo s. m. direction.

rumor', s. m. murmur; rumour.

rural, adj. rustic, rural.

ruso. adj. & s. m. Russian.

ruta, s. f. route, way.

rutina, s. f. routine.

S

sábado, s. m. Saturday.

sábana, s. f. sheet.

saber, v. a. know; taste; ¿ sabe usted español? do you know Spanish?; esto sabe mal this tastes bad; a ~ namely; — s. m. knowledge.

sabio, adj. wise; — s. m. learned or wise person.

sabor, s. m. taste, flavour.

saborear, v. a. taste, relish.

sabroso, adj. savoury, tasty.

sacacorchos, s. m. corkscrew.

sacar, v. a. draw (out), take out, put out; get, win; ~ copia make a copy; ~ una fotografía take a picture.

sacerdote, s. m. priest.

saco, s. m. sack, bag; jacket.

sacudir, v. a. shake; jolt.

sagrado, adj. sacred, holy.

sainete, s. m. one-act farce.

sal, s. f. salt.

sala, s. f. living room, parlour; ~ de espera waiting-room.

salario, s. m. salary, wages.

salchicha, s. f. sausage.

salchichón, s. m. (large) sausage.

saldo, s. m. balance; sale.

salero, s. m. salt-cellar.

salida, s. f. departure; exit; expenditure; callejón (s. m.) sin ~ blind alley, cul-de-sac.

salir, v. n. go out, leave; come off, disappear (spots); rise (sun); grow, come up; come out, be published; stick out; ~ de compras go shopping.

salmón, s. m. salmon.

salón, s. m. living-room, hall.

salsa, s. f. gravy, sauce.

saltar, v. n. jump, spring; bounce.

salto, s. m. jump.

salud, s. f. health; ¡ a su ~! to your health!

saludar, v. a. greet; salute.

saludo, s. m. greeting, salute.

salvaje, adj. savage, wild.

salvar, v. a. save, rescue.

salvo, adj. sound, unhurt.

san, adj. saint.

sanar, v. a. heal, cure.

sangre, s. f. blood; ~ fría composure, coolness of mind.

sangriento, adj. bloody.

sano, adj. healthy.

santidad, s. f. holiness, sanctity.

santo, *adj. & s. m.* holy; saint.

sardina, *s. f.* sardine.

sastre, *s. m.* tailor.

satisfecho, *adj.* satisfied.

sazón, *s. f.* ripeness, maturity.

sazonar, *v. a.* season; ripen.

se, *pron.* oneself; (to) himself, herself, itself; (to) themselves, yourselves; (to) each other; ~ *dice* they say, it's said; *se habla español* Spanish spoken.

secante, *s. m.* blotter.

secar, *v. a.* dry; wither.

sección, *s. f.* section.

seco, *adj.* dry; dried.

secretaría, *s. f.* secretary's office.

secretaria, *s. f.* secretary.

secretario, *s. m.* secretary.

secreto, *s. m.* secret.

sed, *s. f.* thirst; *tengo mucha* ~ I'm very thirsty.

seda, *s. f.* silk.

seguida; *en* ~ *adv.* immediately, right away.

seguir, *v. a.* follow; continue; *siga a la derecha* keep to the right.

según, *prep.* according to; as; it depends.

segundo, *s. m.* second; — *adj.* second.

seguridad, *s. f.* security.

seguro, *adj.* sure, certain: sale, secure; steady; — *s. m.* insurance.

seis, *adj. & s. m.* six.

selección, *s. f.* selection, choice.

selva, *s. f.* woods, forest.

sellar, *v. a.* stamp; seal.

sello, *s. m.* stamp; seal.

semana, *s. f.* week.

semanal, *adj.* weekly.

sembrar, *v. a.* sow; spread.

semejante, *adj.* similar; such; — *s. m.* fellow-man.

semejanza, *s. f.* resemblance, similarity.

semilla, *s. f.* seed.

sencillez, *s. f.* simplicity.

sencillo, *adj.* simple, plain; unaffected.

senda *s. f.* path.

sendero, *s. m.* footpath.

sensación, *s. f.* sensation.

sensato, *adj.* sensible, wise.

sensible, *adj.* sensitive, keen.

sentar, *v. a. & n.* seat; fit; ~*se* sit down; *siéntese usted* sit down.

sentencia, *s. f.* sentence.

sentido, *adj.* sincere; moving; — *s. m.* sense; meaning; direction.

sentimiento, *s. m.* sentiment, feeling; sorrow, grief.

sentir, *v. a.* feel; hear; regret; be sorry; *lo siento mucho* I'm very sorry; *v. n.* ~*se* feel; *me siento mal* I feel ill.

seña, *s. f.* sign; mark; ~*s pl.* address.

señal, *s. f.* signal; mark; ~*es de tráfico* traffic signs.

señalar, *v. a.* point out, mark.

señor, *s. m.* sir; ¿ *está el* ~ *Pérez?* is Mr. Pérez in?; man, gentleman.

señora, *s. f.* madam; *quisiera hablar con la* ~ *González* I'd like to speak to Mrs. González; lady.

señorita, *s. f.* Miss; young lady.

señorito. *s. m.* young gentleman; master of

the house.

separar, v. a. separate; divide; move away; lay aside; v. n. ~se separate.

septiembre, s. m. September.

séptimo, adj. seventh.

sepultar, v. a. bury, inter.

sepultura, s. f. grave.

sequedad, s. f. aridity, dryness.

ser, v. n. be; soy médico I'm a doctor; él es de Madrid he is from Madrid.

serenata, s. f. serenade.

sereno, adj. clear, fair; calm, serene; — s. m. night-watchman; dew.

serie, s. f. series.

serio, adj. serious, solemn; en ~ seriously.

servicio, s. m. service; set.

servidor, s. m. man-servant.

servidora, s. f. servant.

servidumbre, s. f. (staff of) servants; servitude.

servilleta, s. f. table napkin.

servir, v. a. & n. serve; wait on; ~ para be good for; ~se help oneself.

sesenta, adj. & s. m. sixty.

sesión, s. f. session; meeting.

setenta, adj. & s. m. seventy.

severo, adj. severe, rigorous.

sexo, s. m. sex.

sexto, adj. sixth.

sexual, adj. sexual.

si, conj. if, whether.

sí¹, yes; ~ que certainly.

sí², pron. oneself.

sidra, s. f. cider.

siempre, adv. always; ~ que whenever; para ~ forever.

sien, s. f. temple (anatomy).

sierra, s. f. saw; mountain range.

siesta, s. f. afternoon nap.

siete, adj. & s. m. seven.

siglo, s. m. century.

significado, s. m. meaning.

significar, v. a. mean.

significativo, adj. significant.

signo, s. m. sign, mark, symbol.

siguiente, adj. following, next.

sílaba, s. f. syllable.

silbar, v. n. whistle.

silencio, s. m. silence; guardar ~ keep quiet.

silencioso, adj. silent.

silla, s. f. chair; ~ de montar saddle.

sillón, s. m. armchair.

simpatía, s. f. sympathy.

simpático, adj. congenial, nice, pleasant.

simple, adj. simple, easy.

simular, v. a. & n. simulate.

sin, prep. without; ~ embargo however, nevertheless.

sincero, adj. sincere.

sindicato, s. m. trade-union.

singular, adj. & s. m. singular.

siniestro, adj. sinister.

sino, conj. but; except; no ... ~ not ... but.

síntoma, s. m. symptom.

siquiera, adv. at least; ni ~ not even.

sirvienta, s. f. maid, servant.

sistema, s. m. system.

sitio, s. m. spot, site;

place, seat; room, space: siege.

situación, *s. f.* situation; location, site.

smoking, *s. m.* dinner jacket.

sobornar, *v. a.* bribe.

sobra, *s. f.* excess, surplus; *de ~* more than enough; *estar de ~* be superfluous, be in the way.

sobrar, *v. n.* be in excess; be superfluous.

sobre, *prep.* over; on, upon; about, concerning; — *s. m.* envelope.

sobrina, *s. f.* niece.

sobrino, *s. m.* nephew.

sobrio, *adj.* sober, temperate.

social, *adj.* social.

socialismo, *s. m.* socialism.

sociedad, *s. f.* society; *~ anónima* joint-stock company.

socio, *s. m.* partner (in business); member (of club).

socorrer, *v. a.* help.

socorro, *s. m.* help, aid.

sofá, *s. m.* sofa.

sofocar, *v. a.* suffocate; stifle; choke.

soga, *s. f.* rope.

sol, *s. m.* sun; sunlight.

soldado, *s. m.* soldier.

soldar, *v. a.* solder, weld.

soledad, *s. f.* solitude.

solemne, *adj.* solemn.

soler, *v. n.* be in the habit of, have the custom of; *suelo levantarme a las seis* I usually get up at six o'clock.

solicitar, *v. a.* request, apply for.

solicitud, *s. f.* solicitude; application, request.

sólido, *adj.* solid, firm.

solo, *adv.* alone; — *adj.* lonely; — *s. m.* solo.

sólo, *adv.* only.

soltar, *v. a.* loosen; let out, let go.

soltero, *s. m.* bachelor.

solución, *s. f.* solution; result.

solucionar, *v. a.* solve

sollozar, *v. n.* sob.

sombra, *s. f.* shade; shadow; dark, darkness.

sombrero, *s. m.* hat.

sombrilla, *s. f.* parasol.

sombrío, *adj.* gloomy, sombre.

son, *s. m.* sound.

sonar, *v. n.* sound, ring; strike (clock); *~se* blow one's nose.

sonido, *s. m.* sound.

sonoro, *adj.* sonorous.

sonreir, *v. n.* smile.

sonrisa, *s. f.* smile.

soñar, *v. n.* dream.

sopa, *s. f.* soup.

sopera, *s. f.* tureen.

soplar, *v. n.* blow.

soplo, *s. m.* blow(ing), puff, gust (of air); breath; tip, hint.

soportar, *v. a.* bear; suffer.

sorber, *v. a.* sip.

sorbo, *s. m.* sip.

sordo, *adj.* deaf; muffled; dull.

sordomudo, *adj. & s. m* deaf and dumb; deaf-mute.

sorprendente, *adj.* surprising.

sorprender, *v. a.* surprise.

sorpresa, *s. f.* surprise.

sortear, *v. n.* draw lots.

sortija, *s. f.* ring.

soso, *adj.* tasteless; insipid.

sospecha, *s. f.* suspicion.

sospechar, *v. a.* suspect.

sospechoso, *adj.* suspicious.

sostén, *s. m.* bra.

sostener, *v. a.* hold; support; maintain.

sótano, *s. m.* basement.

su, *pron.* your, his, her, its, their; *sus pl.*

suave, *adj.* delicate, soft, gentle, light; smooth; mellow, mild; meek, docile.

subasta, *s. f.* auction.

súbdito, *s. m.* subject.

subir, *v. a.* bring up; put on, set on; lift up, raise; *v. n.* go up; amount; rise, increase; ascend.

súbito, *adj.* sudden.

subrayar, *v. a.* underline.

su(b)scribirse, *v. n.* subscribe.

su(b)scripción, *s. f.* subscription.

su(b)stituir, *v. a.* replace.

su(b)stituto, *s. m.* substitute.

subterráneo, *adj. & s. m.* underground (railway).

suburbio, *s. m.* suburb.

suceder, *v. n.* succeed; happen.

suceso, *s. m.* event.

sucio, *adj.* dirty; unfair.

sudamericano, *adj. & s. m.* South American.

sudar, *v. n.* sweat.

sudeste, *s. m.* southeast.

sudoeste, *s. m.* southwest.

sudor, *s. m.* sweat.

sueco, *adj.* Swedish; — *s. m.* Swede.

suegra, *s. f.* mother-in-law.

suegro, *s. m.* father-in-law.

suela, *s. f.* sole.

suelo, *s. m.* floor; soil; ground.

suelto, *adj.* loose; free; — *s. m.* (loose) change.

sueño, *s. m.* sleep; dream; *echar un* ~ take a nap.

suerte, *s. f.* fate, luck; *por* ~ fortunately.

suéter, *s. m.* sweater.

suficiente, *adj.* sufficient.

sufrir, *v. a. & n.* suffer; endure, put up with; undergo (operation).

sugerir, *v. a.* suggest.

sugestionar, *v. a.* influence.

suicida, *s. m. f.* suicide (person).

suicidarse, *v. n.* commit suicide.

suicidio, *s. m.,* suicide (act).

suizo, *adj. & s. m.* Swiss.

sujetar, *v. a.* hold; fasten.

sujeto, *adj.* fastened; — *s. m.* subject; fellow, guy.

suma, *s. f.* amount, sum; *en* ~ in short.

sumar, *v. a.* amount to.

sumo, *adj.* great; *a lo* ~ at most.

suntuoso, *adj.* sumptuous.

superficie, *s. f.* surface

superior, *adj.* superior, better; higher; — *s. m.* superior.

superioridad, *s. f.* superiority.

supersticioso, *adj.* superstitious.

suplente, *s. m.* deputy; substitute.

súplica, *s. f.* request; supplication.

suplicante, *s. m.* petitioner.

suplicar, *v. a.* request; entreat, implore.

suponer, *v. a.* suppose, assume; imagine.

suprimir, *v. a.* suppress; abolish; omit.

supuesto, *adj.* assumed, supposed; *por* ~ of course.

sur, *s. m.* south.

surtido, *s. m.* assortment, collection.

surtidor, *s. m.* fountain; ~ *(de gasolina)* petrol station.

surtir, *v. a.* supply.

suspender, *v. a.* suspend, stop; hang.

suspirar, *v. n.* sigh.

suspiro, *s. m.* sigh.

sustituir, *v. a.* substitute, replace.

sustitudo, *s. m.* substitute.

susto, *s. m.* fright, scare; *dar un* ~ frighte

sustraer, *v. a.* subtract.

susurrar, *v. n.* murmur.

sutil, *adj.* thin; shrewd.

suyo, *adj.* (of) his, hers, theirs; *los* ~*s pl.* his (her, your, their) folks.

T

tabaco, *s. m.* tobacco.

tabaquero, *s. m.* tobacconist.

taberna, *s. f.* tavern.

tabla, *s. f.* board, plank; list, table (of contents, prices); ~*s pl.* stage (theatre); draw (in a game).

tablero, *s. m.* (chess) board.

taburete, *s. m.* stool.

tacón, *s. m.* heel (of shoe).

tacto, *s. m.* touch; tact.

tajada, *s. f.* slice.

tajo, *s. m.* cut.

tal, *adj. & pron.* such (a);

con ~ *que* provided that; ~ *como* just as; ~ *cual es* as it is; — *s. m., f.* such a thing *or* person; *un* ~ *Alvarez* a certain Alvarez.

talco, *s. m.* talc.

talento, *s. m.* talent, brains.

talón, *s. m.* heel (of foot); stub (of check).

talonario, *s. m.* chequebook.

talle, *s. m.* waist, figure.

taller, *s. m.* workshop; factory, mill.

tamaño, *adj.* so great, such a big; — *s. m.* size.

también, *adv. & conj.* also, too.

tambor, *s. m.* drum.

tampoco, *adv.* neither, not either.

tan, *adv.* so; ~ *tarde* so late.

tanque, *s. m.* tank (military and for liquid).

tanto, *adj.* so much, so many; — *adv.* so long; so often; — *s. m.* point (in games); *entre* ~ meanwhile; *por lo* ~ so, therefore.

tapa, *s. f.* lid, cover.

tapar, *v. a.* cover; cover up; obstruct; *v. n.* ~*se* wrap (oneself); cover oneself.

tapete, *s. m.* small rug; table-cover.

tapia, *s. f.* wall, mud fence.

tapiz, *s. m.* tapestry; carpet.

tapizar, *v. a.* paper.

tapón, *s. m.* cork, stopper.

taquigrafía, *s. f.* shorthand.

taquígrafo, *s. m.* stenographer.

taquilla, *s. f.* ticket-office, ticket-window.

taquimecanógrafa, *s. f.* shorthand typist.

tardar, *v. n.* delay, be long.

tarde, *adv.* late; — *s. f.* afternoon, early evening; *buenas ~s* good afternoon, good evening.

tarea, *s. f.* task.

tarifa, *s. f.* rates, tariff; list of prices.

tarjeta, *s. f.* (post)card, visiting card.

tarta, *s. f.* cake, tart.

tasa, *s. f.* rate, tax; fee.

tasar, *v. a.* rate, tax; estimate.

tauromaquia, *s. f.* art of fighting with bulls.

taza, *s. f.* cup.

te, *pron.* (to) you; yourself.

té, *s. m.* tea (beverage).

teatro, *s. m.* theatre.

técnica, *s. f.* technique.

técnico, *adj.* technic(al); — *s. m.* technician.

techado, *s. m.* roof; cover.

techo, *s. m.* ceiling; roof.

tejado, *s. m.* roof.

tejer, *v. a.* weave.

tejido, *s. m.* fabric, textile.

tela, *s. f.* cloth, material.

telaraña, *s. f.* cobweb.

telefonear, *v. n.* telephone.

telefonema, *s. m.* telephone message.

telefonista, *s. m., f.* telephone operator.

teléfono, *s. m.* telephone.

telegrafiar, *v. a. & n.* send a telegram.

telégrafo, *s. m.* telegraph.

telegrama, *s. m.* telegram.

televisión, *s. f.* television.

televisor, *s. m.* T. V. set.

telón, *s. m.* theatre curtain.

tema, *s. m.* subject, topic, theme; translation.

temblar, *v. n.* tremble, shiver.

temer, *v. n.* fear, be afraid.

temerario, *adj.* rash; unwise.

temor, *s. m.* fear.

temperamento, *s. m.* temperament.

temperatura, *s. f.* temperature.

tempestad, *s. f.* storm, tempest.

tempestuoso, *adj.* stormy.

templado, *adj.* temperate, mild; tuned; tepid.

templar, *v. a.* tune.

templo, *s. m.* temple, church.

temporada, *s. f.* period of time, season.

temporal, *adj.* temporary; — *s. m.* storm.

temprano, *adj. & adv.* early.

tenazas, *s. f. pl.* tongs.

tender, *v. a.* stretch; spread out; hang (clothes); extend, offer (one's hand); *v. n. ~se* stretch out, lie at full length.

tendero, *s. m.* shopkeeper.

tenedor, *s. m.* fork, holder, keeper; *~ de libros* book-keeper.

tener, *v. a.* have, possess; hold; contain; *tengo treinta años* I'm thirty years old; *~ cuidado* be careful; *tengo frío* I'm cold; *tenemos hambre* we are hungry; *~ que* have to, be obliged to; *tengo que irme* I must go.

teniente, *s. m.* lieutenant.

tenis, *s. m.* tennis.

tentar, *v. a.* touch, feel; tempt.

tentativa, *s. f.* attempt.

teñir, *v. a.* dye.

teoría, *s. f.* theory.

tercero, *adj.* third.

tercio, *s. m.* one third.

terciopelo, *s. m.* velvet.

terminar, *v. a.* end, finish.

término, *s. m.* end.

termómetro, *s. m.* thermometer.

ternera, *s. f.* female calf; veal.

ternero, *s. m.* male calf.

terrateniente, *s. m.* landed proprietor.

terraza, *s. f.* terrace, drive.

terremoto, *s. m.* earthquake.

terreno, *adj.* earthly; worldly; — *s. m.* piece of ground, lot; soil.

territorio, *s. m.* territory.

terrón, *s. m.* lump (of sugar); clod (of earth).

tertulia, *s. f.* gathering, party, conversation.

tesorería, *s. f.* treasury.

tesorero, *s. m.* treasurer.

tesoro, *s. m.* treasure.

testamento, *s. m.* will (document).

testificar, *v. a.* testify.

testigo, *s. m., f.* witness.

testimonio, *s. m.* testimony.

tetera, *s. f.* teapot.

textil, *adj.* textile.

texto, *s. m.* text; textbook.

tez, *s. f.* complexion.

ti, *pron.; a* ~ (to) you; *para* ~ for you.

tía, *s. f.* aunt; old woman.

tibio, *adj.* tepid, lukewarm.

tiburón, *s. m.* shark.

tiempo, *s. m.* time; period, epoch; weather; *a* ~ on time; *ganar* ~ save time; *hace* ~ long ago; *hace mal* ~ it's bad weather.

tienda, *s. f.* shop, store; tent.

tierno, *adj.* tender, soft.

tierra, *s. f.* earth; ground; land; soil; native land, country.

tifus, *s. m.* typhoid fever.

tigre, *s. m.* tiger.

tijeras, *s. f. pl.* scissors, shears.

timbre, *s. m.* electric bell; seal, tax stamp.

tímido, *adj.* shy, timid.

timón, *s. m.* helm; rudder.

tinta, *s. f.* ink.

tinte, *s. m.* shade, tint.

tintero, *s. m.* inkpot.

tinto, *adj.* coloured; *vino* ~ red wine.

tío, *s. m.* uncle; fellow, guy.

típico, *adj.* typical, characteristic.

tiple, *s. f.* soprano.

tipo, *s. m.* type; pattern; fellow.

tirante, *adj.* tight, taut; tense; — ~s, *s. m. pl.* pair of braces.

tirar, *v. a. & n.* throw; throw away, discard; shoot, fire; draw (a line); print; ~ *coces* kick; ~ *de* pull.

tiritar, *v. n.* shiver.

tiro, *s. m.* shot; drive; team of horses; *errar el* ~ miss the mark.

tirón, *s. m.* jerk; jolt.

tisis, *s. f.* consumption.

títere, *s. m.* marionette, puppet; dwarf.

titubear, *v. n.* hesitate.

título, *s. m.* title, name;

headline (newspaper); diploma, degree; security.

tiza, s. f. chalk.

toalla, s. f. towel.

tobillo, s. m. ankle.

tocado, s. m. hair-style.

tocador, s. m. dressing-table.

tocar, v. a. touch; play (an instrument); knock; call (at a port); *por lo que a mi toca* as far as I am concerned.

tocino, s. m. bacon.

todavía, adv. still; yet; even; ∼ *no* not yet.

todo, adj. & pron. all; the whole; ∼ *el mundo* everybody; ∼s pl. all of them; ∼s *los dias* every day.

toldo, s. m. awning; tarpaulin.

tolerar, v. a. tolerate; overlook.

tomar, v. a. take; drink, eat, have; hire; adopt; capture; ∼ *por la derecha* go to the right.

tomate, s. m. tomato.

tomo, s. m. volume.

tonel, s. m. cask, barrel.

tonelada, s. f. ton.

tonelaje, s. m. tonnage.

tono, s. m. tone; note; manner; shade; *darse* ∼ put on airs.

tontería, s. f. foolishness, nonsense.

tonto, adj. silly, foolish; stupid, dumb; − s. m. fool; *hacerse el* ∼ play the fool.

topo, s. m. mole.

torbellino, s. m. whirlwind.

torcer, v. a. twist, turn.

torero, s. m. bullfighter.

tormenta, s. f. storm.

tormento, s. m. torment, pain.

tornarse, v. n. turn, become.

tornasol, s. m. sunflower.

tornillo, s. m. screw.

toro, s. m. bull.

torpe, adj. slow; stupid.

torre, s. f. tower.

torrente, s. m. torrent.

torta, s. f. cake.

tortilla, s. f. omelet.

tórtola, s. f. turtle-dove.

tortuga, s. f. tortoise; turtle.

tos, s. f. cough.

toser, v. n. cough.

tostada, s. f. toast.

tostado, adj. tanned (by the sun).

tostar, v. a. toast.

total, adj. & s. m. total.

trabajador, adj. industrious; − s. m. worker.

trabajar, v. n. work.

trabajo, s. m. work; labour.

trabar, v. a. entangle; ∼ *amistad* get acquainted with sy.

tradición, s. f. tradition.

tradicional, adj. traditional.

traducción, s. f. translation.

traducir, v. a. translate.

traer, v. a. bring; fetch; carry.

tráfico, s. m. traffic.

tragar, v. a. swallow.

tragedia, s. f. tragedy.

trágico, adj. tragic.

trago, s. m. swallow; drink; *echar un* ∼ take a drink.

traje, s. m. dress; ∼ *de baño* bathing-costume; ∼ *de etiqueta* evening dress.

tramontana, s. f. north wind.

trampa, *s. f.* trap.

trance, *s. m.* critical moment; *a todo ~* at any cost.

tranquilizar, *v. a.* calm, tranquilize; *v. n.* ~*se* calm oneself.

tranquilo, *adj.* quiet.

transatlántico, *s. m.* transoceanic steamer, liner.

transcurrir, *v. n.* pass, elapse.

transcurso, *s. m.* lapse, course.

transeúnte, *adj.* passient; — *s. m.* passer-by.

transferir, *v. a.* transfer.

transigir, *v. n.* settle, compromise; agree.

tránsito, *s. m.* passage; thoroughfare.

transmisión, *s. f.* transmission; broadcasting.

transmisora, *s. f.* broadcasting station.

transmitir, *v. a.* transmit, broadcast.

transportar, *v. a.* transport, carry.

transporte, *s. m.* transport, transportation.

tranvía, *s. m.* tram.

trapo, *s. m.* piece of cloth; rag.

tráquea, *s. f.* trachea.

tras, *prep.* behind.

trasero, *adj.* rear, back; — *s. m.* rear, hind part.

trasladar, *v. a.* transfer; *v n.* ~*se* move, change place of residence.

traslado, *s. m.* removal, transfer.

trasnochar, *v. n.* be up *or* spend all night.

traspasar, *v.a.* go through, pierce; transfer, trespass.

trasto, *s. m.* household furniture; ~*s pl.* implements.

tratado, *s. m.* treaty; treatise.

tratamiento, *s. m.* medical treatment; form of address.

tratar, *v. a.* treat; handle.

trato, *s. m.* treatment; behaviour, manners; pact, agreement; close friendship.

través, *prep.; a ~ de* through, across; *de ~ adv.* sideways.

travesía, *s. f.* voyage, crossing.

trayecto, *s. m.* distance; stretch; line.

trazar, *v. a.* draw, outline.

trébol, *s. m.* clover.

trece, *adj. & s. m.* thirteen.

treinta, *adj. & s. m.* thirty.

tremendo, *adj.* terrible, dreadful; huge, tremendous.

tren, *s. m.* train.

trepar, *v. n.* climb.

tres, *adj. & s. m.* three.

tribu, *s. f.* tribe.

tribuna, *s. f.* tribune.

tribunal, *s. m.* law-court.

trigo, *s. m.* wheat.

trillar, *v. a.* thresh.

trimestre, *s. m..* quarter (of a year); term.

trinchar, *v. a.* carve (meat).

trinchera, *s. f.* trench.

trineo, *s. m.* sledge.

tripa, *s. f.* tripe; i ntestines.

tripulación, *s. f.* crew.

triste, *adj.* sad; gloomy.

tristeza, *s. f.* sadness.

triunfar, *v. n.* triumph, succeed; win.
triunfo, *s. m.* triumph, victory.
trompeta, *s. f.* trumpet, bugle; — *s. m.* bugler.
tronar, *v. ŋ.* thunder.
tronco, *s. m.* trunk, stalk, stem.
trono, *s. m.* throne.
tropa, *s. f.* troop.
tropezar, *v. n.* stumble; ~ *con* run into, come upon.
tropical, *adj.* tropical.
trópico, *adj.* tropic(al); — *s. m.* tropics.
tropiezo, *s. m.* obstacle, hitch.
trotar, *v. n.* trot.
trote, *s. m.* trot.
trozo, *s. m.* piece; part, fragment; selection, passage (of books).
truco, *s. m.* trick.
trucha, *s. f.* trout.
trueno, *s. m.* thunder.
tu, *adj.* **tus** *pl.* your.
tú, *pron.* you.
tubería, *s. f.* pipeline.
tubo, *s. m.* tubo, pipe.
tuerca, *s. f.* nut (hardware).
tuerto, *adj.* one-eyed.
tumba, *s. f.* tomb.
tumbar, *v. a.* knock down; *v. n.* ~*se* tumble.
tumbo, *s. m.* tumble, somersault.
tumor, *s. m.* tumour.
tumulto, *s. m.* mob; noisy crowd.
tunante, *s. m.* idler, rascal, rogue.
túnel, *s. m.* tunnel.
turbar, *v. a.* disturb, upset; confuse.
turbina, *s. f.* turbine.

turco, *adj.* Turkish; — *s. m.* Turk.
turismo, *s. m.* tourist traffic.
turista, *s. m.,* *f.* tourist.
turno, *s. m.* turn; *de* ~ on duty.

tutear, *v. a.* use the familiar *tú* in addressing a person.
tutor, *s. m.* guardian.
tuyo, *adj.* (of) yours.

U

u, *conj.* (for *o,* before *o* or *ho*) *siete u ocho* seven or eight.
úlcera, *s. f.* ulcer, abscess.
ultimar, *v. a.* finish, end.
último, *adj.* last; final; latest.
ultramar, *s. m.* overseas.
ultramarinos, *s. m. pl.* colonial produce, groceries.
un, *m.;* **una,** *f.* a, an; one.
undécimo, *adj.* eleventh.
ungüento, *s. m.* ointment.
unico, *adj.* only, only one.
unidad, *s. f.* unity; unit.
unido, *adj.* united.
unificar, *v. a.* unite.
uniforme, *adj.* & *s. m.* uniform.
unión, *s. f.* union; unity; joining, joint; matrimony.
unir, *v. a.* tie together; link, attach; *v. n.* ~*se* unite, join.
universal, *adj.* universal.
universidad, *s. f.* university.
universo, *s. m.* universe, world.
uno, *adj.* & *s. m.* one;

somebody; ~s pl. some, a few.

untar, v. a. spread (butter); bribe; ~ con grasa grease; v. n. ~se la cara use cream on one's face.

uña, s. f. nail, fingernail, toenail; claw; ser ~ y carne be fast friends.

urbanidad, s. f. good manners.

urbano, adj. urban; urbane.

urgencia, s. f. urgency, hurry.

urgente, adj. pressing, urgent.

usado, adj. used, secondhand.

usanza, s. f. usage, custom.

usar, v. a. use; wear; v. n ~se be in use.

uso, s. m. use.

usted, pron. you.

usual, adj. usual, customary.

usura, s. f. usury.

utensilio, s. m. utensil; ~s pl. tools, implements.

útil, adj. useful; profitable.

utilidad, s. f. utility, usefulness.

utilizar, v. a. utilize.

uva, s. f. grape.

V

vaca, s. f. cow; beef.

vacación, s. f. vacation, time of rest; ir de vacaciones take a holiday.

vacante, adj. vacant; — s. f. vacancy.

vaciar, v. a. empty; drain.

vacío, adj. void, empty; unoccupied, vacant; — s. m. empty space, vacuum.

vagabundo, s. f. tramp.

vagar, v. n. rove, wander.

vago, s. m. loafer, tramp; — adj. vague, hazy.

vagón, s. m. railway carriage, goods-van, wagon.

vagoneta, s. m. lorry.

vainilla, s. f. vanilla.

vajilla, s. f. set of dishes.

vale, s. m. note; sales slip; coupon.

valentía, s. f. courage.

valer, v. n. cost; cause, result; be of value; be worth; — s. m. worth, merit.

valiente, adj. valiant, brave, courageous.

valioso, adj. valuable.

valor, s. m. value; price; courage; ~es pl. stocks, bonds, securities.

vals, s. m. waltz.

válvula, s. f. valve.

valle, s. m. valley.

vanidad, s. f. vanity.

vano, adj. vain; shallow; en ~ in vain.

vapor, s. m. steam; steamship.

vaquero, s. m. cowboy.

vara, s. f. twig; yardstick; rod, shaft.

varar, v. n. run aground.

variación, s. f. variation, change.

variado, adj. various, manifold.

variedad, s. f. variety, diversity.

vario, adj. various, varied; several.

varonil, adj. virile, manly.

vasija, s. f. container, receptacle.

vaso, *s. m.* (drinking) glass.

vatio, *s. m.* watt.

vaya! *int.* ¡~ *una idea!* what an idea!

vecindad, *s. f.* vicinity, neighbourhood.

vecindario, *s. m.* population of a district.

vecino, *adj.* neighbouring, near-by; — *s. m.* neighbour; tenant.

vegetal, *adj. & s. m.* vegetable.

vehículo, *s. m.* vehicle.

veinte, *adj. & s. m.* twenty.

vejez, *s. f.* old age.

vejiga, *s. f.* bladder; vesicle.

vela, *s. f.* candle; sail.

velada, *s. f.* evening party.

velar, *v. n.* stay up, stay awake.

velo, *s. m.* veil; film (thin coat).

velocidad, *s. f.* velocity, speed.

veloz, *adj.* swift, fast.

vena, *s. f.* vein.

venado, *s. m.* deer.

vencer, *v. a.* vanquish, defeat; overcome; prevail; win; *v. n.* ~se control (one's feelings).

venda, *s. f.* bandage.

vendar, *v. a.* bandage, dress.

vendedor, *s. m.* vendor, seller.

vender, *v. a.* sell.

veneno, *s. m.* poison, venom.

venenoso, *adj.* poisonous, venomous.

venganza. *s. f.* revenge, vengeance.

vengar, *v. a.* avenge; *v. n.* ~se take revenge.

venir, *v. n.* come; la semana que viene next week; ~ *bien* suit; ~ *mal* be inconvenient.

venta, *s. f.* sale, selling.

ventaja, *s. f.* advantage, profit; lead.

ventajoso, *adj.* advantageous.

ventana, *s. f.* window.

ventanilla, *s. f.* ticket or car window.

ventilación, *s. f.* ventilation.

ventilador, *s. m.* electric fan, ventilator.

ventilar, *v. a.* air, ventilate.

ventoso, *adj.* windy.

ventura, *s. f.* happiness, luck.

ver, *v. a.* see; ¡a ver! let's see!; *hasta más* ~ see you again; *v. n.* ~se meet, see each other.

veraneante, *s. m., f.* holiday maker.

veranear, *v. n.* spend the summer.

veraneo, *s. m.* vacation, summer holiday.

verano, *s. m.* summer.

veras, *s. f. pl.* reality, truth; *de* ~ in truth, really.

verdad, *s. f.* truth; ¿~? isn't it so?

verdadero, *adj.* true; real.

verde, *adj.* green.

verdura, *s. f.* vegetables.

vereda, *s. f.* path.

vergüenza, *s. f.* shame; shyness; *me da* ~ I'm ashamed.

verificar, *v. a.* verify.

versión, *s. f.* version; translation.

verso, *s. m.* line of poetry; poem.

vestíbulo, *s. m.* vestibule; lobby.

vestido, *s. m.* dress; garments, clothing.

vestir, *v. a. & n.* dress; wear; ~se dress, clothe oneself.

veterinario, *s. m.* veterinary (surgeon).

vez, *s. f.* turn (in line); time; *una* ~ once; *dos veces* twice; *muchas veces* many times, often; *a la* ~ at once, simultaneously; *alguna* ~, *algunas veces* sometimes; *a veces* occasionally; *cada* ~ each time; *en* ~ *de* instead of; *otra* ~ again; *tal* ~ perhaps.

vía, *s. f.* track; route; — *adv.* via, by way of.

viaducto, *s. m.* viaduct.

viajar, *v. n.* travel.

viaje, *s. m.* travel; trip; *¡buen* ~*!* have a good trip!

viajero, *s. m.* traveller; passenger.

víbora, *s. f.* viper.

vibrar, *v. n.* vibrate.

vicio, *s. m.* vice, defect.

vicioso, *adj.* defective, given to vice.

víctima, *s. f.* victim.

victoria, *s. f.* victory.

victorioso, *adj.* victorious, triumphant.

vid, *s. f.* vine.

vida, *s. f.* life; way of living; liveliness.

vidrio, *s. m.* glass (material); pane of glass.

viejo, *adj.* old; — *s. m.* old man.

viento, *s. m.* wind.

vientre, *s. m.* belly.

viernes, *s. m.* Friday; *Viernes Santo* Good Friday.

vigilar, *v. a.* watch, guard.

vigor, *s. m.* vigour, strength; *en* ~ in effect, in force.

vil, *adj.* vile, mean:

villa, *s. f.* town; country house, villa.

vinagre, *s. f.* vinegar.

vino, *s. m.* wine.

viña, *s. f.* vineyard.

viola, *s. f.* viola.

violento, *adj.* violent, impulsive; *sentirse* ~ be embarrassed; feel out of place.

violeta, *s. f.* violet; lilac (colour).

violín, *s. m.* violin.

violinista, *s. m., f.* violinist.

violoncelo, *s. m.* violoncello.

viraje, *s. m.* curve, bend; cornering, turning.

virar, *v. n.* turn. curve.

virgen, *adj. & s. f.* virgin.

viril, *adj.* male, virile.

virtud, *s. f.* virtue, good quality; efficacy.

virtuoso, *adj.* virtuous; — *s. m.* virtuoso.

viruela, *s. f.* smallpox.

visar, *v. a.* visa.

visible, *adj.* visible.

visión, *s. f.* vision; view, opinion.

visita, *s. f.* visit; *hacer una* ~ pay a visit.

visitar, *v. a.* visit, call on; make a call; inspect.

víspera, *s. f.* eve, day before.

vista¹, *s. f.* eyesight; sight; view; *corto de* ~ nearsighted; *de* ~ by sight; *en* ~ *de* in view of; *¡hasta la* ~*!* so long!

vista², *s. m.* customs

officer.

visto, pp.; por lo ~ apparently; está ~ it's evident; — s. m. approval.

vistoso, adj. showy; good-looking.

viuda, s. f. widow.

viudo, s. m. widower.

¡viva! int. long live!

víveres, s. m. pl. provisions.

vivienda, s. f. dwelling.

vivir, v. n. live, exist; dwell.

vivo, adj. alive; vivid; intense; a lo ~ vividly.

vocablo, s. m. word.

vocabulario, s. m. vocabulary.

volante, s. m. steering wheel.

volar, v. n. fly; blow up.

volcán, s. m. volcano.

volcar, v. a. overturn; v. n. turn over.

voltio, s. m. volt.

voluntad, s. f. will; buena ~ good will.

voluntario, adj. voluntary; — s. m. volunteer.

volver, v. a. turn (pages); return, give back; v. n. return, go back; turn (road); ~ en sí recover consciousness; volveré a escribirle I'll write him again; ~se loco become crazy.

vomitar, v. n. vomit.

vómito, s. m. vomiting; vomit.

vosotros, pron. m. pl. you.

voto, s. m. vote.

voz, s. f. voice.

vuelo, s. m. flight.

vuelta, s. f. turn, revolution; curve; change;

a la ~ upon returning; a la ~ de correo by return of post; dar una ~ go for a walk.

vuestro, adj.& pron. yours

vulgar, adj. vulgar, coarse; common.

vulgo, s. m. mob, populace.

X

xenofobia, s. f. xenophobia.

xilografía, s. f. xylography.

Y

y, conj. and.

ya, adv. already; ~ no no longer; ~ que since; ~ lo creo of course; ¡ya, ya! sure!; ~ voy I'm coming!

yacimiento, s. m. layer; stratum.

yanki, s. m. yankee.

yegua, s. f. mare.

yema, s. f. bud; yolk.

yerba, s. f. herb; grass.

yerno, s. m. son-in-law.

yerro, s. m. error, mistake.

yeso, s. m. plaster.

yo, pron. I; ~ mismo I myself.

yodo, s. m. iodine.

yugo, s m. yoke.

yunque m. anvil.

yute, s. jute.

Z

zafiro, s. m. sapphire.

zagal, *s. m.* shepherd boy.

zaguán, *s. m.* entrance, hall, vestibule.

zalamería, *s. f.* flattery.

zambo, *s. m.* half-breed (Negro and Indian).

zambullida, *s. f.* dive, plunge.

zambullir, *v. a.* plunge; *v. n.* ~se dive.

zanahoria, *s. f.* carrot.

zanco, *s. m.* stilt.

zanja, *s. f.* ditch, trench.

zapatería, *s. f.* shoemaker's shop.

zapatero, *s. m.* shoemaker.

zapatilla, *s. f.* slipper.

zapato, *s. m.* shoe.

zarpa, *s. f.* paw, claw.

zarpar, *v. n.* weigh anchor; sail.

zarza, *s. f.* bramble.

zarzuela, *s. f.* musical comedy.

zona, *s. f.* district, zone.

zoológico, *adj.* zoological; *jardín* ~ zoological gardens.

zorra, *s. f.* vixen.

zorro, *adj.* cunning, crafty; — *s. m.* fox.

zozobrar, *v. n.* capsize, founder, sink.

zurcir, *v. a.* darn, mend.

zurdo, *adj.* left-handed.

zurrir, *v. n.* whizz, buzz.